I0882673

Home-Based Work and Home-Based Workers (1800–2021)

Studies in Global Social History

Series Editor

Marcel van der Linden (*International Institute of Social History, Amsterdam, The Netherlands*)

Editorial Board

Kate Alexander (*University of Johannesburg, South Africa*)
Sven Beckert (*Harvard University, Cambridge, MA, USA*)
Dirk Hoerder (*University of Arizona, Phoenix, AZ, USA*)
Chitra Joshi (*Indraprastha College, Delhi University, India*)
Amarjit Kaur (*University of New England, Armidale, Australia*)
Barbara Weinstein (*New York University, New York, NY, USA*)

VOLUME 45

The titles published in this series are listed at *brill.com/sgsh*

Home-Based Work and Home-Based Workers (1800–2021)

Edited by

Malin Nilsson, Indrani Mazumdar and Silke Neunsinger

BRILL

LEIDEN | BOSTON

This is an open access title distributed under the terms of the CC BY-NC-ND 4.0 license, which permits any non-commercial use, distribution, and reproduction in any medium, provided no alterations are made and the original author(s) and source are credited. Further information and the complete license text can be found at https://creativecommons.org/licenses/by-nc-nd/4.0/

The terms of the CC license apply only to the original material. The use of material from other sources (indicated by a reference) such as diagrams, illustrations, photos and text samples may require further permission from the respective copyright holder.

This book was realised with the support of Riksbankens Jubileumsfond (grant number F17-1341), the Lund University Book Fund, and the Jan Wallanders och Tom Hedelius Stiftelse (grant number W2015-0375:1).

Cover illustration: *The broken line: Jeans – I sew the best I could,* by Frida Hållander, 2018. Technique: sewing and embroidery. Material: cotton. Photo Frida Hållander, 2018.

The Library of Congress Cataloging-in-Publication Data is available online at https://catalog.loc.gov
LC record available at https://lccn.loc.gov/2021044682

Typeface for the Latin, Greek, and Cyrillic scripts: "Brill". See and download: brill.com/brill-typeface.

ISSN 1874-6705
ISBN 978-90-04-49944-7 (hardback)
ISBN 978-90-04-49961-4 (e-book)

Copyright 2022 by Malin Nilsson, Indrani Mazumdar and Silke Neunsinger. Published by Koninklijke Brill NV, Leiden, The Netherlands.
Koninklijke Brill NV incorporates the imprints Brill, Brill Nijhoff, Brill Hotei, Brill Schöningh, Brill Fink, Brill mentis, Vandenhoeck & Ruprecht, Böhlau Verlag and V&R Unipress.
Koninklijke Brill NV reserves the right to protect this publication against unauthorized use.

This book is printed on acid-free paper and produced in a sustainable manner.

Contents

Acknowledgements

This book would not have been possible without the support and much more of not only the contributors, but many other individuals, institutions, and organisations who worked together for the 2018 conference at Stockholm that gave rise to the idea of the book, and then helped develop that idea up to the stage of final publication in 2021. We would like to thank Jane Barrett and Nina Trige Andersen for all their partnership and work put in before, during and after the conference, as well as their contribution towards making the book relevant and up to date. We also thank Union to Union, ABF, and IF Metall in Sweden for the interest and support they gave to the conference that enabled the coming together of activists and academics that has made this book what it is.

The Labour movements archive and library (ARAB) in Stockholm, Centre for Women's Development Studies in Delhi (CWDS), and Women in Informal Employment: Globalizing and Organizing (WIEGO), three different types of institutions made for a memorable collaboration both for the conference and the cross continental thinking together that has gone into this book. Institutional collaboration between ARAB and CWDS, and cooperation from the Economic History department at Lund University, allowed for meetings among editors in Stockholm, New Delhi, and Lund that facilitated collective thinking and editorial solidarity that is so much a part of this book. Grants from Riksbankens Jubileumsfond made it possible to arrange the conference on home-based work in Stockholm in May 2018; Lund university book fund helped us publish the book open access, the Jan Wallanders och Tom Hedelius Stiftelse has given Malin some time to work.

We would like to thank Janhavi Dave, Chris Bonner, and Jane for their willing promptness in contributing a post-script even as the pandemic raged and posed new challenges. To Indira Chandrasekhar of Tulika, we express our appreciation for great copyediting. To Jonas Söderqvist for his excellent job with the index of this book. We would like to thank Barbro Budin for helping us to get in contact with so many of those who have been valuable to this process. We would also like to thank the people at Brill who have helped us to get this book on the road. Thank you Alessandra Giliberto for kindly answering all our questions; thank you to the anonomous reviewer for useful comments. We would also like to thank Marcel van der Linden for encouraging this book project from the start.

At last, we are so happy that HomeNet international let us be part of their first congress. Your fight along with many others has been a main source for motivation and inspiration for this book. With love and solidarity, thank you.

Lund, New Delhi and Stockholm in June 2021
Malin Nilsson, Indrani Mazumdar and Silke Neunsinger

Figures, Tables and Graphs

Figures

Tables

Graphs

Notes on Contributors

Nina Trige Andersen
is a freelance journalist and historian (MA from Roskilde University) affiliated with Society for Labour History (SFAH) in Denmark. She writes about labour, migration, unionizing, women's lives, and cross-border movements, historically and contemporary, in the Nordic countries and Southeast Asia. Her latest book is 'Labor Pioneers. Economy, Labor, and Migration in Filipino-Danish Relations 1950–2015', Ateneo de Manila University Press, 2019.

Jane Barret
took over the Directorship of the Organising and Representation Programme of WIEGO in early 2016. Jane has worked in workers' organisations since the early 1980s. These include the South African Transport and Allied Workers Union (SATAWU), the International Transport Workers Federation (ITF) and the Congress of South African Trade Unions (COSATU). Jane has an Honours Degree in Industrial Sociology from the University of Witwatersrand and a Masters in Philosophy from SOAS, University of London. She is currently a research associate in the Society, Work and Development Institute at the University of Witwatersrand.

Janine Berg
is Senior Economist at the International Labour Office in Geneva, Switzerland, where she conducts research on the economic effects of labour laws as well as provides technical assistance to ILO constituents on policies for generating jobs and improving working conditions. She is the lead author of the recent ILO report, *Non-standard employment around the world: Understanding challenges, shaping prospects*. She received her Ph.D. from the New School for Social Research in New York, USA.

Eloisa Betti
is Adjunct Professor of labour at the University of Bologna. She serves as co-coordinator of the Feminist Labour History Working Group of the European Labour History Network (ELHN) and Scientific Advisor of the Emilia-Romagna Network of Udi Archives.

Chris Bonner
worked as WIEGO's Organization and Representation Programme Director between 2004–2016, supporting informal workers' organizations, contributing

to research and writing on organizing in the informal economy, and producing worker education materials. She is currently a WIEGO Programme Advisor, and has been working with home-based worker representatives from five regions to develop Home-Net International, a global network of home-based workers. Prior to joining WIEGO she worked as organizer and educator in the South African trade union movement.

Eileen Boris
is Hull Professor in the Department of Feminist Studies and an affiliate professor in the History, Black Studies, and Global Studies Departments at the University of California, Santa Barbara, specializing on home-based work and the racialized gendered state. Her latest book is *Making the Woman Worker: Precarious Labor and the Fight for Global Standards, 1919–2019* [2019]. She was President of the International Federation for Research in Women's History, 2015–2020.

Patricia Coñoman Carrillo (Patylu)
has been a trade unionist since 1975. She belongs to an indigenous community in Chile. She was President of Contextil (union of textile workers), and her union representative in CUT (national union federation) for 22 years- being the first woman representative in CUT after the dictatorship. She is now a home-based workers' representative of Coordinadora Nacional de Trabajadores en Domicilio, CONATRADO, and a member of the International Working Committee of HomeNet International.

Janhavi Dave
is the International Coordinator of HomeNet International. Prior to this she was the International Coordinator of HomeNet South Asia for over five years. There she played a key role in expanding its membership, ensuring good governance and increasing accountability. She also played an important role in the Working Group that led the process towards the formation of HomeNet International. Janhavi has worked with women workers in the informal economy for over fourteen years, and holds a Master's degree in Social Work from the Tata Institute of Social Sciences, Mumbai.

Saniye Dedeoğlu
is Professor of Social Policy in the Department of Labour Economics and Industrial Relations at the University of Mugla, Turkey and was a Marie Curie Fellow at the Center for Research in Ethnic Relations at Warwick University, UK. She is the author of Women Workers in Turkey: Global Industrial Production in

Istanbul (2007) and Migrants, Work and Social Integration. Women's Labour in the Turkish Ethnic Economy (2014).

Laura Ekholm
is Postdoctoral Researcher fellow in the faculty of social sciences with a specialization in economic and social history at the University of Helsinki. She is currently working on the history of the ready-to-wear industry in Sweden and Finland. She is country editor for Scandinavian Economic History Review.

Frida Hållander
is a craft artist and holds a Ph.D. from Konstfack and HDK-Valand The Faculty of Fine, Applied and Performing Arts, University of Gothenburg, Sweden. Her doctoral thesis *Whose Hand is Making? A Sister-Text about Craft, Class, Feminism and the Will to Contest* (2019), includes a case study which addresses the thematics of textile and the collective story of women that have worked in sewing factories and homebased industry.

Jenna Harvey
coordinates WIEGO's Focal Cities Initiative, which provides research, capacity-building and advocacy support to informal workers' organizations in five cities. She is an urban planner by training, and spent several years working with feminist organizations on community development initiatives in Costa Rica and Nicaragua prior to joining WIEGO. Her specific areas of expertise are in participatory planning, critical education, and inclusive models of urban economic development.

K. Kalpana
is Associate Professor in the Humanities and Social Sciences Department, IIT Madras. Her research and academic publications are in the intersecting fields of gender, poverty, microcredit, women's work in the informal sector, women's trade unions and collective action in solidarity economies. Her book 'Women, Microfinance and the State in Neo-liberal India' was published by Routledge in 2017.

Srabani Maitra
is a Senior Lecturer in the School of Education at the University of Glasgow, UK. She holds a PhD in Adult Education and Community Development from OISE/University of Toronto, Canada. Her research focuses on the issues of education/learning, workplace learning, race and racism, skill and transnational migration.

Indrani Mazumdar
is Senior Fellow at the Centre for Women's Development Studies, New Delhi. Her research focus has been on gender, labour, migration in India. Her publications include 'Homebased Workers in 21st century India', CWDS, 2018 and *Women Workers and Globalization: Emergent Contradictions in India Street, Kolkata* (2007), which has a chapter study of home-based workers in Delhi.

Gabriela Mitidieri
is a Ph.D. candidate in the Department of History at the University of Buenos Aires, researching a dissertation about labor experiences of tailors, dressmakers and seamstresses in Buenos Aires City (1848–1870), for which she had received a scholarship from the National Council for Scientific and Technical Research. She works at the Interdisciplinary Institute of Gender Studies (University of Buenos Aires), she is a member of the Social History and Gender institute's group and she is the editorial assistant of Revista Mora, the institute's annual scientific journal. She has published papers on several Latin American historical journals. She also works as a History teacher.

Sona Mitra
is Principal Economist at the 'Initiative for what works to advance Women and Girls in the Economy' (IWWAGE) - An initiative of LEAD at Krea University, India. Sona has previously worked with several government and non-government think-tanks and research centres including the Centre for Women's Development Studies (CWDS). She has been an independent consultant with multilateral organisations working on women's empowerment and has served as member and technical adviser to the Committee on Gender Responsive Budgeting in India, Ministry of Women and Child Development, Government of India. She was also adjunct faculty at Ambedkar University, Delhi till recently, teaching Labour and Development under the Master's in Economics program. Sona regularly publishes articles in peer-reviewed journals, chapters in books, and opinion pieces in leading newspapers and magazines.

Silke Neunsinger
is Director of Research at the Swedish Labour Movement Archives and Library. She gained her Ph.D in 2001 at the department of History Uppsala University and is since 2009 associate professor in economic history. She has worked extensively on feminist labour history, global labour history and methodology. She is also the editor of the Swedish labour history journal *Arbetarhistoria*.

Malin Nilsson
is a teacher and researcher at the Economic History Department at Lund University, Sweden. Her current research is focused around gender, textile production and early processes of industrialization. Her doctoral thesis: "Taking work home: Labour dynamics of women industrial homeworkers in Sweden during the second industrial revolution" won the Rudolf Meidner-award for studies in the history of the trade union movement.

Narumol Nirathron
is Associate Professor in Labour Development and Welfare at the Faculty of Social Administration, Thammasat University, Bangkok, Thailand. Her research focuses on informal workers, informality and social policy. She is currently exploring the issue of informality in street food vending in Bangkok.

Åsa Norman
is a textile artist educated at HDK Steneby, Dals Långed, Sweden, and Konstfack, Stockholm, Sweden. Her work deals mainly with how different female organizations and formations have been formed socially and politically throughout history, but also in the present. She is often researching how ways of working within the field of textile can organize acts of resistance.

Leda Papastefanaki
is Associate Professor of Economic and Social History at the University of Ioannina and Collaborating Faculty Member at the Institute for Mediterranean Studies – FORTH. Her research concerns the social and economic history of industrialisation and labour in the Mediterranean context, social history of technology, gender history, urban history.

Archana Prasad
is Professor at the Centre for Informal Sector and Labour Studies, JNU. She specializes in research on the contemporary history of adivasi livelihoods, labour and resistance, women and labour, environmental and labour history. She has also been helping many grassroots organisations in their work with homebased workers.

Marlese von Broembsen
is the Director of WIEGO's Law Programme and has a Masters Degree in Development Studies and Law Degrees from the Universities of Cape Town and Harvard Law School. Previously she convened a Masters Programme in

Social Justice at the University of Cape Town. She writes on global value chains, labour law and informal employment.

Maria Tamboukou
is Professor of Feminist Studies at the University of East London, UK. Her research activity develops in the areas of feminist theories, narrative analytics and archival research. Writing histories of the present is the central focus of her work, currently configured as an assemblage of feminist genealogies.

Saludo A Las Trabajadoras En Domicilio

Las veo día a día trabaja que trabaja con el pie en el pedalSon mujeres trabajadoras que trabajan y trabajan encerradas en el hogar,
Son mujeres invisibles. Que solo quieren trabajar y
Ser reconocidas como tal

Son las nuevas formas del modelo neoliberal, las sacaron de las empresas
Para enquistarlas en su comunidad,
No saben de descanso, trabajan día y noche.
Produce que produce, para la empresa formal.

Les dicen que son emprendedoras, para mantenerlas en la invisibilidad,
Pero son mujeres trabajadoras, que trabajan en su hogar
Sin tener derechos de seguridad social,
No tienen vacaciones como todas las demás.

E; trabajo en domicilio no es nuevo ni formal
Hoy con mucho orgullo nos podemos pronunciar
Tenemos sindicatos a nivel nacional, y seremos
Reconocidas como todas las demás.

Para eso nos organizamos para salir de la invisibilidad
Junto con aliados que nos socorrieron a recuperar dignidad
A salir de cuatro paredes de nuestro hogar.
Hoy decimos estamos vigentes.

Y a este Congreso las venimos a saludar
Somos la trabajadoras en domicilio
Que organizadas, venimos a participar
Para hacer más fuerte la organización sindical

PATYLU

Greetings to Home-based Workers

I see them day in, day out; with the foot on the pedal
Women home-based workers, who do their job locked in homes,
They are invisible women who just want to work and
be recognized as such.

These are the new forms of the neoliberal model,
They were taken away from enterprises and placed within communities,
They do not know about rest, and work all day & night.
Producing and producing, for the formal enterprise.

They are told they're entrepreneurs, but are kept in invisibility,
They are working women, who work home-based and have no social
security or rights,
They do not have vacations, like other workers with rights.

Home-based work is neither new or formal
Today we can proudly pronounce ourselves,
As we have unions at the national level,
and we will be recognized as other workers alike

This is why we organize, to get out of invisibility
Together with allies who have helped us recover our dignity
We leave the four walls of our home, and
Today we are here.

We come to this Congress to salute
We are Home-based Workers
Organized, we are here to participate and
To strengthen our union

PATYLU

Introduction

History–Visibility–Recognition–Organizing

Malin Nilsson, Indrani Mazumdar, Silke Neunsinger and Nina Trige Andersen

All over the world there are women and men who work and produce for the market within the space of their own homes, or together with neighbours in collective local spaces. They stitch shoes, sew and embellish garments, weave carpets, make baskets, prepare and sell food, assemble electronics and perform computer-based tasks amongst other forms of labour. They produce for a wide range of industries and services: textiles, pharmaceuticals, automobiles, tech– such as assemblage of parts for technological devises – tobacco, wood, food, education, as well as more recent forms of digital work, for instance, graphic design, programming, text production and translation. In 2019, drawing on household surveys in 118 countries, the International Labour Organization (ILO) estimated that there were around 260 million home-based workers worldwide, representing 7.9 per cent of global employment.[1] Yet an accurate count of the actual number of people—particularly women—who earn their living by working in their homes is still elusive, since many labour force surveys do not take this type of work into account, or fail to define and include it adequately. Buried in statistical obscurity and often omitted from labour laws, the conditions of their work are hidden from public view as an effect of its location in private spaces, and even their worker status is often denied through misrepresentation of home-based productive labour as leisure activities. No doubt, the overwhelming social perception of public spaces such as the factory, the office, the classroom, the laboratory, the shopping mall or arcade—all designated "workplaces" as distinct from what is considered the private world of "homes"—has reinforced the neglect of the home as a site of production and labour. Despite having contributed significantly to production in basically all sectors of the economy through centuries, home-based workers have remained largely invisible, unrecognized and undervalued.

1 International Labour Organization (ILO), *The home as workplace: Trends and policies for achieving decent work* (Geneva, 2020).

© MALIN NILSSON ET. AL., 2022 | DOI:10.1163/9789004499614_002
This is an open access chapter distributed under the terms of the CC BY-NC-ND 4.0 license.

FIGURE 0.1 Mayuri Suepwong, a single mother, took up home-based work in order to look after her children while generating income. Her daughter, Chamaiporn, helps her after school. Like other home-based workers, she sometimes has to work long hours to meet tight deadlines with irregular pay.
PHOTO: PAULA BRONSTEIN/GETTY IMAGES REPORTAGE BANGKOK

At the same time, there has been growing awareness regarding the persistence of home-based production. Well-documented evidence on how modern industries at local, national and even global levels have both fed and fed on the practice of outsourcing production to home workers is now available. While it was earlier assumed that home-based work would disappear with the deepening of industrialization, the persistence and, in some cases, expansion of home work in the second half of the twentieth century challenged this view, as do current practices of outsourcing labour to private homes like the one which is illustrated in fig. 0.1. If earlier assumptions are being disproven by the prevalence of home-based work in contemporary times, the significant part played by home-based work—including its role in the industrialization process itself—has also been brought out by historical research into the work of women in industrialized countries. Often overlooked in official records, these histories—excavated by feminist historians—show that outsourced production in the homes of women emerged as a significant intersection of paid and unpaid work, between home and workplace, and between formal and informal employment, in the past as well as the present.

The persistence of home-based work has been particularly challenging for trade unions whose typical form of organization is less attuned to homes as workplaces and hostile to atomized forms of labour. Further, with most home-based workers located in the impoverished and informal margins of the capitalist economy, it is perhaps not surprising that they have remained without an effective organizational voice. Yet, the past few decades of renewed and distinctively women-oriented forms of organizing and activism among home-based workers have indeed provided a vehicle for the representative voices of home-based workers, including at an international level.[2]

With all its demonstrable commonalities across the globe and over more than two centuries, home-based work also shows considerable variety across sectors and regions of the world as well as in forms of struggle and organization, from the past to the present. A wider sweep across time and space is thus called for, with openness to dialogue between research and activism. Towards this, a beginning was made at a workshop called "Long-term Perspectives on Home-based Work" held in Stockholm in May 2018, organized in a collaboration between The Labour Movements Archive in Stockholm (ARAB), Centre for Women's Development Studies (CWDS) in Delhi, and the global network "Women in Informal Employment: Globalizing and Organizing" (WIEGO). Across three days, academics and activists from India, Sweden, South Africa, Kenya, Argentina, Norway, Denmark, the United Kingdom, the United States, Finland, Spain, Greece, Bulgaria, Thailand, Turkey and Chile shared and discussed research papers on home-based work from the nineteenth century to the present day.

This volume offers a selection of the papers presented at the Stockholm workshop. They draw on a range of disciplines, including but not limited to Statistics, Anthropology, Sociology and History. They address the past and present conditions of specific forms of home-based work, institutional and legal histories of regulations for home-based workers, their modes of organization and resistance, as well as the cutting edge of new aspects of contemporary home work in both traditional and newly developing sectors. As was the case for the workshop, the volume is both a result of and a contribution to the struggles of home-based workers for visibility, recognition and representation, and for dignified conditions of life and labour.

---

2 For example, see Renana Jhabvala and Jane Tate, "Out of the shadows: Homebased workers organize for international recognition", *SEEDS*, no. 18 (New York, 1996); A. Delaney, J. Tate and R. Burchielli, "Homeworker Initiatives: Gaining Recognition and Rights as Workers through Organizing, National and International Standards", in N. Lichtenstein and J. Jensen (eds), *West Meets East* (Geneva, 2016).

1 Conceptualizing the Invisibility of Home-based Work

The "invisibility" of home-based work has been a concern common to the struggles of home-based workers. It is a refrain in the research contributions to this volume. That home-based workers see themselves as invisible and so, to even get to a place where they can fight for their rights as workers, must mobilize for action to become visible, is apparent from the poems that are also included in this volume. Yet, what is meant by invisibility is itself a question that has several interpretations and which opens up a range of issues.

Ela Bhatt, founder of SEWA (Self Employed Women's Association) in Gujarat, India, who emerged as a powerful voice speaking on behalf of home-based workers from the 1980s, described India's home-based workers as invisible in terms of the absence of "official or even unofficial records of their existence, their conditions, and their contribution to the national economy".[3] Further, "confined within their homes for economic, social, or cultural reasons", home-based workers "are invisible to the nation—in 'purdah', both literally and statistically".[4]

Writing about the history of industrial home work in the United States, feminist historian Eileen Boris argued that "waged labour at home shares the same invisibility as housework" as both are part of the "gendered structuring of employment, whereby occupations, processes and places of labour become designated as male and female". Also that employers, "taking advantage of gender ideology that identified the home as the domain of motherhood and housework by women, increased profits by shifting the burdens of production on to the [home] worker, whose payment by piece encouraged sweating".[5]

More than a century earlier, based on descriptions of the conditions of home workers in nineteenth-century Britain, Karl Marx had referred to the "invisible threads" by which capital sets in motion an army of workers as an "outside department of the factory, the manufactory, or the warehouse", where "the power of the resistance in the labourers decreases with their dissemination".[6]

Conceptions of invisibility can thus be seen to encompass hidden dimensions of power and gender injustice, of poverty, and of the structural and

3 Ela Bhatt, "The Invisibility of Home-based Work", in Andrea Menefee Singh and Anita Kelles (eds), *Invisible Hands: Women in Home-based Production* (New Delhi, 1987), pp. 33.

4 Ela Bhatt, We are poor but so many: The story of self employed women of India (New Delhi, 2006) pp. 44.

5 Eileen Boris, *Home to Work: Motherhood and the Politics of Industrial Homework in the United States* (Cambridge, 1994), p. 2.

6 Karl Marx, *Capital*, Vol. 1 chapter 15, section B.

systemic features of capital that underlie and propel the sweated conditions of home-based workers, the cultures and ideologies of gender that lay the ground for it, and the disempowering effect of the processes that inhere in its growth and expansion. From our perspective, and as evident from several papers in this volume, questions as to whose work is made visible or how visibility is framed, and what forms of invisibility become issues of struggle—when, how, why—need to be constantly asked, contextually situated and interrogated by researchers to guard against reinforcing invisibility of one kind or another. In this, questions of how home-based work and workers are defined and perceived, where they are recorded and counted and where they are not, are of particular salience. Critically and imaginatively interrogating and correlating different types of sources and sets of data have been useful and are necessary to lift the veil of invisibility in which home-based workers are so often shrouded. Such methods have been used to considerable effect in some of the papers in this volume, for both excavating the past of home-based workers and understanding their present situation.

The Stockholm workshop was held at a time when the issue of data and statistics on employment and work in the informal economy was being mainstreamed. Approaches to the collection of employment statistics had reached a critical juncture and were poised for change.[7] Inevitably, the issue of how home-based workers could acquire greater visibility and recognition through these changes in statistical definitions and practices became a subject of intense discussion.

1.1 *Visibility and Recognition: Debating the Power of Definition*

Definitions have always been central to the struggle for recognition and visibility for home-based workers. Delineation of the home as a place of work and defining the nature of employment relations or status of employment have been key issues in the journey towards visibility. Home worker, industrial home worker, home-based worker—these are various terms and nomenclatures that have been in use. These different nomenclatures were not necessarily distinguished from each other in historical usage, as is evident in the choice of terms used by authors in this book, yet they do sometimes denote differences with reference to status of employment or the nature of employment and/or contractual relations.

7 See "Resolution concerning statistics of work, employment and labour underutilization' of the 19th International Conference of Labour Statisticians, 2013, and "20th International Conference of Labour Statisticians resolution concerning statistics on work relationships", 2018.

At the core of many debates around definitions is the question of whether the home-based worker works for an employer directly or through a chain of intermediaries—typically at some form of piece-rate—or is self-employed on her own account with (some degree of) decision-making power over what to produce, how and at what price. Making a distinction between own account self-employment and wage work for a trader, manufacturer, contractor or service provider is of course crucial for analytical, regulatory, strategic and organizational purposes—even though the distinctions can often be blurry in home-based production.

"Home worker" is the term used in ILO Convention No. 177—Home Work Convention, 1996—that came into force in 2000. It defines home work as work carried out by a person, to be referred to as a home worker, in his or her home or in other premises of his or her choice other than the workplace of the employer, and as work that is carried out for remuneration and results in a product or service as specified by the employer irrespective of who provides the equipment, materials or other inputs used. The term "employer" refers to a person, natural or legal, who either directly or through an intermediary gives out home work in pursuance of his or her business activity.[8] The ILO's Home Work Convention therefore does not apply to own account self-employed home-based workers, and a dependent relationship between the home worker and employer is written into its definition. It explicitly excludes workers who have a degree of economic autonomy that is necessary to be considered an independent worker under national laws, regulations or court decisions.

The umbrella term "home-based worker", on the other hand, has been more in use in developing countries and regions, particularly South Asia, where household industries, independent home-based production for markets *and* outsourced home work coexist on some scale. Home-based workers here include not only waged home workers (as per the ILO Convention), but also independent artisans working at home and other forms of own account (self-employed) workers who are involved in the marketing of their products. Of course, many own account workers may also have a dependency relationship based on, for instance, debt or market dominance by those who order or buy their products. A line between dependence and independence in the world of home-based work is thus not easily drawn, and organizations of home-based workers tend to include all subcategories within their ambit.

8 Available at https://www.ilo.org/dyn/normlex/en/f?p=NORMLEXPUB:12100:0::NO::P12100_INSTRUMENT_ID:312322, last accessed 7 April 2021.

It is exactly the grey zone between self-employed and waged workers, and between independent and dependent workers, that has been central to recent debates on changes in definitions that apply to home-based workers in employment statistics. The issue itself is not new. It was reflected, for example, in the Swedish and Finnish Business Censuses in the early twentieth century (see chapter 1.2 by Laura Ekholm, "Reading the Margins of Business Censuses"). Yet, a hundred years later, the way the issue has been sought to be resolved has thrown up a new controversy, which was, in a sense, previewed in the Stockholm workshop debates.

The necessity of distinguishing between those who work in the home at piece-rates for some other employer and own account small entrepreneurs or independent artisans in home-based production has long been recognized, in that conceptualizing worker rights and regulations for the former would require recognition of the relationship with employers, while for the latter the focus would have to be on arrangements for purchase of raw material, for marketing, for credit, for storage, for better prices, etc.[9] In the decades following the ILO Convention, some scholars further amplified a terminological and definitional distinction between *dependent home workers* (subcontracted home-based workers) and *independent self-employed home-based workers.* The former, in this perspective, are seen to be contracted by individual entrepreneurs or firms, often through an intermediary, usually given the raw materials and paid per piece, and not involved in selling the finished goods to the end customer, even though they may typically cover a large part of the costs of production: workplace, equipment, supplies, utilities and transport. The latter, on the other hand, are viewed as assuming all the risks of being independent operators, buying their own raw materials, supplies and equipment, paying utility and transport costs, and selling their own finished goods—either to an end consumer or to an intermediary—mainly to local customers and markets but sometimes to international markets, and while they rarely hire other workers, they may have unpaid family members working with them.[10]

9 See, for example, Bhatt, "The Invisibility of Home-based Work", and also the 1988 *Shramshakti* report of the Government of India-appointed National Commission on Self-Employed Women and Women in the Informal Sector that was headed by Ela Bhatt.

10 Joann Vanek, "Home-based Workers: Progress in the Development of Statistics", paper presented at the Stockholm workshop on Long-term Perspectives on Home-based Work, mimeo (2018). We may note here that large proportions of unpaid helpers have also been recorded among those who would be included in the category of dependent home workers. See, for example, Labour Bureau, Government of India, *Report on Evaluation Studies on Implementation of the Minimum Wages Act in Bidi Making Establishments in Madhya Pradesh* (2003), available at labourbureau.nic.in/ Report_on_Beedi_Industry_2015.pdf.

The hitherto standard practice of categorizing dependent subcontracted home workers as self-employed in employment statistics has of course long obscured and frustrated a clear view of the actual number of wage-based home workers, whose rising proportions have been obvious to activists and evident in most field studies of contemporary home-based work. With the aim of remedying this situation, WIEGO (Women in Informal Employment: Globalizing and Organizing) representatives who were part of the team working on revising the International Classification of Status in Employment (ICSE) had supported the introduction of a new category of "dependent contractors", defined as "workers employed for profit, usually by way of a commercial transaction, who are dependent on another entity for access to raw materials, capital items or clients that directly benefits from the work performed by them and exercises explicit or implicit control over their activities". However, when this was announced at the Stockholm workshop, which was held a few months before formal approval of the revised ICSE by the International Conference of Labour Statisticians (ICLS), it evoked a stormy debate. Questions were raised particularly by the South Asian participants, who argued that the term contractor applies to infamous middlemen or agents of employers who hire workers for particularly exploitative conditions of work, and therefore designating all home workers as contractors would be a misnomer. The debate, which remained unresolved in Stockholm, continued to reverberate in the following years. It merits some explication, since a revised ICSE may indeed lead to global changes in the conceptualization of home workers in employment statistics and beyond.

ICSE 18, which was approved by the 20th ICLS in October 2018, posits two characteristics of jobs and work activities as relevant to differentiate them by status at work and status in employment. One is based on "type of authority" and the other on "type of economic risk". Type of authority is used to classify workers as dependent or independent, under which "dependent contractors" are classified as dependent workers and own account workers in household market enterprises without employees as independent workers. Type of economic risk is used to classify workers as in employment for profit or in employment for pay (including piece-rate wages), under which both dependent contractors and own account workers are classified as in employment for profit. If, under the former characterization, home workers emerge as distinct from self-employed home-based workers, in the latter typology a home worker's earnings are defined as profits, thereby conceptually blurring the important distinction between profits and wages.

Some of those who had instinctively recoiled at the nomenclature of dependent contractor for home worker during the Stockholm workshop later came to be persuaded that the new category was "essential". On the grounds that the definition included "dependent workers who do not have a contract of employment … are paid only by the piece or commission, and do not benefit from social contributions paid by the economic unit paying for the work", they accepted that such a definition fits subcontracted, piece-rated home workers, and is better able to capture home workers as distinct from other self-employed home-based workers. It was also argued that as an international standard it would help make comparable assessments and analysis of global, regional and national trends, and that governments could legislate, plan and programme for the security and empowerment of home-based workers using the data. These arguments rested on a sense of reassurance that the definition indeed refers to the dependent contractor as a worker, and even though the term dependent contractor is "not ideal" from their point of view, they believed that it would not lead to home workers losing any rights and entitlements under labour law, and, further, that the definition of home worker provided by ILO's Convention 177 would continue to hold.[11]

Yet, the question as to why the term contractor was brought in to define workers remained pertinent and continues to be contested by others. "Independent contractor" is the prevalent term in the US for some of the new, non-standard forms of work such as Uber drivers, where the inequalities of the employment relationship and the process of profiting from the labour of drivers are camouflaged as a commercial relationship between independent equals.[12] The insertion of a separate "dependent" category in ICSE was thus thought to be a victory for the informal workers' lobby.[13] However, it could equally be argued that insertion of the term "contractors" to signify workers introduces a new confusion of categories. If all home workers begin to be counted as dependent contractors, how, for example, would a piece-rated wage worker be distinguished from a contractor who merely farms out work to home workers but may have a dependent relationship with another employer? That renaming

11 "Understanding the statistical term 'Dependent Contractor': A Q&A with Firoza Mehrotra", https://www.wiego.org/blog/understanding-statistical-term-%E2%80%9Cdependent-contractor%E2%80%9D-qa-firoza-mehrotra.

12 Only recently, in February 2021, the UK Supreme Court ruled that Uber drivers designated as independent contractors by Uber Technolologies Inc. would be considered as workers (although not employees) with entitlements, in a case that was settled after more than six years of litigation. However, the decision only applies within the scope of definitions under a specific UK law.

13 Leslie Vryenhoek, "Major Step Forward for Informal Workers with New ILO Employment Categories", available at https://www.wiego.org/blog/major-step-forward-informal-workers-new-ilo-employment-categories.

workers as contractors would also symbolize a political retreat from a labour perspective on home-based work was one of the arguments that was raised at the Stockholm workshop. Further, since the wages of such dependent contractors are defined as profit, a question remains as to whether it would promote conceptual falsification and a roll-back of the advances made in understanding the hidden political economy of outsourced home work that has been brought out by scholars and activists over decades.

A related concern is that this categorization may provide an excuse for traditional trade unions reluctant to deal with home workers to further retreat from this field of organizing, just as it may further cloud the already contested area of how (in)dependent contractors may be conceived in relation to competition laws, which in some parts of the world is a potential threat to the right of such workers to organize and bargain collectively.

The significance of these questions is far-reaching for future strategies of women home-based workers. They acquire particular salience in the prevailing context of an offensive against the politics of labour movements, as neoliberal regimes across the globe are engaged in restructuring labour relations as well as labour laws at the cost of the rights and entitlements of workers. ICSE 18 now has the authoritative backing of ICLS. Nevertheless, the tense debates at the Stockholm workshop and after suggest that the renaming of workers as contractors might encounter further resistance and interrogation in various countries. The unease with the term "dependent contractor" even among those who have accepted it may deepen when it is placed before the varied terrain of workers' organizations, including of home-based workers, who have not been part of the consultations for the revision of ICSE.

The issue of contractors and their various tiers is of course complex, particularly in the formerly colonized and now developing countries of South Asia.[14] Here, where larger contractors are primarily agents and labour mobilizers for employers, many low-end contractors may indeed be home workers

14 The emergence of the figure of the labour contractor has long had a connection with the way colonial rulers mobilized labour from and within the countries they colonized. In India, labour historians have used the term of "labour lord" for such contractors, and the persistence of the figure of the oppressive contractor resonates with the figure of the oppressive overseer of slaves in other contexts. See Lalita Chakravarty, "Emergence of an Industrial Labour Force in a Dual Economy: British India, 1880–1920", *Indian Economic and Social History Review*, vol. 15, no. 3 (1978); Tirthankar Roy, "Sardars, Jobbers, Kanganies: The Labour Contractor and Indian Economic History", *Modern Asian Studies* (September 2008); and for the debate on the role of contractors in the informal economy in the post-colonial and recent period, Jan Breman, "Labour, Get Lost: A Late-Capitalist Manifesto', *Economic and Political Weekly*, Vol. 30, No. 37 (1995).

themselves. The question, however, is that in their case, should the contractor identity be foregrounded over the worker identity or vice versa? Further, how would home workers' organizations approach the issue of denial of adequate wages or wage theft by contractors if both are clubbed in the same category? This relates to another important question: where would home workers redesignated as contractors place themselves in the building of larger worker solidarities, particularly against the neoliberal restructuring of labour relations that affects all workers and excludes none?

In such a fraught, complex and contested terrain, insights from historical research and a long-term perspective, the ways in which home-based work was conceived and represented, and the debates that took place at various points in the history of home work, acquire special relevance. Where the platform of the Stockholm workshop created a particularly vibrant and intersected space for debating meanings of the current framing of definitions and terms for home work, the papers in this volume bring out the interplay of vicissitudes of power, capital and dominant ideologies in shaping approaches to home-based work and workers over a longer period. These provide a critical foundation for thinking around some of the questions raised by the current conjuncture.

1.2 *Shifting Sands: Research on Home-based Work Across Time*

A long-term view has to bear in mind also that home-based workers have been largely invisible in the production of knowledge on labour markets and work, barring some notable exceptions and occasional surges in public interest across different phases and points of time in "industrialization" or "development". Around the turn of the nineteenth century, for example, home-based work was intensively investigated and studied in Europe, and even displayed at large exhibitions. A large number of national and regional surveys and reports were written up by organizations and governmental actors at the time, when home-based work was approached as part of "the social question"—an expression describing the discourse around organizations, policy and publications trying to find solutions to the new forms of poverty and related problems among the urban working class in the late nineteenth century.[15]

15 See, for example, Marcel Allexandre, *L'industrie à domicile salariée* (Université Caen, 1906); Investigation Committee of the Women's Industrial Council, *Home Industries of Women in London: Report of an Inquiry* (1908); J. Beck, "Die Schweizerische Hausindustrie: Ihre Soziale Und Wirtschaftliche Lage" (1909); Franz Fiedler, "Die Heimarbeit Und Deren Bekämpfung in Der Kleider-Und Wäsche-Industrie" (1908); Heinrich Koch, "Die Deutsche Hausindustrie" (1905); *Svensk Hemindustri* [*Le Travail à Domicile En Suède*] (Stockholm, 1917).

Between the two World Wars home work received renewed attention in Europe and other parts of the world, not least because the wars had momentarily disrupted economic development towards workplace centralization. Indeed, the discussion on home work was taken up in the very first decade of the ILO's existence, resulting in the The Minimum Wage-Fixing Machinery Convention from 1928, which encouraged member-states to set fixed rates of minimum wages, "in particular in home working trades", for sectors where "no arrangements exist for the effective regulation of wages by collective agreement or otherwise and wages are exceptionally low".[16] Before the First World War the idea of minimum wages, especially for home workers, had been contested in most European states as well as the US. But pressure from trade unions and other social movements as well as the exposure of the harsh and unhealthy conditions of home workers had prepared the ground for agreement that minimum wages were a reasonable way to control some of the negative effects of the home work practice.[17] Except for the inclusion of home workers in the 1952 Maternity Protection Convention,[18] the ILO did not adopt more conventions dealing directly with home work until The Home Work Convention (177) in 1996, although a Tripartite Meeting in the Clothing Industry in 1964 called for the abolition of home work because of low wages, long hours, unhealthy sanitary conditions and inadequate safety standards. This position was reversed in 1980, however, when the Tripartite Meeting decided that home workers should be treated on an equal footing with regular workers.[19]

By this time attention towards home workers was again on the rise, gaining international momentum from awareness of and research on the significant role of home work in global commodity chains and developing country exports. In the 1980s the momentum came from the developing world, where the textile and garment industry, stitching and embroidery were particularly in focus, and where resurgent women's movements and the newly developing field of Women's Studies were pushing research agendas towards engaging with undercounted and hidden dimensions of women's work.[20] The backdrop

16 Minimum Wage-Fixing Machinery Convention, C026. See also Eileen Boris, *Making the Woman Worker: Precarious Labor and the Fight for Global Standards, 1919–2019* (New York, 2019), pp. 28–29.

17 Elisabeth Prügl, *The Global Construction of Gender: Home-Based Work in the Political Economy of the 20th Century* (New York, 1999), p. 41.

18 *International Labour Review*, Vol. IXX (1954), p. 544.

19 Internationales Arbeitsamt and Internationales Arbeitsamt (eds), *Home Work*, vol. 8, Conditions of Work Digest 2, (Geneva, 1989), pp. 22, 164–65.

20 See, for example, Vijay Rukmini Rao and Sahba Husain, "Invisible Hands: The Women behind India's Export Earnings", in Singh and Kelles (eds), *Invisible Hands*.

of this period, as noted by Gisela Schneider de Villegas,[21] was persistently high levels of unemployment in large parts of the world, which meant that home work had become an increasingly important way of earning incomes, and even industrialized countries that had earlier seen stagnant or decreasing involvement in home-based work had started to see significant increases, especially because of its wide use in the services sector.[22]

It was this latter period that also saw pioneering feminist research and academic writing on home-based work in both developing and developed countries: Maria Mies' study, *Lace Makers of Narsapur* (1982) and Lourdès Benería and Martha Roldan's book on industrial home work in Mexico City (1987) being two prominent examples.[23] The early edited compilation *Invisible Hands: Women in Home-based Production* (1987) by Andrea Menefee Singh and Anita Kelles, which included piece-rated workers as well as self-employed home-based workers within its ambit, was a first attempt at providing a view of home-based women workers across a range of industries in South Asia. Ground-breaking historical studies on industrial home work in the US and Europe were also a part of this phase of feminist academic engagement with home-based work, as for example the anthology *Homework: Historical and Contemporary Perspectives on Paid Labor at Home* by Eileen Boris and Cynthia R. Daniels (1989).[24]

The surge of political interest in home work in the 1990s was of course propelled by structural changes in the organization of international capitalism, and the liberalization and globalization context. Boris and Prugl[25] pointed out that the bodies of thought that were pertinent to locating home workers in academic discourse at the time included feminist scholarship on women

---

21 Gisela Schneider de Villegas, 'Home Work: A Case for Social Protection', *International Labour Review* 129 (1990) and 'Home Work: And overview' in Internationales Arbeitsamt and Internationales Arbeitsamt (eds), *Home Work*.

22 Internationales Arbeitsamt and Internationales Arbeitsamt (eds), *Home Work*, pp. 5–6.

23 Maria Mies, *The Lace Makers of Narsapur: Indian Housewives Produce for the World Market* (London, 1982); Lourdes Beneria and Martha Roldan, *The Crossroads of Class and Gender: Industrial Homework, Subcontracting, and Household Dynamics in Mexico City* (Chicago, 1987); Eileen Boris and Cynthia R. Daniels, *Homework: Historical and Contemporary Perspectives on Paid Labor at Home* (Urbana, 1989); Lourdes Beneria, Gunselli Berik and Maria Floro, *Gender, Development and Globalization: Economics as if All People Mattered* (New York, 2003).

24 Eileen Boris, "Regulating Industrial Homework: The Triumph of 'Sacred Motherhood' ", *The Journal of American History*, 71:4 (1985), pp. 745–63; Boris, *Home to Work*; Boris and Daniels, *Homework*.

25 Eileen Boris and Elisabeth Prügl, *Homeworkers in Global Perspective: Invisible No More* (New York and London, 1996).

and work, a focus on documenting the work of third world women within the rubric of women in development, and gender and social policy. To this must be added the growing body of literature that had developed around concepts of the informal sector, the informal economy and informal workers, within which studies on home-based workers inevitably found a place. As "globalization" entrenched itself in several countries, altering the terms of discourse and frames of engagement, a number of studies also emerged in the context of the engagement between home-based work and globalization, in which Boris and Prugl's volume *Homeworkers in a Global Perspective* from 1996—which, like the present volume, deals with long-term perspectives on home-based work—is a classic anthology.[26] It was in this period of internationalization that the home-based workers question reached a turning point around and for ILO's Convention 177, in which the connections between activism and research moved outside national boundaries to the international.[27]

Another round of nuanced scholarly work came around the turn of the next century: for example, Ping-Chun Hsiung's study (1996) of gender, class and home-based work in Taiwan that perhaps for the first time brought out processes of class differentiation taking place within and among home-based workers; or Naila Kabeer's comparative study (2000) of Bangladeshi women workers which juxtaposed their increasing involvement with home-based work in London with their increasing involvement in factory work in Dhaka. Radhika Balakrishnan's edited book, *The Hidden Assembly Line* (2002), engages with the situation of home-based workers in South Asia and Southeast Asia, and presents an NGO perspective, reflecting a sense that the ILO Convention is ineffective while consumer-based.[28]

Since the turn of the century, a growing number of writings have emerged within a wide range of disciplines: papers developing standard labour market

26 Martha Chen, Jennefer Sebstad and Lesley O'Connell, "Counting the Invisible Workforce: The Case of Homebased Workers", *World Development*, 27:3 (1999), pp. 603–10, <https://doi.org/doi: 10.1016/S0305-750X(98)00154-5>; Marilyn Carr, Martha Alter Chen and Jane Tate, "Globalization and Home-Based Workers", *Feminist Economics*, 6:3 (2000), pp. 123–42 <https://doi.org/10.1080/13545700750020164>; Boris and Prügl, *Homeworkers in Global Perspective*; Elisabeth Prügl, *The Global Construction of Gender: Home-Based Work in the Political Economy of the 20th Century* (New York, 1999).

27 See Jhabvala and Tate, "Out of the shadows".

28 Ping-Chun Hsiung, *Living Rooms as Factories: Class, Gender, and the Satellite Factory System in Taiwan* (Philadelphia, 1996), <https://www.jstor.org/stable/j.ctt14bssv8>, accessed 11 December 2020; Naila Kabeer, *The Power to Choose: Bangladeshi Women and Labour Market Decisions in London and Dhaka* (London, 2002); Radhika Balakrishnan, *The Hidden Assembly Line: Gender Dynamics of Subcontracted Work in a Global Economy* (Bloomfield, CT, 2001).

models to include home workers, like Edwards and Field-Hendrey's study on women's labour market decisions in the US; or "Counting the Invisible Workforce: The Case of Home-based Workers" by Chen, Sebstad and O'Connell, which brings the lack of available statistics on home-based workers to an international scale and has become a central work for many scholars.[29]

However, much has shifted over the past two or more decades, both on the ground and in the field of research. Home-based workers face new issues that need to be understood. While this volume is still only a beginning, it aims to contribute to and update existing knowledge by bringing together cross-generational activists, artists and researchers, combining new sources with new research ideas, and bringing together perspectives of the past and the present so that we may look to the future: the future of home-based work as such, the future of its place in the broader political economy and the future of organizing home-based workers.

An expanded terrain of investigation into the materialities of gender culture that historically shaped, and indeed continues to shape, the labour process in home-based work has imparted a distinctive multicultural texture to this volume that speaks to the current juncture of an evolving relationship between home-based work and race, ethnic and immigrant community identity-based discrimination in labour markets. Cutting-edge insights into how the introduction of new technologies in the past and in the present have propelled home-based work and mechanisms of social control and subordination, from the sewing machine to algorithmic management, has re-grounded perspectives on the relationship between technology and home-based work with new data. Cross-country analyses of laws and regulations that address home workers in global supply chains combine with an unpacking of the complex interaction of global, national and local economies that move beyond an exclusive focus on supply chains towards the influence of macroeconomic policies, structures and processes at national and international levels, as factors affecting trends in home-based work. Case studies and histories of institutional and organizational perspectives in interaction with women's agency and organization bring out a variety of forms of organizing and alliances.

Coinciding as it does with the movement of regional networks of home-based workers towards the formation of a global network, this volume marks

29 Linda N. Edwards and Elizabeth Field-Hendrey, "Home-Based Work and Women's Labor Force Decisions", *Journal of Labor Economics*, vol. 20, issue 1 (2002), pp. 170–200; Martha Chen, Jennefer Sebstad and Lesley O'Connell, "Counting the Invisible Workforce: The Case of Home-based Workers", *World Development*, 27:3 (1999), pp. 603–10, <https://doi.org/doi: 10.1016/S0305-750X(98)00154-5>.

a crossroads moment of interchange between historical perspectives and current-day activism. The decision to form an international network was actually mooted in a parallel set of discussions among four regional networks—HomeNet Africa, Contraldo Alac (Latin America), HomeNet Southeast Asia, and HomeNet South Asia—that took place around the Stockholm workshop in 2018. It culminated in the constitution of HomeNet International that was formally launched at a congress held in February 2021.[30]

Engaging with home-based work is a complex affair, but one thing is certain: this type of labour is here to stay. It is being utilized and reinvented—by employers and states, as well as workers themselves—in production dynamics around the world and across industries and sectors.

1.3 *Towards a Global History of Home-based Work under Capitalism*

Writing the history of home-based workers contributes to their visibility and a clarified view of the confluence of historical processes that have propelled home-based work to its current condition. History sheds light on the persistence of exploitative and particularly difficult working conditions among home-based workers, on the underlying social and economic compulsions behind home-based work, and on how the worker identity of particularly women in home-based work and their economic contributions have been pushed to the margins. Moreover, a long-term perspective can deepen our understanding of the political economy of home-based work, its relations with the state, with other forms of work, with trade unions and with international organizations. It can also contribute to an analysis of the forms of regulation that have been applied—and to what effect—and why some issues tend to sustain or repeatedly recur. In other words, what changes, what remains the same and what falls by the wayside across time, and why.

In mainstream historiography, it has often been assumed that home-based work belonged to an early phase of industrialization and disappeared as the process of industrialization advanced.[31] A large number of historical studies have focused on home-based work as proto-industrial work, especially in the

30 A HomeNet International was also formed as part of the efforts pushing for the ILO Convention on home work, but that network did not survive the 1990s. The structure of a new HomeNet International was thus put in place during the Stockholm conference in 2018, with a formal launching congress planned for 2020, which got delayed because of the Covid-19 pandemic. Finally, the congress was held virtually on 23–24 February 2021.

31 See for example Richard A. Easterlin, *Growth Triumphant: The Twenty-First Century in Historical Perspective* (Ann Arbor, MI, 1998) pp. 79.

European context.[32] Yet, the remarkable persistence and reinvention of home work well into the twenty-first century across all parts of the world challenged the understanding of home-based work as simply a feature of a passing phase of "proto-industrialization".

Where contemporary studies mostly engage with the situation of home-based workers in the global South, the historiography of home-based work has been dominated by research on the situation of workers in the global North.[33] This, in a sense, set the stage for a standard historical description of home-based work, mirroring the view of home-based work as simply a form of production that disappears as factory production advances. However, as the studies in this volume show, the relationship between home-based industrial production and the processes of industrialization is far more complex, and was so even in the past.

One aspect that is missing in our book, and in much of historiography at large, relates to the former colonized regions, particularly in Africa. This lack in no way reflects anabsence of home-based work in Africa's modern history. On the contrary, home-based work is prominent throughout the region and contemporary studies are available on home-based work in African countries.[34] However, historical studies remain scarce. There are some studies that are records of home-based rural craft work in South Africa that was initiated by vocational missionary schools to stimulate "native home industries" in the countryside. Self-help crafts schemes were developed by churches and

32 Hans Medick, "The Proto-Industrial Family Economy. The Structural Function of Household and Family during the Transition from Peasant Society to Industrial Capitalism", *Social History*, 1 (1976), pp. 291–315; Peter Kriedte, Hans Medick and Jürgen Schlumbohm, *Industrialization before Industrialization: Rural Industry in the Genesis of Capitalism* (Cambridge, 1981); Maxine Berg and Pat Hudson, *Manufacture in Town and Country Before the Factory* (Cambridge, 2002).

33 Marilyn J. Boxer, "Women in Industrial Homework: The Flowermakers of Paris in the Belle Epoque", *French Historical Studies*, 12:3 (1982), pp. 401–23; Sheila C. Blackburn, " 'No Necessary Connection with Homework': Gender and Sweated Labour, 1840–1909", *Social History*, 22:3 (1997), pp. 269–85; Malin Nilsson, "Seasonal Variation of Hours Worked in Home-Based Industrial Production: Evidence from Sweden 1912", *Economic and Industrial Democracy* 40:4 (2019); Jessica S. Bean, " 'To Help Keep the Home Going': Female Labour Supply in Interwar London", *The Economic History Review*, 68:2 (2015), pp. 441–70; Malin Nilsson, "Needles and Cribs: Becoming a First-Time Mother and Starting Industrial Homework in Early Twentieth-Century Sweden", *Journal of Family History* 45:3 (2019).

34 Kalpana Hiralal, "The 'Invisible' Workers of the Informal Economy: A Case Study of Home-based Workers in Kwazulu/Natal, South Africa", *Journal of Social Sciences*, 23:1 (2010), pp. 29–37; Martha A. Chen and Shalini Sinha, "Home-Based Workers and Cities", *Environment and Urbanization*, 28:2 (2016), pp. 343–58 .

humanitarian organizations. Production was mainly concentrated in the rural areas and the products sold in urban markets, and workers were paid by the piece.[35]

The relation between colonization and home-based work is in itself an understudied but interesting topic. The idea of craft production as a development strategy initiated by the colonizers has often been regarded as a tool for the empowerment of women by international organizations during decolonization. It was also used by the apartheid regime in South Africa, which created incentives to move the clothing and textile industry to the so-called homeland areas with the lowest wages in the country. Between 1995 and 2001, mass retrenchment led to informalization of the textile industry in South Africa, as many of its workers became home workers. The effects of this history persist with design houses in South Africa able to get access to retrenched but skilled textile workers even today. However, as these workers start to retire, it seems that it is becoming increasingly difficult to find equally skilled workers for the same tasks.[36]

The economic history of colonized countries in the nineteenth and twentieth centuries is among other things marked by a shift from local production and export of finished products towards export of raw materials and severe disruption, often destruction, of the dynamics of local production. But there are exceptions. Economic historian Elise van Nederveen Meerkerk suggests that in Java, women continued to produce textiles in their homes for the local market.[37] A study of unemployment in Tunisia indicates the prevalence of women home-based workers in the "inner regions of Tunisia".[38] Interestingly, Ethiopia has a growing garment/textile industry, but a recent attempt by WIEGO to identify home workers in supply chains could not progress; it was found easier to locate workers who still do traditional spinning and weaving for local markets. The experience suggests that perhaps the role of global supply chains is less predominant and more limited than the literature suggests, and points to the need to develop greater understanding of the political economy of home-based work in hinterlands that are less integrated into global circuits of labour

35 Ruth Castel-Branco, "Research and Analysis of Home-based Work in South Africa: An overview report", unpublished WIEGO report, 13 September 2013.

36 Ibid.

37 Elise van Nederveen Meerkerk, *Women, Work and Colonialism in the Netherlands and Java: Comparisons, Contrasts and Connections, 1830–1940* (Cham, 2019).

38 Hamadi Sidhom, "Le travail feminin à domicile, taux de chômage et productivité : Le cas de la Tunisie", in Jacques Charmes and Mohamed Saïb Musette (eds), *Reflets de l'économie sociale* (Alger, 2006), pp. 199–223.

and capital, and whose interaction with globalization may be of a different nature. There is indeed a vast field to explore in future research regarding the role of the colonized and colonizers in home-based work in colonial and post-colonial times.

1.4 *Engaging with the Work, Life and Organizing Experiences of Home Workers across Time and Space*

The papers in this volume provide new perspectives and new case studies to a relatively scarce academic literature. Together with other papers and participants of the Stockholm workshop, they also contribute by identifying questions that are relevant to where we are now. That is not to say that the earlier literature is outdated, it remains an important ground from where we take off; however, just as capitalist production re-invents itself, so must the production of knowledge.

The preparation for the Stockholm workshop, including deciding on themes and papers, was done at meetings with representatives from WIEGO, CWDS and ARAB (The Swedish Labour Movement's Archive and Library). Co-production of knowledge through dialogue between activists and researchers has growing relevance for a global historical perspective on home-based work. Activists and researchers can benefit from each other's different outlooks, experiences and approaches in building and using knowledge. Such co-production of knowledge is perhaps still at a preliminary stage, though it has been an ongoing process for the past three decades in the case of home-based workers. Organizations such as WIEGO have worked systematically to collect data and information through a core programme on statistics in order to mobilize, organize and support home-based workers in their struggles for recognition and decent working conditions.[39] The current development of activist networks and organizations of home-based workers at local, regional and international levels, parallelled by a growing research interest in home-based work, paves the way for an intensified exchange. Knowledge-building regarding commonalities and particularities in home-based work across regions is of course still at a nascent stage. What is clear, however, is that research in this

39 See, for example, the report, *Mapping Home-based Workers in Kenya and Egypt*, February 2014, published by WIEGO and World Fair Trade Organization Africa: "The mapping exercise, conducted in 2013, aimed at expanding the global networking amongst HBWs by identifying home-based workers and support organizations in Egypt and Kenya that could be brought to WIEGO's HBWs Programme and the developing network of home-based workers" (p. 5). For statistics as one of WIEGO's core programmes, see https://www.wiego.org/our-work-impact/core-programmes/statistics.

area calls for greater engagement with the experiences, outreach and histories of organizations and networks of home-based workers, and how these are related to specific political–economic contexts in various parts of the world at various times in history.

Some key issues in the dialogue between activists and researchers at the Stockholm workshop are of significance for both global labour history of the new century and for ways in which workers' movements can respond to the changing relations between labour and capital. These include the following.

(a) How urban development is reshaping home-based work, particularly as population density increases, living spaces become smaller and thus space-intensive labour can no longer take place in the home; furthermore, home workers are being displaced to the outskirts of cities as informal settlements are demolished to make way for new formal housing—work conditions become harsher and incomes decline, since more time is spent on infrastructural challenges.

(b) The emergence of entrepreneurial ideologies and "start-up" concepts that encourage individualization rather than organizing.

(c) Where earlier home-based work was a supplement of regular employment, workers are becoming more dependent on home-based work as the option of regular employment disappears; as it is becoming increasingly difficult to make a living from one type of work, many are simultaneously taking on subcontracting, vendoring, going to the market, farming, cooking for sale, etc.

(d) People are still organizing and forming communities and networks—also without the formal organizations. Collectives among home-based workers are utilized to, for instance, counter violence from contractors and middlemen, to land bigger contracts, to gain access to finance and savings, to achieve recognition and increase bargaining power as well as the likelihood of getting paid on time—or getting paid at all—and getting orders ready in time.

(e) Barriers to unionizing/organizing home workers can be self-identification (as entrepreneurs or contractors rather than workers) and, in the case of women, opposition from families (mainly husbands) who try to prevent them from joining collectives.

(f) While ILO Convention 177 does play a role as a reference for the struggle, few countries have ratified it, and lack of legal recognition of home-based workers as workers with unionization rights is a recurring problem in many parts of the world, leading to their lack of access to the ILO's tripartite structure.

Global labour history has been criticized for its lack of spatial focus and over-emphasis on universalizing phenomena across spatial contexts. Research on home-based work—the most local form of production—helps to situate research at the local level and to follow the entanglements from there. Global labour history has a tendency to look more at structures and organizations, and less at activists and movements, sometimes making workers on the floor, and even more so women workers, disappear from the narrative. Focusing on a micro-historical approach and looking into agency and resistance amongst home-based workers is a way to give workers a voice in the shaping of global labour history. It is from such a perspective of co-produced knowledge that this volume locates its relevance in the narratives of global labour history.

2 Looking to the Future from the Past and the Present

During the last year of working on this book, the world was swept by the Covid-19 pandemic, which placed the home as a workplace at the centre of public attention in unprecedented ways. Several chapters in this book discuss how the introduction of wage labour under capitalism eventually led to the (ideological) separation of home and workplace. We discuss how the formal workplace—as a physical place separated from the home—became the norm that framed both (state) regulation and organizing practices. This dichotomy is of course problematic in many ways. It codes unpaid care work as non-work, and it obscures the fact that home is still the most common workplace. With the pandemic, the home returned as the workplace for new groups of workers. Even as the home reclaimed its status as workplace in the public mind, the pandemic also laid bare and enforced many old structures of inequality—not least those of class and gender.

The pandemic not only made the theoretical dichotomies of home and workplace more relevant than ever, it also came with a very real aggravated economic crisis. The relationship between informal work and economic crisis has been discussed in both previous research and in many of the chapters in this volume. Informal and irregular workers are disproportionately exposed during economic crises. They are in several ways more economically vulnerable and unprotected as compared to other groups of workers. In this pandemic, many informal workers have faced additional risk for their health. For some— street vendors, for instance—the risk came from working in crowded public spaces. For others, like domestic workers, the risk came from working in other people's homes; and for still others, such as delivery workers, the encounter with many different homes put them at great risk. All informal as well as irregular workers once again found themselves outside the scope of social security as they were excluded from—or rather, not considered at all in—various forms of economic compensation from the state during lockdowns.

Home-based workers, of whom many are informal workers, were also severely affected by the pandemic. As global demand falls, so do orders for home-based workers in global supply chains. In countries where the state provided some form of economic compensation to workers affected by the lockdowns and economic crisis, even high-skilled home-based workers in the formal economy had difficulties applying for support because of the lack of standard employment relations and thus an inability to "prove" what kind of wage they would have received under normal circumstances. This was even more the case for home-based workers in low-status industries and the informal economy. Several organizations of home-based workers have called for targeted relief from their government. In India, migrants among the home-based workforce in urban metropolises, unable to feed themselves or pay their rents, and facing basic survival issues, fled to their home villages, some making journeys of hundreds of miles on foot. In Eastern Europe and Central Asia, HomeNet called for minimum wages, treatment for workers affected by Covid-19—including those without social and health insurance coverage, and temporary relief from payment of taxes, rents and mortgages. They also called for support centres to provide services and information to home-based workers.

In Uganda, the "Home-based Workers Network" issued a statement about the economic impacts of COVID-19 for home-based workers. Here they describe how Covid-19 and related lockdowns have severely affected their work. For example, orders were halted without clear terms or information on how and when they would be resumed. The lockdowns and disruption of public transportation also severely limited the possibilities to pick up raw materials and to reach customers to sell their products. They also describe how funding for their business became even more scarce as money otherwise saved in group savings schemes were now being used for daily livelihood expenses.

Conditions within the home during lockdowns and increased incidence of working from home brought other issues to the fore, including what has been called the shadow pandemic of greater domestic violence, where current evidence suggests an increasing scale of intensity. The increase in domestic violence and gender-based violence was not a problem confined to only home-based workers. Nevertheless, as there is a relationship between economic stress and domestic violence, home workers as a particularly vulnerable section are also more exposed to domestic violence. Curiously, it was only when wage workers from formal workplaces suddenly had to work from home that the public eye saw the shadow effects of working at home. This was true not only for the problem of domestic violence, but also for work environment issues in general. Home-based workers—whether in manufacturing, crafts, computer-based work or other sectors—have always struggled with the challenges of how to make their (often limited) home space into a decent workplace that minimizes health risks, but now wage workers from formal workplaces were facing the same situation. This dramatically increased the public interest, including traditional trade union interest, in the work environment of the home.

Evidence on the increasingly volatile location of home workers—in, for example, the apparel industry—suggests that an overdetermined emphasis on global chains may be less useful in the future for manufacturing home workers. Detailed empirical analysis of in-country macroeconomics indicates the need to focus on the domestic market drivers of home-based manufacturing in this century within the larger historical shaping of home-based work under capitalism. At the same time, where home-based work has expanded and moved along new and internationalized service trajectories and higher skills, shortage of work is an experience common to new digital services as well as traditional home-based work in manufacturing. The book thus addresses new forms of home-based work and new data, and questions dominant paradigms regarding traditional forms of home work, as well as shifts and changes in forms of organizing.

2.1 *The Structure of This Volume*

The volume is organized into four sections around the following themes in home-based work: long-term connections, regulations, resistance and contemporary issues. The subject of each chapter is briefly outlined and contextualized in introductions to each section.

The first section presents examples of long-term continuity by describing similarities in the dynamics of gender, place and skill in four different settings between the 1860s and 2000: Buenos Aires in the mid-nineteenth century; Greece between late nineteenth and early twentieth century; Finland and Sweden in the mid-nineteenth century; and Turkey in a late twentieth and early twenty-first century setting. The section brings out the importance of context and how a seemingly similar experience can cover widely different experiences related to particularities of context.

The second section includes contributions that highlight the reasons for prolonged lack of regulation of home workers' conditions. From the end of the nineteenth century until the 1980s many unions wanted to ban home-based work. It was with the expansion of home-based work under neoliberalism that unions at national as well as international levels started to support the struggles of home-based workers for recognition as ordinary workers with access to workers' rights. The contributions illustrate this development by analysing the various ways of regulating home-based work, the ILO Convention as well as a number of instruments of multinational companies where the rights of home-based workers are treated as human rights.

The third section on resistance brings the struggles of home workers to the forefront. These struggles have been mostly neglected in earlier accounts of the history of workers' struggles and movements. The contributions here show how resistance is indeed a significant feature in the past and the present of home-based workers, whether inside, outside, against or with the support of unions. The section illustrates how alliances with women's organizations and sometimes governments have added to the visibility of home workers' struggles and in the long run have also gained international support from unions, leading to regional and international organizing as a strategy. The chapters highlight how the collection of documents, experiences and statistics has provided struggles of home-based workers with greater power in defining their situation and conditions, and in acquiring visibility. Such investigations of the history and the present of home-based workers have been useful in framing strategic points of intervention to improve the situation of home-based workers.

The fourth section presents some cutting-edge research on features and dynamics of contemporary forms of home-based work. New forms of employment of home workers dispersed over several countries through the intermediary of the digital platform are shown to display both commonalities with traditional home-based work, yet crucial differences in the highly centralized and opaque processes of selection and rejection of work and workers, and close monitoring of workers through algorithms. For the otherwise extensively researched field of home-based work in the apparel sector, a new perspective shows that recent restructuring of the global apparel industry sets limits on the use of home workers in India, with leading firms preferring sweatshop factory production where workers' labour productivity is more tightly controlled, enabling extraction of greater value from the unpaid component of labour time for capital accumulation. A multisectoral and detailed view of home-based work in India also suggests that domestic demand and its macroeconomic context is a more significant driver of home-based work than global dynamics at present. A focus on the turn towards self-employed home-based work by highly educated immigrant women from South Asia in Canada, forced into home-based work by ethnicity and race-based exclusion from the job market, suggests that women workers display entrepreneurial skills and creative satisfaction in providing catering and clothing for a clientele of similar ethnicity, where the work is laborious and time-consuming, yet the product is a complete creation.

PART 1

CHAPTER 1

Introduction Continuity and Change

Gender, Place, and Skill Formation in Home-based Production

Malin Nilsson

Home-based sewing and knitting are a type of in-between work – in-between home and workplace, in-between production and reproduction, in-between craft and industry. It takes many shapes and forms. However, despite its constant fluidity there is also stability across time and place. This section contains four papers from four very different settings: Finland and Sweden in the mid-twentieth century, Buenos Aires in the mid-nineteenth century, Greece between the late nineteenth and early twentieth century, and Turkey in the late twentieth and early twenty-first century. The four papers illustrate the complex interactions between discourses of gender, domesticity, and production in widely different settings across time and space. They however also emphasize the importance of context, and how a seeming similarity in fact covers very different experiences.

One of the most prominent features common to home-based workers across time and space is the connection between gendered discourses and the organization of production. This connection is clearly illustrated in all four chapters in this section. Gabriela Mitidieri's chapter describes the world of seamstresses in Buenos Aires of the 1850s and 1860s. She shows how this labour was performed through a multitude of labour relations, and how all these labour relations were informed by as well as formed by notions of gender. Leda Papastefanaki's chapter centers around the diffusion of the sewing machine. She shows how technical developments were adapted to fit with prevailing ideals of gender. Commercial advertisements targeted married women, emphasizing that the sewing machine helped them to produce goods for their family efficiently. Such a description made it possible to uphold the breadwinner norm, since no mention was made in the advertisements about how the sewing machine could help in working for the market although it was often also used for paid production by married women. The single breadwinner norm also appears in Laura Ekholm's chapter, which focuses on industrial statistics. She shows how married industrial home workers were registered as housewives in the censuses despite the fact that they did paid work. In Saniye Dedeoğlu's chapter,

© MALIN NILSSON, 2022 | DOI:10.1163/9789004499614_003
This is an open access chapter distributed under the terms of the CC BY-NC-ND 4.0 license.

gendered discourses are shown to underpin the entire organization of home-based garment production in Turkey.

The place of production is of course at the core of home-based production. Other industries are defined by what they produce, but home-based industries are defined by where they produce it. Mitidieri emphasizes another important aspect when she looks at the question of what is a home. Could it be the institution where you stay temporarily or is it a permanent residence? Asylums and institutions have formed an important venue for paid production throughout history. Workers in such institutions form a specific group that is, more often than other home-based workers, excluded from labour statistics. Mitidieri also discusses how the same type of work can be understood as home work, a domestic task or leisure. These different positions are formed not only by gender but are also inter-related with individual characteristics like class position, age, ethnicity, and functionality.

The chapters in this section also point to another important place of production – the atelier. The atelier forms a special kind of in between, both in terms of labour relationships and definitions. It is often located within or adjacent to someone's home. However, not all atelier workers live there, and there are different kinds of labour relationships within the atelier. Workers in an atelier can, for example, be unpaid kin, paid kin, employed workers, or apprentices learning the occupation. Ateliers form an important part of Dedeoğlu's chapter, but they are also significant in Mitidieri's descriptions of more than 150 years earlier. Atelier workers are also referred to in Ekholm's chapter as they pose a challenge to mainstream industrial statistics in terms of how they are to be counted. In Papastefanaki's chapter, ateliers like the one in fig. 1.1. appear as small business ventures in urban or semi-urban areas of Greece in the interwar period.

Skill formation is an important but understudied part of industrial home-based work. In previous research, industrial home work is often described as unskilled work with low entry-level bars. Two objections may be made to this description. First, feminist scholars have argued that the perception of skill does not always have to do with training or ability to perform a task, but rather is "an ideological category imposed on certain types of work by virtue of the sex and power of the worker performing it".[1] An important point made by all four papers in this section is that although often seen as an unskilled occupation, there are greatly varying levels of skill in home-based production. There are highly skilled home-based workers who make complicated, high-quality

1 Deborah Simonton, *A history of European women's work: 1700 to the present* (London, 1998), pp.76.

FIGURE 1.1 At the workshop of the seamstress Meropi Meraskenti in Kalloni, Lesvos island, c. 1930
SOURCE: CHRISTOS TRAGELLIS, *Η ΚΑΛΛΟΝΗ ΤΗΣ ΛΕΣΒΟΥ ΜΕΣΑ ΑΠΟ ΠΑΛΙΕΣ ΦΩΤΟΓΡΑΦΙΕΣ* (ATHENS, 2009)

garments, and there are workers who mass-produce products requiring less skill, like matchboxes or burlap sacks. Another interesting aspect of home-based work that we learn from the chapters in this section is that there is considerable integration of training within the home-based production system.

We can also see this from a life-cycle perspective, with many of the workers invested in skills that they could use in different capacities and labour relations in the course of their working lives. A seamstress could work as an apprentice in an atelier, as a seamstress in someone else's atelier, as a seamstress on the factory floor, as a seamstress working for an employer but in her own home, as a seamstress sewing for her own family or for others. However, as Papastefanaki shows in the example of working for the market or for pay, which of these capacities are made visible has to do with the context in which they are performed.

When we make long-term comparisons over time and space, it is important to not become deterministic. The experiences of home-based workers in the process of industrialization in Europe is not a road map for home-based workers in other contexts. If anything, home-based work illustrates a process of transformation and re-invention in order to function within the capitalist system. We see this clearly in Papastefanaki's chapter: home-based production was viewed as an outdated form that would quickly be replaced by factory production. However, with the mass diffusion of sewing machines and small electric engines, we saw the opposite happening. Production moved from the factory floor back into the home, and remains there, as is illustrated by fig. 1.2. These four chapters thus present examples of both continuity and change, the connection with gender, the complex position of paid production in the home within a system that creates a false dichotomy between home and workplace. But they also show how diverse the workers in home-based labour really are, not only in terms of skill, but also the multitude of labour relations that are hidden within the term "home-based workers".

FIGURE 1.2 Ahmedabad, India: Bhavna Ben Ramesh sews handmade purses out of her home. Her work is essential to her family's income, though women's home-based work often goes unrecognized. Bhavna joined the Self Employed Women's Organization (SEWA), a trade union that works to secure the rights of workers in the informal sector, and Mahila Housing Trust (MHT), a NGO that improves the housing conditions of poor, informally employed women, and received training on how to better market her products and to whom
PHOTO CREDIT: PAULA BRONSTEIN/GETTY IMAGES REPORTAGE

CHAPTER 2

Reading the Margins of Business Censuses

The Garment Industry and Home-based Industrial Work in Sweden and Finland, 1930s to 1960s

Laura Ekholm

This chapter analyses how home-based work and home workers were treated in specific nationwide business censuses in Sweden and Finland, especially in regard to the garment industry. This chapter attempts to study how the business censuses of 1931 and 1951 for Sweden, and of 1953 and 1964 for Finland, collected, defined, categorized, and reported data on home-based work and home workers.[1]

A basic premise of the chapter is that statistical censuses, just as with any other type of information, represent produced knowledge: governmental statistical agencies make a number of decisions and compromises when planning and implementing surveys and arranging the collected data. Statistical tables, therefore, are always a social construction and a compromise between many contradictory demands. What types of questions are asked and how the collected information is defined and categorized often reflect the structures, values, and needs of contemporary society. Conducting nationwide censuses is a laborious and expensive process. Hence all such collected information needs to bear social relevance, and herein lies the twist: the statistical tables always reflect social values.

The attempts and decisions regarding how to account for small-scale, arts and crafts industries illustrate a basic challenge in evaluating statistical information. To begin with, no published statistical table can include all the collected information. In addition, statistics are constantly changing. On the one hand, statistics need to describe trajectories over time; on the other, they should grasp new trends. New categories emerge while older ones become marginal. In this respect, the classification categories that disappear over time from published tables and the information that gets omitted can be as interesting as the published data.

1 1931 års företagsräkning (Stockholm, 1935); 1951 års företagsräkning (Stockholm 1955); 1953 års företagsräkning (Helsinki 1960); Företagsräkningen 1964 (Helsinki 1970).

© LAURA EKHOLM, 2022 | DOI:10.1163/9789004499614_004
This is an open access chapter distributed under the terms of the CC BY-NC-ND 4.0 license.

The availability of ready-made clothing symbolizes the rise of a modern consumer society where almost everyone can afford new garments and adopt novel fashions. Between the 1930s and the 1960s in Sweden and Finland, there was a shift from traditional, artisanal manufacturing of clothes to a standard-sized, ready-to-wear garment industry. Many major transformations occurred and intensified over these decades, ranging from how people lived, worked, and dressed, how often and where they bought new clothes, to how garment production was organized.

The garment industry played a significant role in the making of modern industrial Nordic societies. In 1951, in Sweden, textile and apparel companies comprised more than 20 per cent of all industrial firms, and the sector employed 15 per cent of the industrial workforce. In terms of providing employment, the garment industry was second only to the metal and machinery industries.[2] In Finland, in the early 1960s, the textile and garment industry employed approximately 15 per cent of the industrial workforce.[3] Above all, in both countries it was by far the most important industrial employer of women.

Whereas one of the most common themes associated with the history of European clothing concerns the "evil of sweating",[4] Swedish and Finnish scholarly literature has emphasized the rapid technological developments that took place in garment manufacturing in the interwar period.[5] In contemporary discourse, the objective of rational, efficient manufacturing coincided with ideas about public and individual health; the press promoted factory production as a guarantee of good hygiene.[6] At the same time, for Swedish ready-to-wear companies home workers were a crucial part of the story. In Sweden of the 1950s, the norm for married women was to stay at home.[7] This raises the question

2 1951 årsföretagsräkning [hereafter 1951 Census of Production, Distribution, and Services] (Stockholm: Kommerskollegium, 1955), p. 33.

3 Företagsräkningen 1964 [hereafter 1964 General Economic Census I] (Helsinki: Tilastokeskus 1971), pp. 42–43.

4 Andrew Godley, "The development of the clothing industry: Technology and fashion", *Textile History*, 28 (1997), pp. 3–10, 6–7.

5 For example, Erik Dahmén, *Svensk industriell företagarverksamhet: Kausalanalys av den industriella utvecklingen 1919–1939*, I (Stockholm, 1950), pp. 152–53; Piippa Lappalainen and Mirja Almay, *Kansakunnan Vaatettajat* (Helsinki, 1996).

6 Ulrika Kyaga, "Swedish fashion 1930–1960: Rethinking the Swedish textile and clothing industry", Ph.D. dissertation (Stockholm University, 2017), pp. 187–88.

7 Carina Gråbacke, *Kläder, shopping och flärd: Modebranschen i Stockholm 1945–2010* (Stockholm, 2015), pp. 102–03.

of the significance of home-based work for the growing garment industry in Sweden.

Finland, with a population roughly half that of Sweden, not only had a smaller economy, but was also a predominantly rural society until the late 1960s. For the Finnish garment industry, anecdotal evidence draws from the years of the Second World War and the postwar material scarcity. The theme of home work is more or less absent in twentieth-century Finnish literature.[8] The rationalization for such an outcome is a perplexing mixture of underindustrialization and rapid social and economic transformation, raising many new questions about the role of home-based work in postwar Finland.

This chapter, then, examines the following questions. How were home workers and home-based work accounted for in the original surveys in Sweden and in neighbouring Finland? How, if at all, was this information taken into account in the published census tables? To what extent were the tables able to cover different forms of work in the apparel industry of Sweden? Was Finland too underdeveloped or too modern for home industry? If the category of home workers disappears, does it tell us about the marginalization of home-based work, or does it, rather, reflect contemporary conceptions of predictable and relevant outcomes in the future?

1 Business Censuses as Sources

Supplementing the annual industrial and manufacturing statistics were the business censuses, conducted at intervals of approximately ten years, which aimed to collect information on all entrepreneurial activities. Due to the very nature of the garment industry, questions concerning home workers and home-based work are not necessarily easy to answer. Industries at the intersection between traditional arts and crafts production, industrial manufacturing, and trade contain multiple, overlapping meanings. Reconstructing developments in the apparel industry is challenging because it essentially functioned in small and micro-sized units. To begin with, small firms were often short-lived since they existed with the intent of providing a livelihood for the owners without any ambition for expansion. They left behind less data than larger corporations. Further, industries where contractual work was commonplace presented a challenge for statistical agencies. Were self-employed

8 Minna Salmi, "Finland Is Another World", in Eileen Boris and Elisabeth Prügl (eds), *Homeworkers in Global Perspective: Invisible No More* (New York, 1996), pp. 143–67.

business owners in effect subcontractors for larger firms? What was the threshold beyond which very small, craft-based manufacturers were omitted from the list of part-time workers? Many seamstresses, for instance, distinguished as independent proprietors, worked in positions that were indistinguishable from that of home workers.

The International Convention relating to economic statistics of 1928 obliged countries to collect company-level information on economic activities. The Convention stated that all countries should publish statistical information on such economic indices as professions, businesses, and company-level data.[9]

One of the main aims of the business censuses was to collect data on all enterprises, from large corporations to small proprietary firms including craft-based manufacturers, at a time when there was no up-to-date register of entrepreneurial activities. Whereas individuals constituted the unit of focus in population censuses, business censuses focused on firms of all kinds, from fishing and gardening firms to industrial manufacturing and small-scale arts and crafts firms, to finance, retail, transportation, and service providers. Agriculture was excluded because other statistical entries covered agriculture and forestry, and so also was the case for services pertaining to health, education, and religious institutions.

The business censuses supplemented the population censuses and, more important, the annual industrial and manufacturing statistics. Both Sweden and Finland have collected yearly industrial statistics since the nineteenth century. Collecting information from small manufacturers, especially in the countryside, was both expensive and laborious. Due to rapid industrialization, what had been a normal-sized industrial unit in the 1880s was considered a small company by the 1910s. Beginning in 1913, Swedish industrial statistics included only establishments with at least ten employees, or annual production volume of SEK 10,000 or turnover of SEK 3,000.[10]

In practical terms, the business censuses relied on the same methods as annual industrial accounts, but *all* registered firms, including the smallest ones, had to fill in the business census forms. The business censuses have proven to be better than industrial statistics for identifying home workers. For example, in 1951, the industrial statistics for Sweden identified only 21,101 home workers in the industrial and manufacturing sectors, while the business censuses reported 32,589 home workers.[11]

9 United Nations Treaty Collection, Chapter XIII: Economic Statistics, available at www.treaties.un.org, last accessed 8 December 2020.

10 Dahmén, *Svensk industriell företagarverksamhet*, II, p. 7.

11 1951 Census of Production, Distribution, and Services, pp. 42–43, 180–81.

Each company was sent a form with instructions on how to fill in the required information—there were two kinds of forms, one for firms with one to five employees, and the other for larger firms. Generally, the larger companies had more resources (and perhaps interest?) to complete the task. The small companies, on the other hand, were more likely to give non-descriptive and contradictory responses, or to ignore the questions altogether. Nevertheless the census returns, the forms that each company had to complete, offered glimpses of how small-scale businesses functioned, while also reflecting the boundary-lines between home-based workers managing their own accounts and industrial subcontracting. Some companies provided additional information through detailed source material, even if fragmentary in nature.

In order to understand the organizational reality behind the published tables, a sample of census returns is assessed here. I include a sample of business census forms from the ready-to-wear companies in the cities of Gothenburg and Borås in western Sweden from 1931 and 1951, and in Helsinki from 1953 and 1964. The west of Sweden formed a clear cluster of the textile and ready-to-wear industry.[12] Of the Finnish ready-to-wear producers, 70 per cent operated in Helsinki in the early 1960s.[13]

Needless to say, not all home workers were in the garment industry. It may nevertheless be argued that no other sector was as prone towards home-based work as the garment industry. For example, in 1931, Swedish industry and manufacturing consisted of 90,449 firms employing 713,274 people (excluding the owners) and, in addition, 14,123 home workers. In the same year, more than 80 per cent of home workers reported in the business census of Sweden were employed in the textile and garment industry.[14] In the same vein, not all home workers were women. Nonetheless the numbers show how questions about home-based work and female employment are intertwined: women accounted for 82 per cent of all home workers in 1951.[15]

The census returns have been organized into published tables. It is difficult to compare the tables over time, let alone how Sweden compares to neighbouring Finland. For instance, in the 1930s, *knitwear* could refer to small-scale production of knitted garments, which were typically home-made, as well as

12 Carina Gråbacke and Jan Jörnmark, *Den textila modeindustrin i Göteborgsregionen: En Kartläggning* (Göteborg, 2008); Kent Olsson, *En västsvensk industrihistoria: tiden fram till 1950* (Göteborg, 2012), pp. 51–88.

13 Central Archive for Finnish Business Records, Mikkeli, Central Federation of the Finnish Clothing Industry (Vateva), membership lists 1945–1976, B1:1, B2:1.

14 1931 års företagsräkning, pp. 42–43.

15 1951 Census of Production, Distribution, and Services, p. 59.

to light garments made of synthetic fibres with the production process located in textile mills. By the 1960s, knitwear increasingly referred to the latter. Consequently, the product categories and units changed over time. Practical considerations of whether, or to what extent, to report craft-based activities are far from consistent in the records. Comparing tables from one business census to another beyond just aggregated data requires a process of rearranging. For example, whereas in Sweden, the production of men's, women's, and children's ready-to-wear garments was reported separately in 1931 (115–117), the ready-to-wear industry had been combined into a single category by 1951 (164). The Finnish censuses operated more on an aggregated level—there were no separate categories for artisans, making it difficult to assess what kind of firms operated under the label of the garment industry.

Even more problematic is the fact that the different publications applied various means for reporting the owners, unpaid family members, managerial positions, and different subcategories of employees engaged in production. In 1931, the Swedish census grouped owners and managers into a separate category, whereas in 1951 it listed self-employed business proprietors and any assisting family members first, providing a detailed list of qualifications for different types of employees including those in managerial positions. In the tables given in this chapter, the data have been rearranged to enable comparisons over time. A home worker, as defined in the Swedish and Finnish business censuses, was a contracted outworker, someone working at his or her own premises but under contract to an employer. The one category that remained constant was that of home workers since they were always listed separately.

2 Reported but Not Published

All four census forms in the two countries contained a line about the (potential) number of employed home workers in the questionnaire. In the 1931 census, home workers were mentioned as a separate category in all the published tables. Rural women who earned incomes by producing handicrafts, washing and repairing clothes, and other small activities were omitted from the statistics. The same applied for those who held short-term, temporary jobs in a company—for example, seasonal workers at a restaurant or theatre.[16]

16 1931 års företagsräkning, pp. 27–28.

Twenty years later, the census of 1951 only mentioned home workers briefly: "in addition, special information on so-called home workers is included".[17] It depicted the category of home workers in one table: the number of persons engaged on 7 September 1951, classified according to occupation, etc.[18]

To obtain information on the small-scale arts and crafts industry, the statistical agencies in Finland collected data on handicraft-based small businesses every ten years. Collecting and interpreting the data was complicated, and Finnish authorities noted in 1934 that the results were not comparable to proper business censuses such as the 1931 business census of Sweden.[19]

The Finnish business census of 1953 basically contained the same information on home industry as the Swedish census. It defined home industry in parentheses, as consisting of "workers who work at home for a company". Two published tables provided information on home workers: "personnel of establishments" and "average personnel and wages and salaries of establishments".[20] Finally, in the 1964 Finnish business census, the only reference to home-based work noted that "Home industrial workers, working for the factories from their homes, are not included in the total number of workers". Only one published table provided information on "the personnel and the wages and salaries of establishments".[21] The 1964 census explained this by noting that "the only sector in which home workers appear are some specific fields of the apparel industry [...]. This above-mentioned group is just a small part of the textile industry". In fact, some 9,000 companies were removed from the 1964 census at the time, since the workers appeared to be working for someone else most of the time, or the company for one reason or another appeared twice in the register.[22]

In theory, the definition of a home worker was precise. In practice, atelier owners, bespoke tailors, and other artisanal manufacturers typically ran very small businesses. Especially in the countryside, they often had home-based operations. At an empirical level, the difference between a self-employed business owner working in his or her own residence and a home-based outworker working for a single employer is not easy to distinguish.

17 1951 Census of Production, Distribution, and Services, p. 26.
18 Ibid., p. 103, 180–213.
19 Finlands Officiella Statistik, XVIII B Hantverkstatistik år 1934 (Helsinki, 1936), p. 3.
20 1953 General Economic Census, I (Helsinki, 1960), p. 16.
21 1964 General Economic Census, pp. 52–57.
22 Ibid., pp. 33, 37.

Both contemporary scholars and economic historians in Sweden have pointed out that historical censuses underestimate the role of women in the labour market and as business proprietors.[23] The censuses only took into account full-time work by drawing a clear distinction between an employer and an employee, whereas women were engaged in part-time work and home-based work more often than men.[24] Hence, the census data reported married women as being housewives.[25] This invisibility of the economic impact of women has been one of the main themes of feminist activists campaigning for women's rights.[26] One of the main reasons for this oversight was that women were more inclined to do home-based work.[27]

A study of the Swedish textile sector in the 1930s revealed a total of 1,100 companies with 90,000 employees and an additional 15,000 home workers.[28] Measured in this way, home workers accounted for approximately 14 per cent of the workforce in the textile and garment manufacturing industry. The same study also noted that trying to make a distinction between home-based work and home industries is problematic as the garment manufacturing industry is fluctuating and seasonal by nature, and so the boundary between the two categories is quite fluid. The established larger firms relied on the help of independent bespoke tailors and seamstresses whenever the demand was higher than their normal production capacity.[29] These independent workers might, in turn, contract other self-employed women to help them meet deadlines. In other words, the industry relied to a great extent on subcontracting and home workers, but this reality is barely visible in any of the statistical censuses.

Describing a completely different geographic, historic, and temporal context, Elisabeth Prügl has analysed the situation of a Mexican seamstress working for a contractor in the suburbs of Mexico City in the 1990s. In her example, the seamstress identified herself as an entrepreneur. Sometimes she subcontracted her orders to other women to meet deadlines during the high season. At the same time she could not afford to legalize her operations, because that

23 Lena Andersson-Skog, "In the shadow of the Swedish welfare state: Women and the service sector", *Business History Review*, 81 (2007), pp. 451–70, p. 460; Margo Anderson, "The history of women and the history of statistics", *Journal of Women's History*, 4 (1992), pp. 14–36.

24 Nilsson, "Taking work home".

25 C.-E. Quensel, "Antalet förvärvsarbetande gifta kvinnor i Sverige: Några kommentarer till data från folkräkningen 1945", *Ekonomisk Tidskrift*, 53 (1951), pp. 244–57.

26 Anderson, "The history of women and the history of statistics".

27 Nilsson, "Taking work home".

28 Kristensson, *Studier i Svenska Textila Industriers Struktur*, p. 115.

29 Ibid., pp. 152–53.

would have required her to pay taxes.[30] Despite obvious non-response biases, it is still easy to account for the number of home workers. In contrast, it is very difficult to assess the role of independent self-employed workers. Hence, it is also important to look at the introductory sections of the published censuses; do they discuss such classification problems and how to solve these problems?

The 1931 census for Sweden contains a lengthy discussion on the difficulties of defining home workers. In terms of occupational categories, the census made an interesting distinction between "industry and handicrafts" and "industry and handicrafts combined with other livelihoods".[31] This kind of combined category, of which a typical example would be dressmaking and retailing, captured the hidden dynamics underpinning normal classifications wherein officials often forced complex economic activities into simplistic, easily definable categories. In this category, every tenth employee was a home worker.

Interestingly, the 1951 business census explained that initially, the aim had been to distinguish home workers from self-employed "business owners". It was not possible, however, to realize this aim, because "*the data did not allow for such a distinction to be made*".[32] The Finnish statistics seemed to be wholly reliant upon the assumption of a single employer employing individuals. The statistics lacked standard categories for contractors and intermediaries that would take into account the multilayered chains of employment. Hence, home workers moved to the margins of the business censuses, almost disappearing, which indicates that the importance of these workers was declining. In absolute terms, however, between 1931 and 1951, the reported number of home workers in Sweden increased from 14,000 to 32,500.[33] Similarly, in Finland, whereas the 1953 business census listed 3,800 home workers, the number of reported home workers almost doubled in eleven years and in 1964, the census counted more than 6,000 home workers. It is not entirely clear how these numbers were derived.[34] This rise seems to have been due to changes in how the data were organized under the various categories. For instance, the 1964 census included electricians from remote areas in the countryside, who were employed by large power plant companies yet worked on their own and lived near the power stations, in the category of home workers. Many home industry

30 Elisabeth Prügl, "Biases in labor law", in Boris and Prügl (eds), *Homeworkers in Global Perspective*, pp. 210–11.

31 1931 års företagsräkning, p. 33.

32 1951 Census of Production, Distribution, and Services, p. 28.

33 Ibid., p. 181.

34 1964 General Economic Census, pp. 52–53.

jobs were to be found listed under the category of consumer goods, such as the making of toys. The English-language summary in the census explained this oversight as follows: "Omission occurs in the case of very small enterprises, mainly such which have no enduring business premises".[35] This suggests that such omissions pertained mainly to people who were employed elsewhere, yet occasionally earned income on their own account. The next sections will put these numbers into context.

3 The Return of Home Industry in Interwar Sweden

Historically, Swedish home industry was a rural phenomenon: it belonged to the putting-out system of textile weaving that took place on small, unproductive farms in the nineteenth century.[36] A contractor would bring the materials to a farm, which the family worked on to earn extra income to supplement their farming work, especially during the long winter months. The contractor would then pick up and sell the finished products.[37] The mechanization of the textile industry gradually replaced this type of home work in the later part of the nineteenth century.[38]

In the 1930s, persons employed in the Swedish manufacturing and services sectors outnumbered those working in the agricultural sector. Electrification and the manufacture of motor vehicles in the interwar period also led to a spread of small businesses.[39] The surveys recorded a large number of micro-sized businesses: cafeterias, laundries, tailoring, shoemaking, and retailing. The majority of census returns at the time came from micro-sized companies and workshops run by self-employed proprietors and their family members. The Swedish business census of 1931 reported more than 90,000 manufacturing establishments.

Publications of the 1950s, looking back to the interwar period, reported innovations in materials, such as new synthetic fibres, logistics, and retailing

35 Ibid., p. 40.

36 Maths Isacson and Lars Magnusson, *Proto-Industrialisation in Scandinavia: Craft Skills in the Industrial Revolution* (Berg, 1987).

37 Gertrud Grenander-Nyberg, "Sömnadsindustrien: En översikt av dess uppkomst och utveckling i Sverige", in Torsten Althin (ed.), *Daedalus: Tekniska museets årsbok* (Stockholm, 1946), pp. 75–120, p. 80.

38 Ibid., p. 83; see also, Olsson, *En västsvensk industrihistoria*, pp. 52–53.

39 Lennart Schön, *An Economic History of Modern Sweden*, Routledge Explorations in Economic History 54 (Abingdon, 2012), p. 226; Andersson-Skog, "In the shadow of the Swedish welfare state", p. 457.

methods. Most notably, the entire concept of how to plan needlework completely changed towards taylorism-inspired management, standardization and measurement of different, specific tasks, unit pricing, and a more rational organization of production lines. One of the biggest changes in the interwar era was the introduction of the assembly line. These changes transformed the garment industry so completely that the economist Erik Dahmén wrote, in the early 1950s, that it was debatable whether it belonged to the same field of industry as earlier.[40]

Anecdotal evidence clashed with the images of speed and modern scientific management among scholars writing about the new working methods and assembly lines. Several major Swedish companies celebrated their success and published company histories as tribute volumes on the occasion of their anniversaries. These publications, written for their social peers, merely conveyed the image the company wanted to advertise. Interestingly, such volumes, published in the 1930s and 1940s, often mention home workers as an important resource in their formative years.

For instance, according to the company history of Erikson & Larsson, two young men, O. Erikson and P. Larsson, moved to Borås from the countryside to start a small-scale business in ready-made work clothes. In the beginning, the entire production relied on home-based work. As the business grew, the firm hired representatives and soon thereafter, they opened an impressive factory in the town.[41] Similarly, the Gothenburg-based Firma Gunnar Lind only had a warehouse when it started, with all production subcontracted to home workers.[42] In Uddevalla, Schwartzman & Nordström became, within a short period of time, the second largest industrial manufacturer in town. One consistent feature during its years of growth was the role of home workers. In 1920, the company had 260 employed workers and some 100 home workers.[43]

Most Swedish seamstresses ran ateliers with quite modest profits. How did they identify themselves in the 1931 census? When filling in the survey forms, some of the respondents had trouble identifying themselves as business proprietors. A sample consisting of seamstresses from Gothenburg reveals their confusion. Carolina Emilia Andersson, 64 years of age, reported that she was "sewing at home for private persons". Selma Matilda Gustafson used the exact

40 Dahmén, *Svensk Industriell Företagarverksamhet*, II; Kristensson, *Studier i Svenska textila industriers struktur*.

41 *Aktiebolaget Erikson & Larson, Borås 1892–1942: En minnesskrift* (Göteborg, 1942).

42 *Firma Gunnar Lind 1924–1949* (Göteborg, 1949), pp. 6–7.

43 Olsson, *En västsvensk industrihistoria*, p. 125; Robert Schwartzman, *Aktiebolaget Schwartzman & Nordström* (Göteborg, 1943).

same words, but then continued as follows: "I don't think this task refers to me; should I only report that I am sewing without any employees, while I am taking care of the household?" A third respondent, Alma Andersson, clarified her work status in the following manner: "[...] no other activity than home-based sewing, in an apartment of one room and a kitchen, no license to trade, no employees, thus I can hardly be identified as a business proprietor or anything like that".[44]

The business census categorized such women as self-employed workers who managed their own accounts under the heading of seamstresses. It is not possible, however, to know the extent to which they had control of their own work. The term "private persons" most probably indicated customers who commissioned bespoke clothing from a seamstress, and may refer to the custom of visiting the homes of customers. It is likely, however, that occasionally the same seamstresses undertook piece-work for private persons. Herein lies the difficulty of distinguishing between home workers and self-employed business proprietors. The emergence of the "modern" Swedish garment industry also meant a boom in the demand for home-based sewing.[45]

4 Postwar Economic Growth and the Home Industry in Sweden

The 1950s were the golden years of the Swedish garment industry. Compared to the situation elsewhere in war-torn Europe, Sweden's infrastructure remained intact at the end of the Second World War. The garment industry produced goods for domestic use. This was a market with constantly increasing purchasing power, but also more leisure time among all classes. Demand rose for new types of clothing.[46] For the Swedish garment industry, the most pressing problem in the postwar years was an acute shortage of workers.[47]

By the 1950s, the total number of employees in the Swedish manufacturing sector (including owners and managers) reached the milestone figure of 1 million. The ready-to-wear garment industry alone employed nearly 44,000 people.[48] Beneath the surface, though, the Swedish textile industry was

44 Swedish National Archives [hereafter SNA], Stockholm, Kommerskollegium, Företagsräkningen 1931, Ha: 372, translated from the original Swedish by the author.

45 Grenander-Nyberg, *Sömnadsindustrien*; see also Nilsson, "Taking work home".

46 Gråbacke, *Kläder, shopping och flärd*, p. 102.

47 Johan Svanberg, "Migration at the multi-level intersection of industrial relations: The Schleswig-Holstein Campaign and the Swedish garment industry in the early 1950s", *Scandinavian Economic History Review*, 66 (2018), pp. 54–72, pp. 62–63.

48 1951 Census of Production, Distribution, and Services, p. 191.

undergoing thorough structural changes. While the total number of employees across the textile and garment industries remained stable, the textile industry was reducing the number of employees. Most new jobs were to be found in the garment industry.[49]

Table 2.1 illustrates three overlapping changes in the growing ready-to-wear sector, and how bespoke tailoring and seamstresses were affected. The table shows the disappearance of small tailors: between 1931 and 1951, 2,869 traditional tailors had disappeared. At the same time, the number of dressmakers remained practically the same. It is credible, but hard to prove, that some of them did commissioned work under contract for larger manufacturers.

Furthermore, where the 1931 business census showed approximately 13,500 jobs in the ready-to-wear manufacturing sector, as compared to 8,853 tailors and 600 seamstresses, by 1951, the number of employees in the ready-to-wear sector had increased to over 52,000, when more than 8,000 home workers made ready-to-wear garments at home.

Through the postwar years, economic rationalization was a declared objective. The general wage level needed to improve, and this was possible due to the industrial renewal which kept productivity high. The balance and consensus for the rationalization measures were achieved through negotiated collective agreements between employers' organizations and workers' unions.[50] Such policies favoured larger businesses. In the retail sector, small retailers experienced increased pressure from larger chains. Over the next two decades, an entire generation of small businesses disappeared.[51] The logic underlying the existence of the garment industry was in conflict with the general economic policy of Sweden. In the garment industry, large firms were outliers rather than the norm and small companies continued to dominate. No matter how much the Swedish political system encouraged employers to negotiate with the unions, typically many ready-to-wear firms remained outside the employers' organizations.[52]

The 1951 business census returns offer a glimpse of the way in which production was organized. In 1951, the Swedish company Oscar Jacobson reported:

> [We employ] home industrial workers /10/ plus commissioned work by independent firms and establishments. Our sales reported on page 3 also include products that we commission on piece-work from our

49 Gråbacke, *Kläder, shopping och flärd*, p. 344.

50 Schön, *An Economic History of Modern Sweden*, pp. 218–20.

51 Andersson-Skog, "In the shadow of the Swedish welfare state", p. 457.

52 Svanberg, "Migration at the multi-level intersection of industrial relations", pp. 62–63.

TABLE 2.1 Proprietors, employees and home workers in the Swedish ready-to-wear garment industry, bespoke tailoring and seamstresses, 1931 and 1951

Cateogries	**Proprietors**				**Employees**				**Home workers**			
	1931*	**1951****	*Difference*	*%*	**1931**	**1951**	*Difference*	*%*	**1931**	**1951**	*Difference*	*%*
Ready-to-wear (115–119); (164–168)	492	595	*103*	*21*	13,535	52,928	*39,393*	*291*	4,757	8,128	*3,371*	*71*
Bespoke tailoring (120–122); (169–170)	7,069	4,200	*-2,869*	*-41*	8,853	4,658	*-4,195*	*-47*	1,241	502	*-739*	*-60*
Seamstresses (123); (171)	5,609	5,832	*223*	*4*	674	194	*-480*	*-71*	21	61	*40*	*190*
Total	**13,170**	**10,627**			**23,062**	**57,780**			**6,019**	**8,691**		

Notes: * Proprietors and paid managers; ** Self-employed proprietors

SOURCES: 1931 ÅRS FÖRETAGSRÄKNING, PP.102–03; 1951 CENSUS OF PRODUCTION, DISTRIBUTION AND SERVICES, PP. 188–92.

> subcontractors. For instance, Karlskrona Aktiebolaget, from Karlskrona, has 95 workers producing [for us]. [...] whether and in what form our other subcontractors reported their work, we do not know, but we will take this issue up so as to avoid double accounting.[53]

Additionally, Oscar Jacobson reported that the company retained ten home workers on "commission to their own firms and residences". Thus we know that Karlskrona AB produced goods for Oscar Jacobson. Most likely, the mention of "other subcontractors" refers to small firms near the factory premises in the company's hometown of Borås.

Some firms specialized as intermediaries. For instance, Handelsfirman Källa, owned by Allan Källqvist, employed nineteen women home workers. Its field of business was "subcontracting needlework".[54] The other companies running needlework workshops were less clear as to what their needlework included and who was doing the sewing. For instance, Syfabriken Textil, owned by Karin Gunnarson, seems to have been doing work for a larger company. The firm did "shirt sewing" and had six employees. Videx Konfektionsfabrik announced that it "runs a piecework business in the needlework business". Videx was owned and managed by Roland Widlund, and had five seamstresses and twenty home workers.[55] Another company, Ab Erik Winter, employed four men and thirty-eight women. In addition, it had "160 seasonal home workers".[56]

Runéakonfektion, a small firm, declared that its operations involved home-based needlework: "in addition, I have in my own workplace done piecework for E G Eriksons Konfektionsfabrik in Sjömark [...] all work is done by me alone".[57] What we do not know is whether this company reported its owner as a home worker or as a business partner. Table 2.2 illustrates the estimated shares of home workers in the textile and garment sectors in the years 1931 and 1951.

As shown in the table 2.2 below, from 1931 to 1951, the proportion of home workers among all employees in the garment manufacturing business hardly changed and did not show any drastic decrease. It seems safe to say, then, that throughout the golden years of the Swedish garment industry, the industry continued to rely on subcontracting and home work. The next section looks at the situation in Finland in the same period.

53 SNA, Stockholm, Kommerskollegium, Företagsräkningen 1951, Ha: 552.
54 Ibid.
55 Ibid.
56 Ibid.
57 Ibid.

TABLE 2.2 Estimated numbers and proportions of home workers in the textile and garment sectors of Sweden, 1931 and 1951

	1931		1951	
	(105–127)	%	(141–178)	%
Employed workers*	65,138	85.0	1,20,842	85.3
Home workers	11,520	15.0	20,835	14.7
Total	76,658	100.0	1,41,677	100.0

Note: Not including administrative and other office staff.

SOURCES: 1931 ÅRS FÖRETAGSRÄKNING, TABLE 1, PP. 42–43; 1951 ÅRS FÖRETAGSRÄKNING, TABLE A, PP. 30–31.

5 Was Finland too Underdeveloped or too Modern for Home Industry?

The take-off point of the Finnish ready-to-wear industry dates to the post-Second World War years. The wartime economy boosted the nascent clothing industry, as all firms involved in textile or garment production were obliged to deliver goods for military purposes.[58] In the early 1950s, the Finnish clothing industry was still struggling under heavy postwar constraints. Consequently, domestic consumption and the demand for clothing were at considerably lower levels than in Sweden. Attitudes towards the garment industry were contradictory. In the immediate postwar years, an organization called the Central Organization of Cottage Industry Associations (Kotiteollisuusjärjestöjen Keskusliitto), promoted cottage industries as extra means of livelihood for unproductive rural farms. The government consciously established tens of thousands of small holdings for farmers who had lost their land to the Soviet Union. Cottage industry advocates persistently focused on the virtues of craft-based industry. According to their world view, craft work would bring much needed extra income to poor rural small-holders.[59]

58 Piippa Lappalainen and Mirja Almay, *Kansakunnan Vaatettajat* (Helsinki, 1996).

59 Eliza Kraatari, "Finnish Cottage Industry and Cultural Policy: A Historical View", *Nordisk Kulturpolitisk Tidsskrift*, 1 (2013), pp. 137–52.

Home-based work in small farms leads one to ask if parallels can be drawn to the precarious conditions, high seasonality, and unaccounted work by unpaid family members that are typical of home industries.[60] The self-accounts of the Finnish garment industry have, however, focused on mass-production techniques that enabled companies to produce large volumes of good-quality items at low prices. The clothes represented postwar recovery as well as modern Nordic values. Finnish design was about bright colours, futuristic forms, and comfortable, casual, mass-produced but well-designed, high-quality clothes for men, women, and children alike. The symbolic value of modern Finnish clothing was perhaps even greater than its economic value. When the First Lady of the United States and fashion icon Jackie Kennedy posed in a dress made by the Finnish company Marimekko in *Sports Illustrated* in 1960, the impact certainly was at a national level, well beyond the small clothing manufacturers of Helsinki.[61] The implicit assumption was that the production line followed the norms of the Nordic policy models. The celebrated Marimekko found a niche in the U.S. market, while many more companies gained an advantage as a result of the 1961 European Free Trade Agreement. Finland, had a significantly lower wage level than Western Europe.[62] For a brief period in the 1970s and early 1980s Finland was a garment exporter, making clothes for companies like Britain's Marks & Spencer, but also for the huge Soviet market.[63]

Notably, an outstanding collection of short histories of nearly all the major ready-to-wear producers in Finland, *Kansakunnan vaatettajat*, does not pay any attention to home workers or home-based work.[64] The volume was compiled by Piippa Lappalainen and Mirja Almay, both designers with long careers in the Finnish clothing sector, as popular history looking back in time to the mid-1990s, when Finnish producers were either shutting down operations or outsourcing production to cheaper countries. Hence, it is a collection of short

60 M.J. Boxer, "Protective Legislation and Home Industry: The Marginalization of Women Workers in Late Nineteenth–Early Twentieth-Century France", *Journal of Social History*, 20 (1986), pp. 45–65.

61 "1960 Jackie Kennedy buys seven Marimekko dresses", www.company.marimekko.com, last accessed 5 May 2020.

62 Pirkko Haavisto, *Suomen Vaatetusteollisuus: Kehitys vuosina 1965–1978 ja kehitysvaihtoehdot vuoteen 1990* (Helsinki, 1980).

63 Lappalainen and Almay, *Kansakunnan Vaatettajat*, pp. 123–25, 201–03; for the relative ranking of Finland as an apparel exporter, see Kitty Dickerson, *Textiles and Apparel in the Global Economy*, third edn (Upper Saddle River, N.J., 1999), p. 194.

64 Lappalainen and Almay, *Kansakunnan Vaatettajat*.

histories celebrating the heyday of Finnish clothing, and highlighting its modern and innovative design.

Finnish economists in the 1960s noted that Finland, in comparison with the Scandinavian countries, had fewer industrial subcontracting jobs.[65] As Fougstedt, Berndtson, and Lindståhl write: "The most important reason [for larger firm size] is no doubt that, in Finland, the process of industrialization has taken place later than in the other Nordic countries, so that, from the beginning, the industrial establishments given larger dimensions corresponding to the demands of the time".[66] The economists observed that in many of the important branches of the economy, from mining to forestry and paper mills, economies of scale favoured mass production. The putting-out system was common in industrial sectors with relatively low mechanization and technical requirements. Since Finland industrialized later than the other Nordic countries, its industrial development "jumped over" the phase of many small-scale manufacturers typical of Swedish and Danish economic history. Finnish postwar taxation and credit policies further favoured big businesses.[67]

This analysis looked at the entire industrial manufacturing sector at an aggregate level. What may have been true for forestry and paper mills, though, seems less credible for garment manufacturing. At an empirical level, in the business censuses, the ready-to-wear producers of the mid-1950s were small, family-owned companies. The line between artisanal work and industrial manufacturing was fluid. Many manufacturers were bespoke tailors or dressmakers rather than factory owners.[68] Precise numbers are, however, hard to obtain. While the Swedish census reported the number of tailors and seamstresses, the Finnish census had no category for artisans. Therefore, in the Finnish case, it is not possible to estimate how many independent, self-employed proprietors might have worked in positions similar to that of home workers. Looking at the few tables that do mention home workers, such workers seem to have been rare and played no significant role in the development of the clothing industry-or in any other sector, for that matter. The numbers on their own suggest that the share of home industry in the Finnish garment industry was rather insignificant, and towards the mid-1960s it diminished further.

Table 2.3 suggests that both the textile industry and ready-to wear industry used home workers. The table also indicates that the clothing industry provided

65 G. Fougstedt, H. Berndtson, and S. Lindståhl, *Industrins storleksstruktur i Finland* (Helsingfors, 1961).

66 Ibid., p. 57, English summary.

67 Ibid., p. 32.

68 National Archives of Finland, Helsinki, Liikeyrityslaskenta, LyL K18F: 38.

TABLE 2.3 Proprietors, employees, and home workers in the Finnish garment industry, 1953 and 1964

Categories	Proprietors				Employees				Home workers			
	1953	**1964**	*Difference*	%	**1953**	**1964**	*Difference*	%	**1953**	**1964**	*Difference*	%
Textile (23)	1,351	676	*-675*	-50	26,399	27,807	1,408	5	2,010	1,437	*-573*	-29
Ready-to-wear (24)*	5,964	3,893	*-2,071*	-35	19,412	26,484	7,072	27	1,199	1,099	*-100*	-8
Total	**7,315**	**4,569**			**45,811**	**54,291**			**3,209**	**2,536**		

Note: * Without shoe and fur manufacturing.

SOURCES: 1953 ÅRS FÖRETAGSRÄKNING, PP. 34–35; 1964 ÅRS FÖRETAGSRÄKNING, PP. 52–53.

most of the new jobs. The number of home workers, however, decreased over time.

Table 2.3 shows that in less than a decade, from 1953 to 1964, half of all the proprietors in the textile industry disappeared. In the garment manufacturing industry, more than 2,000 firms disappeared, while the number of jobs and employment in the manufacturing sector increased. The number of home workers in both sectors, textiles and garments, dropped. The fact that the census specifically mentions the industries removed from the list—the garment industry, construction work, and retailing—makes the matter more complicated. Both the garment industry and construction work were prone to subcontracting; and the line between employer and employee was often blurred in these sectors. This raises the question of whether "work for someone else" or, in English, "no enduring business premises" might still refer to home industry work.

The failure to mention home-based work in all published sources suggests that home workers indeed had little significance in Finland. The results may also correspond to underlying contemporary aspirations regarding the future of industrialization and economic growth. Rereading the business censuses suggests that at least in the initial stages, Finnish garment companies too relied on piece-work, contracts, and home workers. What, for example, did the iconic Finnish design house Marimekko report in the 1953 business census? The newly established firm described itself as an "apparel shop making women's wear of printed materials relying foremost on contracted work". Marimekko, in its early days, had a manager and three employees, two of whom were home workers.[69]

6 Conclusion

In many respects, extant literature on the Swedish and Finnish clothing industries countered the near-universal themes generally associated with the industry. The literature emphasized the "modern" aspect of Nordic clothing, namely, the introduction of assembly line-produced synthetic textiles and knowledge-intensive management in the larger companies. This part of the story fits well with the general narrative on the rise of the Nordic model, industrial rationalization, high productivity levels, and rising standards of living.

According to anecdotal evidence, home-based work formed a major part of the business strategy for start-ups in the Swedish apparel industry. Only as

69 National Archives of Finland, Helsinki, Liikeyrityslaskenta K18F:38/2445.

the business grew did companies begin investing in modern facilities, or buy and convert existing small-scale textile factories into modern ready-to-wear businesses.[70] The enthusiasm for electrification and mechanization ignored this continuity and the renewal of home industry.

Censuses, like any form of knowledge production, are a sum of decisions and compromises. The Swedish and Finnish business censuses were clear in their definition of home workers, yet in practice it was often difficult to draw a line between home industry workers and self-employed business owners. Information disappears into the margins of the census tables due to an assumed decrease in social relevance.

The 1931 census in Sweden distinguished between different modes of production, including home production. In contrast, the 1951 census mostly ignored home-based work. The original census forms suggest that during the heyday of the locally oriented domestic garment industry, industrial subcontracting and home workers or a combination of these two types of labour were an integral part of garment production.

The literature on the Finnish garment industry recognizes neither home-based industrial work nor industrial subcontracting. The statistical accounts may have failed to provide information because it was not "out there" in the first place. At the outset, this seems to apply to the home worker question in Finland. Home workers barely appear in any of the sources. This makes for a story of an outlier category initially comprised of workers "too poor" for proto-industrialism, until the industry suddenly became defined by technology-driven and quality-based modern producers. The problem with the story line is its linear frame with the implicit assumption that any industrial sector must grow from small-scale firms to larger corporations. Despite all these shortcomings, the original forms of the business censuses are as close as one can get to information on short-lived, small companies in the ready-to-wear business. What kind of data were collected, and how they were measured, distinguished, and categorized, often affected the findings.

Acknowledgements

The research for this article was supported by the Emil Cedercreutz Foundation (Esko Rantanen grant) and by the Academy of Finland (grant 185640).

70 Grenander-Nyberg, *Sömnadsindustrien*, p. 102.

CHAPTER 3

"A Virtuous Woman Knows How to Sew"

Labour, Craft, and Domesticity in Buenos Aires During the 1850s and 1860s

Gabriela Mitidieri

In July 1855 a local newspaper, *El Nacional*, published a small piece asking for protection for those "virtuous mothers" who were used to sew certain items in return for a small amount of money every once in a while in the city of Buenos Aires.[1] The protection was needed because, due to a recent tax law, these women could be mistaken for *actual* seamstresses or dressmakers, and therefore be asked to pay the government for their right to work and produce. At around the same time, the French dressmaker Madame Perret-Collard arrived in the country, settled in a shop near the commercial area of the city, and started to look for young female apprentices who would live with her while she trained them in the craft.[2] A few years later, the Battle of Cepeda (October 1859) and the Battle of Pavón (September 1861) broke out between Buenos Aires and the Confederación Argentina.[3] Besides the numerous women who sewed uniforms on piece-work at their places of dwelling, young girls belonging to the elite classes donated bandages they sewed at home for the Buenos Aires army.[4] As did the female patients of the local lunatic asylum, who made shirts as part of their daily tasks of rehabilitation.[5] All these activities involved female labour, in which notions of femininity and virtue were intertwined. They were performed within places of dwelling, blurring the lines between paid and unpaid labour or home and workplace.

This chapter discusses the interactions between paid needlework and urban life, class, race, gender, and age in Buenos Aires City during the 1850s and 1860s. It focuses on the meanings assigned to women's work—linked to notions of virtue, honour, motherhood—and tries to understand the role played by these significations. Over the past few decades, historical studies with a gender

1 *El Nacional*, 5 July 1855, p. 2.
2 Mme. Perret-Collard advertising her new shop, published in *El Nacional*, 20 October 1856, p. 3.
3 A block of provinces that struggled against the customs monopoly of Buenos Aires. From 1862 onwards, Buenos Aires and the Confederación became part of the same national territory.
4 *El Nacional*, 4 September 1861; 3 October 1861; 7 October 1861, p. 2.
5 *El Nacional*, 3 September 1857, p. 2.

© GABRIELA MITIDIERI, 2022 | DOI:10.1163/9789004499614_005
This is an open access chapter distributed under the terms of the CC BY-NC-ND 4.0 license.

perspective have illuminated the dynamics of previously dismissed work spaces. As Eileen Boris demonstrates, home-based needlework and the system of sweated labour—among other kinds of industrial home-based work—showed how manufacturing and living could become "intimate".[6] Therefore, an analysis of home work provides the opportunity to question popular meanings of home and to expand the categories of work and worker, further extending the boundaries of labour history.[7]

Needlework in mid-nineteenth century Buenos Aires was one of the main ways of earning a living for women. It was also the craft with the largest presence in the city, with over 160 shops where people could buy ready-made or tailored clothing. However, needlework was ignored by historical studies on Argentinean labour until the 2000s, when feminist historians decided to explore the work and struggles of seamstresses and textile workers from the early twentieth century onwards, in the context of the growth of national industrialization.[16] Earlier manifestations of the labour of seamstresses, tailors, and dressmakers had not yet been analysed in depth. Although the interest of historians in domestic house work has increased over the past few years, it has not involved an analysis of sewing as part of the daily chores required in a house. There are two factors that might explain the absence of proper research in this field. One is the complex process of the circuit of labour in the garment industry and the artisanal workshops of tailors and dressmakers during the second half of the nineteenth century, in Western Europe as well as those North American and Latin American cities where European immigrants were starting to arrive. The main characteristics of that process were the fragmentation of traditional crafts (such as tailoring) and the industrialization of activities through outworking and feminization of the labour workforce.[17] Because of this, as some researchers have suggested, the boundaries between business and labour, exploiter and exploited, home and work, domestic and professional, public and private, skilled and unskilled, and even woman and seamstress seemed to get blurred. As Susan Ingalls Lewis showed in the case of Albany, New York in the 1850s, which parallels the trajectories of many dressmakers of Buenos Aires that will be revisited in this paper, "[…] these women: 1) ran both workshops and stores within their own dwelling places, 2) trained apprentices, and sometimes lived in extended households with their employees, 3) hired or worked alongside family members, and 4) mixed domestic tasks with commercial activities throughout the day".[19] Another

6 Eileen Boris, *Home to Work: Motherhood and the politics of industrial homework in the United States* (New York, 1994), p. 52.

7 Ibid., p. 5.

element is related to the obstacles that appear when we focus our attention on the domestic sphere and what women did there. As Eileen Boris stated, "waged labour at home shared the invisibility of housework".[20]

My aim in this paper is to enter the world of sewing in the city of Buenos Aires in the mid-nineteenth century, using the theoretical and methodological tools of Social History with a gender perspective. By doing so, I intend to analyse one of the main female occupations in the job market and its vastly heterogeneous forms: "real" seamstresses, occasional ones, and young girls being trained in one of the few crafts open to women in those days. This implies also a questioning of how certain activities using the needle at home could be understood as home work, a domestic task or leisure, sometimes paid and sometimes not. It is a chance to recover the historical meanings assigned to women's work and how they played a role within the margins of actions of different women. How those meanings were sometimes used in their favour, helping these women to earn a living or to demand—of the government, of their employers—what they believed was rightfully theirs. By examining their demands, I try to reflect upon the formation of a new state in South America, presented as "modern" and "liberal" and on how the state adapted itself to the demands of a capitalist international division of labour and assigned very specific roles to women in the framing of public policies—as poor women—embodied by the ladies of the Sociedad de Beneficencia, or as mothers and hardworking women worthy of benefits.

I explore a variety of primary sources in my attempt to understand activities related to needlework performed by women and girls in mid-nineteenth-century Buenos Aires. The main source for this analysis is the local newspaper, *El Nacional*, which was started on 1 May 1852, a moment of renewed public and political life in which the press played a key role. My attention is focused on its advertisement section, that is, the last two pages of the four-page newspaper. I analyse advertisements relating to the supply and demand of needle workers; advertisements of tailors and seamstresses, or of slop-shops advertising services or goods that could be found in their shops; and the very first advertisements of sewing machines. The men in charge of newspapers and magazines in Buenos Aires also took the lead in moulding public opinion and forging common notions of identity within the state. *El Nacional* had high-profile politicians as journalists and editors, such as Domingo Sarmiento, future President of Argentina, and Dalmacio Vélez Sarsfield, who would be named Minister of Internal Affairs in Sarmiento's government. Their connections with the government of Buenos Aires gave them access to various subsidies and benefits.[8] Therefore, this chapter also focuses on the debates on women's work,

8 Alberto Lettieri, "La república de la opinión: Poderpolítico y sociedad civil de Buenos Aires entre 1852 y 1861", *Revista de Indias*, vol. LVII, no. 210 (1997), pp. 497–99; and Fabio

motherhood and feminine virtues that appeared in this newspaper, to get a sense of how these subjects were matters of interest to the new liberal government. Also, by taking into consideration not only the articles of journalists but also the little comic pieces in the form of short dialogues where seamstresses and tailors were portrayed, it is possible to reconstruct a vivid image of the dynamic world of needlework at that particular time and place.

Another source I analyse is the 1855 Buenos Aires census, which was one of the first actions taken by the new state in order to have a record of its population. Along with the Statistical Records of the State of Buenos Aires, these sources allow us to take a look at the social and economic life of the city.

In order to assess the learning process of needle skills by little girls, I explore sources such as handbooks, apprenticeship contracts, journalistic accounts, and testimonies of women of the Sociedad de Beneficencia (Welfare Society) regarding the raffles of needlework pieces sewn by girls and women who attended the institutions administered by the Society—students, orphans, and patients from the asylum. The Sociedad was the main welfare institution of the government of Buenos Aires devoted to women and children, and it was headed by powerful women from the local elite. It was set up by the government of the province in 1823, and it depended on the government both legally and financially until it was nationalized in 1880.[9] In a political context framed by the making of a new liberal project after the downfall of the Juan Manuel de Rosas government in 1852, the Sociedad de Beneficencia played a key role as the welfare arm of the state, led by ladies of the elite. Through these institutions, the women in charge gave meaning to the notions of female republican virtue, encouraging industrious labour such as sewing and embroidery among poor working women, orphan girls and patients of hospitals.[10]

I also explore the demands made to the Buenos Aires City Hall by women asking for tax exemptions, many of them widows after the battles of 1859 and 1861. These are also important sources to look at since we can find here notions of virtue, motherhood, and sewing as an honourable occupation for women, but one that paid very little to support a family. By considering the trajectories of different women who sewed to make a living, I follow the traces of a wide circuit of a highly feminized labour force. Seamstresses sewing at home, girl

Wasserman, "Prensa, política y orden social en Buenos Aires durante la década de 1850", *Revista Historia y Comunicación Social*, vol. 20, no. 1 (2015), pp. 174–180.

9 Valeria Pita, "Nos termos de suas benfeitoras: encontros entre trabalhadoras e as senhoras da sociedade de beneficência, Buenos Aires, 1852–1870", *Revista Mundos do Trabalho*, vol. 1, no. 2 (2009), p. 42.

10 Ibid.

apprentices living with their dressmaker mistress, young women learning to embroider, inmates of the local asylum stitching shirts for the Army—each of these activities deserves a chapter of its own, but the purpose of bringing them together is to connect the dots and to analyse the social experiences and cultural meanings embedded in the work of the needle at this particular time and place.

1 Buenos Aires in the Mid-nineteenth Century

At the beginning of the second half of the nineteenth century, Buenos Aires was a city undergoing great political changes. In 1810, the territory belonging to the Viceroyalty of Río de la Plata declared its independence from the Spanish crown. By the end of the 1820s, a precarious stability had been accomplished, with the landowner and military leader Juan Manuel de Rosas ruling over Buenos Aires and its countryside. He was committed to cattle farming which connected the region with different foreign markets, and this activity became the main source of customs revenue. Rosas entered into alliances with other provincial leaders, was part of a network of diplomatic ties with allied native communities, and had hostile relations with liberal intellectuals and politicians, most of who went into exile during his regime. The decades I analyse here were marked by a conflictual process in which two different national projects attempted to re-establish order after Juan Manuel de Rosas's coup: one of the Confederación Argentina and the other of the state of Buenos Aires. The new liberal elite in power in Buenos Aires City would not change the economic foundation of the system, cattle farming, with the newer sheep-breeding. However, with the growth of the city and demographic expansion due to immigration, some industries and artisans' workshops started to increase in number.[11]

After the end of the Juan Manuel de Rosas government, the city started to implement measures of renovation, following the idea of modernity pursued by the liberal elite in power. The expansion of the Colon Opera Theatre, the building of a new pier to receive the growing flow of migrants, enhancement of the system of gas-powered lights, the laying of the first railroad line, new urban

11 Hilda Sábato and Luis A. Romero, "Artesanos, oficiales, operarios: trabajo calificado en Buenos Aires. 1854–1887", in Diego Armus (comp.), *Mundo urbano y cultura popular* (Buenos Aires, 1990), p. 221.

markets, and greater attention to public hygiene and health were some of the innovative measures that were introduced.[12]

By the mid-nineteenth century Buenos Aires had a population of approximately 90,000 inhabitants;[13] 41 per cent of that number were immigrants.[14] Of the 43,000 women listed in the 1855 census, 30,000 were born in Buenos Aires, 7,000 came from Europe, 3,000 migrated to the city from the provinces, 2,000 were migrants from neighbouring countries, and nearly 1,000 were listed as Africans,[15] meaning that they were part of the enforced slave population that came to the region largely from the end of the eighteenth century up until the decade of the 1840s.[16] Of course, there was a larger African-Argentinian population, since the children of former slaves were not registered as "black" or "mulatto" as they were in previous censuses.

European immigrants and African-Argentinian natives did not settle in the same areas of the city. The former were mainly located in the central area, that is, the blocks surrounding the central square, Plaza de la Victoria. On Perú Street, a block away from the square, as a French traveller stated in the beginning of the 1850s, were located the main commercial establishments and several elegant stores, such as those belonging to French and Spanish tailors and dressmakers.[17]

The English, Irish, German, French, and Spanish established themselves in the northwest area of the city, near the Plaza de la Victoria. The San Miguel parish, west of the Plaza, had a high density of craftspeople, mostly French. Among them were many tailors and dressmakers. There was a high concentration of Italian immigrants in the southeast area, as well as Basque, Spanish,

---

12 Juan F. Liernur, "La ciudad efímera", in Juan F. Liernur and Graciela Silvestri (comp.), *El umbral de la metrópolis: Transformaciones técnicas y cultura en la modernización de Buenos Aires (1870–1930)* (Buenos Aires, 1993), pp. 180–187.

13 According to researcher Gladys Massé, the Buenos Aires census of 1855 listed no less than 92,709 individuals. These were estimations since there were no census records for quarter no. 2 in the General National Archive (AGN). See Gladys Massé, "Inmigrantes y nativos en la ciudad de Buenos Aires al promediar el siglo XIX", *Población de Buenos Aires: Revista semestral de datos y estudios demográficos*, no. 4 (2006), p. 13.

14 Gladys Massé, *Reinterpretación del fenómeno migratorio hacia la ciudad de Buenos Aires a mediados del siglo XIX.*, PhD dissertation (Universidad de Luján, 1993), pp. 55–56.

15 Gladys Massé, "Participación Económica Femenina en el Mercado de Trabajo Urbano al promediar el Siglo XIX", *La Aljaba, segunda época*, no. 1 (1996), pp. 82–84.

16 On the persistence of slave-trafficking up until 1840 in Buenos Aires, see Miguel Rosal, "La esclavitud en Buenos Aires y sus fuentes", paper presented to the round table: Fontes para o estudo da escravidão, em 5º Encontro Escravidão e Liberdade no Brasil Meridional, Universidade Federal do Rio Grande do Sul (UFRGS) (2011), p. 13.

17 Xavier Marmier, *Buenos Aires y Montevideo en 1850* (Buenos Aires, 1948), pp. 25–28.

and Portuguese men and women, who were involved in activities related to the docks. African, African-Argentinian, and Brazilian people settled in the western area of the city, in the parishes of Monserrat, La Piedad and Balvanera. These were suburban areas that led to the rural areas.[18] Thus, men and women from different backgrounds managed to earn a living in the city. Many women found in needlework a way to make ends meet.

2 Needlework in Buenos Aires in the 1850s–1860s

Eighty per cent of the working women who lived in Buenos Aires City identified themselves as either seamstresses or as employed in domestic work.[14] With respect to the world of needlework labour, it is hard to say how many of the women listed as seamstresses worked out of workshops and how many from homes. But information contained in the Statistical Register of Buenos Aires Province for 1855 allows us to quantify the garment industry in the city: there were 150 businesses included under the categories of tailor shops, slop-shops, and millinery shops, and 18 dressmaker shops. In a comparative assessment of all artisanal activities, the Register stated that there were 119 shoemakers' shops; 78 blacksmiths' workshops; 39 tin workshops; 72 jewellery stores, clockmakers' shops, and silversmiths' workshops; and 5 printing shops.[15] Thus needlework was the largest artisanal activity in this time and place.

3 Sewing in Your Own House or Someone Else's

There were different ways in which one could earn a living as a seamstress. Women who knew the craft could be hired in shops or ateliers under the supervision of tailors or dressmakers. They would be in charge of sewing pieces of dresses, trousers or vests previously cut by their masters. If the clothing was standardized or ready-made, the number of pieces to sew would be larger. Women with stitching skills could pick up these pieces regularly or sporadically to work at home, and then deliver the finished garments. To be hired as a maid could include mending outfits of the masters of the house. To be trained as an apprentice could mean helping a dressmaker with daily work.

18 Massé, "Reinterpretación", pp. 58–59.

4 Own Account Workers Sewing by the Piece

In August 1861, the newspaper *El Nacional* published a fictional dialogue between a Spanish tailor and a group of seamstresses. The scene takes place at the tailor's shop at the break of day, when the seamstresses arrive to deliver the pieces they had sewn and to receive the corresponding payment.

A SEAMSTRESS: When should I send my son to get the pieces to sew?

TAILOR: Your son can come tomorrow morning; you'll have the pieces fixed by then. Several seamstresses: Master! ... Master ... let us go. [...] Pay us tonight because we won't be able to come tomorrow.

TAILOR: Evil ladies! Always with "pay" on your lips! Tonight I can pay no more, it is late.

A SEAMSTRESS: Master, at least pay me tonight, I live very far away from here.

TAILOR: If you live far, move closer. Ea! Outside, everybody! Tonight there's nothing more to be done. Domingo, turn off the gas, it is very late.[19]

Even though the dialogue was made up and had a humorous tone—in the original there were markers of the typical northern Spanish accent of the tailor—its setting had realistic elements: mention of the gas-powered light system, an example of European craftsmen setting up a store in the city, and reference to the organization of garment production that involved occasional hiring of seamstresses who did piece-work sewing in their own homes. The dialogue reveals that the workers were all women, and that some of them had children who helped them by picking up the pieces to sew. Also, the fact that one of them mentions the distance that separated the shop from her house is an opportunity to reflect on how many women seamstresses had to walk across the city regularly to earn a living.

This type of labour, work with the needle, grew side by side with the conflicts between Buenos Aires and the Confederación Argentina. As mentioned above, their complex relations during these decades culminated in two battles, in October 1859 and September 1861. This political confrontation was also to have an impact on work with the needle: besides the massive recruitment

19 *El Nacional*, 31 August 1861, p. 2.

campaigns that led to many tailors and apprentices leaving their positions to serve in the battlefield, the government of Buenos Aires started to issue calls for the making of uniforms for the army. In 1859 the Buenos Aires army had nearly 9,000 men and two years later the number had more than doubled, to 22,000 men.[20] To be able to provide that many uniforms implied the existence of standardized, "ready-made" garments. It opened up the possibility of disaggregating the different tasks involved in the making of garments, and allowed the outsourcing of needlework from shops to the homes of seamstresses.[21] Even though a local magazine commented on the arrival of the first sewing machines as early as 1854,[22] proper advertisements of these machines that were put up for sale and offered to tailors, seamstresses, and households were not widely published until 1861.[23] There is evidence that until the early twentieth century, sweat-labour systems of garment manufacturing involved hand-sewing. The making of a hand-stitched shirt could take approximately fourteen hours.[24]

During these years, the calls issued by the government for the supply of army uniforms were regularly published in the newspaper, and the names of the selected tailors or entrepreneurs in charge of providing them were also communicated by these means.[25] The men would undertake the task of cutting the fabric, while subcontracted women would sew by piece. The spread of this form of production had an effect on the requirements of the labour that was in demand. The advertisements mentioned the necessary qualifications of the workers: "To the lady seamstresses. You can come pick up pieces to sew at the slop-shop, 28 San Martín Street. Those who are not seamstresses, please provide certification of your good performance".[26]

20 General Mitre Archive, Book XVI, Battle of Cepeda: 1858–59 / y Battle of Pavón (Ed. La Nación, 1912).

21 On the links between war and state promotion of standardized army uniforms, see for the French case Judith Coffin, *The Politics of Women's Work: The Paris Garment Trades* (Princeton, 1996), pp. 56–57.

22 *La Revista del Plata*, abril 1854, mentioned in Luis A. Romero and Hilda Sábato, *Los trabajadores de Buenos Aires: La experiencia del mercado: 1850 –1880* (Buenos Aires, 1992), p. 204.

23 *El Nacional*, 1 January 1861, p. 4.

24 Marcela Nari, "El trabajo a domicilio y las obreras (1890–1918)", *Razón y Revolución*, no. 10 (2002), p. 3.

25 See, for example, "Propuestas aceptadas" (Accepted proposals), open call for the making of uniforms, *El Nacional*, 19 May 1860, p. 3.

26 *El Nacional*, 26 December 1860, p. 3.

According to this, the job was available for "seamstresses", that is, women who have been trained in the craft of sewing, but also for less skilled women who could use the abilities gained by learning from their mothers or at school.

Also in August 1861, another fictional dialogue was published in *El Nacional*. This time it involved an entrepreneur, Don Ángel, his clerk, Mr Vazquez, and a large group of seamstresses. "Please accept my sewing for I'm in a hurry", says one. "Me, Mr. Vazquez, I've left my six boys all alone since this morning. Tell the book-keeper to pay me so I can buy bread for my children", yells another. When a third one intervenes asking to be paid soon, saying she came with a special recommendation, the other seamstresses interrupt her and shout, "Get out! There are no privileges here. Look this little miss wearing a fancy hat, sewing on a whim to buy herself a piece of jewellery. She's not happy with taking our jobs away, she also wants to be the preferred one! Get out, fancy girl!"[27] Finally, Mr Ángel makes an entrance in an attempt to calm the tension, and he tells the women there aren't any more pieces of sewing to give out, but he could give them a recommendation to go to Lozano or Peralta, other entrepreneurs like himself.

Soon after these fictional dialogues were published, in October 1861, a journalist's account described an equally loud scene where a group of women workers stood in line from 6 in the morning to 10 at night in front of the entrepreneur Ángel Martinez's store (perhaps the man who inspired the "Don Ángel" of the previous dialogue) to receive pieces of fabric to sew army uniforms. According to the journalist, one of the women shouted, "War for everybody so poor women can keep receiving pieces to sew!"[28]

The work of these women overlapped with the daily tasks they had as mothers. Simultaneously with the increasing recruitment of men into the army, many of the women found themselves having to be in charge of the family. Also, in this context of necessity, when these women asked for more sewing pieces to earn a living for themselves and their children, it appeared that there was a convergence of identities—as workers, as women trying to earn a living on their own—among them, in opposition to those who only occasionally used their skills with the needle to collect some extra money.

The notions of what to expect from a working mother changed during this period, if we take a look at the words of men writing in the press. As I mentioned previously, in 1855 a new tax was applied on local manufacturing. Worried about the abuses this might cause, a journalist of *El Nacional*

27 *El Nacional*, 27 August 1861, p. 2.

28 *El Nacional*, 29 October 1861, p. 2.

wrote: "there are taxes that have wrongfully classified women as seamstresses or dressmakers behind doors. This is extraordinary; this is inhumane; to afflict a virtuous mother and to drive her to despair [...]".[29]

According to this journalist, there was a big difference between the virtuous mother and the full-time seamstress or dressmaker. The work performed by the former after finishing her unpaid domestic tasks should be protected and not taxed. In his perspective, that activity did not make a seamstress out of her, because it was her role as a mother that primarily defined her identity.

Five years later, in December 1860, in a reader's letter published in the newspaper, the reader, a concerned citizen, reported his horror at witnessing how a cart driver ran over an "innocent creature" that was eating a piece of bread in the middle of the street. He claimed, "There are certain mothers in these neighbourhoods who, in order to free themselves from their children, give them a piece of bread and throw them to the streets, causing the obstruction of the public road with over fifty boys, from age 2 to 10 [...]".[30] The letter-writer, from the perspective of a citizen, intended to reprimand what, according to him, was a lack of commitment to motherhood. The fault was not of the cart driver but of those mothers who should have been taking care of their children inside their houses. Instead, they were probably busy sewing or going to the tailor's shop to ask for payments. Moral admonitions like this one began to gain a presence in the press, even though there were no specific public policies yet allowing intervention into the private spaces of workers' families.

However, these women also attempted to contest certain meanings ascribed to their work. In the year 1861, the seamstress Isabel Lugones decided to approach the nearest church to demand from the leading priest, Juan Paez, a note certifying that she was "poor with no resources", and that she relied solely on her sewing labour to earn a living. In this way, Isabel tried to get the city hall to grant her exemption from paying tax for night watchmen and gas-powered light. A similar claim was made by the widow Petrona Lagarza, represented by a lawyer in her neighbourhood. This lawyer wrote that she and her daughter "work at sewing pieces, which doesn't add up to enough money to even buy clothing. They are virtuous women, very committed to their work and because of that are very much worthy of a tax exemption".[31] To commit themselves to work, to toil as seamstresses, was for her and her daughter a way to lay claim to

29 *El Nacional*, 5 June 1855, p. 2.

30 *El Nacional*, 10 December 1860, p. 2.

31 Archive of Buenos Aires City, Box 5 1861-Government, Demands of light and nightwatch tax exemption from Isabel Lugones and Petrona Lagarza.

notions of virtue, and a chance to demand from the government an exemption from tax that would relieve the burden of having to support their families.

5 Productive Leisure: Middle-class Wives and Daughters

By the mid-nineteenth century, young *Porteño*[32] women who were financially supported by parents or husbands devoted a considerable amount of time to daily training in the art of sewing and embroidery, a common practice among females belonging to the elite classes. Bearing evidence of this were the numerous advertisements for haberdashery stores, offering sewing and embroidery items and patterns. In April 1857, Madame Ana Fontana, the owner of such a store, posted an advertisement saying that because of the variety of embroidery items she offered, the store "truly deserved to be visited by our elegant ladies".[33] There was also the presence of foreign imported magazines in the city, like the *Museo de las Familias*, a monthly illustrated newspaper in Spanish that had a "Fashion Bulletin" "with sewing patterns and drawings to embroider".[34]

However, in times of armed conflict like the battles of 1859 and 1861, the occupation of needlework found another purpose. In several editorials published throughout September and October 1861 specific demands were made of young women of the elite to sew and donate bandages to army hospitals.[35] Women of the Sociedad de Beneficencia were in charge of the receipt of such donations.

6 Between Craft and Industry: Sewing in Shops and Ateliers

The year 1856 was a time of intense work for the French dressmaker Madame Perret-Collard. A year earlier, the 35-year-old woman from Paris had arrived in the city and settled in the urban centre along with two compatriots.[36] She had decided to quit her lucrative position in the Parisian shop Maison

32 A person born in Buenos Aires City.

33 *El Nacional*, 27 April 1857, p. 3.

34 *El Nacional*, 17 September 1856, p. 1.

35 *El Nacional*, 4 September 1861; 3 October 1861; 7 October 1861, p. 2.

36 Buenos Aires census, 1855, Census sheet No. 184—quarter 12°—San Miguel parish. According to the census, there were three other French individuals living with the dressmaker.

Popelin-Carré[37] in order to open her own shop in Buenos Aires. Her brand new store, on the first floor of no. 50 Perú Street, above the Spanish tailoring shop of Paladio Sanglás, soon moved a few blocks south.[38] From the moment she arrived she started to post advertisements in the local newspapers, *El Nacional* and *El Orden*, offering her services in dressmaking, but also asking for female apprentices to train and seamstresses who would work for her.[39] And there were ads in response: at no. 225 Federación Street, across the street from Indian's Apothecary, someone wished to place "a 12-year-old girl as an apprentice in a dressmaker house".[40]

During this period, there were European craftswomen—seamstresses and dressmakers—who trained local and immigrant girls as apprentices. And for that purpose, they decided to specifically ask for them in the newspapers: "Required a little girl to teach how to sew",[41] or "a little girl who understands a bit of the craft of dressmaker",[42] were some of the ads posted in a similar tone to those posted by Mme. Perret-Collard. To "understand a bit of the craft" referred to the basic sewing skills that girls learnt in their own homes from their mothers or older sisters. Those skills could have also been taught to them in the public schools for little girls managed by the Sociedad de Beneficencia. By 1858 that agency, run by women of the Buenos Aires elite, was in charge of fourteen public schools for girls in the city and forty-two in Buenos Aires province, in addition to the Women's General Hospital, the Women's Asylum, and an orphanage for little girls.[43]

The craft of a dressmaker, or a tailor, involved the knowledge of skills far beyond those learnt in school or at home.[44] The ability to take measurements,

37 *Le Moniteur de la Mode : Journal du Grand Monde: Modes, littérature, beaux-arts, théatres*, 1854, available at www.mediafire.com last accessed 30 May 2021. On the front cover of issue no. 2, 1854, there is a mention of the store where Mme Perret-Collard worked in Paris.

38 Advertisement of the dressmaker notifying the move of her store to her customers. *El Nacional*, 20 October 1856, p. 3.

39 See the advertisements posted by the dressmakers in *El Nacional*, 27 March 1856, p. 3; 27 April 1856, p. 3; 12 May 1856, p. 3; 4 November 1856, p. 3; 26 November 1856, p. 3; and in the newspaper *El Orden*, 25 April 1856, p. 3.

40 *El Nacional*, 5 December 1855, p. 3.

41 *El Nacional*, 5 October 1859, p. 3.

42 *El Nacional*, 10 April 1856, p. 3.

43 Pita, "Nos termos de suasbenfeitoras …", p. 42.

44 As historian Marcela Nari stated in the case of seamstress Milagros de Soria, in late 1800 in Buenos Aires: "Finally, she had to borrow money from her brother to be able to learn the craft properly in a sewing workshop. That is, there was an unrecognized gap between domestic sewing for the family and needlework for the market". Nari, "El trabajo a domicilio y las obreras (1890–1918)", p. 8.

to translate the vital statistics of a customer into a two-dimensional pattern, to properly use scissors in order to make the best out of a piece of fabric, to know the different types of stitches and be able to sew meticulously, or even to master the art of embroidery—these were skills that could only be mastered within artisanal training.[45]

Why should we analyse the training of apprentices into the craft as home-based work? As the US historian Susan Ingalls Lewis posited it in the case of nineteenth-century Albany, it was common to find home-based artisanal businesses with people toiling in both the shop at the front of their dwellings and the backroom in living quarters that must have doubled as workrooms.[46] In mid-nineteenth-century Buenos Aires, craftsmen and women could sign apprenticeship contracts with the parents or guardians of a minor, like this tailor did in the month of May in 1861.[47] In that contract, signed in the Protection of Minors Office, the tailor Mr Rathke committed himself to teach the art of tailoring to a young man named Julio Fortunato, and also to provide food, housing and pay him a monthly salary of $200, which at that time was about 20 per cent the monthly income of a tailor in Buenos Aires City.[48]

To be accepted in a dressmaker's workshop meant for little girls the possibility of learning a craft, but also, as Julio Fortunato did, their expenses being covered and receiving a minimum wage as payment for their hours of amateur work. Even though there were usually no formal requirements for boys and girls to be hired as apprentices, there were ads that confirmed a racial bias on the part of the masters. In 1855, an ad that asked for a little girl to be trained said she had to be foreign.[49]

7 Looking for a Maid Who Can Sew

On 9 October 1855, an ad was posted in the last pages of *El Nacional* for "a cook and a maid knowing how to sew, do the laundry and iron".[50] There was nothing extraordinary about this since it was usual to find ads looking for men and

45 Marla Miller, "Gender, Artisanry, and Craft Tradition in Early New England: The View through the Eye of a Needle", *The William and Mary Quarterly*, vol. 60, no. 4 (2003), p. 759.

46 Susan Ingalls Lewis, "Business or Labour? Blurred Boundaries in the Careers of Self-Employed Needlewomen in Mid-Nineteenth-Century Albany", in Beth Harris (ed.), *Famine and Fashion: Needlewomen in Nineteenth Century* (London, 2005), p. 228.

47 AGN, Secretaría de la Niñez, Adolescencia y Familia, Book 183, p. 172, May 1861.

48 Records of monthly wages of workers in Buenos Aires city, *El Nacional*, 1 August 1855, p. 1.

49 *El Nacional*, 22 September 1855, p. 3.

50 *El Nacional*, 9 October 1855, p. 3.

women to be hired as house servants. But this particular ad listed the main tasks that the woman in question had to do in order to become a housemaid. Among those tasks, she was supposed to sew and mend clothes. Along with expectations regarding the abilities of sewing, cleaning, and ironing, the ad also asked for certification of the candidate's suitability and good habits. She was also supposed to be "alone" and willing to live inside the employer's house. According to Brazilian historian Flavia Fernandes de Souza, who has analysed the work of domestic servants in Río de Janeiro at the end of the nineteenth century, the requirement of good habits was not directly linked with the quality of the work that women were supposed to perform, but to a consideration of her moral behaviour.[51]

Who were these women with needlework skills, hired to be maids? According to the 1855 census, there were a significant number of women from Africa—that is, former slaves, Irish women, and migrants from the province of Corrientes working as domestic servants.[52] There seems to have been ethnic hierarchies among them. An ad of January 1855 which asked for a maid to take care of children and to sew emphasized that the woman in question should be Basque.[53] The demand for "alone" candidates might have referred to a preference for single women or widows. Also, it is possible that it was a search for workers who would not ask to be hired along with relatives—daughters, sisters, husbands—as usually happened.[54]

Five years later, in April 1860, an ad required "a mistress who can take care of a house and the clothes of a small family and kitchen".[55] It is possible here to get a glimpse of the daily tasks of such a maid, but also of how caring for clothes was a task in itself. This could mean to do the laundry, to iron, and to mend holes, in the same way as these tasks were performed by seamstresses and tailors who had stalls at the urban market, mending holes on demand.[56]

51 Flavia Fernandes de Souza, "Entre a convivência e a retribuição: Trabalho e subordinação nos significados sociais da prestação de serviços domésticos (cidade do rio de janeiro, 1870–1900", *Revista de História Comparada*, vol. 4, no. 1 (2010), p. 115.

52 Ibid., p. 81.

53 *El Nacional*, 9 January 1855.

54 Ibid.

55 *El Nacional*, 14 April 1860, p. 3.

56 *El Nacional*, 2 December 1857, p. 3.

8 Institutions

There were many other places were women could be found sewing. For example, to be institutionalized in an asylum, an orphanage or a school if you were female meant to learn how to sew and to be obligated to sew on a daily basis. In a way, it was quite similar to the activities of elite girls, embroidering as a feminine pastime, but with better defined structures of work intended to produce profits for the managers of those public institutions.

9 Schools

In August of 1855, the women in charge of the Sociedad de Beneficencia decided to spread the word through the pages of *El Nacional* about a raffle of pieces of needlework hand-stitched by orphan girls who were students in their public schools. This was supposed to be an encouragement to the young girls to develop their craft, but also a way to collect funds for the schools and institutions run by the Sociedad.[57] In addition, it was a way to invite members of the elite to donate funds to these projects. *Porteño* men and women of the upper and upper-middle classes participated in such humanitarian causes as a part of their recreational social activities: balls, the theatre, or charity raffles like the one mentioned in the newspaper.[58]

By the end of the 1850s, there were different public and private educational institutions for children in Buenos Aires, segregated by sex. As earlier mentioned, the Sociedad de Beneficencia was in charge of the administration of fourteen of these public elementary schools for girls in the city and forty-two in the rural areas of the province. The syllabus comprised reading, writing, arithmetic, and basic lessons on sewing and embroidery. And the teaching of those basic lessons demanded a specific type of person who had mastered needlework skills but was also capable of transmitting them. In the year 1823, when the Sociedad was established, they translated and introduced a French school book for girls: *school book for elementary schools of girls with the basics on mutual learning applied to Reading, Writing, Math, and Sewing.*[59] Among the many skills that were supposed to be taught there were the sewing of turn-ups, sleeves; five different types of stitches; the making of buttonholes and

57 *El Nacional*, 27 August 1855, p. 1.

58 Valeria Pita, *La casa de las locas: Una historia social del Hospital de Mujeres Dementes, Buenos Aires, 1852–1890* (Rosario, 2012), p. 83.

59 Biblioteca Nacional, Tesoro, Colección Libros, Imprenta de los Expósitos, año 1823.

the sewing of buttons. During the 1850s girls also learned how to embroider.[60] Lessons on how to make a pattern, a cut-out or how to cut fabrics were not included. Those were skills that could only be learned through an apprenticeship. But the simpler abilities could surely allow them to earn a living sewing by piece or even as maids mending clothes.

In April 1857, an ad was posted by a British mistress "with the most respectable recommendations" who wished to "find a job with a family to be in charge of the education of some young girls, to whom she will teach English, French, Spanish, piano and singing lessons, embroidery and sewing [...] you can find her in the School for Young Girls, no. 10 Suipacha Street".[61] Here was a woman, previously occupied as a teacher of needlework, looking for another job as a governess, where sewing and embroidery abilities were also expected.

Even though needlework was something to be learnt in both public and private schools for young girls, this did not mean they were supposed to learn these skills in the same way. In a short article published in *El Nacional* in August 1855, a journalist pointed out that "there is a gap between well-educated wealthy classes of all societies and the common people, between the taste of the first ones and the industry of the latter, that can rarely be filled".[62] According to the journalist, the women of the Sociedad de Beneficencia attempted the important mission of filling that breach within the frame of public schools for poor girls: "as soon as the patterns arrive from Europe, these ladies offer them to the school, under the direction of teachers and the taste exercised by the ladies themselves [...] thus putting within reach a productive industry and a mean of civilization and culture". Certain assumptions about sewing as a pastime, as leisure, or as work to earn a respectable living lay beneath the ideas of "taste" and "industry". The same act of needlework could be a tool for working women, or a feminine virtue and daily task for young girls from the elite classes. What the journalist forgot to mention was the work experience of the women involved in teaching those skills. Women such as that British governess and many other women with needlework abilities found jobs as teachers of young ladies in public and private schools of the city.

60 AGN Sociedad de Beneficencia, Educación, Escuelas de Ciudad, 1825–1884, Legajo No. 260, Records of the public schools for girls in Balvanera parish, 30 May 1859.

61 *El Nacional*, 6 April 1857, p. 3.

62 *El Nacional*, 27 August 1855, p. 1.

10 Convalecencia

Meanwhile, the distance between labour and non-remunerated work remains unclear in another institution of the Sociedad: the asylum for mentally ill women, or Convalecencia. According to the reconstruction of historian Valeria Pita, this institution opened its doors in March 1854. During that year, 64 women were admitted as patients and there were 90 of them by 1857. Half of the inmates in 1857 were local women and 9 per cent of them immigrants from Spain;[63] half a dozen of them had a small amount of money, while the rest were part of a wider group of poor women with no family or belongings of their own. Their state of dementia, which was not always clearly defined or diagnosed, was marked by delusions, loss of reasoning, and violent or scandalous behaviour. Before their admission into the institution, it was common for these women to have served time in a public jail or women's hospital, or for them to have been among the homeless in the city, interrupted by relocation to the asylum ordered by a police officer or public night watchman. Thus, the Convalecencia for mentally ill women functioned as an institution that committed a section of the female population, known for their state of poverty or indigence.[64]

The process of rehabilitation in the institution proposed by the Sociedad and the doctors working with them involved a daily routine of different productive tasks, where sewing played a key role. The patients woke up at dawn and cleaned the facilities, then they gathered in the collective dining room to have the morning *mate*,[65] after which they were assigned specific activities: some of them had to work in the vegetable garden, others had to do the laundry, but most of them had to toil in the sewing workshop, making shirts and underpants for men. After the lunch break, they resumed their activities in the afternoon until 5 pm, when they had dinner, said their prayers and then went to bed.[66]

For the women in charge of the Convalecencia, sewing was a virtuous activity and a way towards "regaining reason". As an additional benefit, it earned profits for the institution.[67] The profit could be, for example, from money collected after raffles of the pieces sewn by the patients, just like the needlework

63 Pita, *La casa de las locas*, p. 94.

64 Ibid.

65 Typical Argentinian hot beverage.

66 Pita, *La casa de las locas*, p. 94.

67 Annual Report, Sociedad de Beneficencia, Buenos Aires, 31 December 1856, AGN ISB-yAS, Memorias, Estadísticas y Exposiciones, 1824–1903, Legajo 3, Tomo 1, F.28.

pieces from the orphanage or the public schools of the Sociedad were raffled. In August 1856, a brief mention in *El Nacional* stated that among the pieces of needlework raffled by the Sociedad, there were "two dozens of simple shirts, hand-made by the poor crazy women of the Convalecencia".[68] The making of these many pieces of clothing suggested, unlike the pieces embroidered by young girls, a larger scale of production of standardized clothing.

Ready-made clothes were sewn by patients of the asylum and acquired by the local government for the army and the police force, at much lower prices. An article in the local newspaper on this matter in 1857 stated as follows:

> Sewing of clothes by the demented women. We know that the miserable demented women of the Asylum have sewed 912 pieces of clothing for the army and for that, the government has ordered to pay $6840 to the Sociedad de Beneficencia. This shows how the unhappy lunatics are being usefully occupied in such a disgraceful asylum.[69]

The Sociedad quoted a lower price than that put forward by contemporary textile entrepreneurs when submitting applications in response to public calls or tenders.[70] Unlike the seamstresses hired by these businessmen, the patients of the asylum were not supposed to receive cash for their work. Instead they were compensated with goods such as cigars, *yerba mate*,[71] maybe a dress or some extra free time outdoors in the garden of the institution.[72] The administrators of the asylum received an average of $7 for each piece of clothing delivered. The stitching of a shirt by hand, as mentioned above, took approximately fourteen hours of work.[73] And the daily wage for a seamstress in Buenos Aires City at that time was in the range of $25 to $40.[74] Thus, for this mode of production of clothing using cheap labour, the Sociedad received less than a third of the customary minimum wage.

A year later, in 1858, a newspaper article reported that the inmates had sewn 500 linen shirts and 670 underpants. "These sewn pieces represent an

68 *El Nacional*, 29 August 1856, p. 2.

69 *El Nacional*, 3 September 1857, p. 2.

70 In the budget assigned to the year 1861, for the purchase of uniforms for 215 police officers, the state of Buenos Aires expended $109.650. See Budget 1861 of the State of Buenos Aires, available at www.hcdiputados-ba.gov.ar, last accessed 30 May 2021.

71 The leaves of the plant known as *yerba mate* are steeped in hot water to make a beverage known as mate.

72 Pita, *La casa de las locas*, p. 96.

73 Nari, "El trabajo a domicilio y las obreras", p. 3.

74 *El Nacional*, 1 August 1855, p. 1.

immense amount of patience, charity, and caring given to the disgraced under the maternal support of the Sociedad de Beneficencia".[75] "Patience", "charity", "maternal support": even though the article mentioned the work of women who were inmates of the asylum, the general tone of writing moves from that notion of labour to a series of considerations about the Sociedad itself as a "motherly" institution.

Within this structure of work, there were also manifestations of resistance and negotiation between the patients and the administrators. In 1857, a woman named Andrea Guardia was admitted to the institution with a diagnosis of dementia. A few months later, according to the inspector in charge, the patient showed the disposition and good judgment to "coordinate the routines of the other patients working in the sewing workshop".[76] It was therefore decided to designate her as temporary manager, receiving a monthly wage of $150. She stayed for over two years in that job. She coordinated the production in the workshop and was so successful in doing so that she managed to collect around $15,000 in profits for the institution. In March 1860, Andrea Guardia requested a wage increase of an extra $100 per month, which was at first denied. But after evaluating the report of the inspector, the administrators changed their minds: "there is no way to find a woman with such commitment to work for that salary". It would have been more onerous for them to hire a new coordinator than to grant Guardia the raise she asked for.[77]

Bandages, embroidery pieces, shirts and underpants for men, these were all items produced by women who devoted time to sewing in mid-nineteenth-century Buenos Aires. In the name of patriotic honour, virtuous industry, and rehabilitative productivity, women of different ages, backgrounds, and social conditions contributed non-remunerated labour, most of which was coordinated by the Sociedad de Beneficencia for the benefit of their welfare institutions. Even though it meant hard work, for some of these women to perform such activities implied the possibility of disputing notions of virtue for themselves, to receive prizes and financial aid from the Sociedad. Or even to widen the margin of autonomy in spaces of confinement.

75 *El Nacional*, 14 October 1858, p. 3.
76 Pita, *La casa de las locas*, p. 98.
77 Ibid., p. 99.

11 Conclusion

The development of a capitalist labour market in Buenos Aires City in the mid-nineteenth century did not follow a linear trajectory. What counted as work or not-work—but was still crucial to the reproduction of the system—implied engendered notions of labour and could be seen in the words used by journalists and in the measures taken by the women of the Sociedad de Beneficencia, the welfare arm of the new political project. Needlework is an example that allows us to analyse the very fluid but complex borders that separated leisure from work, reproductive work from productive activities, and occasional ways to earn a living from full-time skilled labour.

Throughout this chapter, my attempt has been to recreate a labour circuit that had a crucial presence of women and which was also performed inside dwelling spaces: workshops that were also places to live in, homes where women sewed pieces or learnt how to embroider, spaces of confinement where sewing was a part of daily life. Gaining an entry into these places of work allowed me to alter the scale of my analysis and bring in elements of complexity to the study of a historical period that marked the beginning of a national modern State in South America. My purpose here is to give a glimpse of the everyday life and ordinary spaces where these very different women were engaged in sewing.

In this context of transition, I posit that using rigid or extemporaneous notions of "home", "domesticity", "motherhood", "work" or "feminine labour" might come in the way of a reasonable comprehension of the experiences of a heterogeneous group of women who earned a living by sewing. With that in mind, I have attempted to describe those trajectories in a way that did justice to their activities in Buenos Aires, during the 1850s. I have tried to understand, first, the meaning of "earning a living" in a broad sense, acknowledging how needlework was an ability expected from women of different backgrounds. This did not imply, as I hope to have shown, an underestimation of the social and economic distance between women who needed to receive payment for their needlework and those who did not. In other words, I have sought to recognize the common traces of a female activity, but also the different meanings behind sewing as an honourable industry, as a patriotic virtue, as a way to rehabilitate women. To restore a historical context to social subjects that, thanks to specific skills with the needle, were able to support their families, demand rights from civil authorities, or dispute notions of virtue and industry has been an objective of this chapter as well.

Maids knowing how to sew, young girls embroidering in schools and orphanages, patients of the asylum hand-stitching shirts—all these experiences of female needlework may as well receive the name of home-based labour, since many of them were performed by girls and women either in the house where they worked and lived in as servants, or inside institutions like the orphanage or the asylum where they spent their lives. These were activities that were not always considered as work that deserved wages; instead they involved notions of feminine republican virtue and industrious honourable labour.

If we change the focus and look closely at what these women did inside their homes, going back and forth from the shops that hired them to sew uniforms by the piece, we can see how they played a role in the nineteenth-century wars that took place in this region. These conflicts did receive the attention of political historiography, which in turn forgot to pay attention to the invisible feminine work they required. Women's work behind closed doors, in spaces where labour was intertwined with domestic and motherly chores, deserves a place in history. Hopefully, this chapter will make a contribution on that score.

CHAPTER 4

Sewing at Home in Greece, 1870s to 1930s

A Global History Perspective

Leda Papastefanaki

The sewing machine is an object familiar to most people worldwide: almost every house in Europe in the twentieth century had a sewing machine and almost everyone has memories of mothers or grandmothers sewing on their machines. These days, the return of the "do-it-yourself" culture caused by the global economic crisis has contributed to a revival of the use of modern sewing machines, while the old machines are viewed as collectible items or objects of decoration.

The sewing machine was the first mass-produced and mass-marketed consumer good of the twentieth century, and the first to be globally disseminated even before 1914. Moreover, it could be said that the sewing machine was the first machine to bring the industrial revolution into the home.[1] It was the first durable, technologically complex household appliance to find a national market first in North America, and soon after in Europe, India, and South America.

In this chapter, I explore the gendered aspects of the technology of the sewing machine in their interaction with the divisions of labour (paid and unpaid) within the Greek family, and the ways in which gendered hierarchies influenced the forms of labour and systems of payment in the clothing trade. I approach these questions following the Indian social-cultural anthropologist Arjun Appadurai's ideas on modernity and the cultural dimensions of globalization. According to Appadurai, technologies cannot be understood without taking into account the local societies and cultures in which they came to be embedded; and globalization needs to be understood as a *localizing process* (not simply a homogenizing one).[2] Following also the discussion on how global labour history should be examined in connection with local histories, this chapter tries to combine theoretical approaches regarding modernity with historical research on the diffusion and appropriation of technology in

1 Cf. Ruth Schwartz Cowan, "The 'Industrial Revolution' in the Home: Household Technology and Social Change in the 20th Century", *Technology and Culture*, 17/1 (1976), pp. 1–23.

2 Arjun Appadurai, *Modernity at Large: Cultural Dimensions of Globalization* (Minneapolis, 1996).

© LEDA PAPASTEFANAKI, 2022 | DOI:10.1163/9789004499614_006
This is an open access chapter distributed under the terms of the CC BY-NC-ND 4.0 license.

different contexts, and the transformation of labour through the use of new, mass-produced technology.

Work in the home—paid, but more commonly unpaid—cannot be easily traced in the literature. For this reason, research that seeks to throw light on aspects of women's work in the home has to investigate a variety of sources: illustrated, literary, and autobiographical testimonies. The sources for my research here are catalogues of international expositions, advertisements, the press (women's press, daily newspapers), feminist reports, trade union archives, literary accounts and photographs.

The first section of the chapter refers to previous studies that focused on the sewing machine from the differing perspectives of business and labour history, while providing a general overview of Greek historiography on labour. The second section examines the introduction and dissemination of sewing machines around the world; the third section—as a parentheses—provides an overview of Greek manufacture, labour and population movements during the nineteenth century and the interwar period in order to better understand the economic and social context of the spread of sewing machines in Greece. The fourth section of the chapter examines the promotion, advertisements and training for the use of sewing machines in Greece, while the last section studies work at home and some efforts at regulation.

1 Studies on Business and Labour History

A number of historical studies from the perspective of economic and business history, the history of technology and labour history/migration history/gender history, especially for the United States and Western Europe, have been published over the last thirty to forty years. The sewing machine has been at the centre of major debates in business and economic history, ranging from the invention of mass-produced technologies, and the development of modern advertising, managerial, and marketing strategies, to the origins of multinational firms[3] and the emergence of the sewing machine as a global consumer

3 Fred V. Carstensen, *American enterprise in foreign markets: Studies of Singer and International Harvester in imperial Russia* (Chapel Hill, 1984); Andrew Godley, "The Development of the U.K. Clothing Industry, 1850–1950: Output and Productivity Growth", *Business History*, 37 (1995), pp. 46–63; Andrew Godley, "Pioneering Foreign Direct Investment in British Manufacturing", *Business History Review*, 73 (1999), pp. 394–429; Mark Casson and Andrew Godley, "Revisiting the Emergence of Modern Business Enterprise: Entrepreneurship and the Singer Global Distribution System", *Journal of Management Studies*, 44/7 (2007), pp. 1064–77.

good.[4] Recently, business history has studied the gender strategies of marketing by the multinational firm Singer.[5] New studies have examined the appropriation of technology in Europe and consumers' experience.[6] There is also research on the advent and appropriation of the sewing machine in India, the Ottoman empire, Turkey, and the Middle East.[7]

The sewing machine has also been at the centre of major debates in social and cultural history, ranging from the distinctive character of female labour as a combination of paid and unpaid work[8] to the "sweating" of garment industry workers;[9] from the feminization of the garment trade to the idealization of home life and the "separate spheres"[10] of gender relations, the social consequences of flexible labour for women and immigrants,[11] and the effect of the sewing machine on workers' health and sexual

4 Barbara Burman (ed.), *The Culture of Sewing: Gender, Consumption and Home Dressmaking* (Oxford, 1999); Andrew Godley, "The Global Diffusion of the Sewing Machine", *Research in Economic History*, 2 (2001), pp. 1–45; Andrew Godley, *Fabricating Consumers: The Sewing Machine in Modern Japan* (Berkeley, 2011).

5 Paula A. de la Cruz-Fernández, "Multinationals and Gender: Singer Sewing Machine and Marketing in Mexico, 1890–1930", *Business History Review*, 89 (Autumn 2015), pp. 531–49.

6 Ruth Oldenziel and Mikael Hård, *Consumers, tinkerers, rebels: The people who shaped Europe* (New York, 2013).

7 Uri M. Kupferschmidt, "The Social History of the Sewing Machine in the Middle East", *Die Welt des Islams*, 44/2 (2004), pp. 195–213; David Arnold, "Global goods and local usages: The small world of the Indian sewing machine, 1875–1952", *Journal of Global History*, 6/3 (2011), pp. 407–29; Ayşen Işler Sarioğlou, "My faithful machine: The role of technology in daily life. The case of Singer sewing machine in Turkey", MA dissertation, School of Social Sciences, Middle East Technical University (2011).

8 Karin Hausen, "Technical Progress and Women's Labour in the Nineteenth Century: The Social History of the Sewing Machine", in G. Iggers (ed.), *The Social History of Politics: Critical Perspectives in West German Historical Writing since 1945* (Dover N.H., 1985), pp. 259–81.

9 Andrew Godley, "Homeworking and the Sewing Machine in the British Clothing Industry 1850–1905", in B. Burman (ed.), *The Culture of Sewing: Gender, Consumption and Home Dressmaking* (Oxford, 1999), pp. 255–68; Nancy Green, "Fashion, Flexible Specialization and the Sweatshop: A Historical Problem", in D. Bender, R.A. Greenwald (eds), *Sweatshop USA: The American Sweatshop in Historical and Global Perspective* (New York, 2003), pp. 37–55; Colette Avrane, *Ouvriéres à domicile: Le combat pour un salaire minimum sous la Troisième République* (Rennes, 2013), pp. 69–73.

10 Judith C. Coffin, "Credit, Consumption and Images of Women's Desires: Selling the Sewing Machine in Late Nineteenth Century France", *French Historical Studies*, 18/3 (1994), pp. 749–83; Eadem, *The Politics of Women's Work: The Paris Garment Trades, 1750–1915* (Princeton, N.J., 1996); Eadem, "Consumption, Production and Gender: the Sewing Machine in Nineteenth Century France", in L. Frader and S.O. Rose (eds), *Gender and Class in Modern Europe* (Ithaca, 1996), pp. 111–41.

11 Nancy Green, *Du Sentier à la 7e Avenue: La Confection et les immigrés, Paris–New York 1880–1980* (Paris, 1998).

politics.[12]

Since the mid-1980s, the history of labour has generated substantive renewal of the social history of Greece from the viewpoint of the history of women and gender.[13] New research underlines the impact of gender in the formation of labour markets, in labour relations and the division of labour, and reports the female presence in business and in different sectors of the formal or informal economy. Studies of women and gender from a social history perspective have offered numerous case studies, reflecting the methodological and theoretical richness of the critiques of existing sources and the search for new sources. Moreover, the incorporation of culture in these approaches has enriched the field, with a focus on the historical construction of the gendered labour experience.[14] There are lacunae still, however, and a large number of questions await answers: questions having to do with work at home, the composition of household incomes, the strategies of families to enter labour markets, paid and unpaid work at home and in family business are some of them.

2 Introducing the Sewing Machine into a Global Market

The new sewing machines were used, first of all, by garment manufacturers, but the sewing machine manufacturers realized that their largest potential market was the millions of families who intended to have a sewing machine in their homes when they could afford it. An advertisement campaign was launched

12 Karen Offen, "'Powered by a Woman's Foot': A Documentary Introduction to the Sexual Politics of the Sewing Machine in Nineteenth Century France", *Women's Studies International Forum*, 11/2 (March 1988), pp. 93–101.

13 For historiographical accounts of women's and gender history in Greece, see Efi Avdela, "L'histoire des femmes au sein de l'historiographie grecque contemporaine", in Gisela Bock and Anne Cova (eds), *Ecrire l'histoire des femmes en Europe du Sud, XIXe–XXe siècles / Writing Women's History in Southern Europe, 19th–20th Centuries* (Oeiras, 2003), pp. 81–96; Efi Avdela, *Le genre entre classe et nation: Essai d'historiographie grecque* (Paris, 2006), pp. 13–25; Eleni Fournaraki and Yannis Yannitsiotis, "Three Decades of Women's and Gender History in Greece: An Account", *Aspasia, The International Yearbook of Central, Eastern, and Southeastern European Women's and Gender History*, 7 (2013), pp. 162–73; A. Dialeti, E. Fournaraki, and G. Gotsi, "Εισαγωγή", in A. Dialeti, E. Fournaraki, and G. Gotsi (eds), *Το φύλο στην ιστορία. Αποτιμήσεις και παραδείγματα* (Athens, 2015), pp. 7–52; Nikolaos Papadogiannis, "Gender in modern Greek historiography", *Historein*, 16, no. 1–2 (2017), pp. 74–101.

14 For a recent historiographical account on gender and labour, see Leda Papastefanaki, "Labour in economic and social history: The viewpoint of gender in Greek historiography", *Genesis: Rivista della Società Italiana delle Storiche*, XV/2 (2016), pp. 59–83.

from the mid-1850s to the 1860s in order to distribute sewing machines to households in the US and all over Europe, and introduce new methods of payment. Among the manufacturers who introduced sewing machine models for families were the US firm Singer, which introduced the "New Family" model in 1865; the North American firm Smith & Egge MFG Co., which manufactured the model "Household" model sewing machine in the 1880s with a "Family" buttonhole attachment (Figure 4.1);[15] and the Belgian house Sinave-Mignot, which specialized in different kinds of small machines for home industries (*industrie à domicile*) (Figure 4.2).[16]

Already by 1870, the sewing machine was capable of making 600 stitches per minute whereas a good dressmaker could not make more than 25 stitches per minute. The consequences were a rise in productivity and greater division of labour in workshops and home-based manufacture. The sewing machine brought about a "conciliation" of work for women working from home: household tasks could now coexist with paid work in the house. The introduction of the sewing machine into ateliers and households, it was believed, would have the following advantages: amelioration of the lives of numerous women workers who would now receive more satisfactory salaries, and augmentation of consumption and general well-being.[17]

The disadvantage was the relatively high price of the sewing machines, making them too expensive for workers and working-class households. Merchants and manufacturers began to sell the sewing machines on long-term credit, while the buyers paid for them through profits earned by using the machines.

Andrew Godley, in his study about the global distribution of sewing machines, has shown that Germany was the leading European consumer in the 1870s and 1880s, after Britain. However, by 1914, Ireland and Scandinavia had overtaken Germany, with the Netherlands, France, and Spain close behind. In Switzerland, Belgium, and Portugal, the distribution of the sewing machine was significant before 1880, while Italy and Russia experienced rapid distribution in the 1900s. Estimates on the distribution in the Ottoman empire and Greece point to more than 10 per cent of all households having sewing machines before the First World War.[18] The development of an easy payment

15 *United States Sewing Machines Times*, 29 June 1889.

16 *Catalogue illustré de l'exposition internationale du petit outillage avec la description des machines exposés* (Ghent, 1904).

17 See, for example, this rhetoric in Association pour le développement de l'industrie ouvrière et des fabriques dans les Pays-Bas, *Exposition internationale d'économie domestique, Amsterdam 1869* (Hague, 1873).

18 Godley, "The Global Diffusion".

scheme contributed to the rapid distribution of the sewing machine in France, where department stores pioneered credit systems, in Britain, in the Middle East, in the Ottoman empire, and in Greece.[19] Although Singer dominated the world market around 1900, it appears that other brands from the United States, United Kingdom, Germany, and Italy continued to be imported in the interwar period (and even after the Second World War) in Turkey, Middle East, Greece, and the Balkans. Singer's marketing success at the turn of the century was connected to the introduction of a monthly payment system. Most sewing machine manufacturers established a large network of agents and salesmen throughout France, Greece, the Ottoman empire, and the Middle East. These agents offered potential customers the machine, some lessons, credit, and possible work from local clothing manufacturers.

3 The Greek Economy, Manufacture, Labour, and Movement of Populations in the Nineteenth Century and the Interwar Period

The newly founded Greek state of 1830 was a predominantly agricultural country, with just a few small urban centres. It was a typical monetized economy of the Mediterranean, integrated with the region's commercial networks, with old cash crops (grain, olive oil, wine) and well-developed maritime communications. The expansion of cash crops for exports (olive oil, wine, currants, etc.) was a main feature of the economy of Greece in the nineteenth century, giving rise to movement of populations from the mountain regions to the lowlands, polarized social backgrounds, and rapid integration of a large part of the agricultural population into the market economy. The intensive cultivation of the Corinthian currant in particular combined well with the structure of small property ownership that prevailed in the Greek countryside, leading to the gradual descent of the mountain populations to the lowlands, and also absorbing a large part of the increasing population and available labour resources.[20]

During the nineteenth century the older cottage industries began to decline. Home-based thread manufacturing, which met the needs of households,

19 Donald Quataert, *Manufacturing and Technology Transfer in the Ottoman Empire 1800–1914* (Istanbul,1992); Coffin, "Credit, Consumption"; Eadem, *The Politics of Women's Work*; Godley, "Homeworking and the Sewing Machine"; Kupferschmidt, "The Social History of the Sewing Machine in the Middle East".

20 Christina Agriantoni, "Οικονομία και εκβιομηχάνιση στην Ελλάδα του 19ου αιώνα", in V. Kremmydas (ed.), *Εισαγωγή στη νεοελληνική οικονομική ιστορία (18ος–20ός αι.)* (Athens, 1999), pp. 145–176, especially pp. 148, 150.

gradually disappeared from all regions of Greece, but textile manufacturing survived and its commercial character expanded not only to regions that did not have sufficient cultivation but throughout the country after the agricultural crisis of the late nineteenth century.[21] The transfer of the capital to Athens and the general transformation of the economy gave an impetus to the growth of new port cities. Piraeus, Patras, Hermoupolis, and later Volos, provided with initial incentives to develop external trade, were to become centres for the reception of industry. The construction of towns absorbed a large portion of domestic public and private resources during the nineteenth century. Similarly, significant domestic resources in cash and labour were absorbed by the first public works in the Greek state.[22] The first wave of systematic industrial investment can be dated to the years 1865–1875; industrialization was then quickened and expanded to several sectors: there were 110 steam-powered factories in 1875 distributed across a number of towns and different sectors (cotton-makers, flour producers, oil producers and soap-makers, tanneries).[23]

The crisis in rural areas throughout the Mediterranean in the last two decades of the nineteenth century resulted in falling prices for agricultural products, increasing migration, and the search for supplementary incomes by rural households. The current crisis, which hit the Greek agricultural economy in the 1890s and contributed to mass transatlantic migration, illustrates the rural crisis most emphatically. The second wave of industrialization was supported by rapid urbanization, but was also accompanied by great inequality and social polarization. It followed various paths, primarily by using the available labour force but without, of course, being able to absorb all of it. The second wave concluded with the emergence of the country's first large industrial enterprises.[24]

The revival of industrial activity in the late nineteenth century also occurred through the distribution of small production units throughout Greece. Given the prevailing conditions of poverty and emigration, small businessmen began to make more systematic use women's home-based work, organizing networks to commercialize home-made textile products or to establish

21 Ibid., pp. 150–52; Eadem, "Βιομηχανία", in K. Kostis and S. Petmezas (eds), *Η ανάπτυξη της ελληνικής οικονομίας κατά τον 19ο αιώνα (1830–1914)* (Athens, 2006), pp. 222–23; Socrates Petmezas, "Patterns of Protoindustrialization in the Ottoman Empire: The Case of Eastern Thessaly", *Journal of European Economic History*, 19/3 (1990), pp. 575–603.

22 Christina Agriantoni, *Οι απαρχές της εκβιομηχάνισης στην Ελλάδα τον 19ο αιώνα* (Athens, 1986), pp. 77–105; Eadem, "Οικονομία και εκβιομηχάνιση", pp. 154–57; Eadem, "Βιομηχανία", in *Η ανάπτυξη*, p. 223.

23 Agriantoni, *Οι απαρχές*, pp. 111–28; Eadem, "Βιομηχανία", in *Η ανάπτυξη*, pp. 224–25.

24 Agriantoni, "Οικονομία και εκβιομηχάνιση", p. 172; Eadem, "Βιομηχανία", in *Η ανάπτυξη*, pp.226–27.

seasonal agricultural processing factories (mills, oil mills, distilleries, currant processing), which provided supplementary daily wages to rural households. Correspondingly, the system of home-based work and small workshops expanded in urban centres as well. Patras, Volos, Hermoupolis, and, above all, Athens became filled with small knitting and garment workshops.[25]

Industry soon followed the activities of the cottage industries, which in several cases had created a new demand for intermediate products. In the late nineteenth century, new textile industries were opened (Hermoupolis, Volos, Athens, and Piraeus in Greece, and Salonica, Veroia, Naoussa, and Edessa in Ottoman Macedonia),[26] while, thanks to the availability of raw materials at exceptionally low prices, alcoholic beverages, in particular Greek brandy, enjoyed significant exports. New distilleries were founded in Piraeus, Elevsina, Kalamata, and elsewhere. Small machinery workshops were established in all the important towns, while the largest facilities in the industrial centres were expanded to serve shipping and the railways. The most spectacular rise was that of the mining sector in 1895–1907, thanks to the increasing demand for minerals from the industrially developed countries.[27]

In the interwar period the demand for industrialization became all the more urgent. In the absence of migration opportunities, industrial development became the only hope for absorbing the unemployed among both refugees from Asia Minor and the indigenous population. The 1920s were characterized by a high rate of establishment of new industries, especially cottage industries. The smaller units increased in number while the larger ones became more powerful.[28]

The Greco–Turkish War (1919–22) resulted in a huge wave of refugees, of whom women, children, and elderly people comprised a major proportion. More than 1,221,000 Greek refugees came to Greece from Asia Minor in 1922 and settled in a country which had 5,531,474 inhabitants in 1920. Studies have pointed to the large number of refugee women who were employed mainly in textile, tapestry, and tobacco manufacturing, both in factories and workshops. According to the 1928 population census, 36.2 per cent of the total number

25 Agriantoni, "Οικονομία και εκβιομηχάνιση", p. 173.

26 Agriantoni, *Οι απαρχές*, pp. 331–35, 343; Christos Hadziiossif, *Η γηραιά σελήνη: Η βιομηχανία στην ελληνική οικονομία (1830–1940)* (Athens, 1993), pp. 90–95; Leda Papastefanaki, *Εργασία, τεχνολογία και φύλο στην ελληνική βιομηχανία: Η κλωστοϋφαντουργία του Πειραιά, 1870–1940* (Herakleion, 2009), pp. 121–23.

27 Agriantoni, "Οικονομία και εκβιομηχάνιση", p. 173.

28 Christos Hadziiossif, "Το προσφυγικό σοκ, οι σταθερές και οι μεταβολές της ελληνικής οικονομίας", in Christos Hadziiossif (ed.), *Ιστορία της Ελλάδας του 20ού αιώνα: Ο μεσοπόλεμος, 1922–1940*, vol. B1 (Athens, 2002), p. 26.

of industrial workers consisted of female workers, of which a large number were refugees.[29] Yet, the policy of state institutions and private organizations that directed women and children to home work and domestic labour is underestimated.[30]

The use of statistical sources for women's participation in the labour force of the developing labour market in Greece has specific limitations. Identifying the "dark" spots and uncertainties in the censuses leads to the hypothesis that wage relations in Greece in the nineteenth century and the beginning of twentieth century were far more widespread than originally assumed. Wage relations operated within the context of disconnected or fragmented local or sectoral labour markets, which were distinguished by a gender division based on the gender divisions among the members of working and farming families.[31] Family strategies regarding the selection of members who would 'proletarianize', migrate, enter into the service of third parties or remain within the family smallholding were determined by the gendered family division and resulted from the needs of the market.

4 Sewing Machines in Greece: Promotion, Advertisement, Education

Sewing machines, when introduced into the Greek market, were paid for in instalments or in cash. "Easy payments" (in instalments) were launched by sewing machine companies in the nineteenth century in order to make it possible for men and women of the working class to buy the machines. Easy payments were introduced into the Greek market by shops selling sewing machines from the 1870s onwards.[32] In 1897, Singer advertised payment "in cash and on credit",[33] while in the years that followed, it advertised payment on credit in small, weekly instalments.[34] Retailers stressed weekly instalments in advertisements throughout the country.

The rapid spread of sewing machines was due not only to easy payments and the system of instalments it introduced, but also to the training provided

29 Papastefanaki, *Εργασία*, pp. 90–91.

30 Pothiti Hantzaroula, *Σμιλεύοντας την υποταγή: Οι έμμισθες οικιακές εργάτριες στην Ελλάδα το α΄ μισό του 20ού αιώνα* (Athens, 2012).

31 Leda Papastefanaki, "Μισθωτή εργασία", in K. Kostis and S. Petmezas (eds), *Η ανάπτυξη της ελληνικής οικονομίας κατά τον 19° αιώνα (1830–1914)* (Athens, 2006), pp. 278–79.

32 Newspaper *Ποσειδών*, 25 April 1874.

33 Newspaper *Εμπρός*, 30 December 1897.

34 Newspaper *Εμπρός*, 20 June 1906.

to their users and the provision for their repair. Retailers and agencies sold the machines and, together with these, a "package" of services, including training in how to use them and repair. "Training, teaching and repairs entirely free of charge" or variations on this wording are to be found in advertisements dating from the early twentieth century.[35]

The spread of the use of the sewing machine in Greece was accompanied by systematic advertising in the Athenian and provincial press, as well as articles by journalists, many of which were paid for. The robust and simple features of the machines and the ease with which their use could be learnt were stressed in order to convince consumers—chiefly female consumers—that it was worthwhile to buy a sewing machine, for it was durable and simple to use. Advertisements for machines which sewed "any kind of textile or leather without a change of needle, thread or any modification" promoted gender-based conceptions of technology: the machine has to be simple in order to be operated by women.[36] At the same time, most of the advertisements of all the companies had references to the family, which women have to look after: machines for the family, for family use, was a repeated motif in all of them. Jones sewing machines were advertised, in 1908, as "the most durable machines for a family";[37] Eldredge sewing machines advertised as the only "true friends of family harmony",[38] because they are noiseless and when being used, do not annoy the husband when he is sleeping or doing his accounts.

In the paid articles inserted in newspapers, the sewing machine was promoted as a philanthropic and beneficial invention, which, as it increases productivity, allows women who use it to work and easily earn their living, but also to carry out the family's sewing tasks with comparative ease.[39]

> In earlier times, impoverished widows and unfortunate orphan girls, unable to resort to any other occupation to earn a living, devoted themselves day and night to needlework by hand, but although they wasted away as a result of their labours, were just about able to survive; but now, thanks to the beneficial invention of the sewing machine, an industrious woman can comfortably sew enough to enjoy an income of up to eight drachmas a day. A middle-class housewife engaged in the upbringing of her children and the running of her home was unable also to carry out the

35 Newspaper *Μακεδονία*, 29 January 1912, p. 4.
36 See, for example, the newspaper *Ποσειδών*, no. 481, 4 September 1876.
37 Newspaper *Εμπρός*, 25 October 1908, p. 6.
38 Advertisement of Eldredge sewing machine, newspaper *Εμπρός*, 30 March 1908, p. 6.
39 "Οικιακή βιομηχανία", *Ποσειδών*, no. 719, 17 July 1877, p. 3.

FIGURE 4.1 The model "Household" sewing machine with a "Family" buttonhole attachment
SOURCE: *UNITED STATES SEWING MACHINES TIMES*, 29 JUNE 1889

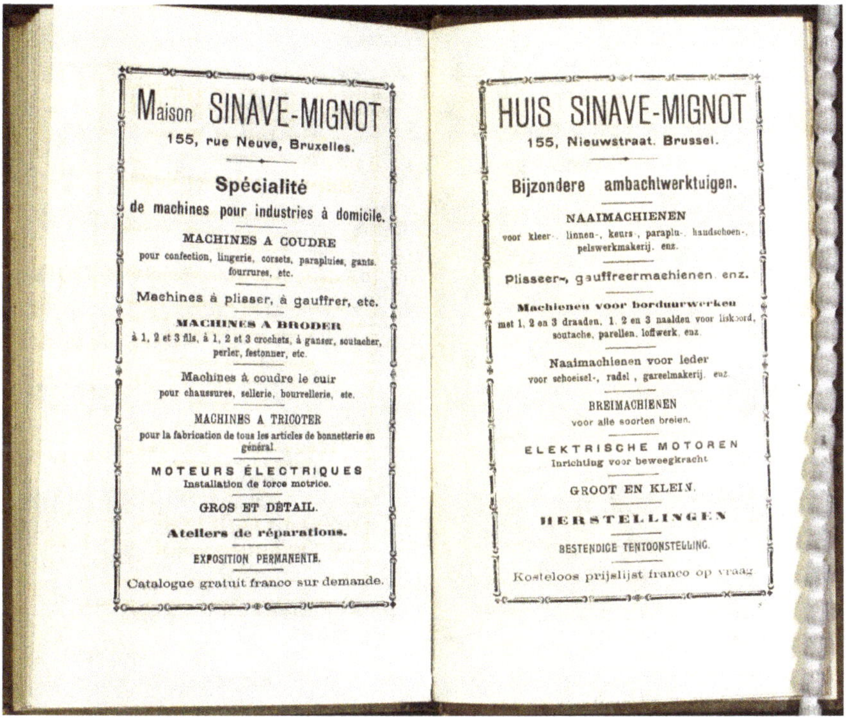

FIGURE 4.2 Advertisement of the Belgian house Sinave-Mignot, which specialized in different kinds of small machines for home industries
SOURCE: *CATALOGUE ILLUSTRÉ DE L'EXPOSITION INTERNATIONALE DU PETIT OUTILLAGE AVEC LA DESCRIPTION DES MACHINES EXPOSÉS* (GHENT, 1904)

> necessary sewing tasks, and so was put to additional expense. Now, by means of the machine, she can happily overcome this deficiency.[40]

The motif of the mother who can, by working at home, contribute to the family income without neglecting her maternal and household duties was repeated in similar articles for the promotion of sewing machines in the American and European press in the second half of the nineteenth century.

Of all the companies selling sewing machines in Greece, it was Singer that carried out advertising campaigns of the longest duration. The publications stressed the possibilities afforded by Singer sewing machines to craftsmen, tailors, seamstresses, and housewives, as they supported "healthy, useful, and gainful" labour.[41] Emphasis was also laid on the lightning speed of the sewing

40 Ibid.

41 "Το δώρον των καλών νυμφών", *Εμπρός*, 12 March 1903, p. 3.

FIGURE 4.3 Advertisement of Singer sewing machine for families in the daily press of Athens, *c.* 1910

machines, which were driven by electricity, and the great ease of handling the machines for factory and craft-industry use; the ease of use was impressive even in the case of more bulky sewing machines, so that even a "smaller girl" could use them "without any trouble".[42] The machines for family use sewed noiselessly, with the same speed and perfection as the professional models, and produced the most perfect stitches in all kinds of materials, both coarse and fine, with the same needle. Thus, the machines for household use repaired tablecloths, napkins, etc., but also produced a variety of artistic embroidery. Consequently, the use of the simple family sewing machine made "skilled and artistic embroidering" accessible to all.

42 "Η Εταιρεία Σίγγερ εις την Διεθνή Έκθεσιν", *Εμπρός*, 8 June 1903, p. 3.

FIGURE 4.4 Advertisement of the commercial firm Benmayor, Molho and Cohen in Thessaloniki, for sewing and knitting machines for home industries and manufacturers, *c.* 1930
SOURCE: *ΓΕΝΙΚΟΣ ΕΜΠΟΡΙΚΟΣ ΟΔΗΓΟΣ ΘΕΣΣΑΛΟΝΙΚΗΣ* (THESSALONIKI, 1930)

Apart from being a means of paid labour for poor male and female workers, the sewing machine was, for well-to-do women, a marvellous means "whereby an artistic talent is created and formed and tasteful inclinations and proclivities are interpreted with grace and perfect precision".[43] Philanthropic bourgeois ladies who were members of associations and sisterhoods that provided assistance to orphan girls and widows, as well as principals of schools and institutions, were enjoined to appreciate and lend practical support to the work of Singer, that is, "the shaping, in this way, of good taste and an artistic spirit in the works of handicraft of our female youth".[44]

Artistic embroidery was addressed not only to middle-class women but also to those of the working class, who, by producing embroideries, would be able to find additional means of making a living. The multinational company Singer,

43 Ibid.
44 Ibid.

as early as the 1870s, had expanded into the manufacture of sewing machines which produced embroidery in order to address American and European women of the middle class. In addressing women of this category, Singer promoted the idea of female work as a form of "art", while the company projected itself as a trustee of domesticity, of the "private sphere". In the 1890s, Singer set up its Embroidery Department, which would function on a world-wide scale to adapt the company's embroidery machines to specific local conditions.[45]

In Greece, as also in cities of the Ottoman empire, in order to boost the market for embroidery sewing machines, exhibitions were held in which embroideries produced by Singer machines were displayed. On the new artistic forms created through the use of the Singer "New Family" embroidery sewing machine, the Athens newspapers commented, "more importance must be given to production by the sewing machine of women's handicrafts, and the introduction of these into charitable institutions and girls' schools is a necessity".[46]

In 1910–11, an advertising campaign was launched for a new Singer family sewing machine, the "66" model, describing it as the machine of the twentieth century, since it had even more labour-saving accessories, such as a tool that performed the difficult task of darning to perfection.[47] What is of interest is that in this new advertising campaign, the sewing machine is treated as an ornament to the household. The specific machine for family use could make the best Christmas present for any family, "of whatever class".[48]

Advertising campaigns in the local and women's press, especially from Singer, addressed both workshop owners and private consumers, women and men.[49] A Singer advertisement *c.* 1910 in an Athens daily (Figure 4.3) and that of a commercial house in Thessaloniki selling sewing and knitting machines for houses and manufacturers *c.* 1930 illustrate this double orientation (Figure 4.4).

45 Paula A. de la Cruz-Fernández, "Marketing the Hearth: Ornamental Embroidery and the Building of the Multinational Singer Sewing Machine Company", *Enterprise and Society*, 15/3 (2014), pp. 442–71.

46 "Η νέα καλλιτεχνία", *Εμπρός*, 24 November 1904, p. 4.

47 Advertisement, "Η ραπτομηχανή του 20ού αιώνος", *Εμπρός*, 16 December 1910, p. 5.

48 Ibid.

49 Elisabeth Frierson, "Cheap and easy: The creation of the consumer culture in late Ottoman society", in D. Quataert (ed.), *Consumption studies and the history of the Ottoman Empire: An introduction* (New York, 2000), pp. 243–60.

5 Education and Training in Sewing

The art of sewing was a substantive item in the curriculum for women's education in private girls' schools and state schools in most European countries from the nineteenth century onwards. This was because sewing was considered a part of a woman's household duties, but also a suitable way of making a living for married and unmarried women.

In Greece, practice in "womanly arts" formed a basic constituent of the primary and secondary education of girls from the nineteenth century to the interwar period.[50] With the appearance of the sewing machine from the 1870s onwards, many educational institutions and charitable foundations undertook to introduce sewing lessons with the use of these machines, and then introduced cutting. This development occurred not only in institutions of the Greek state, but also in Greek institutions in the Ottoman empire.

Singer organized regular instruction in the use of its sewing machines in Athens and in the provinces. The company announced, in the press, to ladies of the cities of Aighio, Agrinio, Aitoliko, and Mesolonghi that one of its special teachers of embroidery would teach, free of charge, embroidery with the "Central Bobine" sewing machine. The "Central Bobine" machine for family use was suitable for sewing for family needs, for repairs and darning, as well as for embroidery. The specialist embroidery teacher would stay five to eight days in each city. Teaching would be daily and would take place at Aighio in the city's two girls' schools and at the Singer agency of Athanasios Mentzelopoulos; in Agrinio at the linen draper's shop of M. Yerapanda and at the embroidery school of Photeini Karayianni; and at Mesolonghi at the Xenokrateio Girls' School. The teacher would be accompanied by an employee of the company. In the subsequent period, similar teaching of embroidery was scheduled for Zakynthos, Cephalonia, Corfu, Gastouni, Amaliada, and Lechaina.[51] Embroidery teaching was also conducted in the Zagora villages of Pelion, in the villages of Crete, of Lesvos, Euboea, and in many other agricultural and provincial areas of the country.[52] Commemorative photographs which are to this day to be found in houses, museums, and small-circulation publications of local interest provide evidence of this activity (Figure 4.5). "Schools" for

50 Sidiroula Ziogou-Karastergiou, *Η μέση εκπαίδευση των κοριτσιών στην Ελλάδα (1830–1893)* (Athens, 1986); Alexandra Bakalaki and Eleni Elegmitou, *Η εκπαίδευση εις τα του οίκου και τα γυναικεία καθήκοντα: Από την ίδρυση του ελληνικού κράτους έως την εκπαιδευτική μεταρρύθμιση* (Athens, 1987), pp. 33–65.

51 Newspaper *Εμπρός*, 9 October 1902, p. 2; newspaper *Σκριπ*, 3 October 1902, p. 2.

52 Newspaper *Εμπρός*, 3 December 1905, p. 4.

FIGURE 4.5 School of embroidery by Singer in Lesvos island, c. 1930
SOURCE: FILIA MUSEUM IN LESVOS

training, free of charge, in the use of sewing machines were also organized by other manufacturers between the beginning of the twentieth century and the first decades after the Second World War.

Cutting and tailoring were also taught by seamstresses in women's clothing and fashion stores.[53] However, learning under a seamstress was not without problems. Until the interwar years, it appears that girls worked with seamstresses without being paid or receiving only tips from customers when they delivered dresses or hats. Young girls went to women's clothing workshops as apprentices with a view to becoming professionals. It was however well known that the first, and perhaps the second, year of their "apprenticeship" would be spent in running errands and performing menial tasks for the seamstress–employer.[54] Apparently, the employer–teacher taught little or nothing of her art to the girls, so as to keep them longer in the workshop as unpaid or low-paid apprentices. The demands voiced by the feminist Labour Inspector and member of the Resistance, Maria Desypri-Svolou,[55] in the early postwar years

53 Newspaper *Σφαίρα*, 8 October 1902, p. 2; 31 January 1905.

54 Contemporary Social History Archives (ASKI), Archive Maria Svolou, f. 1, "Έκθεση για τη γυναικεία απασχόληση" (1936), p. 17.

55 Maria Desypri-Svolou (1892–1976) was a leading member of the Greek feminist movement in the interwar period, and a member of the Resistance during the Nazi occupation of Greece (1941–44). As a Labour Inspector in the interwar years she wrote broadly about

regarding apprentice seamstresses were concerned with precisely the institutionalization of the apprenticeship system. She sought an apprenticeship agreement that would determine: (i) the qualifications of the individuals who were to undertake the role of teachers to give professional training to male or female apprentices; (b) the duration of the apprenticeship; (c) the monitoring of the apprenticeship. Maria Desypri-Svolou also wanted unpaid apprenticeship to be banned in instances where the apprentices provided their labour.[56]

6 Working at home

For men and women in the periphery of industrialized countries, the domestic sewing machine might have had a more direct impact on their daily lives than steam technology. The use of the sewing machine made possible the continuation of home-based manufacture right up to the end of the twentieth century. In the Ottoman empire, the diffusion of sewing machines contributed to the revival of small-scale garment and shoe manufacturing in Istanbul and Salonica (Thessaloniki) until 1914, while in Greece, from the 1890s until the interwar period, it contributed to the production (at home or in small workshops) of uniforms for the army and to the systematic organization of mass production of garments.[57] In France, Italy, and Greece, the relatively cheap sewing machine allowed manufacturers, until recently, to hire (married or unmarried) women who could work for lower wages at home for the garment or leather industry.

The social consequences associated with the diffusion of domestic sewing machines led also to the development of sweatshops and home-based work (*travail à domicile*). A whole invisible (informal) sector of urban and rural economies developed thanks to cheap female labour that operated sewing machines at home to gain some additional family income. From the nineteenth

the working conditions of women workers. See Efi Avdela-Angelika Psarra, "Εισαγωγή", in *Ο φεμινισμός στην Ελλάδα του Μεσοπολέμου: Μία ανθολογία* (Athens, 1985); Efi Avdela, "Contested Meanings: Protection and Resistance in Labour Inspectors' Reports in 20th c. Greece", *Gender & History*, 9/2 (1997), pp. 310–32; Dimitra Samiou, "Svolou, Maria", in Francisca de Haan, Krasimira Daskalova, and Anna Loutfi (eds), *Biographical Dictionary of Women's Movements and Feminisms in Central, Eastern, and South Eastern Europe: 19th and 20th Centuries* (New York, 2005), pp. 552–57.

56 ASKI, Archive Maria Svolou, f. 2, "Εισήγηση πάνω στην οικονομική και κοινωνική θέση της Ελληνίδας", 2 May 1946, p. 6.

57 Quataert, *Manufacturing and Technology Transfer*; Agriantoni, "Βιομηχανία", pp. 173–221; Eadem, "Οικονομία και εκβιομηχάνιση", p. 173.

century in Greece, the sewing machine gradually became a much desired element included in the dowries of women getting married. Ownership of a sewing machine was important as it gave economic initiative to the owner and even some economic power to women of the working class. Women in urban or semi-urban environments in Greece in the interwar period could run an *atelier* (with young seamstresses), or enter into a business contract with an urban shop-owner, or become itinerant seamstresses selling their services from house to house. Women of the middle class and working class could also use the machine in unpaid domestic work for the needs of the family economy (as clothes needed to be repaired).

Work carried out in the home was an important alternative for the bourgeois morality of the nineteenth and early twentieth century. Furthermore, in capitalist relations of production, home-based work had important advantages, as working women did not have control over their labour or any significant scope for bargaining—advantages which explain the delay in the mechanization of this branch in Western Europe. In Greece, even in the case of women of the middle class with their limited career opportunities, paid work in the home in arts that were "noble and refined" (in various forms of small-scale handicrafts) seemed a "respectable" solution, according to the bourgeois feminist Kallirrhoe Parren.[58]

More or less simultaneously with the appearance of sewing machines on the Greek market, a relatively high-profile (at least in the press and advertising) piece-work network also made its appearance. How else do we interpret the advertisement for the sewing work branch operated by the Central Sewing Machine Warehouse of Dimitrios Constantinou, which accepted orders for sewing jobs of all kinds: for dowries, linen, clothing, etc., sewing work for tailors and shoemakers, and work by the yard, carried out "with precision and speed".[59] The sewing machine, then, served not only for the carrying out of sewing work within the family, but also for the execution of orders. This is noted, in his own way, by the writer Alexandros Papadiamantis in his short stories about working-class families living in the neighbourhoods of Athens at the turn of the nineteenth century: the wife of the drunken carpenter Manolis is "industrious"; she has a sewing machine at home with which she makes shirts; in this way, she earns five drachmas a week, approximately one-third of what her husband earns.[60]

58 Kallirrhoe Parren, "Γυναικείαι τέχναι και επαγγέλματα", *Εφημερίς των Κυριών*, 19 September 1899; Quataert, *Manufacturing and Technology Transfer*, pp. 22–25; Frierson, "Cheap and easy", pp. 243–60.

59 Newspaper *Ποσειδών*, no. 481, 4 September 1876.

60 Alexandros Papadiamantis, "Πατέρα στο σπίτι!" (1895), *Άπαντα*, v. Γ′ (Athens, 1984).

Workers' collective action against the working conditions in home industry and piece-work in the garment industry was frequent in the interwar period, though often without success. Collective action by the Workers' Association in the garment industry of Piraeus (tailors and seamstresses) since 1937 remained unsuccessful, as employers' pressure to the piece-workers was important.[61] In the workshops making women's clothing and in the various craft industries concerned with clothing in Athens and Piraeus, where the workers were mainly female, the legislation on working hours was not observed until the interwar years. Although this legislation stipulated an eight-hour working day for women and children, this was usually not observed and they worked eleven to twelve hours a day; at the same time, overtime was often not paid at the rate of an additional 25 per cent of the daily wage as laid down by the legislation, or was not paid in full. In workshops that operated from homes, in particular, the ten hours of work were systematically exceeded, as the feminist Labour Inspector Maria Desypri-Svolou noted in her report in 1936. The conditions of periodic unemployment in the majority of these small establishments forced their employees to accept work on any terms in the hope of keeping their jobs for longer, and they even resorted to working in shifts in times of great shortage of work. In occupations that required a long period of training, the working woman joined with the intention of becoming qualified as soon as possible, because she hoped the situation would change when she worked on an individual basis or when she realized the dream of later becoming an employer herself. Thus, generally, she did not pay much attention to the conditions of work, however crushing they were, calculating that they would be temporary. However, the situation of young seamstresses who worked on their own account or did sewing work in the houses of others was "lamentable". Their daily working hours were twelve or more, rather than ten. Moreover, the work was intensive, in order to satisfy the customers and to ensure, as far as possible, constant employment. It is not surprising that the majority of seamstresses, when still very young, were consumptive, while many of them suffered from stomach or heart conditions resulting from their posture during endless hours of intensive work, beginning in childhood.[62]

The craft industries in this field, which included a large number engaged in producing linen, children's clothing, embroidery and lace, as well as carpets and textiles woven by hand, operated in conditions that were harsh for

61 ASKI, Archive of the Workers' Association in garment industry of Piraeus (tailors and seamstresses). On the extension of the piece-work system in many sectors of manufacture and home industry during the interwar years, see Papastefanaki, *Εργασία*, pp. 249–58.

62 ASKI, Archive Maria Svolou, f. 1, "Έκθεση για τη γυναικεία απασχόληση" [1936], pp. 10–12.

the women employees. In the interwar period, no legislative provision was made for them, nor was there any thought of making such provision for home-based occupations. It was a known fact that it was to these sectors of work, particularly embroidery, lace-making, simple kinds of sewing, etc., that thousands of refugee housewives who had not worked in their places of origin had recourse. Similarly, as a large number of widows arrived without any source of income, they were forced to engage in occupations that were most accessible to them, and, of course, to offer their labour in what were known as women's occupations: embroidery, simple needlework, etc. It was precisely because of the existence of this population of workers and the unemployment due to the economic crisis that plagued these sectors in the interwar years, that the working conditions, which were poor to begin with, became even more wretched. Further, the minimal profit for endless hours of work by the woman who produced men's, women's and children's clothing for a starvation wage—if she had work—was absorbed by intermediaries between the working woman and the trader.[63] And daily wages fell to an incredible extent since many housewives engaged in these occupations as supplementary work and accepted whatever payment was offered.[64] At the same time, there was total neglect of the workforce on their work premises with respect to welfare measures such as public health, in spite of legal regulations.[65]

7 Conclusion

A global technology that was gender-specific, that of the sewing machine, invented for manufacturers, home industries, and families, was embedded in multiple ways in different countries by North American and European firms. In Greece, a whole network of agents and traders offered the sewing machine to women customers with the promise of training, credit (in instalments), and possible employment offered by local garment manufacturers. Advertisements, publications, and educational institutions emphasized in various ways the need for every woman to have her own machine, to either repair clothes for the family or to earn a living. In the case of Greece, ownership of the sewing machine stressed the gender division of labour in families (of the working class and the middle class), both in cities and in the countryside. Furthermore, adoption of the sewing machine in home industries stressed the class relations

63 Ibid., p. 12.
64 Ibid., p. 13.
65 Ibid., p. 15.

between women of the working class and bourgeois women and men (who acted as clients and entrepreneurs). The technological modernization of the garment industry contributed to the feminization of the profession throughout Greece, while piece-work as the payment mode in home industries tended to extend the working day and to increase the yield from labour.

Focusing on the sewing machine as a tool mass-produced and mass-marketed throughout the globe, this study explores home work in Greece as a meeting point for paid and unpaid labour, and the ways in which this modern technology has been integrated and *localized* in the historical context of Greek society in the period from 1870s to 1930s. The diffusion and adoption of the global technology of the sewing machine in Greece constitutes a good example of the interconnections between the global and the local regarding the transformation of labour for men and women in home industries.

Acknowledgements

The main part of this study was conducted during a sabbatical in the Fall semester of 2013–14 at the International Institute of Social History. The author wishes to thank Marcel van der Linden for his unwavering support during the research; ex-librarian Willeke Tijssen who helped greatly with her excellent knowledge of the collections at the IISH; Jacqueline Rutte for helping and organizing everything during my stay there; Jenneke Quast for her friendship and support; and all colleagues in the Netherlands, Greece, and elsewhere who contributed with their comments on this study.

CHAPTER 5

Women's Home-based Work in Istanbul's Garment Industry

Gender Inequalities and Industrial Work

Saniye Dedeoğlu

In many regions of the world, women's work in export industries has been at the centre of interest since the early 1970s, and this interest has further grown with the world-wide trend of 'feminization of employment'. Although there is great variation in the degrees and forms of women's work from country to country, there is a strong association between women's employment and production for export. Turkey went through the process of export orientation of its economy and has registered a growing export performance since the early 1980s. However, women's work in export manufacturing remains highly invisible in the Turkish case, in the context of an overall decline in women's employment.

With the neoliberal turn in economic policies in the early 1980s, the garment industry became one of Turkey's most important export industries. The expansion of the industry is attributed to initial government support, the falling cost of labour, and the renewed capacity of the textile industry to support the rapid expansion in the manufacturing of ready-made garments.[1] As elsewhere, the garment industry in Turkey draws heavily on women's labour, although women's contribution to the success of exports is largely invisible in official employment statistics. Women are the main suppliers of informal labour for the industry, through subcontracted and home-based piece-work. According to TurkStat's Household Labour Force Survey, one-third of all home-based women workers were engaged in textiles-related work in 2016.

This chapter examines women's home-based piece-work in the Turkish garment industry and shows the gender inequalities that underlie the export success of the industry, wherein the organization of production and workplace relations embed and reproduce gender ideology and norms. Women's

1 Ayda Eraydin and Erendil Asuman, "The Role of Female Labour in Industrial Restructuring: New Production Processes and Labour Market Relations in the Istanbul Clothing Industry", *Palace and Culture*, 6 (1999), pp. 259–72; Saniye Dedeoğlu, *Women Workers in Turkey: Global Industrial Production in Istanbul* (New York, 2012).

© SANIYE DEDEOĞLU, 2022 | DOI:10.1163/9789004499614_007
This is an open access chapter distributed under the terms of the CC BY-NC-ND 4.0 license.

engagement in garment production is ensured through the articulation of their subordinate position within the social organization of garment production and the mobilization of kinship relations. The findings of the chapter are based on a field study of Istanbul's garment industry over a fifteen-month period, between early 1999 and mid-2000. The main questions driving the field work were the role of women's labour in the generation of a globally competitive industry, the ways in which women became the main providers of labour for Istanbul's garment firms, and the implications of this integration into export production for gender relations. As part of the field study I interviewed women garment workers, garment workshop owners and their families, factory managers, and those engaged in informal work and other forms of invisible work in the garment industry. I conducted fifty interviews with women garment workers in different segments of the garment industry, and twenty-five interviews with factory managers and workshop owners.

1 Global Commodity Chains and Home-based Work

The commodity-chains approach has contributed to an understanding of the connections between global buyers and informal work in developing countries, and also offers a way of conceptualizing how labour market informalization affects women.[2] Along the same lines, Carr, Chen, and Tate have pointed out that technological change has facilitated "lean retailing", which demands the "quick and timely supply of goods associated with the just in time inventory system".[3] The system is seen as a reason for the increase in home work in the garment sector, particularly in countries close to the main markets of Europe and North America, and points to how women's traditional informal work has been connected to the globalization of industrial production.

The increasing use of home-based work is associated with intensified global competition in industrial production, and with the drive of local exporters and producers to minimize costs and thus accumulate more capital. Home-based work is, therefore, linked to the international production system through a chain of dependent relations between multinational companies, their buyers, and local exporters, and between exporters and contractors and workers.

2 Gary Gereffi *et al.* (eds), *Commodity Chains and Global Capitalism* (Westport CT, 1994).

3 Marilyn Carr, Martha Alter Chen, and Jane Tate, "Globalization and Home-Based Workers", *Feminist Economics*, 6 (2000), pp. 123–42, p. 126.

Benería and Roldan[4] have pointed out how the growing concentration of women in the informal sector was promoted through urban employment policies in Mexico City, and its political and economic implications for women's home-based industrial work. In addition, the diverse range of home-based work activities, including garment production and textile work, undertaken by women was conditioned by class, gender, and the dynamics of social relations in the workplace and household.

Although variations between countries exist, home-based work is an income-generating opportunity for low-income women in developing countries. Due to their limited mobility and the narrower range of options available to them in the labour market, married women especially make up the majority of the home-based workforce.[5] Women do not leave the industrial labour force when they get married, but continue their income-generating activities at home by combining their domestic duties with home-based work.[6] However, home-based work puts them in a vulnerable situation, as they hold very limited bargaining power to improve their working conditions. Also, subcontracting makes it very difficult to hold a single employer responsible for protecting workers' rights due to the many layers of production chains.[7] Thus, these home-based women workers' earnings are lower than in the formal sector, and their employment is characterized by a lack of consistency of work contracts, difficult working conditions, and long hours of work.

Research has shown that gender norms and ideologies are instrumental in generating export success in developing countries. For example, Hsiung's study of Taiwan's "economic miracle" shows how women's labour was drawn into export production in small-scale, family-centred, export-oriented satellite factories in local neighbourhoods.[8] With factory production located either adjacent to or within family living quarters, proletarian men became small factory owners by harnessing the labour of wives, daughters, and women in the neighbourhood. Women may also use their informal work in the export industry as a

---

4 Lourdes Benería and Martha I. Roldan, *The Crossroads of Class and Gender: Industrial Homework, Subcontracting, and Household Dynamics in Mexico City* (Chicago, 1987).

5 Lourdes Benería, *Gender, Development and Globalization: Economics as if All People Mattered* (New York and London, 2013).

6 Benería and Roldan, *The Crossroads of Class and Gender*; Jenny White, *Money Makes Us Relatives: Women's Labour in Urban Turkey* (Austin, 1994); Dedeoğlu, *Women Workers in Turkey*.

7 Lourdes Benería, "Shifting the Risk: New Employment Patterns, Informalization, and Women's Work", *International Journal of Politics, Culture and Society*, 15 (2001) pp. 27–54.

8 Ping-Chun Hsiung, *Living Rooms as Factories: Class, Gender, and the Satellite Factory System in Taiwan*, (Philadelphia, 1996).

way of building their identity and community membership. White[9] highlights how women's home-based, income-producing activities in Istanbul, combined with the more traditional labour of housewifery and motherhood, are being viewed in the community as an expression of their identity as " good' and hard-working Muslim women. As women emphasize their gender identity in order to gain financial security and membership in low-income neighbourhoods, they provide a low-cost labour source for production in the global market. This is also true for women's home-based piece-work in export-oriented industries.

This paper contributes to the existing literature on women's home-based piece-work in Turkey by pointing to the major role of women in Istanbul's garment industry and how this role ends up with an articulation of their subordinate position. It also shows that the mobilization of kinship relations has played a significant role in the integration of gender roles and ideologies into industrial production and in the social organization of garment production in Istanbul. More recent research on women's home-based piece-work in Turkey shows the continued importance of the garment industry in generating employment for women, and the ways in which the devaluation of women's work generates low-cost labour for the industry. In a study analysing why women's home-based work in Turkey remains invisible and hidden, Atasü-Topçuoğlu[10] identifies a process of deliberate obscuring and concealing of women's contributions whereby they gain neither public nor private recognition of their work. This is because women prioritize their roles as mothers and wives over their income-generating activities, which may signal that their husbands cannot provide for their families. Similarly, Balaban and Sarioğlu[11] show that piece-workers regard themselves as housewives who just earn *pazarparasi* (money for weekly shopping at the bazaar). Although women's informal work is hidden and invisible in urban Turkey, these two studies also show that women's income-generating activities are an important source for the well-being of the family, helping to meet household expenses, pay bills and rent, and save money for children's education. The next section of the chapter presents a description of the women who do piece-work in Istanbul's garment industry and their working conditions.

---

9 White, *Money Makes Us Relatives*.

10 Reyhan Atasü-Topçuoğlu, "Home-Based Work and Informal Sector in the Period of Globalization: An Analysis through Capitalism and Patriarchy, The Case of Turkey", Master's dissertation, The Graduate School of Social Sciences, Middle East Technical University (2005).

11 Utku Balaban and Esra Sarioğlu, "Home-Based Work in Istanbul: Varieties of Organization and Patriarchy", Working Paper, Social Policy Forum, Boğaziçi University (2008).

2 Flexible Organization and Subcontracting in Istanbul's Garment Industry

The garment industry in Turkey is a classic example of decentralized production networks with the administrative centres of transnational corporations and international brand names playing a leading role in different segments of the commodity chains.[12] The industry is organized to include different scales of production, whose connections and networks are based on subcontracting linkages. Representatives of international brands, integrated textile production factories, large-scale garment factories, and garment ateliers are the main constituents of garment production in Turkey. Mass and sweatshop production complement each other despite the great contrast between them in terms of market access, power, and competitiveness, as smaller and more informal businesses have less access to resources and markets with less decision-making power over production relations.[13]

An asymmetry between large and small firms governs the subcontracting relations wherein the small firms do not have control over the production process or power over the decision-making process. The findings in Istanbul show that large-scale producers have relatively more power over production processes as compared to small-scale firms, while ateliers are more dependent on orders coming from the large firms or international companies. Although orders are usually passed from large-scale firms to ateliers, horizontal subcontracting relations between ateliers are established if different specializations and skills are needed. For example, garment ateliers producing designer or branded products could subcontract to ateliers that do mainly ironing, packaging, and finishing of garments, or to ateliers acting as distributors of piece-work.

Underlying Turkey's garment export success are networks of subcontractors who help to reduce the fixed costs and provide lower labour costs. These networks not only exist between firms of different scales, but also extend to home-based garment workers. The majority of small-scale workshops operate informally without provision of decent working conditions and evade tax

12 A classic example of buyer-driven global value chains (Gereffi *et al.*, eds, *Commodity Chains and Global Capitalism*). In garment production, mass production is only one type of business strategy, and sweatshop and home-based production act as complementary stages of subcontracting chains in the whole production line (Appelbaum and Christerson 1997).

13 Dedeoğlu, *Women Workers in Turkey*.

duties. As Hernando De Soto puts it, informality is a way of life for the poor[14] and a way of survival for garment firms. Informality often assumes a relatively hidden, illicit, and under-reported character. Firms evade taxation, health and safety regulations, labour rights, and social security rules. Small workshops, in particular, keep themselves officially unrecorded.

Garment workshops stand at the heart of subcontracting chains providing backward linkages to factory production and enable the industry to reach untapped sources of low-wage women and children. The number of garment ateliers in Istanbul has recorded a phenomenal increase since the 1980s, most vividly observable in *gecekondu* neighbourhoods (shanty towns) where abundant cheap migrant labour is available.The location of workshops in basements and in *gecekondu* neighbourhoods allows workshop owners not only to take advantage of the low rents and low-wage labour in the area, but also to evade official inspections. Family ownership is a noticeable feature of these ateliers supported by family labour with the initial capital pooled through familial solidarity networks. Most of the ateliers specialized only in the sewing and trimming of parts of standardized products such as T-shirts and sweatshirts, while a few produced high-quality branded products requiring highly skilled labour and expertise in a certain aspect of production, such as embroidery, lacemaking, needlework, or stitching. The workshops were family businesses owned by men. The workers were immediate family members, more distant relatives, and neighbours, resulting in a high proportion of women working in these workshops.

Garment ateliers manufacture garments for export shaped by the demands of European and American fashion brand names. There are different categories of ateliers in Istanbul and they differ according to the type of market niche they serve. In table 5.1. we can see an outline of the features of these ateliers. A common underlying feature of all these ateliers is their reliance on the work of home-based piece-workers. Although reached in different ways, all the ateliers subcontract piece-work to women, and, in some cases, the number of piece-workers who work for ateliers could be higher than the number of those working in the atelier.

Home-based work takes on three different forms in Turkey: piece-rated work (for an employer, subcontractor, or mediator), order-based work, and own account work.[15] The first two forms are dependent on an employer or

14 Hernando De Soto, *The Other Path: The Invisible Revolution in the Third World*, (New York, 1989), pp. 11–12.

15 Şafak Tartanoğlu, "The Voluntary Precariat in the Value Chain: The Hidden Patterns of Home-Based Garment Production in Turkey", *Competition & Change*, 22 (2017), pp. 1–18.

TABLE 5.1 Garment ateliers in Istanbul

Ateliers working for brand-name exports	Ateliers working for standard exports	Ateliers working for domestic markets
Specialized, quality-oriented products	Production of standardized and simple products (T-shirts, sweatshirts)	Lower quality than exported products
Skilled and experienced labour	Rapid shifts between different subcontractor firms Skilled labour	More diversified product range Intensified utilization of family and kinship relations Greater extent of informalization

Source: Author's own fieldwork findings

mediator, whereas the last one is independent work and earns the lowest income.[16] In the garment industry of Istanbul, the first two forms of home-based work are more widespread in practice.

3 Home-based Piece-work in Istanbul's Garment Industry

Home-based work serves as a driver for the flexibility of the garment industry and its success in global competition. Gaining access to the labour of home-based workers and keeping them within the subcontracting network requires reaching out to the most secluded form of labour in Turkey, that of housewives, and opening the patriarchal lock of private households in the outskirts of Istanbul. The industry employs different strategies to attract home-based workers and retain their labour. This part of the paper identifies the main characteristics of Istanbul's home-based workers and their role in global garment production.

16 Gülsüm Coşkun, "Building women home-based workers, organizations in Turkey", *Global Labour Journal*, 1, Special Issue on Globalization(s) and Labour in China and India (2010), pp. 212–16.

Women's home-based work in Istanbul's garment industry shows that the organization of women's piece-work and atelier production is based on gender and social relations as well as kinship relations in which women's work is embedded. This in turn often leads both men and women to devalue women's home-based work. These relations and ideologies also provide a mechanism whereby women produce cheaply for international and national markets. Thus women's labour, both paid and unpaid, is conflated with their social and gender identity, and their membership of social groups such as the family. Women's informal labour in home-based piece-work or in garment ateliers tends to reproduce the patriarchal character of social relations without any public recognition of the work.

4 Women as Piece-workers

Home-based women workers typically fall within the age range of 30–45 years, have lower levels of education (on average, five years of compulsory schooling), and are married with children. Piece-work is the main work opportunity for these middle-aged women with few qualifications and heavy child-care and domestic responsibilities. They belong to poorer households in their neighbourhoods, in terms of general levels of well-being. Women over the age of 45 are not preferred by intermediaries because speed at work decreases with age and they have deteriorating eyesight not suitable for fine needle and embroidery work. However, the women enlist their daughters to engage in piece-work during their summer holidays.

Life-cycle mobility is more apparent among piece-workers in Istanbul. It is common practice for a mother to be a piece-worker at the workshop where her daughter or other children work. Another form of mobility is for a garment worker to start work in a workshop when she is a young girl, and to become a home-based worker when she gets married or becomes pregnant. Women move in and out of employment, not only because they have weak connections to the labour market, but also because the fluctuating nature of the garment business creates a high turnover of workers. A woman may work in a workshop for a few months or for a year or so, and then, when there is no work and she is made redundant, she could stay at home for some time before looking for another place to work. In some cases, women's employment is interrupted by marriage or children.

Usually associated with the neediest women in the community, piece-work is done by women who have no economic support from husbands, such as divorcees or widows; women whose husbands do not provide for them for a variety of reasons; or women who need extra cash for other reasons such as investing in ownership of a house. Such women were seen as *fakir* (poor), and were usually pitied (*yazik*) in their community. This also reflects how women without men's economic support were conceptualized in society.[17]

Piece-workers are involved in many different activities ranging from packing to cleaning the threads, to sewing beads, and embroidery. The working time of these women changes depending on the volume of work and the deadline. The women stated that they work longer hours particularly during holidays, stock renewal, and the beginning of the season, when orders come in high volumes with tight deadlines. During these periods, the working time increases to 16–18 hours per day. However, on a usual working day, the women said that they worked 12 hours, from 9 in the morning to 9 at night.

In Istanbul, piece-work is distributed to women through intermediaries, and the women usually perform their tasks in their homes. However, during the fieldwork it was observed that the intermediaries sometimes rented a small shop/workspace (*dükkan*) where all the piece-worker women came together to work, and these workspaces were preferably located close to or in the same neighbourhood as the women's homes. Their place of work is important for these women, and they prefer to work out of their homes or small workspaces located close to their homes. Piece-work is a manifestation of women's immobility, domestic responsibilities, and the unavailability of other types of work; "it represents a low-paid and labour-intensive work form primarily conducted by married women, where the productive and reproductive activities of women are juxtaposed both spatially and practically".[18]

During my fieldwork, piece-worker women cited many obstacles that prevented their employment in factories or ateliers: permission from husbands, child care, old age, and being unskilled were the most cited. Child care was the most commonly encountered problem for younger piece-workers. Working becomes possible for mothers only when proper child care facilities are available in the workplace; otherwise a family needs to find alternative modes of child care. For example, the help of other family members and private crèches, even though costly for a working-class family, are other means of handling child care when the mother is out at work. Using these options is viable only in the case of lucrative and stable employment. Women prefer to do home-based piece-work if only marginal and temporary employment options are available.

17 Dedeoğlu, *Women Workers in Turkey*.
18 Balaban and Sarioğlu, "Home-Based Work in Istanbul".

The testimony of one of my informants clearly singles out child care as a major obstacle to women's entry into the labour market:

> How could I go out to work? I have two small children and my husband works all day and comes back late in the evening. I do not have anybody from my family who can look after my children while I work. My husband's family is far from where we live now. So I am doing piece-work and looking after my children at the same time. We live in a one-room flat which was transformed from a kind of storage room or *dükkan* (shop), so it is hard for me to have a relative with us to look after my children. I wish I had better-paid work so we could buy our own flat and live better.

5 Recruiting Piece-workers and Flexibility of Labour

A global surge in new forms of flexible labour relations and fragmentation of the labour force are often associated with feminization of the labour force.[19] In both developed and developing countries, women seem to have been more affected by this trend than men.[20] An increasing number of home-based piece-workers is another phenomenon related to feminization of the workforce. The characteristics of piece-workers and the nature of home-based work are better researched in Turkey than other components of the female labour force.[21] Although some of this research has shown a high number of women engaged in piece-work, little effort has been made to highlight the relationship between industrial production and women's piece-work. This relationship is best illustrated by the recruitment strategies adopted to employ piece-workers, which also show that recruitment creates new forms of hierarchy between co-workers and further flexibility of production relations for employers.

Kinship and community relationships play a significant role in accessing subcontracted work and the labour of home-based piece-workers. In Istanbul's garment industry, some tasks are subcontracted directly from a workshop to

19 Guy Standing, "Global Feminization through Flexible Labour", *Wold Development*, 17 (1989), pp. 1077–95.

20 Maria Mies, *The Lace Makers of Nasapur: Indian Housewives Produce for the World Market* (London: Zed Press, 1982).

21 Emine Mine Çinar, "Unskilled Urban Migrant Women and Disguised Employment: Homeworking Women in Istanbul, Turkey", *World Development*, 22 (1994), pp. 369–80; Dilek Hattatoğlu, "Eveksenliçalişmastratejileri" [Home-based work strategies], in Aynur Ilyasoğlu and Nebahat Akgökçe (eds), *Yerlibirfeminizmedoğru* [Towards a local feminism] (Istanbul, 2001), pp. 173–204; White, *Money Makes Us Relatives*.

women, and others are allocated by middle-women, who are sometimes relatives of the workshop owner. There is a distinct difference between how large-scale factories managed their subcontracting, and how garment ateliers organized their relations with home-based piece-workers. Garment ateliers are mediators for large-scale factories in distributing garment pieces to home-based workers. As dealing with home-based work is a time-consuming and costly activity, large-scale factories preferred to subcontract this to garment ateliers. Despite some factories subcontracting piece-work to ateliers, the ones that specialized in designer and high fashion products had direct relations with home-based workers as the tasks required delicate and skilled handicraft, such as embroidery or stitching ornaments on garments. In order to find the right women for the work, factories established an efficient network of subcontracting.

Here is an example of how a large-scale factory directly managed its subcontracting relations with home-based piece-workers. Two workers were allocated to distribute garments to piece-workers, who were all women and lived in neighbourhoods close to the garment factory. One of these workers was the driver of the van, and he was also in charge of transporting the garments. The other worker was a woman who was in charge of the women piece-workers. She showed the women what needed to be done to the new pieces, and kept records of the garments distributed and the payments to each worker. She could decide independently how many pieces had to be subcontracted and to whom. This woman, Serpil, who was 35 years old and the mother of two children, told her story of how she became the middle-woman of the factory.

> I am good at maths and also a high school graduate. Most of my colleagues are primary school graduates and I was quick to learn every job at the factory. So, our manager (*müdür*) asked me to do this job when they decided to subcontract some tasks to women instead of doing them in the factory. Now, we have 50 women in different *mahalles* around here and some of these women have been working for more than eight years. What I do is very difficult because if a piece is missing or something is wrong with the quality of the work, I am responsible. I try to work with women whom I trust and have known for a long time. In the beginning, there were just a few women whom I reached through my own personal contacts and mostly from my own family and neighbourhood. We need to make sure that women have skills to do the job. Even though most women have skills of sewing and embroidery, it is more important to follow the designs and be precise, clean, and punctual.

Although Serpil was an ordinary worker in the factory, her role as a middle-woman gave her decision-making powers over the piece-workers. She was like a manager of the piece-workers, and demanded information about the progress of their work. She often reminded the women that the time taken to complete tasks was very important, and if the work was not completed on time, payment would have to wait until the following month. She was certainly the boss of the piece-workers, for whom having a good relationship with Serpil was a channel for getting access to regular piece-work.

The relationship between the women intermediaries and piece-workers was usually maintained on the basis of "fictive kinship",[22] which is a form of social relations that mimics kinship relations among non-kin. Since many women get to know about piece-work opportunities by word of mouth, and through existing kin and non-kin networks in their communities, a form of "mutual indebtedness" is maintained between the middle-women and the piece-workers to manipulate social relations in order to ensure a steady supply of work. The important part played by middle-women in giving access to a regular supply of work was emphasized by many piece-workers. Thus, daily survival for piece-workers requires participating in social relations and community networks, and continuously nourishing a web of reciprocal arrangements.[23]

The irregular nature of piece-work and strict rules of work completion have resulted in a complex alliance between women piece-workers and middle-women, which illustrates the extra-economic relations underlying the social organization of piece-work in Istanbul's garment industry. This irregular structure of work has developed a network of women in which a piece-worker, for example, is the main subcontractor of the factory, but also shares her quota with other women in her household or neighbourhood. In cases of surplus work and under time pressure, a piece-worker uses the help of her neighbours and pays them later. This practice of collaboration among women generates further flexibility in the organization of piece-work, and shifts the responsibility of middle-women, in terms of finding new subcontractors, to piece-workers.

I joined Serpil on one of her visits to her piece-workers during which she distributed some work and collected the finished pieces. In one of the neighbourhoods, there were two women piece-workers whom Serpil had known for a long time. When we arrived the two women were together making their garment pieces. Serpil gave them the new garments and explained what was required, and then a third woman suddenly appeared, carefully listening to

22 White, *Money Makes Us Relatives.*

23 Ibid., p. 133.

what Serpil had to say. Later, I asked Serpil who she was and she told me that the first two women shared some of their work with her. When there was too much work and too little time to finish all the pieces, Serpil herself gave work to the third woman. This was one of the ways in which the factory's circle of subcontracted women enlarged over time.

Another model used by garment ateliers is that by which they establish their network of piece-workers using the personal connections of the women in their families. Extended families always have some untapped labour of women that can be drawn into production whenever necessary. For example, the grandmother of the family is usually in charge of child care during the day, while other family members are working in the atelier. Sometimes she also does the finishing of garment pieces by cleaning stitched edges, or, in some cases, she acts as the middle-woman in their immediate environment by distributing garments to other women. Ateliers that are unable to utilize the labour of their own family usually have a number of piece-workers who have worked for them for a long time. These women establish a small network of piece-workers in which they have the leading role as distributor. The networks can be as small as four or five women.

6 Income from Piece-work: Charity or Survival?

Although piece-workers in Istanbul make a substantial contribution to global garment manufacturing, their income is conceptualized as *pazarparasi* (bazaar money) and is seen as charity to poor women. This conceptualization was made clear in the statement of an atelier owner, where he explained how and why he subcontracted to women:

> We subcontract only to women and they sometimes come and ask us if there is any work. Most of the women are regulars and all are from this area. In the past, we hired women to do hand-work of the pieces as full-time workers but the garment business is irregular. Sometimes these women had nothing to do for weeks and we had to pay their salaries. Later, we decided to subcontract the women at home, so that we deliver pieces to them when there is work and pay them on a piece basis. For the women it is better to do piece-work than sit idle at home, so they can earn their *pazarparasi*. I think this work is good for women because *fakir kadin* (poor women) need to feed their children and at the same time they can watch over their children. Times are hard for families, so people are trying hard to make ends meet and everyone has to do something in

> order to survive (*hayattakalmak için*). Piece-work gives the opportunity to live without depending on anybody (*el açmadanyaşama*).

The women involved in home-based piece-work are usually pitied in their community. Workshop owners represent piece-work as a kind of charity to women in need, even though it is entirely a business matter for them.

7 Uneasy Definitions of Work

The piece-work activities of women, such as knitting, sewing, and packaging by women, is arranged around the demands of child care, housework, and other obligations of the home, and they see their income-producing activities as a mere extension of their domestic responsibilities. The type of work women do, the location of their work, and the social context and social relations of their work have tremendous implications for how they define themselves and the meaning of work in their lives. Jenny White's study (1994) of a group of squatter settlement women in Istanbul who engage in home-based piece-work or work in family and neighbourhood ateliers for export and local markets, demonstrates the concentration of married women in the informal sector due to its easy accommodation of women's family responsibilities. White presents a detailed analysis of why the women she studied, although intensely engaged in income-producing activities, maintain a fiction of "not-working". In this regard, women's labour is seen as the property of the group and a woman's gender identity is largely defined by her labour, in the sense that her income-generating labour is conflated with her social roles. Thus the unpaid or poorly paid nature of women's labour is legitimized by the cultural construction of "giving" labour as a contribution to family and community, and an expression of identity.

Intentional concealment of their piecework as domestic work, was observable among the garment workers of Istanbul. Home-based workers, makers of traditional handicrafts, and some of the atelier workers described their activity as a hobby or help to the family business, and did not consider it as "work". That is, women regarded their work as an extension of their traditional housewifely activities by perceiving it to be an expression of solidarity and group identity. Women's invisibility in the labour market, is thus also generated through the uneasy definitions of work that they themselves use.

Women's unpaid or underpaid work as an expression of their social and group identity was also seen by my informants as a means of earning money. Although the expectation of and demand for a fair financial return were not publicly stated, all the women I interviewed were well aware that their work, even as "help", meant a financial gain, and directly or indirectly contributed to the family budget. The financial returns were highly appreciated by the women and their families. Despite being confined to their role of housewives and their marginal incomes as piece-workers, all the women in my sample were conscious of how much money they earned through their work and the dependency of their families on their income for survival. Women's awareness of financial gain from their work does not, however, translate itself into women's perception of themselves as workers and breadwinners of their households.

The case of my informant Ayla illustrates the extent of appreciation of financial gain made through home-based piece-work. Ayla, who was 32 years old and a mother of three young children, was a regular piece-worker for an atelier located in her neighbourhood. She said:

> No one pays you money for sitting idle at home. My husband and all the others know that I earn money for my children and my family. We even managed to save for the future. In case of illness or an emergency, we at least have some money, so we will not be in need of financial help from other people (*elalem*).

Ayten was one of my key informants. I lived close to her and had long conversations with her. She has three sons, and a husband who has irregular employment and often moves from one job to another. Even though he was not unemployed for long spells, the money he made was marginal because of the irregularity of his employment. Therefore, Ayten began to take in piece-work from a large-scale textile factory eight years ago. She said:

> I know that it seems like petty work, but I make as much money as my husband earns every month. Without my contribution we would not have been able to support our sons' education. We have also built the house we live in with my contribution. Although it is very hard and irregular work, everyone knows that without it we would be starving out in the streets. My husband's income is only enough to feed us, the rest is done through the money that I make from the piece-work.

The significance of women's income for the survival of low-income families in Istanbul has not helped to change how women's work is perceived and valued. The uneasy definition of women's paid work as not "work" is also a result of the nature of garment work, which is mainly done at home or in family establishments. For women, the traditional meaning of work requires being present at a workplace and working fixed hours, as observable in the case of factory workers. Piece-work and *elişi* (handicraft) activities are usually perceived as being not "work", but as just passing time and making some cash.

Women manage to preserve a sense of self-respect and the identity of motherhood in the face of the perceived temporariness and marginality of their work by articulating the priority of their domestic roles and responsibilities over their paid work. In Istanbul, women's social identity as mothers and wives does not stop them from turning their skills into income-generating activities that contribute to making ends meet and make a significant contribution to the family budget. The pervasiveness of women's identity as "women of the house", due to which women refrain from carving out a work identity for themselves, is also a result of the negative social image attached to working women.

8 Elişi: A Path from Household to Labour Market for Women

The tradition of women's engagement with handicraft activity (*elişi*) makes it easy for them to acquire garment-making skills. *Elişi* is a common activity covering knitting, embroidery, sewing, and needlework, to make a wide range of materials such as bedspreads, table covers, cardigans, and socks. Most working-class women enter adulthood from girlhood by acquiring the skills of embroidery, knitting, needlework, crochet, and sewing, at the same time as they also learn how to cook, clean, and serve. Making *elişi* has always been the basis of earning money for low-income women, and also builds a bridge to the labour market whereby women can earn some petty cash by making lace or other forms of *elişi*.

These skills, used to prepare an elaborate *çeyiz* (trousseau), are utilized to earn money in two ways. First, women make lace, embroidery, and knitwear for young girls' *çeyiz*; second, women use these skills to take on piece-work or to work in an atelier. Many women in the *gecekondu* areas of Istanbul live on incomes from either lace-making or needlework, similar to Mies's study of Narsapur in India, where lace-makers working from their homes exclusively utilized their skills to integrate the Indian economy into world markets of export production.[24]

Hanife was a lace-maker who lived with her husband and two children in a one-room flat. Her husband had an irregular income and could barely support the family. Hanife kept her income from lace-making a secret from him, in

24 Mies, *The Lace Makers of Nasapur*.

order to force him to try and meet his family's basic necessities. She saved the money she earned in a bank or bought gold for herself. Despite the fact that she was engaged in lace-making for many years, her husband never realized that she was making money out of it, because women's *elişi* (handicraft) was always seen as a hobby and a non-monetary activity.

Filiz, a former garment worker, stopped working when she got married. However, although her husband had regular employment, his income was not enough to support the family. So Filiz started making *elişi* for her neighbours. She said:

> His salary is all right but just enough for rent and food. I want to buy carpets and curtains for my home. … Making *elişi* is better than going out for work. I earn some cash and do my household chores (*evişi*) as well. My husband does not know that I make money with *elişi*. He thinks this is a thing I do to pass my time and entertain myself. … If I work hard I can make 50–75 million TL a month and spend some of this money to buy things for my house. It is not that I want to hide money from my husband, but I do not want to make him feel like he is not capable of earning money to support his family.

Filiz's earnings depend on the price set in the local market for *elişi* among women. For example, there is an approximate price for a ball of yarn (*yumak*). Setting up the price of the lace-maker's labour, two women, the buyer and the seller, negotiate and determine the price each time. A well-known fact among local women was that the prices for *elişi* are set very low. The low prices can be explained by the fact that customers and lace-makers are both from working-class families. If the price is low women can afford to buy, otherwise they would make it themselves since they all have similar skills of lace-making. Thus, low prices make income from *elişi* very low and marginal.

My interviews with women engaged in *elişi*-making show that there was always a demand for *elişi*, either from other women or from traders who specialize in marketing these products. The *elişi* trade took place through two different channels. First, there were shops that sell trousseau items and generate a demand for women's *elişi*. They buy the items from women and sell them in their shops. Second, there were middle-(wo)men who collected items from cities around Istanbul, such as Bursa, Balikesir, etc., and brought them to Istanbul. The second channel was more outward-oriented and internationally marketed, with Arab countries being the main destination especially for women's headscarves, which were tediously decorated with needlework or lace-work.

Engaging in *elişi* (handicraft) was a way for women to express their identity. Women's *elişi* skills, which were normally devoted to making girls' *çeyiz* (trousseaux), were often turned into an income-generating activity that provided significant support for household income. Whenever women needed extra cash, they could rely on income from *elişi*. This work had the advantage of "invisibility", as in the case of Hanife who was trying to build a nest-egg. In some cases, if a woman is trying to establish financial security for the future, for instance, this income becomes vital. However, women's contribution to the household budget has not drastically altered the patriarchal nature of gender relations, and women's perception of their primary roles as mothers and wives.

9 Conclusion

This paper is based on a study that dates back to the early 2000s; however, its findings are still relevant for an analysis of piece-worker women's work in the manufacturing sector in Turkey today. There are similarities between the situation of women described here and that in more recent research on the topic. Current research on home-based work in Turkey is focused mostly on garment production[25] and women's role in the labour process of value chains in the garment industry.[26] Women workers are dependent on mediators for the supply of work and raw materials. They also have no control over the means of production.[27] Gendered control mechanisms make women's obedience easy and implicit, and resistance unnecessary, as they see their relations with the mediator as a part of patriarchal consensus. The gender division of labour is inherent in the organization of home-based work. In this sense, it is very important to understand the dynamics of the organization of home-based garment work in the value chains. Practices of control, in particular, are shaped by the varied patterns of gendered organization of work and the labour process.[28]

The garment industry has been the top exporting sector in Turkey since the early 1980s when Turkey started to adopt economic liberalization policies. Women are the main suppliers of informal labour in the Turkish garment

---

25 Esra Sarioğlu, "Gendering the organization of home-based work in Turkey: Classical versus familial patriarchy", *Gender, Work & Organization*, 20 (2013), pp. 479–97; Tartanoğlu, "The Voluntary Precariat in the Value Chain"; Dedeoğlu, *Women Workers in Turkey*.

26 Saniye Atilgan, "Evden Içeri Bir Ev: Ev Eksenli Üretimve Kadin Emeği", *Birikim*, 217 (2007), pp. 134–40.

27 Balaban and Sarioğlu, "Home-Based Work in Istanbul".

28 Sarioğlu, "Gendering the organization of home-based work in Turkey".

industry through subcontracted and home-based piece-work. This chapter discusses in detail the gender inequalities that underlie the export success of the garment industry, pointing to the organization of production and workplace relations in the industry which embed and reproduce gender ideology and norms. Women's engagement in garment production is ensured through the articulation of their subordinate position with the social organization of garment production and the mobilization of kinship relations. While piece-work is an individual activity and each woman is paid individually for her work, a common argument found in the literature is that women do this work collectively in their homes with neighbours often joining in for an hour or so at a time.

Piece-work in Istanbul's garment industry is defined as women's work because of the assumed characteristics of patience, endurance, lack of mobility, and dexterity associated with women, and also because of the small amount of money paid for each piece. Networks of collaboration created among women are the main source of recruitment of piece-workers, and a further aspect of flexibility in garment production. Women manifest their roles as "good" mothers and wives and express their loyalty to their community by keeping their work invisible and hidden from public eyes. Studies illustrate how patriarchal dynamics restrict women's job opportunities and compel them to engage in home-based work, which is defined by low pay, long working hours, and lack of benefits and job security.

PART 2

CHAPTER 6

Introduction between Ban and Human Rights

The Regulation of Home-based Work Since the Twentieth Century

Silke Neunsinger

The history of home-based work predicts the future of labour, prefiguring the precariousness, the lack of protection, and time and wage theft, as well as the placing of the burden for working conditions on the independent subcontractor. These features are seen in many sectors of the labour market all over the world. While the parcelling out of specific jobs in the production process through subcontracting in such a manner that a part of the production shifted into the homes of workers was characteristic of industrial capitalism from the very start, the bad working conditions, low wages, and poor health and safety conditions did not generate international debate on a large scale until the early years of the twentieth century. This, though home-based work certainly received attention, even if limited, in the nineteenth century. For example, Marx in *Das Kapital* wrote about the predicaments of home-based workers. But it was not until the beginning of the twentieth century that the home-based worker became central to "the social question" in Europe, and a poster-child, as it were, for all the ills associated with industrialization.

For a long time, law and social policy distinguished between family-based work, which was widely accepted, and home work, which was not. Employers argued against the regulation of home-based work on the plea that it would violate the sanctity and privacy of the home. As far back as in 1923, the International Federation of Working Women (IFWW) requested the International Labour Office (ILO) to investigate the conditions of home-based work. However, it was only in the 1980s that trade unions in the global North, which had to begin with demanded the abolition of home-based work, changed their standpoint to push for regulation.

European investigators carried out a large number of national studies in different parts of Europe on the situation of home-based industrial workers. Trade union activist Jeanne Bouvier, whose life and work are discussed in Maria Tambouko's chapter in this volume ("Genealogies and assemblages of resistance: Jeanne Bouvier's struggles in 'le travail à domicile' "), deployed these studies to draw the attention of the international trade union movement to the subject of home-based work and home workers. Several exhibitions were

© SILKE NEUNSINGER, 2022 | DOI:10.1163/9789004499614_008
This is an open access chapter distributed under the terms of the CC BY-NC-ND 4.0 license.

held that displayed the work and situation of home workers in early twentieth-century Europe. These exhibitions, studies, and surveys were arranged and conducted by NGOs, state agencies, and trade unions—at times, by all three in collaboration. All three players, not least the trade unions, seem to have grappled with the same dilemma, namely: how are we to view these workers? Are they "victims" to be "saved", or workers to be organized? Do we argue for a ban or push for better conditions? The dilemma persisted even as many trade unions continued to function on the premise that home workers were "non-workers" serving to drive down wages.

One of the first conferences on industrial home workers was held in Brussels in 1910, when the International Office for Industrial Homework was set up. In 1919, with the foundation of the ILO, home work became a part of the discussions around the subject of regulating work. This section deals with struggles for the recognition of home-based industrial workers and the regulation of their work. In three chapters, the authors discuss why it has been so difficult to regulate home-based labour, and question why the regulations took such a long time.

The home itself has often appeared as the reason for the lack of regulation. Traditionally, the ILO's setting of work standards was concerned with the conditions of male industrial workers in the global North. Many argued that it would be difficult to come up with standards for home work as it would be impossible to monitor work inside people's homes. However, some countries had already passed laws and included home-based workers under wage boards during the interwar period. And a few countries did regulate home work even though monitoring work in private homes was regarded as difficult in general. Depending on the relations between state, union and employers, state inspection of private homes was actually used as a way of regulating home work. This was the case in Norway. In Sweden, the unions were strong and against any form of state intervention; therefore, inspections were not carried out.

Regulation has manifested in three different ways. First, there is special legislation to protect home workers. This was the case with respect to the 1958 law in Italy, analysed in Eloisa Betti's chapter in this volume ("Industrial Home Work and Fordism in Western Europe: Women's Agency, Labour Legislation and Trade Union Action in Golden Age Italy, 1945–75"), and later in Thailand, as shown in Narumol Nirathron's study ("Home Work in Thailand: Challenges to Formalization"). Second, there is the amending of labour laws to include home workers and to make them equal to other workers. Efforts to do this can be seen in the 1973 law in Italy or the Bulgarian legislation, discussed in the chapter by Marlese von Broembsen and Jenna Harvey ("Realizing Rights for Home Workers: Participating in Global Supply Chains"). Third, through regulation of the entire chain of production including the conditions of home-based workers—independently of where they are based—as in the case of Australia, also analysed by von Broembsen and Harvey.

Home-based work and domestic work were the most common occupations of women in the early twentieth century in many urban settings. Both these forms of work also have a common feature: that the workplace is the home. While it is the worker's own home in the former instance, in the latter case it is the house of someone else, who is also the employer. However, regulations relating to domestic work and home-based work took different paths. This could be explained by the growth of the two forms of work at different points of time. Domestic work was never sought to be regulated by a ban, rather the opposite. When women chose to go to factories instead of working as live-in domestic servants, many European states opted for regulation of the working hours of domestic workers, in order to improve their working conditions and to make them stay. The growth of domestic workers in the Northern Transatlantic region during the last thirty years and their organizing on a global scale put the demand of domestic workers for decent work on the ILO's agenda; the ILO convention 189 was adopted in 2011, recognizing domestic workers as ordinary workers. Fifteen years earlier, in 1996, the ILO had recognized home-based industrial workers as ordinary workers. Eileen Boris's analysis of the debates at the ILO shows how initially, a ban on home-based industrial work had appeared inevitable, but changed circumstances after the Second World War eventually led to action. Important factors included a human rights approach, the push for action from staff of the Programme on Rural Women at the ILO, and the strategies adopted by women trade union activists and women's organizations, including the Self Employed Women's Association (SEWA); the former International Confederation of Free Trade Unions (ICFTU), now International Trade Union Confederation (ITUC); *Women in Informal Employment: Globalizing and Organizing* (WIEGO); the International *Union* of Food, Agricultural, Hotel, Restaurant, Catering, Tobacco and Allied *Workers'* Associations (IUF); and the International Textile, Garment and Leather Workers' Federation (ITGLWF). The efforts of these groups brought the issue to the table of the ILO. As in the case of domestic workers, women from the global South played a crucial role in this struggle.

Some unions regarded home work as a system to evade standards, and, as the chapter on Italy shows, employers closed factories and moved work to private homes, replacing men workers with cheaper women workers. Unions acted against such home work, but Betti shows that home workers started to protest the precarity of their working conditions and the lack of recognition.

During the 1970s and 1980s home work was still seen as undermining factory work according to trade unions and international trade secretariats such as the ITGLWF. The change in strategy—from pushing for a ban to regulation—was driven not only by the growth of home work, but also, as Boris presents, by the work put in by feminists at the ILO and networks of female trade unionists, especially SEWA in India, led by the inimitable Ela Bhatt. These, together, managed to push for a focus on the demands of home-based workers, combined with the rural development programme of the ILO.

Other international organizations followed the changes at the ILO, as von Broembsen and Harvey show. Since 2011 new international instruments—primarily guidelines or soft laws to protect home workers—have been developed by the United Nations (UN) and the Organization for Economic Co-operation and Development (OECD). Together with the ILO Convention, these are useful instruments at the disposal of home workers. They are limited recommendations which support the legitimacy of home workers' claims in global supply chains. By referring to the 2011 UN Guiding Principles on Businesses and Human rights, the OECD Declaration on International Investment and Multinational Enterprises indirectly endorses the need for protection of home workers. As per the UN approach, home workers are covered under the framework of human rights, with states and corporations bearing responsibility to respect and uphold human rights and to remedy the situation when violations occur. These two principles refer directly to the ILO Declaration of Fundamental Principles and Rights at work and the UN Declaration of Human rights. This holds businesses responsible for violations of human rights in different parts of the supply chains. Today, 147 countries adhere to the OECD guidelines. The OECD also has guidelines for specific sectors, such as the Due Diligence guidelines for the garment and footwear sector. According to von Broembsen and Harvey, the OECD instruments are the most effective as home workers' organizations can report on companies violating the guidelines.

The chapters by Nirathron as well as von Broembsen and Harvey deal with the results of regulation and the struggles for their implementation. In Thailand, historically speaking, home-based work changed from being concerned with agricultural production to industrial and service products, a process that was accompanied by the informalization of labour. Thai home workers organized themselves under Home-Net Thailand. Legal protection of home workers started in 2004 with the passing of a regulation. This was followed in 2010 by the Home Workers' Protection Act.

The case of Thailand shows the importance of continuous investigations to monitor the situation of home workers and the collection of statistics. More important than the guidelines analysed in von Broembsen and Harvey's chapter is the 2015 ILO focus on the development of regulations for home work, which forms part of the Recommendation on the Transition from Informal to Formal Economies. In the Thai case, home workers were informal workers—similar to home workers in India, South Africa, and Brazil. Since the enforcement of the 2010 Act they are protected by specific laws when working in industrial sectors, but work in the service sector is still excluded from the provisions of the Act. Issues connected with the transition from an informal to a formal economy include a mandate for the collection of statistics to make home work visible, the organizing of home workers, qualitative research on the conditions of home work, and minimum wages for home work. The Thai government has created a tripartite Homework Protection Committee which reports to the Ministry. Protection and promotion of home work falls under the protection of labour courts, and violations can be punished with fines and imprisonment. Similarly, as in the case of food workers in Chennai analysed by K. Kalpana in this volume ("Refusing Invisibility: Women Workers in Subcontracted Work in a South Indian City"), the social protection of home workers—including health care, income security, and personal development—have become an issue for the state, and therefore the struggles of home workers have become a part of larger struggles involving citizens versus the state.

Nevertheless, it should be noted that most laws concerning aspects of labour protection assume an employer–employee relationship, which poses a specific challenge to regulations related to home work. As shown by K. Kalpana in her contribution to this volume, alliances between home workers and unions, as well as the state, become necessary to handle this situation. This appears to have been a successful strategy in South Africa and Brazil.

The fact is that legislation and regulation are not enough if rights are to be ensured. These remain toothless unless they are systematically implemented and violations are regularly reported, which in turn requires active intervention on the part of the respective authorities. Moreover, home workers are excluded from bargaining between brands and transnational/trans-sectoral unions. If the economic contribution of home workers remains unrecognized, they will continue to be neglected and their need to organize ignored.

CHAPTER 7

From Industrial Evil to Decent Work

The ILO and Changing Perspectives towards Home-based Labour

Eileen Boris

The home has haunted the formulation of global labour standards. It has stood for the space of family privacy, the realm of reproduction, where the woman's responsibility for the quotidian aspects of life and for life itself distinguished her from the male breadwinner. * For nearly a century, the International Labour Organization (ILO) attacked the low wages, long hours, and unregulated conditions of outwork indirectly, sometimes including it in its conventions and other instruments, but more often allowing signatory states to exempt myriad forms of home-based labour from coverage. Beginning in 1919, when the ILO emerged out of the First World War along with the League of Nations, until the 1970s, when global supply chains intensified the relocation of manufacturing to the global South, garment unionists and labour feminists pushed for the elimination of home work. By the last decades of the twentieth century, however, they increasingly called for regulation rather than the prohibition of home-based labour. As the body that established norms for the world of work, the ILO appeared as a venue to gain redress.[1]

It is tempting to label this shift in perspective as a progress narrative: from outwork as an evil to be eradicated to home-based work and home workers as deserving decent work like all other labourers.[2] This outcome was hardly inevitable, the victory partial, and its timing pyrrhic. Pushed by trade union federations, feminist campaigners, and its own staff, the ILO formulated what became Convention No. 177, "Home Work", which the International Labour Conference (ILC, one of the ILO's component parts) passed in 1996. But this measure extended labour protections to home workers precisely when the old standard employment relationship was fraying.[3] With more workers even in

* I would like to thank Blair Hull for endowing the Hull Chair in Feminist Studies, which I hold; the archivists and staff at the ILO; research assistant Sharon Dade; and the editors of volume.

1 Gerry Rodgers *et al.*, *The ILO and the Quest for Social Justice, 1919–2009* (Ithaca, 2009).

2 Clare Hemmings, *Why Stories Matter: The Political Grammar of Feminist Theory* (Durham, 2011).

3 David Weil, *The Fissured Workplace: Why Work Became so Bad for so Many and What Can Be Done to Improve It* (Cambridge, 2014); Leah F. Vosko, *Managing the Margins: Gender, Citizenship, and the International Regulation of Precarious Employment* (New York, 2010).

© EILEEN BORIS, 2022 | DOI:10.1163/9789004499614_009
This is an open access chapter distributed under the terms of the CC BY-NC-ND 4.0 license.

"developed" countries defined as independent contractors and shoved into the informal economy, home work's past began to foretell labour's future. The strategies of home-based workers for survival and recognition thus take on added significance in today's gig economy.

The road to Convention No. 177 requires historicization. The 1980s' recognition of home-based labour as worthy of standard-setting, for which activists in India and elsewhere were central, drew upon key players within and around the ILO: international union federations and the ILO tripartite committee for the clothing industry; the staff in the Programme on Rural Women of EMPLOI, one of the technical sections of the International Labour Office (the Office), and grassroots campaigners. These stakeholders—labour feminists, garment unions, development specialists, ILO staff, and home-based worker campaigners—brought their own goals to the table, motivated by self-interest, feminism, and economic justice. That this pathbreaking recognition of the home as a workplace has garnered few signatories (ten as of 2020) should not distract from its impact. It launched international action on other excluded, informal, and "non-standard" workers, and has proven to be an instrument which home workers and their allies, as von Broembsen and Harvey ("Realizing Rights for Home Workers: Participating in Global Supply Chains") emphasize in this volume, have deployed to make changes in national laws and corporate practice.

Scholars and activist commentators have highlighted the role of grassroots and feminist activists who campaigned for the Convention.[4] Yet NGOs could only become observers with limited participation because of the structure of the ILO. This limit comes from the ILO's unique tripartite structure that divides national representation between government, worker, and employer members. Since employers were adamantly opposed and governments had to be convinced, success depended on the willingness of the global trade secretariats and worker delegates to embrace the cause—though Office staff proved crucial for an insider–outsider strategy. The opening up of the ILO to issues of the informal sector and the problem of multinational enterprises further set the stage for their efforts.

Still, ideas matter. Campaigners confronted assumptions and silences about gender difference, the unequal global development of labour relations, and the relationship of women (and men) to productive and reproductive work at the core of ILO activities. The global labour standards regime of the twentieth century took the conditions of industrial workers, predominantly male, in the

4 Annie Delaney *et al.*, *Homeworking Women: A Gender Justice Perspective* (London, 2019).

global North as the norm, turning the woman worker into a problem of difference and treating women in colonialized and developing nations as difference's other, distinct from those in industrial nations. Even though some men also laboured as home-based workers throughout the world, policy-makers judged industrial home work as a feminized practice, conflated with and often discussed with domestic work; the home location of both (and the association of agricultural work with the family farm) obscured commodification and exploitation as these forms of labour became confused with the unwaged family labour of wives, mothers, and daughters. The ILO remained reluctant to address home spaces as places of employment until the self-activities of home-based workers and their advocates forced the issue at the end of the twentieth century.[5]

This chapter divides into four sections. During the interwar years, conventions allowed for outworker exemption. With the United Nations (UN) development decades after the Second World War, action against industrial home work stalled but home handicraft for cultural and social reasons emerged in the ILO imaginary as work most appropriate for women in Asia and other developing regions. The last two sections consider parallel movements: policy pleas of trade union bodies and ILO tripartite committees from the 1970s and the 1980s, and lobbying within the ILO by staff: feminist development experts who sought action from the 1980s until passage of the Convention. The chapter ends with an analysis of Convention No. 177 itself.

1 Interwar Years, 1919–39

Addressing the first ILC in 1919 on the question of the eight-hour working day, the prominent French trade unionist Léon Jouhaux distinguished between work "in which only members of the family are employed" and home work: "a shameful exploitation, against which vigorous action should be taken". The majority of delegates, men accompanied by a few women advisors, seriously doubted the feasibility of monitoring hours in the home—the number of inspectors needed would be too large. The impossibility of regulation meant that suppression was the only solution. But the very rationale for this

5 For greater elaboration, see Eileen Boris, *Making the Woman Worker: Precarious Labor and the Fight for Global Standards, 1919–2019* (New York, 2019), from which a portion of this chapter comes.

impossibility—the home location—also justified doing nothing out of fear of state "control over private life", as another French delegate insisted.[6]

During the interwar years, the ILO considered industrial home work, often referred to as outwork, in relation to compensation and social protection. Commentators generally agreed that this system of production generated abuse and exploitation: low wages and wage theft, long hours, child labour, unhealthy working conditions, and threats to public health. Coming up with standards was difficult. Member states exhibited uneven and scattered coverage despite legislative, union contract, and administrative models of determining minimum wages.[7] Some states had viable laws: Australia and Britain long had used wage boards to regulate the sweated trades; Germany strengthened its trade board act in 1923. Norway's experimental act relied on a central Home Work Council whose leaders could not "have any economic interests in the decisions of the Council". With some 4,500 needle workers concentrated around Oslo, agents conducted home inspections to verify working conditions and examine books in which workers and employers recorded items made, hours worked, and payments.[8] Argentina covered some clothing workers, while Hungry, Canada, and Czechoslovakia claimed to have fixed wages successfully for outworkers.[9]

In the early 1920s, however, not all legislative attempts succeeded. An effort to draft wage and hygiene standards for home work stalled in Belgium.[10] Sweden argued that decreasing numbers and more robust worker organization made the need for legislation less pressing than it was earlier in the century.[11] Other states failed to classify home workers as employees, placing them outside of the law. India based its exclusion on the practices of agriculturalists who took in work secondarily, and the self-employed, specifically own-account workers in the handloom industry.[12]

6 League of Nations, *International Labour Conference: First Annual Meeting* (Washington, 1920), p. 60; International Labour Conference [hereafter ILC], *Minutes of the Commission on Hours of Labour* (Geneva, 1923), p. 10.

7 ILC, *Minimum Wage-Fixing Machinery: Report and Draft Questionnaire*, First Discussion, Item II on the Agenda (Geneva, 1927).

8 Ibid., pp. 88, 91.

9 League of Nations, *International Labour Conference*, Eleventh Session, I (Geneva, 1928), pp. 401, 383–84, 407; Vivien Hart, *Bound by Our Constitution: Women, Workers, and the Minimum Wage* (Princeton, 1994).

10 League of Nations, *International Labour Conference*, Eleventh Session, I, p. 202.

11 ILC, *Report on Minimum Wage Fixing Machinery*, Second Discussion, First Item on the Agenda (Geneva, 1928), p. 31.

12 League of Nations, *International Labour Conference*, Eleventh Session, I, p. 411.

The Office asked in the mid-1920s whether states would support a specific recommendation on home-working trades.[13] As often done, the resulting proposal placed what appeared as a particular practice under an apparently more universal concern. That is, rather than a stand-alone convention, the ILO's Governing Body agreed that a convention on regulating wages would "primarily" cover home-working trades. It would rectify the abuses of home work through the well-established concept of the wage board, setting rates in relation to both general standards and factory equivalents (leaving the determination of equivalency to be resolved).[14] Wage boards usually consisted of workers, employers, and government members. But experts were central to their determinations, reflecting the privileging of quantifiable knowledge on cost of living that embodied concepts of working-class life and the needs of the woman worker.

ILO delegates agreed that home workers were unable to raise their own standards. They lacked the power to engage in collective bargaining, so the state had to become involved in wage-setting. A German worker advisor argued the case for coverage of home workers, whose numbers in his country were "extensive" in textiles, glass, wood, and metal industries, but were difficult to organize "because they fear to lose their employment".[15] To deal with home work as a system of "evasion", as a South African government delegate called it, demanded placing "the same kind of work" carried out in factories and in homes on a similar footing rather than establishing "any special measure of protection". He preferred to abolish the practice and establish crèches to facilitate mothers going out to work.[16] Feminist Betzy Kjelsberg, a Norwegian government delegate and one of three women (out of forty) on the 1928 committee crafting an instrument, explained that Norway's minimum wage legislation intended not "to repress home work" but rather to fix its wages in light of actual conditions, to cover cost of living "and enable the worker to maintain his working capacity".[17] The assumption that home workers were weak, ill-informed, and afraid, that they were casual workers supplementing family income, would persist. They were wives and mothers, and thus, by definition, less organizable.

13 League of Nations, *International Labour Conference*, Tenth Session, I (Geneva, 1927), pp. 657, 661.

14 League of Nations, *International Labour Conference*, Eleventh Session, I, p. 380; Governing Body, *Minutes of the 30th Session* (Geneva, January 1926), p. 36.

15 League of Nations, *International Labour Conference*, Eleventh Session, I, pp. 93, 99.

16 League of Nations, *International Labour Conference*, Tenth Session, I, p. 407.

17 League of Nations, *International Labour Conference*, Eleventh Session, I, p. 401; League of Nations, *International Labour Conference*, Tenth Session, I, p. LXXVII.

The 1928 Minimum-Wage Fixing Convention (No. 26) applied to "trades or parts of trades" with "exceptionally low" wages without collective bargaining.[18] It was generally agreed that all low-waged industries could benefit, but countries had considerable leeway in how they applied their mechanisms and calculated an appropriate minimum wage. Some government delegates (from Austria, Denmark, France, the Netherlands, and Rumania) and the employers' group had wished to restrict such machinery to home workers. Employer opposition, as in Japan, to any instrument came from the relative advantage that low wages held in international trade. A male Japanese worker delegate who saw through such arguments accused employers of mislabelling home work as a family "side-business". Middle-men earned special opprobrium for "depriv[ing] the workers of the greater part of the product of labour". Employers in general claimed that home workers themselves rejected state interference "as a violation of their home".[19] There was an irony attached to the employers' group concession to cover home workers. Inclusion of workers located in factories challenged employer prerogative to determine compensation, but trampling employer rights was moot when it came to home workers. The difficulty of monitoring the home limited the impact of wage board or legislative determinations.

Convention No. 26 addressed women's precarious labour through an apparently gender-neutral mechanism, but which everyone recognized was about women's low-waged work and the conditions in families where husbands brought materials home for wives and children to assemble or sew. As a male French employer delegate explained during the first discussion in 1927, "we are dealing with the work of a family. This work is exceptional, not only because of the nature of the trade, but because of the special category of workers employed".[20] It was to combat women's disadvantaged position in the labour market. Pleaded Miss Wolff of the Berlin Women Home-Workers' Trade Union, a German labour advisor, "There are many women workers in particular—hungry women—whose welfare and the welfare of whose children perhaps depend upon getting adequate wages, and thus upon the application of the

18 ILO, "Minimum Wage-Fixing Machinery Convention", 1928 (No. 26), available at https://tinyurl.com/y4pzw8wk, last accessed 26 November 2020; League of Nations, *International Labour Conference*, Eleventh Session, I, p. 98; Elisabeth Prügl, *The Global Construction of Gender: Home-based Work in the Political Economy of the 20th Century* (New York, 1999), pp. 40–48.

19 League of Nations, *International Labour Conference*, Eleventh Session, I, pp. 98–100, 382, 384.

20 League of Nations, *International Labour Conference*, Tenth Session, I, p. 403.

machinery provided for". She hoped the question would never come down to "giving the workers, and particularly the women workers, a choice between having very low wages and having no wages at all".[21] The adopted instruments targeted women-dominated occupations where few men performed the same jobs as women, while reaffirming the principle of equal remuneration.[22] Recognizing workforces with many women, the accompanying recommendation, No. 30, suggested that there should be a woman among both the worker and "independent" representatives on any wage board.[23]

Regulating home work generated its own special treatment/equal treatment conundrum that has long divided feminists but one in which stakeholders other than the workers themselves defined the options. Feminist proponents of legal equality, institutionally outside of the ILO, made the charge of subversion of the principle of equal pay for equal work without much evidence.[24] In contrast, Kjelsberg claimed compatibility between wage-fixing and the principle that workers "have the right to a living wage" as well as an equal one. Her statements at the ILO revealed the complexity of feminist thought at that time. She both adhered to legal equality between the sexes and based the authority to defend such principles on her duty as a woman, a special standpoint.[25] An accompanying non-binding recommendation similarly adhered to female distinctiveness, common among activist women, when requesting that women be included among worker and independent representatives on wage boards, as previously noted.[26]

During the 1930s, conventions on social insurance recognized outwork in their titles but such naming was no guarantee of coverage. The special status of the home formed a barrier. "Compulsory Old-Age Insurance for Persons Employed in Industrial or Commercial Undertakings, in the Liberal Professions, and for Outworkers and Domestic Servants Convention, 1933" (No. 35), despite its title, allowed nations to exempt "outworkers whose conditions of work are not of a like nature to those of ordinary wage earners" as well as "members

21 League of Nations, *International Labour Conference*, Eleventh Session, I, p. 396.

22 Paula Määttä, *The ILO Principle of Equal Pay and its Implementation* (Tampere, 2008), pp. 89–92; League of Nations, *International Labour Conference*, Eleventh Session, I, pp. 441, 444.

23 ILO, "Minimum Wage-Fixing Machinery Recommendation", 1928 (No. 30) available at https://tinyurl.com/59tmfzek, last accessed 29 November 2019.

24 Boris, *Making the Woman Worker*, chapters 1 and 2.

25 League of Nations, *International Labour Conference*, Eleventh Session, I, p. 402.

26 Ibid., p. 648.

of the employer's family".[27] The same wording limited the applicability of "Invalidity Insurance (Industry, etc.) Convention, 1933" (No. 37) and the earlier "Sickness Insurance (Industry) Convention, 1927" (No. 24), which only mentioned outworkers to allow for their omission.[28] This wink to nations with no intent to include would repeat in the early postwar years with the extension of maternity protection to home-based workers that allowed for postponing implementation.[29]

Delegates tended to group home workers with domestic workers. In 1936, the ILC voted to delay consideration of these groups, along with agricultural workers, in a Holiday with Pay convention. Without any documentation, the employers asserted the administrative difficulty of including home workers. A concurring resolution underscored both "the present lack of any regulation of the hours of work of these workers" as a justification for paid holidays, and "the special character of the relations between employers and home workers" that required "special arrangements". Home work stood apart from existing regulatory frameworks, which justified exclusion from standards.[30]

2 Development Decades, 1944–75

Following the Second World War, during the years when the UN system focused on "third world" development, the ILO explored regulating home labour while advocating home handicrafts for women as a solution to underdevelopment. Questions of trade and factory conditions as well as global competition propelled a fresh look, but the place of the home in culture and society pervaded the discussions. As a French correspondent replied to an Office request for information, "labour inspectors are barred from inspecting the home worker's actual place of work by the principle of the inviolability of private domicile which French social legislation has apparently not modified to any extent".[31] In

27 ILO, "Old-Age Insurance (Industry, etc.) Convention", 1933 (No. 35), available at https://tinyurl.com/vs64pytm, last accessed 28 August 2019.

28 ILO, "Invalidity Insurance (Industry, etc.) Convention", 1933 (No. 37), available at https://tinyurl.com/2k7x2hph, last accessed 28 August 2019; ILO, "Sickness Insurance (Industry) Convention", 1927 (No. 24), available at https://tinyurl.com/3rt8233j, last accessed 28 August 2019.

29 ILC, "Committee on Maternity Protection", June 1952, ILC 35-510-7, International Labour Organization Archives [herafter ILOA], Geneva.

30 ILC, *Record of Proceedings*, Twentieth Session (Geneva, 1936), pp. 465, 639.

31 Governing Body, "Correspondence Committee on Women's Work", *Minutes*, 99th Session (Geneva, September 1946), pp. 70–72; "Industrial Home Work in France", p. 13, WN1001/06,

passing a US-initiated "Resolution Concerning Women's Work" as a "tribute" to the wartime labours and sacrifices of women throughout the world, delegates at the 1947 ILC conceived home work (and domestic work) as part of "the problems of the employment of mothers of families".[32]

In the early post-Second World War years, the ILO only researched home work, despite the request for action by the Correspondence Committee on Women's Work.[33] The Director-General and Governing Board dismissed efforts to do anything else. Calling for more study delayed wrestling with proposals for international instruments. Regarding home work, the Director-General in 1947 felt that "it would be premature for the Office to submit this question pending the actual collection of further information", one of his deputies informed Mildred Fairchild, head of the Section on Women and Young Workers. Instead, he suggested that they publish research authorized by the Governing Body in the *International Labour Review*.[34]

The subsequent report in 1948 continued the tropes of irregularity and danger. Describing the system as "hazardous", it referred to cheap labour amid rampant falsification of records by both employers and workers, suggesting illegality and illegitimacy. States relied on wage boards, government committees, hours laws, distribution regulations, registration mechanisms, and social insurance rules to monitor the practice. Inspectors more often looked at the employer's books than visited the worker's home. But no one was certain of the results.[35]

Home work loomed over initiatives to bring women of the global South into development by encouraging handicraft industries. In the early 1950s, researchers discovered that women "represent a considerable part of the productive capacity of the labour force in handicrafts", though estimating numbers in this mostly informal sector was daunting. Conditions of work were abysmal: long hours, hazardous materials, cramped quarters, and economic exploitation from middle-men.[36] Because crafts production occurred in the household,

---

ILOA. For France, Colette Avrane, *Ourières à Domicile: Le combat pour un salaire minimum sous la Troisième République* (Rennes, 2013).

32 ILC, *Record of Proceedings*, Thirtieth Session, Geneva, 1947 (Geneva, 1948), pp. 404–06, 236.

33 Governing Body, "Correspondence Committee on Women's Work", p. 72.

34 Fairchild to Miller, 15 January 1947, WN1001/06, ILOA.

35 Governing Body, "Correspondence Committee on Women's Work", pp. 36–37; ILO, "Reports and Enquiries: Industrial Home Work", *International Labour Review*, LVIII (December 1948), pp. 735–51.

36 Asian Advisory Committee, "Special Protective Legislation Affecting Women and Its Relation to Women's Employment in Asian Countries", pp. 4–6, AAC/IV/D.5, 24, in WN 2/7, ILOA; "Development of Opportunities for Women in Handicrafts and Cottage Industries", IX Session, pp. 13–20, ESC 77-8, ILOA.

such work posed no challenge to *purdah* or other cultural or religious practices that secluded women from contact with non-family. This hidden quality, as German feminist researcher Maria Mies later argued in an ILO-supported study, allowed for the obfuscation of women's labour as house work, what she termed *housewifization*, and thus the denial of their status as workers even when they were producing under orders of contractors for the world market.[37]

The line between handicraft and industrial home work was a shifting one. Blurring especially occurred when the goods produced by independent artisans and self-employed people resembled those made for an employer using "materials belonging to the employer and undertaken on order, tending to turn the home into a sweatshop", charged Frieda Miller of the US Women's Bureau, who was an active member of the Correspondence Committee and often a delegate to the ILC.[38] With its irregular hours, starvation wages, and proclivity to involve child labour, industrial home work certainly was no solution "to relieve mothers of young children from the necessity of work outside their homes by means of providing paid work they could do in their homes", she contended. In the mid-1950s, Miller would serve as an ILO consultant surveying women's work in Asia.[39] Though she had fought for legislative prohibition in her country, she was open to home-based industry in Asia if authorities safeguarded labour standards.[40]

Pre-Second World War industrial home work, Miller insisted, differed from Asian home-based industry. The first "was a sort of parasitic growth on an established factory system whose purpose it was to escape certain legitimate costs of in-plant production", and to ignore wage, hour, child labour, and safety laws. But Asia's "small scale and cottage industries ... related to capital shortage which makes plant and elaborate equipment hard to get or impossible while the small-scale enterprises substitute underemployed or unemployed workers with a minimum of capital". The Philippines was an exception, with its garment industry, connected to the US economy, full of home work to evade factory law through "exploitative standards".[41]

37 Maria Mies, *The Lace Makers of Narsapur: Indian Housewives Produce for the World Market* (London, 1982).

38 Frieda Miller to Mildred Fairchild, 15 May 1947, WN1001/06, ILOA.

39 Frieda Miller to Ingeborg Waern Bugge, 30 December 1945, WN 1001/07, ILOA; Frieda Miller, ILO Personnel File P 7353 1955-1957, Jacket 1, ILOA.

40 Eileen Boris, *Home to Work: Motherhood and the Politics of Industrial Homework in the United States* (New York, 1994), pp. 247–52.

41 Frieda Miller to Eugene Staley, 31 October 1958, Box 13, Folder 257, A-37, Schlesinger Library, Radcliffe, Cambridge, MA.

The dangers of home work pervaded most discussions on handicraft. Scattered in "private" homes, unregulated and unorganized, and performed by women (often joined by their children) without other options for income and who find it "convenient" to work from home, such labour was ripe for abuse. The ILO staff worried about how to protect handicraft workers "against exploitation by middlemen and against sweated conditions of industrial homework".[42] They suggested developing local supplies of raw material and alternative sources of credit, especially through cooperatives, to eliminate the middle-man. They advised bringing such work under national laws, despite being "easily evaded".[43] The UN Commission on the Status of Women asked the ILO in 1956 "to give special attention to methods found useful to organize on a sound basis handicrafts and cottage industries products", so "to avoid the evils of industrial home work".[44]

3 Trade Unions Take Command, 1970s–1980s

Sectoral committees of the ILO wrestled with the threat of home work undermining factory conditions. These committees brought together Government, Worker, and Employer representatives to discuss conditions in specific industries.[45] The textile trade regularly held tripartite deliberations in the postwar years, but it took lobbying by international union federations, and organized US employers and garment workers, to institute a committee for clothing in 1964. Sixteen years would pass before a second meeting, delayed in part by the economic constraints affecting the sector, which also impeded ILO operations.[46]

The very characteristics of clothing and related industries—"low capital requirements and the ease with which part of the work can be done at

42 Outline, "Development of Opportunities for Women in Handicrafts and Cottage Industries", p. 1, ESC 77-8, ILOA.

43 "Opportunities for Women in Handicrafts and Cottage Industries: Progress Report prepared by the International Labour Office" for X Session, pp. 2–4, ESC 77-8, ILOA.

44 "Note for the Governing Body, 135th Session: Tenth Session of the UN Commission on the Status of Women", p. 7, ESC 1004-11-10, ILOA. ILO capitalizes Employer, Worker, and Government when referring to representatives or delegates.

45 ILO, 1964 Tripartite Technical Meeting for the Clothing Industry, *General Examination of the Labour and Social Problems in the Clothing Industry*, Report I (Geneva, 1964), p. 3; ILO, Second Tripartite Technical Meeting for the Clothing Industry, *Contract Labour in the Clothing Industry*, Report II (Geneva, 1980), p. 1, all in ILOA. Subsequent reports are also found in the ILOA.

46 ILO, 1964 Tripartite Technical Meeting for the Clothing Industry, pp. i–iii.

home"—generated nervousness that the practice flourished despite assertions that industrial home work had "declined in recent years". When responding to Office inquiries in the 1960s and 1970s, nations quantified the extent of home work but could not vouch for the accuracy of their calculations.[47] Much of the production occurred "under the table", as a manoeuvre around trade restrictions, labour standards, and even worker compensation. After the Second World War, home work expanded in newly industrializing regions and offshoring intensified. Reacting to these conditions, the ILO issued a declaration in 1977 on multinational enterprises and their social responsibilities, prefiguring later measures to regulate global supply chains.[48]

Organized workers recorded similar trends. While everyone agreed that women with family responsibilities took in work to earn necessary income, few questioned the assignment of domestic and care work to women. Some affiliates of what in 1972 had become the International Textile, Garment, and Leather Workers Federation (ITGLWF) associated home work with minoritized or dependent groups. The Indian Textile Labour Association (TLA) pointed to "very large numbers of Muslim and other caste women", while US unions connected home work to immigrants from Asia and the Americas (earlier Eastern and Southern Europeans and Puerto Ricans had predominated as outworkers).[49] By the end of the decade, the new Federation boasted 5 million members in 140 unions from 70 countries, numbers that were less than impressive given that there were millions more toiling in these trades.[50] Recognizing unique national circumstances, the Federation hoped to level the playing field through global labour standards while aiding global South affiliates. As one Federation leader insisted, "It is obvious that unions must try to organize all workers, whether they are in factories or at home".[51] But that was easier said than done, given the scattered and episodic form of the labour, the belief

47 Ibid., pp. 34–35, 45, 64–65; ILO, Second Tripartite Technical Meeting for the Clothing Industry, pp. 9, 19, 21–22.

48 Prügl, *The Global Construction of Gender*, p. 102; "The Multinational Enterprises Declaration", available at https://tinyurl.com/say7uwx6, last accessed 27 August 2019.

49 International Textile, Garment, and Leather Workers' Federation [hereafter ITGLWF], *Report on Homework* (Brussels, 1 June 1978), p. 10; ITGLWF, *Employment of Women in the Textile, Garment, and Leather Industries* (Brussels, 1980), pp. 19–20.

50 Charles Ford, Transcript of the Third Sitting, 26 September 1980 Afternoon, p. III/102, IC 17-2-202, ILOA.

51 ITGLWF, *Second World Congress*, 22–26 March 1976 (Brussels, 1976), p. 188.

that these women were not real workers, and the male domination of union leadership.

Sectoral committees of the ILO, which included union delegates, usually proceeded by consensus. Under discussion at the First Tripartite Meeting of the Clothing Industry in 1964 were general conditions of work and social problems that characterized the industry.[52] Employers and workers failed to agree on how to combat home work; the meeting passed a resolution by majority vote rather than unanimously. Employers, workers, and governments were able to concur that "there should be maximum governmental regulation and control", which included registration of employers, middle-men, and workers. But many employers and a few governments still rejected the central claim that the practice "should, as a matter of principle, ultimately be abolished, except as to certain individuals—for example physically handicapped persons—who cannot adapt themselves to factory work". The resolution insisted that prior to abolition, labour standards and social protection for home workers should match those of their factory counterparts. Meanwhile, the ILO should study the problem.[53]

This resolution provided authority for a subsequent measure passed by the Second Congress of the ITGLWF in 1976. The international union "reaffirm[ed] its opposition to the evils of industrial home work", requested affiliates "to press their governments to pursue policies leading to the ultimate abolition", but, until that time, called for "the same legal status as factory workers ... with full entitlement to social benefits". To enforce parity, it demanded full registration of "home workers, agents, and employers". In contrast to the ILO sectoral committee, its resolution maintained the discourse of disgust and outrage that for long had pervaded writings against the sweatshop. It spoke of "evils", "threat", and "pittance". It portrayed workers as "deprived", using language like "appalling" and "deplorable" to describe their fate. Other reports deployed coercion metaphors, referring to "slave labour", "near-slavery", and "people chained".[54]

Nonetheless, the garment unionists were pragmatists. Apparently maintaining a single standard for the developing and developed nations in an era when the Cold War and decolonization challenged western hegemony was more prudent than pushing for immediate abolition. By taking the lead, the US affiliates (International Ladies' Garment Workers Union/ILGWU, Textile Workers Union of America, and Amalgamated Clothing Workers of America) could keep some control over the political process of resolution-making. Arvind Buch, president

52 ILO, 1964 Tripartite Technical Meeting for the Clothing Industry, p. 35.

53 ILO, Second Tripartite Technical Meeting for the Clothing Industry, p. 1.

54 ITGLWF, *Report on Homework*, pp. 1–6, 38–9.

of the India TLA, called for organizing the self-employed, reflecting the activities of its women's section under Ela Bhatt.[55] A few years later, Buch would expel Bhatt's group, which led her Self Employed Women's Association (SEWA) to form close connections with ILO staff and NGOs who pushed forward a home work convention, as we shall see.

The 1980 Second Tripartite Meeting of the Clothing Industry repeated previous calls. It concluded that nations needed to clarify the legal status of such workers, regulate the practice, and limit it "to specific cases where home workers are unable to earn income in any other way". While wanting prohibition ultimately, the resolutions also asked for equivalence between shop and factory workers in terms of wage determination and minimum wages; social security, unemployment, and health benefits; and statutory standards for health, safety, and hours. Holding banning homework and regulating it simultaneously was not contradictory since the general belief was that home work persisted because it was unregulated and cheaper than factory labour; raise its costs, and its advantage for employers would disappear. Lack of direct supervision led to imperfect quality control, which would no longer be merely wasteful but would also become burdensome with regulation. So work would return to factories or workshops. Other items addressed specialized labour inspection and recording of work; "vigilance" with respect to child labour and "illicit or clandestine home work"; "cooperation" among social partners in "control and supervision"; and trade union rights. Finally, the assembled delegates recommended the "possibility of adopting international labour standards concerning home workers"—a tentative gesture towards ILC action.[56]

Tripartite meetings tended to attribute ineffective regulation to unscrupulous contractors and other employers who refused to keep mandated records and cheated workers, rather than to structural problems from offshoring and outwork.[57] But workers knew otherwise. Their livelihoods depended on regulating home work. They were acutely aware of displacement from industrialized to developing countries fuelled by multinationals operating from industrial centres. To avoid exploitation and maintain job security, unionists throughout the world had to demand "fair labour standards" as part of all trade agreements and development programmes.[58] Meanwhile the old gender

55 ITGLWF, *Second World Congress*, pp. 187–88; ITGLWF, *Report of the First World Congress* (Brussels, 1972), p. 10.

56 ILO, Second Tripartite Technical Meeting for the Clothing Industry, p. 74.

57 For example, Mr Bedoya, Transcript of Fourth Sitting, p. IV/42, ILOA.

58 *Joint Congress of the International Shoe and Leather Workers' Federation and the International Textile and Garment Workers' Federation* (London, 1970), p. 8, Library, US Department of Labour, Washington, D.C.

justification for home work, that women choose to take work home to earn supplementary incomes while caring for the family, persisted across political economies. Women trade unionists in the International Confederation of Free Trade Unions (ICFTU) and International Trade Secretariats rejected such a rationale. They agreed "that part-time, temporary or home work" provided no "effective solution to the problems" facing workers with family responsibilities, then under reconsideration by the ILO.[59]

Employer disgruntlement foreshadowed the contentious process that erupted when the ILO entertained standard-setting. Worker delegates (along with governments of socialist states) had lashed out against multinational corporations and, later, worried about the impact of structural adjustment on living standards. In response, at the 1980 Clothing Committee, a UK employer complained,

> We do not believe that we are being oversensitive, but the whole tenor of the presentation seems to us never to miss an opportunity to attack employers in a way which we feel generally diminished the credibility and indeed the impartiality of the ILO to the advantage of no one including the interests of workers, and we would urge, Mr Chairman, that a greater sensitivity be paid to this in future.[60]

The Employers' group rejected abolition of home work "even in the long term". They admitted to having "strong reservations" against the earlier 1964 resolution due to the belief that "home work could play an important role both for the enterprises that resorted to it, as well as for a number of workers".[61] At the Third Tripartite Meeting in 1987, though the Employers' group condemned illegal home work, "performed not in accordance with laws or other protections" and kept from taxation or social security contributions, it agreed "that legitimate home work was a necessary feature of the clothing industry".[62]

Employers had no problem with laws that defined the home worker as self-employed or an independent contractor, depriving them of minimum wages and social security, and placing them outside of health, safety, and hours restrictions. They tried to classify these workers as both micro-entrepreneurs

---

59 "October 4–5, 1979—ICFTU/ITS Consultative Committee on Women Workers' Questions", in ITGLWF, *Report on Activities, Third World Congress* (Brussels, 1980), p. 48.

60 Transcript of the Eighth Sitting, 2 October 1980 afternoon, p. VIII/4, IC 17-2-202, ILOA.

61 ILO, Second Tripartite Technical Meeting for the Clothing Industry, September–October 1980, Paragraph 43, *Note on the Proceedings* (Geneva, 1981), p. 24, ILOA.

62 ILO, Third Tripartite Meeting, 1987, *Note on the Proceedings*, p. 48.

conducting independent businesses and housewives labouring for supplemental income, that is, non-workers. Such definitions created their own obstacles. If the home worker was not an employee, the only justification for entering her home was public health. But scattered workplaces required an army of inspectors even with complaints by unions, consumers' organizations, and women's groups. Even then the ideological sacredness or privacy of the home in many nations created a political if not legal barrier.

Workers also were disgruntled over the outcome of ILO's sectoral deliberations. The 1984 Third Congress of the ITGLWF unanimously charged the Second Tripartite meeting with "retrogression" for reflecting employer demands, accommodating governments where the practice continued, and for no longer speaking in terms of abolition. The Federation once again committed to eradicating "the evils of industrial home work as a threat to the well-being of workers throughout the world", and requested affiliates to seek abolition in their nations. This proposal, urged by the US affiliates, occurred in the middle of the ILGWU fight against attempts by the Reagan administration to lift all federal bans on garment home work.[63]

The move away from abolition/prohibition represented an altered strategy, an accommodation made to the growth of home work.[64] The Canadian section of the ILGWU, the Argentinean National Union of Clothing and Allied Workers, and the UK General and Municipal Workers' Union sought to improve conditions for home workers, while home work sections or unions developed in Venezuela, Uruguay, and India. By the mid-1980s, unions in Australia, India, UK, Netherlands, and Belgium pushed for covering home workers under existing legislation or adopting new laws for them. The Belgian Confederation of Christian Trade Unions, in contrast, never relented from its belief that home work was "a permanent form of 'blackmail' to reduce [union] claims".[65]

---

63 ITGLWF, *Report on Fourth World Congress* (Brussels, 1984), pp. 105, 163–65; Boris, *Home to Work*, pp. 337–61.

64 Jane Tate, "Introduction to Part III", in Margaret Hosmer Martens and Swasti Mitter (eds), *Women in trade unions: Organizing the unorganized* (Geneva, 1994), pp. 63–64.

65 Luz Vega Ruiz, "Homework: Towards a new regulatory framework?" *International Labour Review*, 131:2 (1992), pp. 212–13; Gisela Schneider de Villegas, "Home work: A case for social protection", *International Labour Review*, 129:4 (1990), pp. 429–31; Alexandra Dagg, "Organizing Homeworkers into Unions: The Homeworkers' Association of Toronto, Canada", in Eileen Boris and Elisabeth Prügl (eds), *Homeworkers in Global Perspective: Invisible No More* (New York, 1996), pp. 239–58; Jane Tate, "Canada", in *Women in Trade Unions*, pp. 77–79; ILO, Meeting of Experts, *Social Protection of Homeworkers, 1990* (Geneva, 1991), p. 27.

Feminist campaigners in the UK and Netherlands had pushed their unions, which later provided them access to the ILO.

The 1987 Third Tripartite meeting maintained the question of home work before the ILO. It asked nations to regulate home work, legalize the status of home workers, and involve employer and worker organizations in ending mistreatment. Significantly, it requested that the Director-General convene an "envisaged Tripartite Meeting of Experts on Home Work as soon as possible".[66] Such appeals displayed the kind of global concern that the ILO's Governing Body required to justify action. The Governing Body previously had dropped a meeting planned for 1989 "because of resource constraints". During a period of limited revenues other issues had greater priority, a ranking which suggests that some quarters were unconvinced still about moving on home work.[67] Workers, however, wanted "urgent attention". By the end of the 1980s, as the ITGLWF's Charles Ford explained, it was abundantly "clear not only that workers' standards in the least developed countries fail to improve to reflect greater productivity and exports but standards in importing countries are being undermined by efforts to undercut imports through return to sweatshop and home-work production".[68]

4 ILO Discovers the "New Putting out System"

The international union federations and trade secretariats spoke about industrial home work, but feminist staff within the ILO shared a broader understanding of home-based labour, gleaned from research undertaken on rural women in the global South, often by investigators from the region. These development feminists, located in the Programme on Rural Women and in regional field offices, especially Southeast Asia, pushed for regulating home work from within the bureaucracy. In the 1980s, they partnered with grassroots groups to improve women's lives in the informal sector by investigating the "new putting out system".[69] Through a series of seminars and donor-funded projects, the ILO enhanced the capabilities of rural women's organizations in India, Thailand,

66 ILO, Third Tripartite Meeting, 1987, *Note on the Proceedings*, p. 92.

67 Ibid., pp. 18–19; ILO, Fourth Tripartite Meeting, *General Report* (Geneva, 1995), p. 94, ILOA.

68 ILC, *Proceedings*, Seventy-Fifth Session, 1988 (Geneva, 1989), pp. 16/44.

69 Eileen Boris, "Accounting for Reproductive Labour: Feminist Economists and the Construction of Social Knowledge on Rural Women in the Global South", in Kenneth Lipartito and Lisa Jacobson (eds), *Hidden Capitalism: Beyond, Below, and Outside the Visible Market* (Philadelphia, 2019), pp. 44–63.

Pakistan, Indonesia, and Philippines, the most important being SEWA in Gujarat, India. The feminist development staff at the ILO defended Ela Bhatt and her organization after SEWA's expulsion from the TLA. They convinced others in the Office to fund SEWA projects, but had to prove that SEWA was a trade union and not some other formation.[70]

In early 1982, Dharam Ghai, chief of the Rural Employment Policies Branch (EMP/RU), explained that his unit was "initiating a whole new line of research on home-based industries" due to the results of a project funded by the Programme on Rural Women. He was referring to Mies's "Housewives Produce for the World Market: The Lace Makers of Narsapur", a pathbreaking effort that not only illuminated the workings of the sexual division of labour and intertwining of productive and reproductive labour, but also highlighted the exploitation of the lace makers and the difficulty of organizing a group perceived to be just housewives.[71] In 1980, along with a working paper by Mies, his unit also released a study by Indian sociologist Zarina Bhatty, "Economic Role and Status of Women: A Case Study of Women in the Beedi Industry in Allahabad".[72] Bhatty questioned "the commonly advocated policy of seeking to create employment opportunities for women which allow them to remain at home".[73] Mies demonstrated that a home-based "strategy, by not transforming the production and reproduction relations, may lead to the impoverishment of the women, and a polarization not only between classes but between men and women as well".[74] Over the next few years, Ghai and the women running

70 Zubeida Ahmad, "RBTC Rural Development 1982–83: Request for Funding of SEWA's Action Research Proposal, 'Issues of poor self-employed women'", 13 July 1983, RL 33-3-100, Jacket 1, ILOA; Mal Mukherjee, "Request for Funding of SEWA's Action Research Proposal", 22 July 1983, RL 33-3-100, Jacket 1, ILOA; Zubeida Ahmad, "SEWA", 28 July 1983, RL 33-3-100, Jacket 1, ILOA.

71 Ghai to Petitpierre, Minute Sheet, 24 March 1982, WEP 10-4-04-33-1 Jacket 1, ILOA; Ahmad to Ghai, Minute Sheet, 8 January 1980, WEP 10-4-04-33-1 Jacket 1, ILOA; Ghai to Beguin, 2 April 1989, WEP 10-4-04-33-1 Jacket 1, ILOA; Maria Mies, "Housewives Produce for the World Market: The Lace Makers of Narsapur", World Employment Programme Research Working Paper, December 1980 (Geneva, 1980), ILOA; published by Zed Press as *The Lace Makers of Narsapur: Housewives Produce for the World Market* (London, 1982].

72 Zarina Bhatty, "The Economic Role and Status of Women: A Case Study of Women in the Beedi Industry in Allahabad", World Employment Programme Research Working Paper, December 1980 (Geneva, 1980), ILOA; published as *The Economic Role and Status of Women in the Beedi Industry in Allahabad, India* (Fort Lauderdale, 1981).

73 Dharam Ghai, "Preface", in Bhatty, *The Economic Role and Status of Women*, p. ii.

74 Dharam Ghai, "Preface", in Mies, *The Lace Makers of Narsapur*, p. x.

FIGURE 7.1 Homebased workers representatives during the discussion on Supply Chains at the International Labour Conference in Geneva in June 2016 where a small group of homebased workers participated with WIEGO

the Programme, Zubeida Ahmad and Martha Loutfi, cited Mies and Bhatty to justify standard-setting for home-based labour.[75]

On the basis of these investigations, Ahmad and Loutfi announced that "home-based industries in which women work as contract labour" would constitute a major initiative of the Programme. What to call the practice was in flux, as they spoke of cottage industry, home-based industry, home work, outwork, domestic outworkers, contract work at home, and the putting out

75 For example, Zubeida M. Ahmad, "Employment Opportunities for Poor Women in Rural Areas in Developing Countries", Talk 1980, WEP 10-4-04 Jacket 9, ILOA; Zubeida M. Ahmad, "Mission to Bangkok", 24 August 1982, 4, WEP 10-4-04 Jacket 12, ILOA; Martha F. Loutfi, "Mission, Netherlands", 31 August 1982, WEP 10-4-04 Jacket 13, ILOA; Martha F. Loutfi, "Mission, Belgrade", 14–17 November 1982, 2, WEP 10-4-04 Jacket 14, ILOA; Martha F. Loutfi to Mr Richards, 22 October 1982, WEP 10-4-04 Jacket 14, ILOA; Martha F. Loutfi, "Mission, Washington, D.C., 12–20 October, 1983", WEP 10-4-04 Jacket 16, ILOA; Martha F. Loutfi, "Mission London, 15–19 April 1984", WEP 10-4-04 Jacket 19, ILOA. See also, Eggar to Ms. Belinda Leach, 31 July 1985, WEP 10-4-04 Jacket 25, ILOA, which cites Mies. For the studies' influence elsewhere, see also, Margaret Owen to Martha F. Loutfi, 8 November 1982, WEP 10-4-04-018, Jacket 1, ILOA.

system.[76] Ahmad and Loutfi proposed to commission further case studies and then "to review existing international instruments (Conventions and Recommendations) together with national laws and regulations and their relevance to the situation of women who are forced by social and economic circumstances to work on contract at home".[77] The staff in Geneva pursued the findings of ILO officials and researchers in the New Delhi and Manila regional offices. Into the early 1990s, they shaped ILO multilateral–bilateral projects on technical cooperation as "Self-Employment Schemes for Female-Headed Households" and "Employment Promotion and Social Protection of Home-Based Workers in Asia". As a SEWA organizer referred to ILO New Delhi staffers Anita Kelles-Viitanen and Andrea Singh, "We are colleagues and crusaders together for a common cause".[78]

The Programme pushed other Office units to address the issue. Action required calibrating biennial plans a year or two in advance. As early as 1980–81, in response to sectoral industrial committees, the Working Conditions section (CONDI/T) planned country monographs, though budget considerations delayed them. The Programme placed home work in its 1982–83 plan, but other units dallied. In 1981 Ahmad told an informal meeting that theirs was "a fairly long-term programme which may ultimately culminate in an item on the agendas of either regional or international ILO conferences".[79] In late 1983, Loutfi recommended moving through the ILO bureaucracy to bring the subject to the Governing Body and then, after a questionnaire and draft instrument that EMP/RU would prepare, proposing a convention and/or recommendation in time for the 1986 ILC. Given the worldwide increase in home work but omission of home workers from legal or union protection, and the inability of existing standards on minimum wage-fixing and maternity to reach home workers, she argued that a convention was "a potentially valuable mechanism to improve the conditions of such workers". A basis already existed to formulate a convention from recent legislation enacted by industrialized nations, though the conditions of developing nations required additional discussion. The goal would be the extension of rights that workers in the formal sector

76 Zubeida M. Ahmad and Martha F. Loutfi, *ILO Programme on Rural Women* (Geneva, December 1980), p. 14.

77 Ibid.

78 Anita Kelles-Viitanen to Azita Berar-Awad, 22 January 1992, WEP 10-4-04-028-158, Jacket 3, ILOA; "The Home-Based Are Workers Too", draft typescript, p. 11, WEP 10-4-04-158, Jacket 2, ILOA.

79 ILO, *Programme and Budget for the Biennium*, 1980–1981, Fifty-Seventh Financial Period (Geneva, 1979), p. 90/10; Ahmad to Mr Sidibé, Ghai *et al.*, 7 August 1981, WEP 10-4-04 Jacket 11, ILOA; Sidibé to Ahmad, 29 September 1981, WEP 10-4-04 Jacket 11, ILOA.

enjoyed. "Basically, a convention 'would grant to the home worker the rights of 'employee' ", she argued.[80]

Loutfi and Ahmad shared their findings with units on laws, standard-setting, convention adherence, women, and health.[81] They approached higher-ups, Assistant Director-General Antoinette Béguin and Felice Morgenstern of the Legal Division. In early 1984, Loutfi noted, "Perhaps the extent of ILO capability and planned work relevant to this subject is not sufficiently known and shared". She was not one to shy away from the difficulties of confronting a system whose very organization kept workers invisible or a bureaucracy that slowed down redress. "It is our view that the few references to and weak data on home-based producers are not an indication of an unimportant, minor problem, but the contrary". If the ILO was to live up to its commitment to disadvantaged workers, a "fresh look at possible instruments" was needed because of "the apparent ineffectiveness of the traditional response of prohibiting home-based work and contractor arrangements". EMP/RU had undertaken the field work not only to "define the problem but also [to] identity mechanisms for achieving improved protection"; it had charted innovative programmes. Thus she asked her colleagues to "agree in principle to pursue the possibility of formulating a convention and recommendation in this area".[82]

Loutfi initiated an inter-departmental task force, which, under the leadership of the standard setting department proceeded far more slowly than she wished.[83] The Programme planned reviews of instruments protecting home-based workers and several workshops during 1984–85 on self-employment; CONDI/T started to look at industrialized countries.[84] In early 1985, she circulated preliminary findings on legal status and summaries on relevant sessions from the "Asian Conference on Women and the Household".[85] Other

80 Loutfi to Ahmad, Ghai, Martin, "Items for First Discussion at 72nd (1986) I.L.C"., 19 December 1983, with "Proposal for development of an instrument (Convention/ Recommendation) concerning homeworkers (domestic outworkers)", WEP 10-4-04-018, Jacket 1, ILOA.

81 Informal workshop, "Laws and Policies affecting Home-based Workers under a Putting-Out System", 2 December [1983], WEP 10-4-04-018, Jacket 1, ILOA.

82 Loutfi to Ahmad, Ghai, Martin, "Agenda for 72nd (1986) Session of the Conference", 1 February 1984, WEP 10-4-04 Jacket 18, ILOA.

83 Loutfi, note for file, "Social Protection of Home-Based Workers, '86–87' ", 23 July 1984, WEP 10-4-04-018, Jacket 1; Loutfi to Ahmad, Ghai, Martin, 3 December 84, WEP 10-4-04, Jacket 22, ILOA.

84 "1984–85 Regular Budget Work Programme: Employment of Rural Women", WEP 10-4-04 Jacket 18; "Progress Report on SAREC-Financed Research", 1984, WEP 10-4-04 Jacket 21, ILOA.

85 Loutfi to Rahman, Ghai, Martin, Sidibé *et al.*, "Social protection of home-based producers", 27 February 1985, WEP 10-4-04-018, Jacket 2, ILOA; Andréa Menefee Singh and Anita

departments not so subtly suggested that her program respect other units who worked on the informal sector and self-employment. Loutfi responded by pointing out that the "encouraging" organizing of workers was no reason to reject an ILO instrument as "a valuable tool complementing and supporting practical action by trade unions and other workers' organisations". Indeed, worker groups had called upon the ILO to consider legal measures. She offered as evidence "requests" from SEWA and a recent resolution by the International Union of Food, Agricultural, Hotel, Restaurant, Catering, Tobacco, and Allied Workers' Association (IUF), which SEWA had organized to increase pressure on the ILO.[86]

The task force determined standard-setting to be premature without a more substantive research base. So the Programme published additional working papers on carpet-weavers in rural Turkey, electronic assemblers in Kerala, and rural home work in Latin America.[87] LEG/REL (Legal Regulation) studied precarious employment in 1984–85 and focused on home work in both industrialized and developing countries for 1986–87 to determine if these workers came under labour legislation, collective agreements, or other measures. It questioned whether such workers actually fell into the category of persons working in an enterprise. A number of key branches, including Working Conditions and Environment (known as PIACT), planned to study work uncovered by standards in developing countries, including home work. Office staff drew upon various unpublished country reports for summary articles and "Condition of Work" digests. Comparative analysis, they believed, could lead to adopting new standards.[88] Meanwhile, ILC resolutions on employment and gender equality

---

Kelles-Viitanen, *Invisible Hands: Women in Home-based Production* (New Delhi, 1987). This collection prefigured Shelia Rowbotham and Swasti Miller, *Dignity and Daily Bread: New forms of economic organizing among poor women in the Third World and the First* (London, 1994), and Eileen Boris and Elisabeth Prügl, *Homeworkers in Global Perspective: Invisible No More* (New York, 1996).

86 K.T. Samson to EMP/RU, 16 May 84 (really 85), WEP 10-4-04-018, Jacket 2, ILOA; Loutfi to Samson, 10 May 1985, WEP 10-4-04-018, Jacket 2, ILOA; Hilary Kellerson to EMP/RU, 8 May 1985, WEP 10-4-04-018, Jacket 2, ILOA; Arturo Bronstein to Yemin, EMP/RU (Loutfi), 15 May 1985, WEP 10-4-04-018, Jacket 2, ILOA; A. Taqi to Ghai, 24 May 1985, WEP 10-4-04-018, Jacket 2, ILOA; Rounaq Jahan to Ghai, 12 June 1985, WEP 10-4-04-018, Jacket 2, ILOA.

87 Gunseli Berik, *Women Carpet Weavers in Rural Turkey: Patterns of Employment Earnings and Status* (Geneva, 1987), ILOA; Gita Sen and Leela Gulati, "Women workers in Kerala's electronic industry", WEP Working Paper No. 45 (Geneva, March 1987), ILOA; Maria de los Angeles Crummett, "Rural Women and Industrial Home Work in Latin America: Research Review and Agenda", WEP Working Paper, 46 (Geneva, 1988), ILOA.

88 ILO, *Programme and Budget for the Biennium* 1986–87, Sixtieth Financial Period (Geneva, 1985), pp. 80/7, 90/17–18, ILOA; Prügl, *The Global Construction of Gender*, pp. 110, 191–92, n.31; on legal, H. Boukris, "Conclusion", 2 WEP 10-4-04-018 Jacket 2, ILOA.

in the mid-1980s and on rural employment promotion in 1988 called for improving the conditions of home work; the 1985 resolution on equal opportunities specifically invited future standard-setting.[89] It would take another decade for the ILC to begin a first discussion. Ahmad had retired and Loutfi long left the Programme for other assignments, but new staff, like Rounaq Jahan and Azita Berar Awad, pursued the issue.[90]

Action on home-based labour came as the ILO sought to promote self-employment in the face of unemployment. In June 1990, the ILC passed a broad resolution recommending appropriate labour standards and support for worker organization. The Workers' group pushed for "special measures" to protect home workers and others who were "pseudo self-employed". During general discussion, the ITGLWF's Ford offered a far less positive portrait of such workers than champions of self-employment. He evoked the " 'exploitation' of women in Ahmedabad, India, who spend 15 to 18 hours a day hunched over ancient sewing machines, in order to earn 50 US cents". Repeating the historic tropes of the home as factory, childhood denied, and "family life … tethered to the ever-present work," he urged prompt ILO action on a convention that would soon put home workers on par with factory workers, and regulate "the health and well-being of those forced to work at home". Regulating home work stood as a doable response to the intensified challenge the garment and textile sector faced from free trade zones and globalization untethered from any "social clause".[91]

The ILO also discussed home work as it confronted what the then Director-General Michael Hansenne named "The Dilemma of the Informal Sector". An ILO study had highlighted the irregular, casual, and hidden work of most of the world's people back in the 1970s, bringing the concept into development discussions. Though contributing to economic growth, the informal sector by definition was open to exploitation and other abuses. But it was also a location of economic activity that generated livelihoods.[92] The Nordic countries,

89 ILC, *Record of Proceedings*, Seventieth Session (Geneva, 1984), p. 37/6; ILC, *Record of Proceedings*, Seventy-First Session, 1985 (Geneva, 1986), p. 40/3; ILC, *Record of Proceedings*, Seventy-Fifth Session (Geneva, 1988), p. XCVI; see also, ILO, Meeting of Experts, *Social Protection of Homeworkers*, 1990 (Geneva, 1991), p. 1.

90 Rounaq Jahan to Mr Taqi, 13 June 1985, WEP 10-4-04-018, Jacket 2, ILOA; Azita Berar-Awad, Mission to Philippines, 12 July 1991, for "Rural Women Workers in the New Putting Out System", ACD 53-0-04, ILOA.

91 ILC, *Record of Proceedings*, Seventy-Seventh Session, 1990 (Geneva, 1991), pp. 7–15, 32/7, 19/38–19/39.

92 Prügl, *The Global Construction of Gender*, pp. 79–80; ILO, *Employment, incomes and equity: a strategy for increasing productive employment in Kenya* (Geneva, 1972).

the very nations that funded Programme projects, submitted to the ILC in 1991 a resolution on women workers in the informal sector that asked the ILO to expand "documentation of the conditions of life and work of home-based workers and self-employed women", as well as to consider extending social protection, training, and aid to organize them. Other proposed resolutions targeted the informal sector more generally.[93] During the ILC's first discussion on home work in 1995, the Minister of Labour of Nicaragua would evoke this earlier consideration of informality and its relationship to structural adjustment in arguing for finally confronting the "exploitation which liberalism is imposing in all sorts of countries at this time" through home work regulation. "We are all employers here" ironically underscored the employment relations that many from the Employers' group continued to deny.[94] The experts already had situated home work as part of "increasing casualization of labour, and particularly its impact on women", and so pointed to both discrimination and public policies that disadvantaged women, particularly in terms of family-care work across generations.[95]

5 Conclusion: Towards Convention No. 177

With support from the IUF, ICFTU, ILO development feminists, and some national trade unions (especially in Britain and Netherlands), home work became an agenda item at the ILC. The efforts of SEWA and other women campaigners occurred amid the shift away from viewing home work as so evil that it only could be abolished. Direct appeals to the ILO's Director-General had an impact. Writing after a visit to India to the General Secretary of the ICFTU, then Director-General Francis Blanchard came away "impressed by the work being done by Mrs Ela Bhatt and the Self-Employed Women's Association in Ahmedabad". He asked the ICFTU to "bear their work in mind", while Bhatt herself had asked him to call an experts meeting.[96]

SEWA planned an international campaign, helping to organize Home Net International with British and Dutch activists.[97] These campaigners called

93 ILC, *Record of Proceedings*, Seventy-Eighth Session, 1991 (Geneva, 1992), pp. 5/2, 1/7–1/8, 1/12–14.

94 ILC, *Record of Proceedings*, Eighty-Second Session (Geneva, 1996), p. 27/51.

95 ILO, Meeting of Experts, *Social Protection of Homeworkers*, pp. 76–77.

96 Francis Blanchard to John Vanderveken, 18 March 1987, RL 33-3-100, Jacket 1, ILOA.

97 Annie Delaney, "Organizing homeworkers: Women's collective strategies to improve participation and social change", PhD dissertation, La Trobe University, 2009, pp. 78–97.

for inclusion of the informal sector's self-employed in ILO actions, but "own account" workers fell out of the resulting instruments.[98] To placate governments and employers, the emerging convention and recommendation considered home workers only when they were employees, asking the many nations that failed to count home workers as such to revise their statistics. Employers, for their part, attempted to obscure the deliberations by equating industrial home workers with teleworkers, even though it was generally understood that the convention was to address conditions in developing nations and the informal sector.[99] Refusing to take part in deliberations over the content of the convention, Employer delegates abstained *en masse* during the vote in 1996. But they failed to undermine the needed quorum.[100] Rancour over the appropriateness of this action underscored the breakdown of the tripartism that had governed the ILO from the start. Convention No. 177 brought to a head, then, a long-simmering disjuncture between the organization of the ILO and the employers' negation of its procedures. In the neoliberal moment, employers wanted less, not more, oversight.

In these deliberations, the home worker appeared to be like the woman worker, covered by other conventions and equal to the hegemonic worker of the standard employment contract, but in need of special treatment because of the unique circumstance of her place of labour, the home.[101] The preamble to Convention No. 177 thus spoke of "particular characteristics" and articles referred to "special characteristics", as in safety and health prohibitions. Home work happened outside of the workplace of an employer in a space of the compensated worker's choice. The employee relationship came from the employer specifying the goods or service, no matter whose "equipment, materials or

98 "Resolutions for UN Social Summit 1995 Proposed at SEWA General Body Meeting, 15–17 April 1994", pp. 5–6, EMP 63-4-1-2, Jacket 1, ILOA; "Asian Regional Workshop on the ILO Convention", EMP 63-4-1-2, Jacket 1, ILOA; "Resolution concerning self-employment promotion", in ILC, *Record of Proceedings*, Seventy-Seventh Session, pp. 7, 15.

99 "Report of the Committee on Home Work: Submission, discussion and adoption", in ILC, *Record of Proceedings*, Eighty-Second Session, p. 27/24; Governing Body, "Report of the Meeting of Experts on the Social Protection of Homeworkers", Meeting of the Governing Body, 248th Session, Geneva, 12–16 November 1990, p. III/1–2, GB 248-1—5 GB Sess. 248, ILOA.

100 ILC, *Record of Proceedings*, Eighty-Second Session, pp. 252, 27/19ff; "Record of Votes", in ILC, *Record of Proceedings*, Eighty-Third Session (Geneva, 1996), pp. 7–10.

101 ILC, "Report of the Committee on Home Work: Submission, discussion and adoption", in *Record of Proceedings*, Eighty-Third Session, p. 27/21; ILO, "Home Work Convention", 1996 (No. 177), available at https://tinyurl.com/n5ayxprs, last accessed 28 August 2019.

other inputs". But national legal and regulatory structures could define such a worker as an independent contractor, depending on the "degree of autonomy and economic independence" from the dictates of an employer. Equal treatment with others doing comparable work included "freedom of association, protection against discrimination in employment, occupational safety and health, remuneration, statutory social security protection, access to training, minimum age [guarantees], and maternity protection". To obtain these standards required additional record-keeping by employers, workers, and government agencies, as well as inspection, despite the lingering belief in the privacy of home spaces. But if other workers lacked these rights or the home work was not similar, the convention could not apply.[102]

Convention No. 177 emerged from the converging interests of international union federations and home worker advocates. Both wanted to end exploitation. Unions sought to protect their own gains and stop the undermining of labour standards. Like feminist and NGO campaigners, they also wanted to improve conditions for home workers. For some, improvement depended on bringing the worker to the factory; for others, it meant allowing women to earn an income while remaining in the household. ILO development feminists understood this combining of productive and reproductive labour. By recognizing the home as a workplace, they exposed the private sphere of the home as a space of public struggle.

Thirty-plus years later, we are all becoming home workers. Hours don't count, only completion of the job. In this context, a new generation of ILO staffers has found in Convention No. 177 a tool to modify abusive digital home work as well as to stem outwork in global supply chains. As the burden of production falls on "independent" contractors and other own account workers, as social protection narrows, the struggles of home-based workers offer hope that collective action, new organization, and protest might strengthen a global social wage.

102 ILC, "Report of the Committee on Home Work: Submission, discussion and adoption", pp. 27/32, 34.

CHAPTER 8

Realising Rights for Homeworkers in Global Value Chains

Marlese von Broembsen and Jenna Harvey

Following the Rana Plaza building collapse in 2013 in Bangladesh, labour rights violations in global supply chains, and indeed the governance of global supply chains, have become a pressing global issue. This chapter evaluates key governance mechanisms of existing global and national supply chains from the perspective of the most vulnerable workers in the supply chains—informal home workers.

Home work is as old as capitalism itself. Since the fourteenth century, factories have subcontracted aspects of production to home workers/outworkers to transfer some of their production costs.[1] The contemporary form of subcontracted work differs from previous forms, as global (as opposed to domestic) supply chains often span several continents, with different parts of a single product made in different countries. And, the procurement practices of the most powerful firms in the chain—buyers and retailers—have a more decisive impact on workers' terms and conditions of work than their relationship with the factories from which they receive their orders.

This chapter is interested in whether the emerging rights-based international law instruments for realizing decent work in global supply chains holds any promise for home workers. The academic literature refers to global value chains, global commodity chains, or global production networks. The International Labour Organization (ILO) uses the term supply chains. We will use supply chain and value chain interchangeably.

We begin the paper with a discussion on global value chains so as to contextualize home workers' terms and conditions of work within the political economy of global capitalist production. Thereafter, we discuss the United Nations Guiding Principles on Business and Human Rights and the three human rights-based international instruments on global value chains: the ILO's Tripartite Declaration of Principles concerning Multinational Enterprises and Social Policy [hereafter the ILO's MNE Declaration], the Organization for Economic

1 James Fulcher, *Capitalism: A Very Short Introduction* (Oxford, 2004).

© MARLESE VON BROEMBSEN AND JENNA HARVEY, 2022 | DOI:10.1163/9789004499614_010
This is an open access chapter distributed under the terms of the CC BY-NC-ND 4.0 license.

Co-operation and Development (OECD) Guidelines for Multinational Enterprises, and the OECD Due Diligence Guidance for Responsible Supply Chains in the Garment and Footwear Sector. While only the OECD instrument on the garment and footwear sector explicitly includes home workers, we argue that home workers are covered implicitly by the other instruments. These instruments constitute soft law, meaning that they are legally non-binding. Nevertheless, recognition at the global level is often a precursor to securing recognition, and rights, at the national level. We also explore how home workers in Thailand and Bulgaria used ILO Convention No. 177 on Home Work to fight for the recognition of home workers as workers, at the domestic level.

Our argument is for a plural, overlapping governance perspective that focuses on regulatory mechanisms at local, national, regional, and global levels. Support for the participation of representative organizations of home workers is critical for these regulatory mechanisms to be effective. If home workers are excluded from law and law-making processes, it is likely that multinational enterprises (MNEs) will ban home work. Apart from its implications for home workers, other workers' rights would also be compromised by this.

1 Global Value Chains and Home Workers

A recent International Labour Organization (2017) survey of 1,454 factories from 87 countries that supply MNEs found that suppliers face intense competition to produce goods for as little as possible, and buyers exploit this competition by continually pressuring their suppliers to drop their prices. Up to 52 per cent of suppliers that were surveyed have signed contracts to produce goods at a loss. They did so to secure future orders. Demanding unpaid overtime, keeping wages low, and outsourcing to home workers are the suppliers' primary tactics for keeping their costs low. Home workers can be exploited because they are largely invisible and seldom enjoy legal protection, as this telling statement shows: "The manager candidly admitted that since government inspectors cannot inspect private homes, it is cheaper and easier to simply outsource work to home-based workers".[2]

The question is, how to improve working conditions within these chains? Global value chain scholars argue that countries and firms can appropriate more value by pursuing "upgrading" strategies. Humphrey and Schmitz suggest four different ways in which firms can "upgrade": through product upgrading,

2 M. Zhou, "Pakistan's Hidden Workers: Wages and Conditions of Home-based Workers and the Informal Economy" (Geneva, 2017), available www.ilo.org, last accessed 28 May 2021.

which involves producing a different, more complex product (and therefore being able to charge more for it); production upgrading, which involves improving the efficiency of the production process, often by improving technology (which lowers production costs); functional upgrading, which involves building the capacity and skills of workers to assume more sophisticated functions; and chain upgrading, which involves transitioning to a different industry.[3] What are the implications for home workers if they, or the factory, pursue any one of these strategies?

The Donor Committee for Enterprise Development, comprising the major enterprise development funders, has published case studies showing that functional upgrading (improving home-based workers' skills) leads to higher incomes. Country-level studies, however,[4] show that even when the upgrading strategies of factories are successful, the gains are often short-lived. Consequently, they are resistant to passing on their gains to workers (including home workers). The oligopolistic power of lead firms means that technocratic "upgrading" solutions are not the answer. And, given that the buyers are domiciled in industrialized countries and factories in developing countries, these global supply value chains effectively escape regulation.

In 2011, in response to this "governance gap", the UN Human Rights Council adopted the UN Guiding Principles on Business and Human Rights [hereafter UN Guiding Principles or GPs), which were drafted by UN Special Representative for Business and Human Rights John Ruggie, following global consultation. Ruggie argued that because states are unable to regulate transnational corporations, their activities resulted in human rights abuses.[5] The GPs have been incorporated into the OECD Guidelines for Multinational Enterprises and the ILO's MNE Declaration. In the next section of this chapter, we discuss these rights-based governance mechanisms, and explore whether they hold potential to improve home workers' wages and working conditions. Thereafter we compare the different instruments in terms of their strengths and weaknesses.

---

3 J. Humphrey and H. Schmitz, "How does insertion in global value chains affect upgrading in industrial clusters?" *Regional Studies*, 36:9 (2002), pp. 1017–1027.

4 Reporting on their study of thirty countries and drawing on four other studies, Milberg and Winkler (2011) state that with the exception of a study of the apparel and footwear industry, the data contest the correlation between economic and social upgrading. Ironically, as firms capture more value, the real wages and working conditions of their workers deteriorate. Beinhardt and Milberg's (2011) study of nineteen countries across four sectors concludes that there is a trade-off between employment growth and growth in wages. More jobs mean a decline in wages.

5 John Ruggie, "Guiding Principles on Business and Human Rights: Implementing the United Nations 'Protect, Respect and Remedy' Framework", UNHR Council (2011), A/HRC/17/31:2.

2 International Human Rights Instruments

2.1 *The UN Guiding Principles on Business and Human Rights*

The Guiding Principles represent the first UN endorsed corporate human rights responsibility initiative. The GPs constitute soft law, meaning they do not impose any binding legal obligations upon states or corporations. Nevertheless, they represent an important instrument as the first framework that outlines the duties of national states derived from human rights treaties, and that outline corporations' moral responsibilities. The GPs establish three pillars: states' duty to protect human rights; corporations' responsibility to respect human rights; and access to remedy. Each is discussed in turn below.

2.2 *State duty to protect human rights*

While the GPs are not legally binding, they nevertheless frame states' responsibility to protect human rights as mandatory, based on their obligations under international human rights law to individuals within their territory. The GPs also establish that states should take steps to ensure that their corporations respect human rights in other countries. The GPs recommend that states: Enforce existing laws (including labor laws) that protect human rights and require corporations to "report on their human rights impacts;" Ensure that human rights are respected in their own supply chains; and Establish complaints mechanisms to address alleged human rights violations.

2.3 *Corporate responsibility to respect human rights*

The GPs cite two international legal instruments – the Universal Declaration of Human Rights and the ILO Declaration on Fundamental Principles and Rights at Work – that provide the framework for businesses' responsibility. The GPs state that businesses have a responsibility to address "human rights impacts" which they have caused or contributed to through their own activities, but also to "prevent or mitigate" behavior by actors in their supply chains (such as suppliers or subcontractors) that violate workers' rights, even where they have not contributed to those violations. Businesses are expected to fulfill this responsibility by: Drafting a human rights policy, which should be communicated to all their stakeholders and adhered to in their business practices; Undertaking a due diligence of each supply chain to assess whether any act or omission in the production process might be contravening domestic law and/or causing human rights violations to workers; and Implementing remediation processes, including an operational-level grievance mechanism.

2.4 *Access to remedy*

States are responsible for establishing both judicial and non-judicial grievance mechanisms as part of a "comprehensive state-based system for the remedy of business-related human rights abuse". The GPs outline a set of effectiveness criteria for non-judicial grievance mechanisms. Specifically, these should be: legitimate, accessible, predictable, equitable and transparent. They also state that remediation measures could include "an apology, restitution, rehabilitation, financial or non-financial compensation and punitive sanctions (whether criminal or administrative, such as fines), as well as the prevention of harm through, for example, injunctions or guarantees of non-repetition". Businesses are expected to establish operational-level grievance mechanisms as a first port of call for grievances that should be "accessible directly to individuals and communities who may be adversely impacted by a business enterprise".

The GPs do not explicitly refer to homeworkers. Homeworkers may, however, be covered implicitly, in terms of two provisions. First, the GPs state that a corporation's due diligence should include activities linked to its "operations, products or services by its business relationship". "Business relationship" is defined as "relationships with business partners, entities, in its value chain, and any other .... entity directly linked to its business operations, products or services," which arguably includes sub-contractors who contract to homeworkers. Second, the due diligences process should involve "meaningful consultation with potentially affected groups and other relevant stakeholders". Businesses should "seek to understand the concerns of potentially affected stakeholders by consulting them directly in a manner that takes into account language and other potential barriers to effective engagement". This consultation requirement could present an opportunity for homeworker organizations to participate in due diligence processes. A weakness is a lack of clarity as to the form that consultation should take, which undermines the requirement.

3 The UN Guiding Principles on Business and Human Rights

The Guiding Principles represent the first UN-endorsed corporate human rights responsibility initiative. The GPs constitute soft law, meaning that they do not impose any binding legal obligations upon states or corporations. Nevertheless, they represent an important instrument as the first framework that outlines the duties of national states derived from human rights treaties, and that outline the moral responsibilities of corporations. The GPs establish three pillars: states' duty to protect human rights; corporations' responsibility to respect human rights; and access to remedy. Each of these is discussed in turn below.

4 States' Duty to Protect Human Rights

While the GPs are not legally binding, they nevertheless frame states' responsibility to protect human rights as mandatory, based on their obligations under international human rights law to individuals within their territory.[6] The GPs also establish that states should take steps to ensure that their corporations respect human rights in other countries.[7] The GPs recommend that states: enforce existing laws (including labour laws) that protect human rights and require corporations to "report on their human rights impacts"; ensure that human rights are respected in their own supply chains; and establish complaints mechanisms to address alleged human rights violations.

5 Corporations' Responsibility to Respect Human Rights

The GPs cite two international legal instruments—the Universal Declaration of Human Rights and the Declaration on Fundamental Principles and Rights at Work—that provide the framework for the responsibility of businesses. The GPs state that businesses have a responsibility to address "human rights impacts" which they have caused or contributed to through their own activities, but also to "prevent or mitigate" behaviour by actors in their supply chains (such as suppliers or subcontractors) that violate workers' rights even where they have not contributed to those violations. Businesses are expected to fulfil this responsibility by: drafting a human rights policy, which should be communicated to all their stakeholders and adhered to in their business practices; undertaking due diligence of each supply chain to assess whether any act or omission in the production process might be contravening domestic law and/

6 Penelope Simons and Audrey Macklin, *The Governance Gap: Extractive Industries, Human Rights and the Home State Advantage* (London, 2014).

7 Indeed, one of the principal criticisms of the GP is that it does not go far enough to address the need for extra-territorial regulation. See Simons and Macklin, *The Governance Gap*; Rosaria Burchielli, Annie Delaney, and Maria Montesano, "Regulatory Challenges in the Australian Garment Industry: Human Rights in a Post-Ruggie Environment", *Labour & Industry: A Journal of the Social and Economic Relations of Work*, 23:1 (2013), pp. 69–88.

or causing human rights violations to workers; and implementing remedial processes, including an operational-level grievance mechanism.

6 Access to Remedy

States are responsible for establishing both judicial and non-judicial grievance mechanisms as part of a "comprehensive state-based system for the remedy of business-related human rights abuse".[8] The GPs outline a set of effectiveness criteria for non-judicial grievance mechanisms. Specifically, these should be legitimate, accessible, predictable, equitable, and transparent. They also state that remedial measures could include "an apology, restitution, rehabilitation, financial or non-financial compensation and punitive sanctions (whether criminal or administrative, such as fines), as well as the prevention of harm through, for example, injunctions or guarantees of non-repetition".[9] Businesses are expected to establish operational-level grievance mechanisms as a first port of call for grievances that should be "accessible directly to individuals and communities who may be adversely impacted by a business enterprise".[10]

The GPs do not explicitly refer to home workers. Home workers may, however, be covered implicitly, under two provisions. First, the GPs state that a corporation's due diligence should include activities linked to its "operations, products or services by its business relationship".[11] "Business relationship" is defined as "relationships with business partners, entities, in its value chain, and any other … entity directly linked to its business operations, products or services", which arguably includes subcontractors who contract to home workers. Second, the due diligence process should involve "meaningful consultation with potentially affected groups and other relevant stakeholders".[12] Businesses should "seek to understand the concerns of potentially affected stakeholders by consulting them directly in a manner that takes into account language and other potential barriers to effective engagement".[13] This consultation requirement presents an opportunity for home worker organizations to participate in

8 These grievance mechanisms could include: civil and criminal courts, administrative bodies, human rights institutions, national contact points, labour tribunals, mediation, "or other culturally appropriate and rights compatible processes". See Ruggie, "Guiding Principles on Business and Human Rights", p. 30.

9 Ibid., p. 27.

10 Ibid., p. 31.

11 Ibid., p. 15.

12 Ibid., p. 19.

13 Ibid., p. 20.

due diligence processes. A weakness is the lack of clarity as to the form consultation should take, which undermines the requirement.

7 OECD Guidelines for Multinational Enterprises

The OECD Guidelines for Multinational Enterprises apply to the forty-seven countries that adhere to the OECD Declaration on International Investment and Multinational Enterprises. The Guidelines represent governments addressing MNEs that are operating from or in signatory countries, and constitute "non-binding principles and standards for responsible business conduct in a global context consistent with applicable laws and internationally recognized standards".[14] They cover numerous areas, among them: employment and industrial relations; the environment, bribery and extortion; consumer interests; and competition and taxation. The Guidelines were amended in May 2011[15] to incorporate the UN Guiding Principles by adding a chapter on human rights and including a section in chapter II on supply chain management that applies the GPs' risk-based due diligence process. As the OECD Guidelines mirror provisions in the UN Guiding Principles, they implicitly cover home workers.

The Guidelines respond to the GPs' recommendation that states provide a non-judicial grievance mechanism[16] by requiring signatory countries to establish a "national contact point" (NCP) that can adopt a range of institutional forms. NCPs are tasked with promoting and implementing the Guidelines, and reviewing complaints of corporate non-compliance by trade unions, non-profit organizations, governments, and even members of the public.[17] As of 2017, NCPs in more than 100 countries have handled over 400 cases.[18]

Although participation in the process is voluntary, MNEs engage in order to prevent reputational risk, or to avoid formal legal charges.[19] Some of these

14 OECD, *OECD Guidelines for Multinational Enterprises* 2011 Edition (Paris, 2013), p. 3; available https://www.oecd.org/corporate/mne/, last accessed 12 December 2020.

15 The OECD Guidelines were first signed in 1976.

16 However, authors such as Simons and Macklin have pointed out that the NCPs do not necessarily meet the "effectiveness criteria" outlined in the Guiding Principles for non-judicial grievance mechanisms (see Simons and Macklin, *The Governance Gap*).

17 Ibid.

18 For a full list of cases, see https://mneguidelines.oecd.org/database/, last accessed 27 May 2021.

19 Larry Backer, "Rights and Accountability in Development (Raid) v. Das Air and Global Witness v. Afrimex: Small Steps Toward an Autonomous Transnational Legal System for

complaint processes have resulted in dialogue or mediation between the parties, and in some cases corporations have agreed to remedy the violation and pay compensation to affected individuals or groups.[20]

Assessments of the effectiveness of NCPs are mixed. Backer argues that NCPs can play an important role in changing corporate behaviour, which, over time, could have an effect as binding as hard law.[21] The efficacy of NCPs, he argues, is attributable to their autonomy and their flexibility to apply domestic or international law rules in their findings, while at the same time conducting a decision-making process unconstrained by these very rules. Simons and Macklin are more critical, and argue that a lack of the required procedural standards is responsible for a lack of consistency and accountability among NCPs.[22] For example, there is no requirement that NCPs should establish an appeals process, monitor the implementation of a decision, or issue a decision when parties do not reach agreement. When a dispute resolution process is initiated, there is no required time-frame for concluding it.

We believe that NCPs could be a strategic site of struggle for home workers and their allies, in particular because the OECD Due Diligence Guidance for Responsible Supply Chains in the Garment and Footwear Sector—a key sector for home workers—explicitly recognizes that home workers are legitimate workers in global value chains.

8 OECD Due Diligence Guidance in the Garment and Footwear Sector

The OECD Due Diligence Guidance for Responsible Supply Chains in the Garment and Footwear Sector [hereafter OECD Guidance] was agreed to in 2017,[23] after a multi-stakeholder consultative process. The OECD Guidance includes a module on "Responsible sourcing from home workers", which establishes that home workers are "an intrinsic part of the workforce entitled to receive equal treatment".[24] The module includes both a framework for

the Regulation of Multinational Corporations", *Melbourne Journal of International Law*, 10 (2009), pp. 258–307.

20 Simons and Macklin, *The Governance Gap*.

21 Backer, "Rights and Accountability in Development".

22 Simons and Macklin, *The Governance Gap*.

23 Since the 2011 update to the Guidelines, the OECD has clarified what the due diligence process should involve and developed a due diligence guidance for five different sectors including the garment and footwear sector—which is a key sector for home workers.

24 OECD, *OECD Due Diligence Guidance for Responsible Supply Chains in the Garment and Footwear Sector* (Paris, 2018), p. 182.

"preventing and mitigating human rights and labour abuses when engaging home workers", directed at a range of stakeholders, and a set of recommendations for enterprises to follow in designing their due diligence processes. The framework advocates the formalization of home workers through legal identity, recognition of their worker status, and contracts and/or authorizations that would facilitate legalization of their work. The text notes that formalization is a process, and that legalization should not involve the imposition of requirements that would be prejudicial to home workers. The framework also states that organizing home workers is a critical step towards their participation in social dialogue. Unfortunately, it does not reference ILO Recommendation 204 on Transitioning from the Informal to the Formal Economy, which provides guidelines on achieving progressive formalization with an emphasis on extending labour rights and social protection to informal workers.

Enterprises are encouraged to (i) identify potential and actual harms, and (ii) prevent or mitigate harms that are caused by the enterprise or are present in the supply chain. Under the first objective, enterprises are encouraged to identify production processes and sourcing countries where home workers are likely to be prevalent, and to assess whether suppliers in these areas have procedures in place for responsible sourcing from home workers. Enterprises should build their suppliers' capacity to implement the following measures: (i) a "pre-qualification system" for intermediaries who contract work to home workers; (ii) internal protocols for contracting work to home workers; (iii) training for intermediaries involved in contracting work to home workers; and (iv) contractual transparency requirements from intermediaries that contract work to home workers.[25] Transparency requirements could include keeping records of all workers receiving orders, the details of the orders and of any social benefits provided to home workers—e.g., transporting the raw materials and finished goods.

The recommendations also include supportive measures that MNEs can take, including partnering with local initiatives that support home workers, and engaging with local and national governments to "promote the rights of home workers to access equal treatment [to other workers] under the law".[26]

Although the OECD Guidance represents significant progress in explicitly mentioning home workers, its potential to protect home workers is limited by its soft law status. Also, there are significant omissions in the framework and recommendations. For example, while it mentions the importance of

25 Ibid., pp. 184–85.

26 Ibid., p. 185.

organizing home workers, MNEs are not encouraged to recognize existing representative organizations of home workers as legitimate partners in the due diligence process, including discussions on the form that transparency requirements and grievance procedures should take. And, a key recommendation should be that MNEs require their suppliers to mention the name of their brand in subcontracting agreements—a requirement in the Australian supply chain legislation. Home workers would then be able to identify the brand, research its commitment to decent work, and register complaints through its complaint mechanisms.

Despite these shortcomings, the OECD Guidance represents a potential mechanism for advocacy. Although the recommendations are limited and not binding, they recognize home workers as integral to supply chains and give legitimacy to their claims.

9 The ILO's MNE Declaration

In November 1977, the ILO adopted the Tripartite Declaration of Principles concerning Multinational Enterprises and Social Policy, or the MNE Declaration. The ILO's Governing Body approved amendments to the MNE Declaration in 2000 and 2006 to reflect the changing realities of global production and new international labour standards. The MNE Declaration provides guidelines for "enhancing the positive and social labour effects of the operations and governance of multinational enterprises to achieve decent work for all".[27] It is a voluntary instrument, therefore not binding, and cannot be adjudicated by any international adjudicatory body.[28] Governments, multinational enterprises, and employers' and workers' organizations are simply invited "to observe the principles embodied therein".[29]

After the 2016 International Labour Conference (ILC) general discussion on supply chains, the MNE Declaration was revised to incorporate the UN Guiding Principles. A human rights dimension is now included, which establishes responsibility on the part of corporations to identify, mitigate, prevent,

27 ILO, *International Labour Office Geneva Tripartite Declaration of Principles Concerning Multinational Enterprises and Social Policy* (Geneva, 2017), p. v.

28 If, however, a particular principle in the Declaration reflects an ILO convention that has been ratified by particular countries and the countries promulgated legislation to give effect to the ratification, then that principle would be binding in those countries and capable of adjudication and enforcement.

29 ILO, *Tripartite Declaration of Principles*, p. 1.

and account for adverse human rights impacts in their supply chains. It establishes meaningful consultation with potentially affected groups as integral to the due diligence process. While the Declaration does not explicitly refer to home workers, such a provision covers home workers indirectly.

The MNE Declaration recommends that national tripartite constituents (governments, employers, and workers) establish national focal points[30] to promote their principles, engage in capacity-building and information dissemination, and facilitate tripartite dialogue.

The Declaration does not mention home workers, but given that it is based on the UN Guiding Principles, which we argue includes home workers, the same argument can be made with respect to the Declaration.

10 The Potential of International Instruments to Protect Home Workers

Although only the OECD Guidance on the garment and footwear sector explicitly mentions home workers, there is an argument that the other instruments could also cover home workers. The OECD instruments have the most traction because home worker organizations can report non-compliant companies to NCPs, including their failure to engage in "meaningful consultation" with them (as in the successful Vedanta case) as part of an advocacy strategy with allies.

Our analysis of these international agreements elides the contestations that underpin them, of course. The conclusions of the ILC tripartite general discussion on supply chains recognize that home workers are an ineluctable part of supply chains, which established the basis for their inclusion in the Due Diligence Guidance for Responsible Supply Chains in the Garment and Footwear Sector. This recognition was hard-won: home worker organizations participated in the discussions and the global research advocacy network, *Women in Informal Employment: Globalizing and Organizing* (WIEGO),[31] participated in pre-conference caucuses with the International Trade Union Confederation (ITUC) and in post-conference workshops facilitated by the Global Labour Union.

Despite their soft law (non-binding) status, these instruments are significant for home workers for several reasons. First, human rights rhetoric shifts

30 ILO, *Tripartite Declaration of Principles*, Annex II, 1b.

31 Women in Informal Employment, Globalizing, and Organizing—a research advocacy network of membership-based organizations, researchers, and development practitioners. See www.wiego.org.

public consciousness, which is often a precursor to "enforcement" through social pressure by civil society groups, called "new governance" in legal theory, and it can be used in advocacy to generate the political will necessary to enact legislation at the national level. Second, recognition at the global level is often a precursor to securing recognition, and rights, at the national level. For example, home workers in Thailand and Bulgaria have used ILO Convention No. 177 on Home Work (C177) to fight for the recognition of home workers as workers, at the domestic level.

The next sections reflect on this interplay between national and international law. We start with a discussion on C177, which is followed by a discussion of national legislation in three countries: Bulgaria, Thailand, and Australia. The aim is to remind us that both the existence of the law and its content are an outcome of political struggle, as is its enforcement. Enforcement is contingent upon strong organizations of home workers and support from civil society—most notably from trade unions, but also from non-profit organizations, development organizations, and donors.

11 ILO Convention No. 177 on Home Work and National Legislation to Protect Home Workers

The Self-Employed Women's Association (SEWA) of India, the world's largest trade union of informal workers, facilitated international exchange and dialogue among home worker groups in Southeast Asia and Europe in the 1980s. In the mid-1990s, it spearheaded the formation of an international network, HomeNet, and a global campaign for a Convention on Home Work.

Prior to the adoption of C177 in 1996, the ILO's stance on home work was that it was exploitative, but that home workers were too disparate and isolated to be organized.[32] In the absence of formal representation at the ILO, HomeNet advocated home workers' demands through formal trade union channels, and received support from the International Union of Foodworkers (IUF), the International Confederation of Free Trades Unions (ICFTU) and the International Textiles, Garments and Leather Workers Federation (ITGLWF). The principal demand of home workers was that they should enjoy the same labour rights as other waged workers.[33] The Convention was agreed to in 1996.

32 Renana Jhabvala and Jane Tate, "Out of the Shadows: Home-based Workers Organize for International Recognition", *Seeds*, 18 (1996).

33 WIEGO, "Commemorating Twenty Years of the ILO Home Work Convention 177 (1996–2016)" (Cambridge, MA, 2016), available www.wiego.org, last accessed 28 May 2021.

C177 advocates that home workers must be treated the same as other waged workers. It establishes home workers' rights to freedom of association, occupational health and safety, fair remuneration, freedom from discrimination, social security protection, access to training, minimum employment age, and maternity protection (Article 4). And it states that home workers must be included in national labour statistics. Only eleven countries have ratified the Convention.

After the Convention's ratification in 1996, organizing and network-building efforts shifted from international to regional levels, and HomeNet South East Asia (HNSEA),[34] HomeNet South Asia (HNSA),[35] and HomeNet Eastern Europe were formed.[36] Since the adoption of C177, home workers' organizations and their allies have advocated for legislation at the domestic level. We review these efforts in Bulgaria, Thailand, and Australia below.

Legislation that protects home workers typically employs one of three approaches. The first approach expands the traditional employment and/or labour relations legislation that covers employees to include subcontracted work, including home workers. The legislation therefore creates labour rights for home workers as if they were employees. The second approach is to legislate specifically to protect home workers, as is the case in Thailand. The third approach, which Australia has adopted in the textile, garment, and footwear sectors, is to combine a "due diligence" human rights approach with a mandatory code that contains stringent enforcement mechanisms. Below, we describe each of these approaches, including the political struggle that resulted in the legislation.

12 Bulgaria: Expanding Existing Labour Legislation

Several countries, including Bulgaria, Chile, Brazil, Nicaragua, Uruguay, and South Africa, have amended their labour legislations to incorporate subcontracted work, including home work. We discuss Bulgaria because the

34 HomeNet South East Asia (HNSEA) has five affiliated national organizations from Cambodia, Indonesia, Laos, Thailand, and the Philippines, that represent 25,698 workers.

35 HomeNet South Asia (HNSA) has 57 affiliate organizations representing over 600,000 workers from Afghanistan, Bangladesh, Bhutan, India, Maldives, Nepal, Pakistan, and Sri Lanka.

36 HomeNet Eastern Europe (HNEE) has thirteen affiliates—the largest, AHBW, has 30,000 members (from Albania, Armenia, Bulgaria, Georgia, Kazakhstan, Kyrgyzstan, Macedonia, Montenegro, Serbia, Tajikistan, Turkey, Ukraine, and Uzbekistan) (WIEGO 2017). Organizing efforts are ongoing in Africa and Latin America.

legislation there was amended as the result of campaigning by a movement of home-based workers, and Bulgaria has ratified C177.

The Association of Home-Based Workers, Bulgaria [hereafter Association], a democratic, membership-based organization that was registered as an association in 2002, boasts 35,000 members[37] drawn from twenty-two of Bulgaria's twenty-eight provinces. It is governed by a general assembly, which comprises approximately 150 elected delegates, that meets annually. It elects a national board and chairperson every five years. Each province elects a committee and coordinators who represent the province at quarterly national meetings. If the Association were to be recognized as a trade union, it would be one of the largest trade unions in Bulgaria.[38]

The Association and its allies, including international NGOs, campaigned for the Bulgarian government to ratify ILO Convention No. 177, which it did in July 2009. Subsequently, in November 2010, the government signed a "National Agreement on the Regulation of Home-based Work"[39] that outlined the basis on which the Labour Code would be amended. The Labour Code was amended in 2011 to cover subcontracted "dependent" workers. The Labour Code stipulates that dependent workers must have a contract and must enjoy the same entitlements as employees, including entitlements derived through collective bargaining agreements or through social security legislation.[40]

According to the Association, the government has neither complied with C177 (for example, there is no home work policy and home workers are not visible in the statistics) nor implemented the Labour Code because "the government holds the opinion that because [home workers in Petrich] don't have contracts they are independent units and thus fall outside of the scope of C177".[41] The Association was instrumental in the formation of the union of

37 For a history of AHBW, see Dave Spooner, "Challenges and Experiences in Organizing Home-Based Workers in Bulgaria", WIEGO Organizing Brief No. 7 (2013), available www.wiego.org, last accessed 27 May 2021. Home-based workers comprise both own account workers, and waged workers. Often, the same worker is an own account worker for part of the year and a waged worker in a different season.

38 Spooner, "Organizing Home-Based Workers in Bulgaria".

39 Correspondence between the Association and the ILO's International Labour Standards Department that monitors compliance with conventions (on file with the author); Spooner, "Organizing Home-Based Workers in Bulgaria"; Shelley Marshall, "A Comparison of Four Experiments in Extending Labour Regulation to Non-Standard and Informal Workers", *International Journal of Comparative Labour Law and Industrial Relations*, 3 (2018), pp. 281–311.

40 Ibid.

41 E-mail exchange with Violeta Zlateva on 22 July 2017.

informal workers (Unity), which was founded in May 2014 and which represents several sectors of informal workers.

13 Specific Legislation to Protect Home Workers: The Case of Thailand

HomeNet Thailand, a HomeNet South East Asia affiliate, has been at the forefront of national advocacy efforts in Thailand for the recognition and legislative protection of home workers. Its decade-long struggle resulted in the Home Workers Protection Act of 2010. Below, we discuss the political process that led to the legislation, the terms of the Act, and reflect on whether the Act has made a difference to home workers.

In 1995, Thailand experienced an economic crisis. Factories closed down or laid off workers. Many workers became informal home-based workers, and approximately 80 per cent of all work was subcontracted. HomeNet Thailand, supported by the ILO (whose Thailand representative was previously a trade unionist), began to advocate for the recognition of home workers' contributions and for their being organized. It urged that the Ministry of Labour should extend statutory labour protection to home workers and that the statutory minimum wage should apply to them. Officials argued that this was impossible, since informal workers were not recognized as workers and villagers' livelihood activities did not constitute legitimate employment.

HomeNet Thailand campaigned for a national Act that would establish home workers' labour rights and social protection, with the support of WIEGO, the ILO, HomeNet South East Asia, the Foundation for Labour and Employment Protection (FLEP) and other allies.[42] They pursued the following strategies. First, they focused on increasing the visibility of home workers in the official statistics: "We have statistics, so they cannot deny their existence".[43] Second, they expanded the organizing of home workers to build a democratic, membership-based organization that could be mobilized as a political constituency. Third, they conducted research to identify issues facing home workers, which they used to mobilize the home workers and engage them in legislative processes. Fourth, they drafted legislation with the participation of home

42 WIEGO, "Winning Legal Rights for Thailand's Home-based Workers", Impact Brief (2015), available www.wiego.org, last accessed 27 May 2021.

43 Meeting with ten persons who were part of FLEP and/or HomeNet Thailand, and who recounted the history of the struggle for the Act.

workers. And fifth, they conducted a campaign that included a media strategy and a series of hearings.[44]

In 2010, the Thai Parliament passed the Home Workers Protection Act, which is premised on extending equal protection to home workers and factory workers. The Act is innovative in a number of respects. First, it stipulates that home workers must be given a written contract,[45] and provides that where a contract gives the hirer an "undue advantage", the court has the power to order that the terms of the contract be enforced only in so far as the terms are reasonable (section 8).

Second, the Act makes it a criminal offence to pay home workers less than the statutory minimum wage. Further, payment to home workers must be made at their place of work within seven days of delivery of the finished products, and only limited deductions may be made from such payment (section 19). Third, home workers must be informed if their work is hazardous or involves toxic substances, and the hirer must provide safety equipment. If hirers contravene these provisions, they will have to pay medical, rehabilitation, or funeral expenses (section 24). Fourth, the Act stipulates that the Ministry of Labour must draft "secondary laws" or regulations for the Act to come into effect, which should be overseen by a tripartite committee comprising director-generals from several ministries, three home worker representatives, and three "hirers". At the time of writing, seventeen of the twenty-one laws had been drafted including one dealing with minimum piece-rates. Finally, section 6 of the Act provides that where a particular case by a home worker against a hirer is believed to be *"for the common good"*, the state will appoint a legal representative to represent the home worker in the Labour Court.

Home workers may lodge complaints with the Department of Social Protection and HomeNet Thailand delivers "know-your-rights" training to its members. But no one has complained yet. Interviews with home workers suggest that fear of losing their jobs acts as a deterrent. HomeNet Thailand has put pressure on the Department for the Protection of Informal Workers within the Labour Ministry to engage in a collaborative pilot project in three provinces to "implement" the Act, which is under way.

---

44 The history of the Act was collected through interviews conducted by one of the authors with ten members of HomeNet Thailand who were at the forefront of the struggle, in April 2017.

45 This stipulation addresses a common complaint of home workers. Where a written contract exists, the terms are unilaterally decided and they are not given a copy. In the absence of a written contract, home workers are only given copies of work orders, which only stipulate the number of items to be produced and the rate per piece.

14 Australia's Supply Chain Legislation

In Australia, home workers, who are mostly immigrants from Vietnam and Cambodia, comprise an estimated 40 per cent of the work force in the textile, clothing, and footwear industries.[46] The Textile, Clothing, and Footwear Union of Australia (TCFUA) initiated a campaign to procure labour rights for home workers. It mobilized 4,000 Australian home workers to raise awareness among the public of their work conditions; created an organization called Asian Women at Work (AWATW) and initiated the Fair Wear Campaign (which involved unions, students, community organizations, faith groups, and other civil society allies).[47] The campaign resulted in a public outcry, led to senate enquiries on home work, and placed pressure on industry leaders to support the regulation of supply chains.[48]

Labour law in Australia is composed of legislation—the Fair Work Act of 2009—as well as collective bargaining agreements that establish minimum conditions of employment for the industry.[49] The collective bargaining agreements are negotiated with multi-employer bodies, and have statutory backing as they cover the entire industry including workers and employers not party to the agreements. These collective agreements are known as federal "awards". In 1987, the Federal Clothing Trades Award (now the Textile, Clothing, Footwear, and Associated Industries Award 2010) was expanded to include home workers.[50] Home workers were now entitled to the same labour rights, such as minimum wages, overtime pay, paid vacation, maternity leave, etc., as employees.

Marshall notes that firms responded by requiring home workers to register as self-employed own account workers, which enabled the firms to claim that they were contracting with independent businesses and therefore the award did not apply. In response, the Fair Wear campaign developed a voluntary code of practice—a soft law instrument that companies signed to avoid public scandal. In 2012, lobbying by the union and allies resulted in the Fair Work Act being amended to provide for a federal mandatory code that would require retailers to demand that their suppliers extend the labour rights enjoyed by employees,

46 Michael Rawling, "Cross-jurisdictional and other Implications of Mandatory Clothing Retailer Obligations", *Australian Journal of Labour Law*, 27:3 (2014), pp. 191–215.

47 Ibid.

48 Burchielli, Delaney, and Montesano, "Regulatory Challenges in the Australian Garment Industry",.

49 Marshall, "A Comparison of Four Experiments".

50 Ibid.

to home workers.[51] While the federal mandatory code is yet to be enacted, three states enacted retailers' codes—New South Wales, South Australia, and Queensland (the last of these was repealed in 2012).

The NSW and South Australian Codes are similar, and so we analyse only the former here. In New South Wales, the Ethical Clothing Trades Extended Responsibility Scheme (referred to as the NSW Code) came into effect in December 2004. The NSW Code is a subordinate legislation, enacted by way of proclamation under the Industrial Relations (Ethical Clothing Trades) Act 2001. It is therefore a mandatory code and compliance is obligatory as a matter of law. The NSW Code is not only applicable to the "lead firm" or "effective business controller" at the top of the chain, but also applies to lower levels of the chain, namely suppliers and contractors. This wide coverage in itself is an innovative provision. The terms "retailer", "supplier", and "contractor" are broadly defined, which makes it difficult for these parties to escape their obligations through creative corporate structuring. The Code regulates corporations incorporated in NSW, and retailers that sell clothing in NSW but subcontract production to home workers in any Australian state. It therefore regulates corporations domiciled in other jurisdictions, including international brands.

The Code applies the "due diligence" approach envisaged by the UN Guiding Principles, but it takes this a step further by requiring firms to report both to the state and to unions; non-compliance is a criminal offence.

Retailers have the following obligations under the Code. Before entering into an agreement with a supplier, the retailer must ascertain whether the supplier or any of its subcontractors will contract work to an outworker (home worker).[52] Where an outworker is to be engaged, the retailer must request the supplier to provide the names and addresses of each contractor and of each outworker.[53] Retailers must in turn disclose both to the government and to the NSW branch of the Textile Clothing and Footwear Union of Australia (the NSW Union) the names and addresses of all suppliers, and whether outworkers are engaged in production.[54] Also, "where a retailer becomes aware that an outworker has been engaged on less favourable terms than the conditions described under the applicable award or other industry instrument, the retailer is obliged to report the matter to the NSW Union or the government".[55]

51 Rawling, "Mandatory Clothing Retailer Obligations".

52 NSW Code, sec. 10(1).

53 NSW Code, sec. 10(1)(b), read with Part B of Schedule 2 to the NSW Code.

54 NSW Code, sec. 12(3), read with Schedule 1.

55 NSW Code, sec. 11.

Section 7 of the NSW Code stipulates that the provisions of the Code are mandatory and apply to all persons engaged in the manufacturing of clothing products in Australia, and the supply and retail sale of those products in NSW. Violation of the NSW Code may therefore be prosecuted by the state. We are not aware of any prosecution resulting from a breach of the Code, but according to Rawling,[56] the regulator frequently deploys the threat of prosecution, and retailers comply in order to avoid prosecution and negative media exposure.

The legislation is enforced by means of different mechanisms: government inspectorates, union monitoring, and through voluntary membership of the multi-stakeholder body, Ethical Clothing Australia. Ethical Clothing Australia assists companies to map their supply chains and to establish whether their suppliers and contractors are complying (whether home workers are "receiving their legal entitlements" and accrediting compliant companies).[57]

15 A Comparison of the Different Approaches at the National Level

The three approaches described above are quite different from one another, and rely on different enforcement mechanisms. In the case of Bulgaria and countries such as South Africa, Chile, Brazil, Nicaragua, and Uruguay, existing labour legislation was amended to address disguised employment. Each country has a different legal mechanism by which the home worker can prove that she is an employee, which triggers employee rights. The weakness of this approach is that the legislation assumes an employer–employee relationship. This has two implications. First, if the home worker contracts directly with a factory, the legislation would help her show that she is *de jure* an employee of the factory and entitled to the same rights as other employees. If, however, she contracts with a contractor, subcontractor, or another home worker, she is likely only to be able to establish an employment relationship with the contractor and not with the factory (unless the contractor is a factory employee, or an agency relationship can be proved). This means that the claims for labour rights are against a supply chain actor who often enjoys as little bargaining power as the home worker herself. The Thai legislation has the same effect, in that the "hirer" is liable and the legislation does not deal with the hirer's claim against the factory. There has been no litigation that would enable us to see

---

56 Rawling, "Mandatory Clothing Retailer Obligations".

57 Justine Nolan, "Business and Human Rights: The Challenge of Putting Principles into Practice and Regulating Global Supply Chains", *Alternative Law Journal*, 42:1 (2017), pp. 42–46; Marshall, "A Comparison of Four Experiments".

how the courts are likely to deal with this lacuna. Second, if a home worker works for three different contractors on an intermittent basis, she may not be able to satisfy a court that any one of them is her employer.

Australia's legislation, by contrast, regulates the entire chain rather than only the "employment" relationship. The home worker can make a claim on anyone she regards as the "employer", and if that person is a contractor or subcontractor, he in turn can make a claim on the actual employer.

The three approaches differ in another important respect. In the case of the Bulgarian and Thai legislations, the burden of enforcement rests with the home workers. In Thailand, HomeNet Thailand is putting pressure on the government to enforce the legislation though campaigns targeted at factories complying voluntarily rather than because of inspection, and is loathe to litigate HomeNet Thailand.[58] In Australia, by contrast, several value chain actors bear the responsibility for enforcement. Retailers, factories, suppliers, and contractors, each have transparency and disclosure obligations towards the state and towards trade unions. The state has the duty to inspect and can be a party to litigation, and trade unions participate in enforcement by reviewing the details reported by retailers and other parties, and have powers of inspection.

16 Conclusion

The global instruments recognize that lead firms (retailers and brand merchandisers in buyer-driven chains) exercise considerable power in their supply chains. The instruments are animated by a human rights framework that is based on the Universal Declaration of Human Rights and the ILO Declaration on Fundamental Principles and Rights at Work. They rely on several regulatory techniques, including:

- Normative commitments: MNEs should draft a human rights policy, distribute it to its stakeholders, and provide their suppliers with training
- Disclosure requirements: MNEs need to make disclosures about their own business practices and about their supply chains based on the due diligence of their supply chains. Due diligence includes consultations with "affected parties", which include home workers.

58 One of the authors, von Broembsen, spent two weeks in Thailand with HomeNet Thailand, from 27 March to 7 April 2020. One of the purposes of the visit was to discuss the implementation of the Home Worker Protection Act.

- Using commercial "leverage": MNEs are expected to use their market power to insert labour rights in contracts with their suppliers, and to withdraw from contracts if their suppliers refuse to address human rights violations.
- Grievance mechanisms and remedies where "human rights violations" have taken place.

None of these corporate responsibilities is mandatory, of course. And none of the instruments challenges the procurement practices of corporations, including the pressure for lower and lower prices.

Nevertheless, these global instruments are significant. First, the language of human rights provides a universal standard of behaviour and a floor of rights that is disembedded, to borrow from Polanyi, from market rationales. And importantly, in the case of the OECD instruments, it enables civil society to engage in enforcement processes through national contact points. Second, the global and the national are overlapping: often, recognition of rights at the global level is a precursor to the recognition of rights at the national level and vice-versa. We have discussed home worker legislations in Bulgaria and Thailand as examples of recognition at the global level, in the form of C177, fuelling advocacy efforts at the national level. It works the other way around too—the Australian legislation was cited several times by the workers' group in the ILC General Discussion on Supply Chains as an example of legislation that holds lead firms to account, aspects of which could be replicated at the global level.

With the exception of Australia, national legislation has yet to make a difference to home workers. One of the reasons why the Bulgarian and Thai HomeNets are reluctant to litigate is because they fear that their factories will move to other countries. As Humphrey and Schmidt argue,[59] in the case of "captive supply chains" which are labour-intensive, require little technical skill on the part of the supplier, and therefore few sunk costs on the part of retailers, retailers can, and do, easily move from one country to another. From a governance perspective, what is required are overlapping, plural governance mechanisms at local, national, regional, and global levels. Efforts at creating regional pacts—for example, countries in a region agreeing to legislate and enforce minimum living wages (see the Asia Minimum Wage Campaign)—are therefore as important as focusing efforts on international or national law.

In March 2017, France enacted a corporate duty of vigilance law, which makes supply chain due diligence mandatory for its corporations. The task for

59 Humphrey and Schmitz, "Insertion in Global Value Chains".

home worker organizations is to advocate for their explicit inclusion in such legislation. Otherwise, there is a real risk that MNEs will ban their suppliers from subcontracting to home workers. Home workers are organized, despite significant challenges. But they need (i) support in the form of donor-funding to build strong movements, advocacy campaigns, and to participate in global and national regulatory setting processes; (ii) alliances with formal trade unions; and (iii) their collective organizations to be legally recognized as trade unions.

Alliances between formal trade unions and home workers have proved critical to the adoption of Convention No. 177 and to Australia's comprehensive legislative framework. The institutional power and leverage of formal trade unions lend legitimacy to the claim of home workers that they are an inextricable part of global value chains. While unions are organized internationally along sectoral lines, informal workers (including contractors, subcontractors, and home workers) are largely excluded from collective bargaining between transnational sectoral unions and brands (resulting in global framework agreements), and from tripartite social dialogue at the national level.

The challenges for home workers simply to participate in the rule-making processes are numerous, but their participation is critical. If they are excluded from law (whether soft law at the global level or legislation at the national level), the risk is that corporations will simply ban home work. Apart from the devastating implications of this for home workers, the hard-won rights of factory workers will also be compromised. Home work will not be eradicated—it will simply go underground. Factories will still be under pressure to produce more for less, and they will continue to rely on the age-old mechanism of reducing their costs by subcontracting work. In the words of Zehra Khan, general secretary of the Home-Based Women Workers Federation from Pakistan, in her address to the International Labour Conference plenary on behalf of home worker organizations at the General Discussion on supply chains: "Failure to recognize the economic contribution of home workers as part of global supply chains will simply mean that the bottom of the supply chain remains unregulated".

Acknowledgements

The original version of this paper was commissioned by the Carr Center for Human Rights at the Harvard Kennedy School. The authors thank the Carr Center for permission to reproduce the paper in this volume. Our thanks to the Global Labour University and the Carr Center for Human Rights at Harvard University for providing the funds for this research, and to Firoza Mehrotra and Janhavi Dave from HomeNet South Asia, and Sunataree Saeng-ging from HomeNet Southeast Asia, for their assistance with field work.

CHAPTER 9

Home Work in Thailand

Challenges to Formalization

Narumol Nirathron

This chapter analyses challenges in the transition of home work to the formal economy in Thailand. * It draws on data from different studies on the home work situation, including statistical surveys and findings from a 2015 study covering over 3,000 home workers and 220 employers in 26 job-types from 7 industries, taking into account a series of efforts by the Thai government to provide protection for home workers, the International Labour Organization's (ILO's) Convention No. 177 and Recommendation No. 184—Home Work Recommendation, 1996 (No. 184) as well as Recommendation No. 204 concerning the Transition from the Informal to the Formal Economy.

In most countries, home-based work originated from manufacturing that involved the use of raw materials from the farming sector. The work products were, for the most part, food and local goods. Over time, the manufacturing process and global competition changed; as a result, home work now is no longer confined to products derived from the farming sector, but includes products in the industrial and service sectors.[1]

Home work is a subcontractual form of production. The relationship between the employer and the home worker is not that of an employer–employee, but more like that between an employer and a subcontractor. There are several reasons for the existence of home work: such as, for instance, that a large number of workers are unable to enter the formal economy, for different reasons. Rapid changes in economic conditions and consumption preferences have forced the manufacturing system to adopt a more flexible and practical

* This paper is a revised version of a presentation at the International Conference on "Long-term Perspectives on Home-based Work", organized by the Centre for Women's Development Studies (CWDS), Delhi, the Swedish Labour Movement Archive and Library (ARAB), and Women in Informal Employment: Globalizing and Organizing (WIEGO), Stockholm, 22–24 May 2018.

1 Martha A. Chen, *Informal Economy Monitoring Study Sector Report: Home-Based Workers* (Cambridge, 2004), pp. 1–2; Wendy Cunningham and Carlos R. Gomez, *The Home as Factory Floor: Employment and Remuneration of Home-based Worker*, available at http://elibrary.worldbank.org/doi/book/10.1596/1813-9450-3295, last accessed 23 August 2015.

© NARUMOL NIRATHRON, 2022 | DOI:10.1163/9789004499614_011
This is an open access chapter distributed under the terms of the CC BY-NC-ND 4.0 license.

approach. The subcontractual system also allows business operators to pass along production risks and costs to home workers, thereby saving significantly on costs of labour and storage of goods. It also allows manufacturers to set more competitive product prices for consumers. Therefore, it is not very surprising that the subcontractual approach has become a global practice. At the same time, it has led to greater exploitation of labour in different guises. In subcontractual arrangements, the stakeholders are not confined to employers and contracted workers, but include retailers who enjoy considerable bargaining power in the supply chain and consumers who want cheaper goods.

In 1996, the International Labour Organization (ILO) adopted the Home Work Convention (No. 177) and Home Work Recommendation (No. 184), both emphasizing compliance to international labour standards and respect for workers' rights. Convention 177 is primarily concerned with the protection and promotion of home workers, and the government's role in carrying out necessary acts pertaining to both mandates. The Convention is complemented by Recommendation 184, which provides guidelines to achieve the mandates.

Thailand, which has not ratified Convention 177, nevertheless initiated legal protection of home workers with the Ministerial Regulation on Protection of Home Workers B.E. 2547 (2004), followed by enactment of the Home Workers Protection Act B.E. 2553 (2010), which has been enforced gradually.

In 2015, the ILO's Recommendation 204 concerning the Transition from the Informal to the Formal Economy was adopted. Its main objectives are to promote the transition of workers and economic units from the informal to the formal economy, and to prevent informalization of formal economy jobs. The focus of the Recommendation is on establishing legal and institutional mechanisms designed to promote fulfilment of decent work and development through collaboration between the public sector and different stakeholders. For home workers already protected by legal provisions, the transition means greater legal recognition and access to funding sources necessary for developing their enterprises or working environments.

This chapter presents the situation of home work from the perspective of the transition from the informal to the formal economy using data from the 2015 study, covering 3,105 home workers and 226 employers in 26 types of jobs from 7 industries. In addition, documents related to the home work situation in Thailand are analysed, as well as the essence of labour protection laws, including social protection and welfare systems, for home workers in Thailand. How these serve as a significant vehicle for the transition is analysed, in addition to the ways and means of the transition in the light of Recommendation 204. The chapter unfolds the employment situation; the measures of protection, promotion, and development of home workers; and the opportunities and challenges that result from such transitions.

1 Convention 177 and Recommendation 184: Connecting Core Labour Standards and a Decent Work Agenda

The ILO's Home Work Convention 177 and Home Work Recommendation 184, detailing labour standards and worker rights, were adopted in 1996. Convention 177 offers a framework for protecting home workers, ranging from fundamental tasks such as collecting statistics to formulating national policy pertaining to labour and social protection as well as labour development.[2] Recommendation 184 provides guidelines for implementing the Convention by defining home work, the home worker, and the employer, and formulating core home work policy and its implementation through tripartite mechanisms and collection of data on home workers, employers, and intermediaries. It values the role of employers as compilers of data on home workers and information that home workers should know. The Recommendation also mentions the right to organize and bargain collectively, measures to encourage organization and collective bargaining, and the fixing of minimum wage rates—preferably by collective bargaining or competent authorities, or through agreement between the home worker and employer. At the same time, the remuneration rates should be comparable to those received by workers in formal enterprises. Home workers should also receive welfare, just like other general workers.[3]

Therefore, Convention 177 serves as an international instrument connecting core labour standards and a decent work agenda, promoting equal treatment for home workers as for other regular workers. As of 2019, ten countries have ratified the Convention; Thailand has not yet done so.

2 International Labour Organization (ILO), *Home Work Convention, 1996 (No. 177)*, available at https://www.ilo.org/dyn/normlex/en/f?p=NORMLEXPUB:12100:0::NO::P12100_INSTRUMENT_ID:312322, last accessed 23 August 2019.

3 International Labour Organization (ILO), *Home Work Recommendation, 1996 (No. 184)*, available at https://www.ilo.org/dyn/normlex/en/f?p=NORMLEXPUB:%2012100:0::NO:12100:P12100_INSTRUMENT_ID:312322:NO, last accessed 23 August 2019.

2 Home Work in Thailand before the Enactment of the Home Workers Protection Act B.E. 2553 (2010)

The issue of subcontractual workers or home workers received a certain amount of attention before the implementation of Thailand's Sixth National Economic and Social Development Plan (1987–1991). The Plan specifically mentioned measures to promote the subcontracting system for workers in different provincial towns.[4] In 1985/86, the Department of Labour, then under the Ministry of the Interior, prepared a report on the employment conditions and labour of home workers.[5] The next year, the Justice and Peace Commission of Thailand (JPCT) launched a project to study a shophouse-based tailoring and sewing business in the Dindaeng district of Bangkok as well as a public awareness-raising campaign about how sub-contractual employment might lead to labour exploitation.[6]

From 1988 to 1996, the ILO conducted a project on rural women workers in the putting-out system in Thailand. The eight-year project aimed to promote social protection among home workers and strengthen institutional support for the concerned organizations. Included in it were studies on employment conditions; problems of home work; home worker and employer characteristics in the Northern and Northeastern Regions as well as Bangkok; and the roles of governmental and non-governmental organizations and labour unions in protecting, promoting, and developing home workers.[7] As a result, home-based and non-governmental organizations in Bangkok and Northern Thailand established a network to promote social protection for home workers, own account workers, and other informal workers, known as the Informal Workers Network or HomeNet Thailand,[8] which campaigned for social protection of home workers and other workers in the informal sector. The Network

---

4 National Economic and Social Development Board, *The Sixth National Economic and Social Development Plan (1987–1991)* (Bangkok, n.d.,), p. 94, available at https://www.nesdc.go.th/nesdb_en/ewt_w3c/ewt_dl_link.php?filename=develop_issue&nid=3781, last accessed 23 August 2017.

5 Kongvichakarn Lae Pan [Academic and Planning Division], *Sarubponkarnsuksakarnjangngan Lae Sapapkantumngan Kongpurubnganpaitumteeban Naipratedthai* [Summary Findings of Employment and Working Conditions of Home-based Workers in Thailand] (Bangkok, 1986).

6 *Puthai* (Special Issue), *Rangngannokrabobnaikrungthepmahanakorn* [Informal Workers in Bangkok] (Bangkok, 1994).

7 Lucita Lazo (ed.), *Practical Actions for the Social Protection of Homeworkers in Thailand* (Bangkok, 1996), pp. 94–110.

8 Homenet Thailland, available at https://homenetthailand.org/, last accessed 27 May 2021.

evolved into the Centre for Study and Promotion of Home Workers in 1997, and was registered in 2003 as the Foundation for Labour and Employment Promotion (FLEP). The last-mentioned foundation has played an important role in regularly campaigning for, and promoting, the rights of homeworkers and others in the informal sector.

As changes in the manufacturing system and its impact on workers became more evident, attempts were made in the public and the non-government sector to enact new laws to protect, promote, and develop home workers. Under the Labour Protection Act, B.E. 2541 (1998), "home work" was deemed potentially eligible for labour protection through ministerial regulations different from those broadly prescribed in the Act.

In 2003, the Foundation for Labour and Employment Promotion, in collaboration with Homenet Thailand, NGOs and labour lawyers, drafted a bill designed to protect, promote, and develop home-based workers.[9] One year later, the Thai Ministry of Labour issued a Ministerial Regulation on Protection of Home Workers. However, enforcement was limited in several ways. Both employers and home workers felt that compliance with the Regulation created increased burdens, while government officials experienced certain constraints in implementing the Regulation.[10] Attempts towards a home workers' protection bill continued unabated. Eventually, at the same time as the Ministry of Labour submitted a home workers' protection bill to the government in 2007 for approval, HomeNet Thailand and the Foundation for Labour and Employment Promotion submitted a different bill to the government covering protection, promotion, and development of home workers.

The Ministry of Labour bill aimed to provide protection to home workers as widely and fairly as possible, while that of HomeNet Thailand was designed to protect, promote, and develop home workers, as well as encourage worker organization and participation of all parties concerned in formulating policy and laws to ensure fairness and benefits for all.[11] The Homeworkers Protection Act B.E. 2553 (2010) was adopted on 29 September 2010 and promulgated on 15 May 2011.

---

9 Bundit Thanachaisethawut (ed.), *Leowlunglaena Kodmaikumkrong Sitthipurubnganpaitumteeban* [Looking Backward and Forward: The Law on the Protection of the Rights of Home-based Workers] (Bangkok, 2007).

10 Chalit Meesithi and Poonsap Suanmuang Tulaphan, *Purubnganpaitumteeban Nai Pratedtai: Sitthi Lae Karn Ronnarong Nayobai* [Legal Rights of Home Workers in Thailand] (Bangkok, 2006), pp. 24–25.

11 Thanachaisethawut (ed.), *Leowlunglaena Kodmaikumkrong Sitthipurubnganpaitumteeban* [Looking Backward and Forward], p. 6.

FIGURE 9.1 BANGKOK, THAILAND: Rattana Chalermchai works at her home-based sewing machine where she is able to enjoy the company of her granddaughter, Silisak. A former factory worker, Rattana was laid off during the economic crisis in 1997. She now supplies hand-made flip-flops to a resort. She is a long-time member of HomeNet Thailand and has contributed to several policy campaigns for informal workers, including the Universal Healthcare Coverage Scheme
PHOTO: PAULA BRONSTEIN/GETTY IMAGES REPORTAGE

Prior to this Act's enforcement, statistical surveys of home workers conducted by the National Statistical Office in 1999, 2002, 2005, and 2007, all confirmed the persistence of low compensation, lack of employment continuity, and work safety problems. The National Statistical Office classified home workers into three groups: those who receive work directly, their assistants who are unpaid workers, and (sub)contractual workers. The first group was the largest in number. The survey of 2007,[12] the last year in the survey series, revealed that 0.014 per cent of Thai households were engaged in home work. The percentage of home workers was 0.012 per cent of employed persons in the same year. Over three-fourths of home workers were female, with more than 60 per cent belonging to the 30–49 years age group. In terms of educational qualifications, 75.4 per cent had completed primary school, and 11.8

12 National Statistical Office, *The 2007 Home Work Survey* (Bangkok: National Statistical Office, 2007).

per cent had completed lower secondary school. On average, they worked 7.6 hours a day, but 29.1 per cent of them worked more than 9 hours each day. With regard to remuneration, 84.7 per cent mentioned that the compensation was fixed by the employer, while 9.5 per cent set their own wage rates and only 2.8 per cent had the rate fixed through common agreement. Among those who received home work, 85.7 per cent received work directly. On top of the list of industries with the largest number of home workers was garment, clothes, and textile (45.2 per cent); followed by wood and paper products (8.6 per cent); jewellery (8.1 per cent); food, beverages, and tobacco; leather goods and other goods (16.4 per cent); wholesale, retail, agriculture, and other sectors (12.7 per cent). The annual average income of home workers was 40,555 baht (US$ 1,336.24).[13] On work-related issues, work safety was mentioned most often, followed by low compensation, late payment, and irregular work supply. Assistance most needed was regular work supply, protected compensation, and funding support. The workers also needed further skills training and work improvement, guidance, and health education to meet work safety norms and behaviour protocols. Only 5.1 per cent of them belonged to any association. Those among them who were not affiliated with any organized group stated that they lacked the time for participation, they were satisfied with the compensation they received, and they believed that joining a group would not increase their income.

3 The Way to a Formal Economy: The Home Workers Protection Act B.E. 2553 (2010) and Social Protection

The passage and enforcement of the Home Workers Protection Act B.E. 2553 (2010)[14] was a clear and important step towards protecting, promoting, and developing home workers. Home workers, considered as informal workers,[15] were henceforth legally protected by a specific law. Admittedly, the protection was still rather limited. For instance, the law provides protection only for industrial work, and service work is excluded. Any step taken towards extending protection to other work categories must be prescribed by ministerial

13 The historical exchange rate was 30.35 baht = US$ 1.

14 Krom Sawasdeekarn Lae Kumkrong Rangngan [Department of Labour Protection and Welfare], *Phrarachabunyat Kumkrongrangngan Rubnganpaitumteeban* [Home Workers Protection Act, B.E. 2553 (2010) and Explanations] (Bangkok, 2013).

15 Informal workers are workers who are not subject to protection under the Labour Protection Act and are unaffiliated with the Social Security Fund under section 33.

regulations. The drafting of secondary laws related to occupational safety and health is still in progress. The objective of the Home Workers Protection Act is to lay down measures for supervising, controlling, and protecting treatment of workers by employers, providing occupational safety, and offering remedies when work accidents or injuries occur. The Act also prescribes the establishment of a Home Work Protection Committee that will recommend measures to protect, promote, and develop home workers. Its core functions are defining, registering, and reporting different aspects of labour protection, including the rights and duties of home workers and employers, remuneration, work performance safety, protection and promotion mechanisms, labour inspection, and penalties. In many ways, the Act is in line with Convention 177 and Recommendation 184, which similarly offer guidelines for labour protection, home worker and employer rights and duties, remuneration, registration and reporting, work safety, and labour inspection.

The Home Workers Protection Act defines home work as limited to industrial enterprises or other work as prescribed by ministerial regulations. It also prescribes different aspects of employers' and home workers' rights and duties. For instance, a work contract must specify the following details: contact addresses; agent or subcontractor (if any); rate of remuneration and method of computation; type, quantity, and value of home work; scheduled dates of commencement and completion of each work lot; scheduled delivery date of the work; and date of payment. The law also sets conditions for terminating employment and demanding a performance bond or security against damage.

Regarding remuneration, the Act states that it shall not be less than that stipulated by the labour protection law for work of the same nature and quantity, without any discrimination. Payment of remuneration shall be made within seven days of the date of delivery as per the Act, while Recommendation 184 cites one month as the limit for timely payment. Thai law forbids employers from deducting from workers' remuneration except for payment of taxes and compensation for damages or late delivery penalties. The deduction shall not be more than 10 per cent of the remuneration, and consent must be obtained from the home worker.

The Home Workers Protection Act forbids pregnant women and children under 15 years of age to carry out work that may be hazardous to their health and safety as prescribed in ministerial regulations. It bans work that is dangerous to health and safety as prescribed by ministerial regulations. It also prohibits engaging home workers to perform tasks involving hazardous materials under the Hazardous Substance Act B.E. 2535 (1992), projects producing potentially hazardous vibrations or involving extreme heat or cold, and other potentially hazardous duties that may affect health or the environment. It is forbidden to procure or deliver potentially hazardous raw materials, equipment, or other accessories to carry out the work. Home workers must be given warning notice of the potential dangers of using raw materials, equipment or other accessories associated with projects, as well as offered protective and remedial measures against such dangers, and adequate protective equipment suited to the nature of the work. The employer shall be responsible for medical, rehabilitation, and funeral expenses if home workers suffer from work-related sickness or accidents, in compliance with the criteria, method, and rates prescribed by ministerial regulations.

Nevertheless, a number of issues related to worker protection, remuneration, and safety remain unaddressed in Thai law. In current Thai law, home work is confined to industrial enterprises and does not include the service industry. Nor does it mention the role, duty, and responsibility of those who act as intermediaries concerning payment of remuneration and delivery of records of work. With regard to remuneration, the Thai law does not mention the use of collective bargaining as a primary means to fix the rate of remuneration as a preferable option or to determine compensation for operational costs, such as utilities, and the time spent in maintaining machinery and equipment.

4 Tools of Implementation: Supervision and Protection, Promotion and Development Mechanisms for Home Work

The Home Workers Protection Act stipulates that there shall be a tripartite organization called the Home Work Protection Committee, consisting of the Permanent Secretary for Labour as chairperson and representatives from public agencies, employers, home workers, and experts as members, with the Director-General of Labour Protection and Welfare serving as member and secretary. The Committee's duties are to offer recommendations to the minister about protecting, promoting, and developing home workers; determining home work remuneration rates; encouraging employers and home workers to establish good practice guidelines; promoting cooperation among governmental agencies, the private sector, and other concerned organizations; monitoring home work-related operations of all concerned sectors; and reporting its performance to the cabinet at least once annually, while releasing information to the general public.

The Home Workers Protection Act does not mention forming any national policy on home work, statistical labour surveys covering home workers, registering employers and intermediaries, eliminating constraints or obstacles facing home workers seeking to organize, or measures to encourage collective bargaining in the determination of conditions of work.

4.1 *Dispute Settlement and Penalties*

Under the Home Workers Protection Act, home work-related disputes come under the jurisdiction of the Central Labour Court, while penalties differ from charge to charge. Penalties take the form of fines and/or imprisonment.

After the Act came into force, in 2011, the Foundation for Labour and Employment Promotion conducted a survey of 105 home workers who were members of the informal worker network in nine job categories[16] from seven provinces[17] in the Northern, Northeastern, Central, and Southern regions, and the Bangkok Metropolitan Area (BMA). Home worker characteristics were found to be generally in line with the 2007 survey. The majority of home workers were female (88.6 per cent) with primary school diplomas (58.1 per cent), and in the age-group 31–45 years (56.2 per cent). Most (67.6 per cent) had adopted home work as their main occupation. Some of them (16.2 per cent) had experienced pay deductions because their work was inadequate or the material was damaged or broken; usually, they were given advance notice about the deductions. Over one-third received remuneration upon work delivery, while more than 40 per cent were paid within seven days after delivery. More than half the home workers stated that their pay was lower than it should be,[18] and that they received the same pay for urgently required work. Other problems included: late payment, employers stopping work mid-project, lack of payment, unjustified pay deductions, and termination without prior notice with workers uncompensated for damages. There were cases of discrimination, as when some female workers received less pay than their male counterparts for the same duties.[19]

---

16 The nine job categories were: shoe-stitching, organdy embroidery, garment-making, shoe-making, garment-sewing, gem-polishing, toddy palm-peeling, *hijab* embroidery, and anchovy-gutting.

17 Since 2011, there have been 76 provinces in Thailand, not including the BMA.

18 Research revealed that payment for one bag of anchovy-gutting was 30–40 baht (US$ 0.99–1.32) for thirteen hours of work. Peeling toddy palms earned 50 baht (US$ 1.65) for six hours of work. Gem-cutting earned 130 baht (US$ 4.28) for twelve hours of work. Embroidery of head-scarves earned 160–250 bahts (US$ 5.27–8.24) for ten hours of work. The minimum wage in Thailand is 159–221 baht (US$ 5.24–7.28).

19 Poonsap Suanmuang Tulaphan *et al.*, “Rangngannokrabob Lae Karnkumkrongthangsungkom: Koraneesuksa Purubnganpaitumteeban” [Informal Workers and Social Protection: Case Studies of Home-based Workers], in N. Ativanichpong (ed.), *Rangngan Kub Kwammaipentham: Punha Lae Tang-ok* [Labour and Inequality: Problems and Remedies] (Bangkok, 2012), chapter 3, p.1–64.

Most home workers did not directly access work from the source. Work was mostly obtained from business operators such as garment wholesalers and retailers (33.3 per cent), followed by group agents (25.7 per cent), and contractors/subcontractors (22.9 per cent). The lowest rate of work obtained was from manufacturers (18.1 per cent). There were no written contracts; instead, verbal agreements were made between employers and home workers. The home worker did not obtain work directly from the manufacturer and knew little or nothing about the real employer's name or address. When a non-payment issue arose, the intermediary often claimed that the business owner (the real employer) did not make the payment, resulting in his own inability to pay. Home workers were unable to verify these claims. Some employers did not provide protective gear appropriate to assignments or information about potential risks. With regard to the remuneration rate, the study found that it was fixed by the employer.[20]

The first Home Work Protection Committee was appointed in 2014. In 2016, it issued a notification on the rate of remuneration to ensure that home workers are paid as prescribed by the law, not less than the minimum wage. A second committee was formed in 2017 and participated in an ILO action research project to enforce the Home Workers Protection Act in Thailand. A third committee was appointed in 2019.

In practice, the Home Workers Protection Act is not fully enforceable, for several reasons. The precise definition of home work and employer remains moot. Ministerial regulations necessary for its enforcement are not fully in place, such as on the nature and type of work forbidden to home workers, as well as the criteria, procedures, and payment for medical care, rehabilitation, and funeral expenses for workers who fall ill, are injured or killed by equipment supplied by the employer or due to the employer's failure to provide necessary protective equipment. Some home workers and employers are unaware of the existence of these laws and the relevant rights of protection and employment supervision. In 2019, the Department of Labour Protection and Welfare was in the process of revising and amending the Home Workers Protection Act B.E. 2553 (2010) in light of the changing employment situation.[21]

---

20 Ibid.

21 An officer of the Department of Labour Protection and Welfare, Ministry of Labour, Thailand, interviewed by the author under the condition of anonymity, Bangkok, 11 August 2019.

5 Social Protection

Home workers are entitled to social protection ranging from health care, income security, and personal development. They receive health and medical welfare and health protection from the National Health Insurance Scheme. They are also covered by the Social Security system, although not on a compulsory basis. A home worker between the ages of 15 and 60 may apply for insurance on a voluntary basis under section 40 of the Social Security Act B.E. 2533 (1990). There are three options to choose from, each with a different rate of contribution and benefits with different levels of government support (Table 9.1).

In addition, the National Savings Fund was created to allow self-employed persons with little or no possibility of access to retirement savings to join, enabling them to receive pensions after the age of 60. Members of the Fund should be between 15 and 60 years of age, and should not be beneficiaries of any other retirement fund with contributions from the state or employers. Each member contributes at least 50 baht monthly to the Fund but not more than 13,200 baht annually. The government will reimburse members according to their age at a rate proportional to their contribution to the Fund. In addition, if in any given year they are unable to contribute, the National Savings Fund will retain their membership but not make contributions on its part.[22]

With regard to accessing funding sources, the Department of Employment, Ministry of Labour has established a revolving fund, from which home workers may request loans for procuring production raw materials and equipment or to extend production for their livelihoods. Those entitled to borrow are individual home workers or groups of not less than five home workers registered at the Department of Employment with specified employers and workplace addresses. The loan ceiling is 50,000 baht for individuals and 200,000 baht for groups. Each loan is charged an annual interest rate of 3 per cent. The loan repayment period is from two to five years. As of 2019, 864 cases of individual/groups of home workers were registered at the Department of Employment, making up a total of 5,508 members. The Department had approved loans to 427 groups to the extent of 41,516,000 baht (US$ 1,367,907.75).[23]

For personal development, home workers receive support from the Ministry of Labour's Department of Skill Development, and training through non-formal and informal education provided by the Ministry of Education.

---

22 National Savings Fund, available at https://eservice.nsf.or.th/privilege/list, last accessed 23 August 2019.

23 An officer of Employment Promotion Division, Ministry of Labour, Thailand, interviewed by the author under the condition of anonymity, Bangkok, 11 August 2019.

TABLE 9.1 Options for contribution payment under section 40 of the Social Security Act B.E. 2533 (1990)

Protection	Option 1	Option 2	Option 3
Contribution to be paid	70 baht per month	100 baht per month	300 baht per month
Subsidy from the government	30 baht per month	50 baht per month	150 baht per month
1. *Compensation for lack of earnings in case of accident/sickness*			
In-patient, hospitalized for at least one day	300 baht a day	300 baht a day	300 baht a day
Out-patient (not hospitalized), with a medical certificate prescribing rest from work for at least three days	200 baht a day	200 baht a day	200 baht a day
Conditions for claiming benefits: number of days for in-patient and out-patient together	Not more than 30 days/year	Not more than 30 days/year	Not more than 90 days/year
Out-patient (not hospitalized), stops work not more than three days (not more than three times a year)	50 baht a day	50 baht a day	Not covered
2. *Compensation for lack of earnings in case of disability*			
Receiving a monthly compensation (amount depending on length of contribution time	500–1,000 baht	500–1,000 baht	500–1,000 baht
Length of time for receiving compensation	15 years	15 years	Lifelong
Funeral grant in case of death during disability	20,000 baht	20,000 baht	40,000 baht
3. *Receiving funeral grant in case of death*			
Funeral grant for the person managing the funeral for the deceased	20,000 baht	20,000 baht	40,000 baht

If contributions were made for 60 months before death, additional payment to be received	Additional 3,000 baht	Additional 3,000 baht	Not covered
4. *Receiving a lump sum together with benefits gained in case of old age*			
Accumulating on a monthly basis toward old age pension (savings) from contributions (receiving upon reaching 60 years of age and at the termination of the insurance period)	Not covered	50 baht	150 baht
When contributions have been made for 180 months, receiving additional money	Not covered	Not covered	Additional 10,000 baht
The ceiling for insured person to contribute additional savings on a monthly basis	Not covered	Additional savings of 1,000 baht	Additional savings of 1,000 baht
5. *Receiving monthly allowance for child subsidy*			
Receiving allowance for child from birth to six years (having paid contributions for 24 out of 36 months)	Not covered	Not covered	200 baht per person (not more than two persons at a time)

Note: Under section 40, the insured person makes a monthly contribution, and can make advance payments for 12 months at a time but not back payments.

6 Transition from the Informal to the Formal Economy

Formalization of the informal economy is based on the idea that the existence of informal work leads to violation of worker rights, and poses an obstacle to decent work and inclusive development. Therefore, it is critical that appropriate measures be established urgently to effect the transition of worker and economic units from informal to formal sectors of the economy.[24] In June 2015, at its 104th session, the International Labour Conference adopted Recommendation 204, concerning the Transition from the Informal to Formal Economy. Its main objectives are to move workers and economic units from the informal to the formal economy, and to prevent informalization of formal economy jobs. Recommendation 204 suggests important principles for the transition to the formal economy, namely, emphasizing the diversity of economic units and workers; designing legal and policy frameworks facilitating the transition; and coordination with national development strategies as well as poverty reduction strategies, inclusive growth, and support for generating decent jobs in all dimensions.[25] It affirms application of the Recommendation through a combination of legal mechanisms, enforcement measures, collective agreement, planning and policy development, coordination between government agencies at different levels and stakeholder groups, building institutional capacity, resource mobilization, and other measures in line with national-level mechanisms and the legislature.

For home work, the transition from informal to formal economy entails an understanding of the diversity of employers, workers, and intermediaries; creating legal and institutional mechanisms to improve access for informal workers to decent work; employment opportunities; labour protection; social protection; rights to organize for better learning and empowerment; promotion and development through collaboration between home workers, employers, and government agencies. This is in consonance with the proposals made by Chen[26] that the transition to the formal economy in the case of home workers

24 International Labour Organization, 2015, p. 4.

25 This covers protection, promotion, and development of informal workers as workers and as individuals, entrepreneurship, organization of workers, coordination of agencies at horizontal and vertical levels; employment policies that promote the generation of jobs in the formal economy, including supporting enterprises of all sizes, employment opportunity service for informal workers, and skills development policies that support lifelong learning; guarantee of rights according to fundamental principles including health, occupational health and safety, and social protection.

26 Martha A. Chen, "Informalization of labour markets: Is formalization the answer?", in S. Razavi (ed.), *The Gendered Impacts of Liberalization: Towards "Embedded Liberalism"?* (New York, 2009), pp. 191–218, pp. 207–08.

implies the existence of regular employment; work and delivery based on clear contracts or documents that ensure legal compliance, timely remuneration, payment on a by-piece basis calculated in line with the minimum wage rate; occupational health and safety measures; home workers' ability to access funding for improving the working environment; and availability of infrastructure services including water, electricity, and sanitation for transforming homes into workplaces. All this complies with the provisions of Convention 117 and Recommendation 184, and may eventually lead to the formulation of a national policy related to home workers. Meanwhile Thailand's Home Workers Protection Act B.E. 2553 (2010) covers almost all of the above-mentioned points except access to funding. Although this category is not mentioned in the Act, in practice a fund exists specifically for home workers, as described above.

Although the transition to the formal economy is definitely beneficial for home workers, the diversity of workers and workplaces means that the transition will move at an unequal pace. Besides, a change to the formal economy means increased costs and small-sized businesses may not be able to shoulder greater burdens. There must be measures to support them and ensure that they can adjust accordingly. In this way, work will be guaranteed and workers can get access to basic rights. Further, the change is not something that can take place overnight. Other work-related dimensions must be taken into account, including cooperation from workplaces, workers, and government agencies. On the other side of the equation, not all business enterprises or workers can adjust to the formal economy. Some of them may be unable to do so.[27]

6.1 *Work and Remuneration of Home Workers: Implications for the Transition from Informal to Formal Economy*

In 2015, the author and a research team embarked on a study, "Setting Remuneration Rates for Home Workers in Thailand".[28] The objectives of the study were to study the work/production process, time used in the work process, and time required to complete tasks for twenty job categories (twenty-six types of jobs) in seven industries; the average time used in work/production processes; and rates of remuneration to be used as a basis for calculating different remuneration rates for each type of job. The study adopted a survey

27 Ibid., p. 211.

28 Narumol Nirathron *et al.*, *Karnsuksakarnkumnod Uttrakatobtan Kongpurubngan-paitumteeban Naipratedtai* [Study on Piece-Rate Setting for Home Workers in Thailand: A research report submitted to the Department of Labour Protection and Welfare] (Bangkok, 2015).

approach in conjunction with inputs from academics, experts, stakeholders, and others from the government and private sector.

There were several constraints in the study process, ranging from defining the population to getting access to home workers and employers, all reflecting how challenging the transition to the formal economy could be. At the level of defining target samples, there were essentially no statistics available for reference on home workers. The sampling population was taken from lists of names of home workers and their employers compiled by the Department of Employment, Department of Labour Protection and Welfare, and Foundation for Labour and Employment Promotion, each having its own agenda for statistical compilation. The combined lists of the three organizations remained insufficient. Further network sampling and snowball sampling were required from home workers and local government agencies, including local government organizations and other local government offices under the Department of Employment, Department of Labour Protection and Welfare, and Community Development Department. Attempts were also made to coordinate with civil society, including the Lampang Ceramic Association, which worked in close contact with enterprises, contractors, and home workers in the ceramic industry in Lampang Province. At the same time, the list of employers compiled by the Department of Labour Protection and Welfare from 2013 to 2015, although fairly substantial, was found to be inadequate. Some employers were no longer in business, while others refused to divulge information. Efforts were made to collect more data, including from home workers, by searching the electronic media. This data collection by diverse means yielded a figure of 3,105 home workers and 226 employers across fifteen provinces in four regions of Thailand. The industries under study comprised: (1) food processing (peeling of toddy palms/shallots [red onions]/water chestnuts/garlic cloves, and gutting of anchovies); (2) textiles (garments, clothing, sewing, weaving, seine-making, and embroidery of head scarves); (3) wood processing and basket work (bamboo and rattan wicker work for general use and for decoration); (4) paper products and artificial flowers (production/manufacturing of artificial flowers and garlands); (5) nonmetal products (bricks, flower pots, stone and plaster sculpting, glass and ceramic products); (6) metal products (knife-making and silver-crafting); and (7) miscellaneous (gemstone-cutting, leather goods, chemical products, rubber and plastic products, children's toys, souvenirs, bedding, electrical appliances, electronic parts, and woven products).

The study found similar characteristics for home workers as indicated in the 2007 survey and 2011 studies.[29] In terms of work and income, the study revealed that 94.3 per cent of the samples accepted jobs from one source. Apart from

29 The study found that 80.7 per cent of home workers were female. Most were 40–49 years old (30.8 per cent), followed by 50–59 years (22.0 per cent), and 30–39 years (21.6 per

home work assignments, other important sources of income derived from agriculture and general hired work. Three important suppliers of work were individual operators, contractors/intermediaries, and group representatives/leaders. Only twenty home workers or 0.64 per cent claimed to have some kind of employment document. Most home workers received payment within seven days of work delivery. The number of workers who reported that there was no change in remuneration over the previous three years was almost the same as home workers who stated that they received higher payments, while some workers received lower remuneration.

Of the twenty-six types of jobs examined in the study, sixteen paid less than minimum wage, including jobs related to food processing and the seine industry. Jobs paying higher than minimum wages were skill-related, such as garments, chicken coops, artificial flowers, doll-making, gem-cutting, plastic basket work, and ceramic moulding, or involved hard work, such as soil preparation, knife-making, and mortar-rolling. A study of the work process showed that most of the jobs could be completed within a day, but some jobs took longer to complete, such as basket work and weaving. The working time for these types of jobs was more difficult to calculate. In some types of jobs, the hirer supplied materials and equipment, and the home worker was not required to pay for them. For home workers who used their own materials, remuneration often did not include the cost of materials.

Thirty-five per cent of home workers joined group memberships, with benefits including loan facilities, training opportunities, and funding support for vocational purposes. Those who were not group members gave the following reasons for not joining: lack of time, lack of awareness of opportunities, and no apparent prospective benefits. A large proportion of home workers, 48.9 per cent, averred that they should participate in fixing remuneration rates, and stated that the main problems they faced in their work were occupational safety and health, lack of regular job supply, low remuneration, and inadequate space at the workplace.

Most of the employers were female, too, aged between 50 and 59. Business owners accounted for the highest proportion among them, followed by group chairpersons. Most of the businesses were private operations, registered or unregistered community enterprises, and companies. The varying conditions of operation among these work suppliers led to differing relationships with the home workers. The reasons for the employers assigning them work

cent). For 64.5 per cent of home workers, primary school was the highest level of education, while 18.1 per cent completed lower secondary school.

included making use of local networks, cost reduction, maintaining low inventory levels, coping with high production demands, outsourcing work not produced by their plants, easing labour shortage problems, and utilizing home worker expertise. Nearly all the employers believed that the wages they paid were appropriate, and most of them disagreed with the notion of adhering to minimum wage laws for home workers. Instead, they asserted, remuneration should be based on actual production time; other considerations could include complexity of work, product price and cost, and mutual agreements reached between employers and home workers including on minimum wages. They were of the opinion that remuneration should be determined by employers and home workers, with input from the government sector and experts. Most employers believed that adhering to the minimum wage rate would lead to an adverse impact. They expected the government to develop measures to mitigate such impact, including lower taxes, compensation for cost differences, and price controls for raw materials.

6.2 *Challenges and Opportunities in the Transition to the Formal Economy: Conclusion and Recommendations*

Judging from the proposed work standards under Convention 177 and Recommendation 184, as well as the overall home work situation in Thailand, work protection and social protection mechanisms, proposed guidelines for transition from the informal to the formal economy, and the study of work processes and home worker remuneration in 2015, it can be concluded that longstanding efforts have been made to protect home workers. Although there have been no formally announced protection mechanisms, movements to advance protection have led to productive results, even before the passage of the Labour Protection Act of 1998. That law makes it clear that home work can be accorded labour protection by ministerial regulations distinct from those generally practised. The Ministerial Regulation on Protection of Home Workers in 2004 and the Home Workers Protection Act that followed in 2010 may be said to have significant implications, by no longer placing the issue solely in governmental hands. A number of international organizations have supported different studies, leading to institutional development and creation of non-governmental organizations (NGOs), and triggering movements for protecting, promoting, and developing home workers, thereby strengthening efforts towards the transition from the informal to the formal economy. The current study by the Home Work Protection Committee for the enforcement of the Home Workers Protection Act is also supported by the ILO.

A number of challenges and opportunities remain for the transition to the formal economy that merit consideration:

1. The foremost challenge is the lack of clear statistics on home workers. Statistics collected by Ministry of Labour agencies do not reflect the real situation of home work, as they are collected for a specific purpose, namely to form groups. In practice there is a real need to conduct a survey of the situation, enumerating home workers and employers, remuneration problems, occupational safety and health, and development needs, to ensure protection, promotion, and development as prescribed by law. Therefore, statistics are an important foundation on which a national home workers policy can be built in accordance with Convention 177.

2. Lack of information on types of work, employment, home workers, and employers. This study confirms that (sub)contracting has spread to several production jobs, including the manufacture of very costly as well as inexpensive products. Information on types of work, employment, and employers is crucial for enabling access to the diverse home workers and employers described in this study. Employers include industries with formal production, personal enterprises, and community enterprises with an informal structure. Home workers differ in age, educational level, and skills. Local agencies are important sources of information on home workers and employers. This is especially pertinent when employers and contractors are local residents. The study also reveals that almost all home workers lack employment documents, reflecting their lack of understanding about worker rights as well as the inequalities in bargaining power between home workers and employers.

3. Lack of information on the role of the intermediary. The study provides insight into the important role of the intermediary, or production subcontracting party, relating to the remuneration received by home workers. Setting fair remuneration rates does not guarantee that the home workers will receive fair payment, as production process stakeholders are not limited to home workers and employers. For this reason, Convention 177 stresses a clear role for the intermediary, while Thailand's Home Workers Protection Act B.E. 2553 (2010) does not attach much importance to this role in terms of setting remuneration rates.

4. The Home Workers Protection Act B.E. 2553 (2010) is incomplete and not adequately enforced. There are still no secondary protective laws on occupational safety and health. Employers and home workers are often unaware of the existence of such laws or deliberately avoid compliance. Many employers are small-sized businesses and community enterprises that may have certain limitations to complying with the law, especially in the areas of remuneration and occupational safety and health. On the home workers' side, it is

difficult to form groups and organizations as the workers are widely scattered and the employers still oppose such unions. Finally, the guarantee of regular work supply is influenced by the economic situation, and is beyond the control of agencies responsible for protecting, promoting, and developing home workers.

5. The persistence of problems and obstacles encountered by home workers. The most serious problems identified by home workers continue to be related to their health and regular work supply, not remuneration. The assistance they most need is regular work supply, remuneration protection, and funding. In most cases, these are beyond the control of agencies concerned with protection, promotion, and development. Regular work supply is just one example. At the same time, protection efforts can lead to greater severity of problems, especially when protection means higher costs with no measures in place to support employer adjustment. Certainly, some problems can be managed by means of the existing support system: for example, assistance in access to funding.

Due to the complex interconnectedness of these issues, coupled with conditions beyond individual control, the transition of home work to the formal economy must proceed with caution. It is also necessary to take into account the diversity of home workers and employers, and different types of work engagement, all reflecting different levels of readiness for the transition to the formal economy. In addition, it is important to understand how consumers seek inexpensive products without realizing that it may be related to labour exploitation.

In terms of opportunities, the results included the following:

1. Local governmental agencies can get access to residents at grassroot levels, such as local community development agencies, agencies promoting non-formal and informal education, and Ministry of Labour agencies. These agencies also work under the supervision of provincial governors in addition to their regular duties, making it possible to collect information on home workers, get access to them, and embark on the task of their promotion and development.

2. There is regular cooperation between government agencies, civil society, and international organizations, as seen in the project called Rural Women Workers in the Putting-out System. Undertaken during 1988–96, the project had a significant impact on knowledge generation and institutional development. The tripartite Home Work Protection Committee can also play an important role in simultaneously protecting, promoting, and developing home workers and promoting employers.

3. Workers in Thailand enjoy fairly comprehensive social protection. Although social security benefits to which home workers are entitled as

insured persons may not be as generous as for formal workers,[30] constant attempts have been made by the government and civil society to advocate for additional benefits.[31] There is also a national health insurance system covering medical care and welfare, in addition to services offering informal education and vocational development. Different studies in some of the provinces reveal that these services can help promote vocational development. Lastly, although regular work supply lies beyond the control of agencies responsible for protecting, promoting, and developing home workers, social protection systems and mechanisms exist to provide support to home workers in skills development, acting as important devices to help them adapt suitably. In terms of home worker development, a Home Worker Fund ensures that promotion and development opportunities will be offered.

The following recommendations are made for the transition of home work to the formal economy, taking into consideration the development of home work protection and promotion, challenges and opportunities.

1. There must be a campaign to convey information about home worker protection directly to stakeholders, including employers, contractors, and intermediaries, about roles, duties, and legal responsibilities. The general public as consumers must properly understand the situation of this group of workers who can be exploited by efforts to reduce production costs and produce cheaper goods.

2. Systematic efforts should be made to survey and compile statistics on home workers and to distribute these to the general public. Local agencies should also participate in collecting data about home workers and employers as well as types of work and employment.

3. Studies should be conducted on home work according to different industries, especially those using a high proportion of home workers, such as textiles and jewellery, and those with low remuneration rates, such as farming. Area-specific studies should also be encouraged. All this will help to create better understanding of the situation and the supply chain of the home-based system in Thailand, particularly in terms of the roles, duties, and responsibilities of stakeholders in the supply chain, involving employers, home workers, and intermediaries. It will also help to encourage industries that are ready for the transition to the formal economy.

---

30 Employees in formal establishments are entitled to seven types of benefits: sickness (non-work-related sickness), maternity, invalidity, death, and survivors' benefits; child allowances; retirement benefits; and unemployment insurance.

31 In 2018, the third payment option was introduced. Workers who choose option 3 are entitled to five types of benefits.

4. Local agencies should be encouraged to collect information on home workers and employers (if possible). In addition, local civil society can play a significant role, as seen in the case of the ceramic association which has information on home workers and employers in the ceramic industry in Lampang Province, in making it possible to access employers, intermediaries, and home workers. Such cooperation will lend useful support to protecting, promoting, and developing home workers.

5. Efforts should be made to encourage home workers forming groups or organizations and to strengthen existing ones, including studying conditions conducive to empowerment and improved working conditions in specific categories.

6. Importance must be attached to protecting occupational safety and health through legal measures and cooperating with local agencies to obtain such advice.

7. Labour protection should be extended to cover group formation and group empowerment to strengthen home workers' bargaining powers, integrating with the work of other agencies especially concerned with promoting and improving home worker knowledge and skills, to be readily equipped when there is a change of employment.

PART 3

CHAPTER 10

Introduction between Citizens' and Workers' Rights

Struggles for the Recognition of Home Workers as Workers

Silke Neunsinger

The history of home work carries with it an important history of resistance that makes an important contribution to labour history in general and, specifically, to feminist labour history. The struggles of home workers—whether in the garment sector of the nineteenth century or in today's digital/internet trade channels—show several similarities, such as that they are all dispersed workers, not identified as "real workers", and that they work from their own homes. But they also provide examples of conditions that can be changed. The history of women workers' resistance has for long been under-researched and has not been incorporated into the narratives of resistance within labour history. Rather, the trope of women workers as being "difficult to organize" has been reproduced in the views of both trade unionists and labour historians. This is all the more so in the case of home workers, as they are stamped as "victims" to be saved by placing a ban on their work, rather than being organized.

The contributions in this section of the book are concerned with the history of the struggles, the resistance and the organizing of home-based workers. The forms of organizing include subcontracted workers and self-employed workers; the latter are not covered either by the ILO Convention on Home Work or by labour legislations where they exist. Both groups of workers have many shared concerns and others that differ. The struggles of home-based workers have often been—and still are—linked to the development of regulations related to home-based work, with the aim to improve working conditions and wages. Grievances, to a large degree, were—and are—concerned with the lack of implementation of existing regulations. Home-based workers have mobilized themselves many times in protest. They have also organized in trade unions, though trade unions have not always supported their struggles, with home workers not being regarded as being real workers. As providers of cheap labour, they were seen to be posing a threat to workers' movements.

The grievances of home-based workers were brought to the table of international trade union organizations early on, only to be largely ignored. However, over the last forty years and more, home workers have again started to organize themselves, with an important impulse for this coming from the organizing

© SILKE NEUNSINGER, 2022 | DOI:10.1163/9789004499614_012
This is an open access chapter distributed under the terms of the CC BY-NC-ND 4.0 license.

of self-employed women in the Self-Employed Women's Association (SEWA) in India from the beginning of the 1970s. As Chris Bonner, who has been a part of this organizing process shows, the growth of home-based work in the world has led to new forms of organizing, often at a regional level, growing from local initiatives, first seen in Asia and spread to Latin-America and Africa, that culminated in the formation of an international network, HomeNet International, launched in February 2021. The new regional organizations, as well as the international network, have come out of collaboration with women unionists in global unions, international trade union confederations and women's organizations. The home-based workers' organizations were mainly led by women and supported by NGOs such as WIEGO (*Women in Informal Employment: Globalizing and Organizing*), whereas formal unions with the exception of the IUF (International Union of Food, Agricultural, Hotel, Restaurant, Catering, Tobacco and Allied Workers' Associations) have not been very supportive.

This section seeks to lay out the contextual background for the current struggles being waged by home-based workers all over the world, and to develop an understanding of the specific forms of resistance developed by informal workers. We would like to point to the fact that this is a category of workers brought into the arena of labour history almost exclusively through the works of labour historians in the global South. The essay by Kalpana in this section especially highlights the importance of looking at the struggles of informal workers, and understanding the success and failure of resistance among home workers, by

FIGURE 10.1 May Day Rally organized by the Home Based Women Workers Federation in Pakistan in 2020 during the pandemic with social distancing

focusing on the relationship between citizens and the state in a typical situation marked by the absence of employers.

1 Cherchez la Femme: A Contribution to Labour History

The resistance of home workers has not been part of mainstream labour history. One of the reasons for this is that home workers were struggling at two ends: against exploitation by their employers and, in the best cases neglect and in the worst cases, the undermining of the importance of their struggles by traditional workers' organizations. Stories of failing solidarity in the trade union movement are in general not part of early trade union historiography. The reason for this is simple: these histories were written by the trade unions themselves, and served to mobilize and keep up a sense of solidarity among existing members of the organization. Despite acquiring the character of chronicles rather than historical accounts, these early works played an important part by laying the ground for later academic research. They have been used to delineate the contours of the struggles waged by these organizations, thereby reproducing the absence of women.

The history of Jeanne Bouvier, analysed by Maria Tamboukou in her essay, illustrates this very well. Bouvier, who had worked as a home worker in the garment industry in Paris, had enough experience of the exploitation, bad working conditions and precariousness of home-based work to put it on the agenda of trade unions not only in France but also at the international level, at platforms of trade union organizations. However, despite being one of the most famous trade unionists internationally in her time, Bouvier was dropped by her male comrades in France and excluded from the arena of international struggles, as the union denied her access to the necessary resources.

The history of Jeanne Bouvier illustrates how home workers were silenced not only within trade unions, but also in history. These women workers and their struggles remained unrecorded and unrecognized, yet feminist labour historians critically questioned the absence of women workers in labour history and looked at alternate sources, going beyond traditional trade union documents and histories.

These conditions show clear similarities with developments in home work in Italy after the Second World War, as Eloisa Betti shows. This study points to the fact that the history of declining home work in Europe after the War needs to be rewritten. In Italy, home work was the backbone of the Fordist system. Betti shows how Italian home workers, for a long time, were hesitant to make their work public. One of the reasons for this was the same as elsewhere: when work moved from factories to private homes in order to lower production costs, there were protests by trade unions, for it would be much more difficult to organize workers in their homes. Clearly, it was the important role played by home work during the industrialization process in Italy after the Second World War that enabled home workers, supported by women's organizations, trade unions and political parties, to protest and change legislation in a way that would place them on an equal footing with factory workers.

2 Grievances of Home Workers

What were the main grievances of home workers and how did these change over time?

The primary grievances of home workers, as in the case of other workers, had to do with time and money. At a later stage they increasingly became concerned with the regulation of home work, and then, over time, with the lack of implementation of the existing framework for regulation of their working conditions.

Maria Tamboukou shows in her essay on Jeanne Bouvier how changes in wages were linked to the vicissitudes of insecure incomes in general. Low wages and long working hours were a real problem. Moreover, conditions in the home-centred industry did not follow a teleological development—of progressing towards improved conditions—but in fact became worse by the beginning of the 1900s as compared to the mid-nineteenth century, especially when it came to working hours. In addition to higher wages and the regulation of working hours, Italian home workers demanded the end of informal working conditions, asking for contracts, health and safety-related precautions, formal rules both for employment and termination of employment, and rights such as sick and pregnancy leave. As was the case with the Parisian *lingères*, Italian home workers fought for job and income security, and against precarious working conditions.

The demands concerned issues of workers' dignity, but they were thereby also demands for recognition as workers by the unions and by the state.

3 Strategies of Resistance

The renewed spread of home-based work in the second half of the twentieth century and its continuing growth in the neoliberal era have at the same had a mobilizing effect on the workers. The chapters in this section suggest that it is resistance and coalition-building that enables these workers to refer to international conventions in advancing their rights and changing their situation.

This section marks an important contribution in the effort to make the longstanding grievances of home-based workers and their history of protests visible. Some of the strategies remained the same even as others were added. The chapters show how home workers organized themselves in their own separate organizations and unions, even as they built alliances or coalitions with women and men from other organizations to highlight their cause.

Home workers have used a range of traditional methods of protest, from spontaneous struggles to organized trade union strikes. These actions served not only to project the demands of home workers in the public domain but also made them visible on the streets. This becomes very clear from the instances of striking Italian home workers. In most cases protesting home workers built alliances, with bourgeois women at the end of the nineteenth century—with female members of the Italian parliament, with membership-based organizations such as Home-net Thailand or WIEGO, and with global unions—to build capacity and greater strength, as Eileen Boris has shown in her chapter on the history of international regulations of home work.

A second important strategy has been the collection of data on the number of home workers, which increased in scale and importance after the Second World War, their wages and working hours, through research and an academic approach. As Tamboukous's chapter focusing on the work of Jeanne Bouvier shows, she drew on data from the mid-nineteenth century to write a history of home work. The international conference on home work held in Brussels in 1910, and the International Office for Industrial Home Work, founded in the process leading up to the conference, illustrate the importance of the approach to measure, analyse and make visible.

4 Outcomes of Resistance

The resistance of home workers has resulted in their recognition as workers both locally and internationally, as many contributions to this volume have shown. Their struggles have also contributed to strengthen the citizens' rights of home workers in negotiations with governments about recognition, and also in relation to social rights. In India, SEWA, for instance, has provided home-based workers with identity cards. Home workers have either managed to be registered as informal workers, like in India, which has improved their status, or they have been recognized as formal workers through the law of 1958 and as factory workers through the law of 1973, like in Italy. In South Africa, home workers have become part of the bargaining machinery of industrial councils; however little is known about the implementation. Over time, the attitude of trade unions towards home workers has changed, especially at the international level. Whereas SEWA was expelled from The Indian Textile Labour Association (TLA), a member of the ITLGWF (International Textile, Garment and Leather Worker's Federation) at the beginning of the 1980s, by 1994 the wheel had turned full circle, and, together with the ICFTU (International Confederation of Free Trade Unions), the IUF (International Union of Food, Agricultural, Hotel, Restaurant, Catering, Tobacco and Allied Workers' Associations) and the ILO, the ITGLWF fully supported an initiative to set up an international network of home workers. Overall, home workers have started to gain a political voice, not least through visibility of the exploitative character of home-based production under neoliberalism. Home-based work is no longer seen as backward but as a convenient form of production for employers. With the spread and growth of this form of work, the resistance that home-based workers have built up over the years has been growing as well. While home-based workers are in the main still not recognized as workers, home workers in supply chains have made some progress towards legal recognition, although implementation remains a problem. The pressure on firms to take responsibility for decent work along supply chains may result in a move to do away with home work altogether.

Finally, this section contributes to giving home workers of the present as well as those from the past a place and a voice in labour history.

CHAPTER 11

Genealogies and Assemblages of Resistance

Jeanne Bouvier's Struggles in 'Le Travail à Domicile'

Maria Tamboukou

This chapter draws on extensive archival research into the papers of Jeanne Bouvier, a French trade unionist and activist in the garment industry at the turn of the nineteenth century.[1] Bouvier was a leading figure in transnational debates around the problem of '*le travail à domicile*' or home work, and throughout her life she struggled to place and maintain home-based work on the agenda of the international labour movement. Her work had a major impact not just on the level of state regulations and labour policies, but also within the academic and intellectual circles of her time. In writing a major economic study of the lingerie industry in France, Bouvier also left her imprint on how the problem of home-based work has been studied, understood, analysed and, most importantly, addressed. Many of these questions that were raised at the turn of the nineteenth century are both pertinent and unresolved even today, and thus a genealogical investigation through the lens of assemblage theories can offer rich and useful insights for contemporary research and policies.

In my research into Bouvier's papers, I have followed genealogical trails of her involvement in the politics of *le travail à domicile* as a worker, as a trade unionist and as the author of a major historical study of the lingerie industry in France.[2] While addressing the question of how to inscribe women workers' resistance within the site of home-based work, I suggest that the notion of assemblage is a useful theoretical tool that can help us rethink resistance in the histories of women's involvement in the garment industry and beyond. As I further discuss later on in the chapter, assemblage approaches highlight material and symbolic entanglements of heterogeneous components through

---

1 This chapter draws on my research project of writing a feminist genealogy of the seamstress, looking at submerged and marginalized histories of women working in the garment industry in the nineteenth and twentieth centuries. See Maria Tamboukou, *Sewing, Fighting and Writing: Radical Practices in Work, Politics and Culture* (London, 2015); *Gendering the memory of work: women workers' narratives* (London, 2016).

2 Jeanne Bouvier, *La lingerie et les lingères* (Paris, 1928).

© MARIA TAMBOUKOU, 2022 | DOI:10.1163/9789004499614_013
This is an open access chapter distributed under the terms of the CC BY-NC-ND 4.0 license.

which provisional entities and relations emerge and throw light on the relations between stability, transformation and change.

The chapter unfolds in three parts: first, I follow genealogical lines of lived experiences in the garment industry; then, I consider agonistic responses to the acute problem of industrial home work through the lens of assemblage theories; and finally, I review Bouvier's historical study of the French lingerie industry as an early exemple of assemblage analytics at work.

1 Genealogies and Archives: Jeanne Bouvier's Lived Experiences of Industrial Home Work

As a Nietzschean insight reconfigured in Michel Foucault's analytics, genealogy is concerned with the processes, procedures and apparatuses whereby truth and knowledge are produced.[3] Genealogy writes the history of the present: it problematizes the multiple, complex and non-linear configurations of the socio-political and cultural formations of modernity. In the context of my research, the questions are as follows: What were the conditions of possibility for industrial home work to emerge as the feminine labour problem par excellence? How has it been marginalized and neglected in the social and political movements of the nineteenth and twentieth centuries? Why is this still a troubling issue dividing state policies as well as the international labour movement? And, finally, how can we reassemble traces of resistance in the writing of feminist labour histories?

In addressing the historicity of such questions and problems of the present, genealogy conceives subjectivities and social relations as an effect of the interweaving of discourses and practices, which it sets out to trace and explore. But instead of seeing history as the continuous development of an ideal schema, genealogy is oriented towards discontinuities. Throughout the genealogical exploration there are frequent disruptions, uneven and haphazard processes of dispersion that call into question the supposed linear evolution of history. Industrial home work is a paradigmatic case of uneven historical developments, and its study seriously deviates from the canon of analysing industrial formations in modernity. As Eileen Boris has aptly pointed out, "the history of industrial home work and its regulation over the last century illustrates the historical construction of gender and the gendering of state action."[4]

3 Michel Foucault, "Nietzsche, Genealogy, History", in Paul Rabinow (ed.), *The Foucault Reader* (Harmondsworth, 1986), pp. 76–100.

4 Eileen Boris, *Home to work: Motherhood and the Politics of Industrial Homework in the United States* (Cambridge, 1994), p. 4.

As a methodological approach, "genealogy is grey, meticulous and patiently documentary";[5] it is the art of archival work par excellence. However, Foucault wrote very little about the nuts and bolts of his archival work. It is from his collaborator Arlette Farge's influential text, *Le Gout de l'Archive*,[6] that we can literally have a taste of some of the theoretical, methodological and affective practices in the archive, and it is from Farge's work that my overall "archival sensibility"[7] vis-à-vis forgotten documents, subsumed life-stories and marginalized figures emerges.

Jeanne Bouvier (1865–1964) was one of those marginalized figures that emerged from the archive of women's work in the garment industry. She was born in the south of France to a peasant family and became a silk worker at the age of eleven after a financial disaster that left her family penniless. In 1879 she moved to Paris, where she worked as a domestic and finally trained as a dressmaker. She got involved in labour politics and became an ardent trade unionist in the French garment industry, as well as a leader in the international women's labour movement. After retirement she threw herself in the pleasures of research and wrote four historical studies, as well as her *Mémoires*.[8]

A leitmotif that runs through Bouvier's writings is the problem of industrial home work: it becomes a refrain, a theme that is repeatedly experienced, narrated, contested, analysed, theorized, understood. Her work became so influential that research students would ask her for help and advice: "I am a law student doing my doctoral thesis on the application of the July 10, 1915 law on the minimum salary of industrial home workers", Jeanne Odry wrote to Bouvier, asking for information given her great "competence in the subject".[9] In a later letter she wrote that her thesis had been successfully defended, thanks to Bouvier's invaluable advice and help.[10] Bouvier's papers at the Bibliothèque Historique de la ville de Paris (BHDP) include a series of lengthy letters from researchers asking for her advice, mostly about women's work, well before any

5 Foucault, "Nietzsche, Genealogy, History", p. 76.

6 Arlette Farge, *Le goût de l'archive* (Paris, 1986).

7 Niamh Moore, Andrea Salter, Liz Stanley and Maria Tamboukou, *The Archive Project: Archival Research in the Social Sciences* (London, 2016).

8 Jeanne Bouvier, *Mes Mémoires: Une syndicaliste féministe, 1876–1935* (Paris, 1983 [1936]).

9 Jeanne Odry to Bouvier, Paris, 12 June [no year], Bibliothèque Historique de la Ville de Paris, Archives Marie-Louise Bougle, Fonds Jeanne Bouvier [hereafter BHVP/AMB/FJB], Boite 18, Le Travaille à Domicile.

10 Odry to Bouvier, Paris, 4 February [no year], ibid. Although there is no year in the date of the letter, we know that Odry's thesis was published in 1924. See Jeanne Odry, *Application de la loi du 10 juillet 1915 sur le salaire minimum des ouvrières à domicile* (Paris, 1924).

of her own books had been published. This is what Paul Boyaval, a well-known writer on the home sweating system, wrote to her in December 1920:

> Dear Mademoiselle Bouvier,
>
> Perhaps you still remember the undersigned author of a thick volume entitled "The Struggle against the Sweating System" that I had the pleasure to address to you as a tribute in 1912.
>
> Unfortunately, I have been at war for five years and I was not able to continue following this scary problem of domestic work. I would now like to study the question at the point where it was in 1912 and I could not think of a better person than you to brief me on the current situation of the problem and on everything that has been done on this subject in the last ten years.[11]

It is not surprising that so many researchers got interested in the phenomenon of industrial home work at the turn of the nineteenth century. What is particular to Bouvier, however, is that it became the focal point of her lifelong struggles and agonistic politics. Among the two boxes of her correspondence (Boîte 17/1-2) there is a special Dossier (3) on her epistolary communication with international syndicalists, including letters from the US, the UK, Canada, Argentina, Chile, China, Austria, Belgium, Italy, Spain, Switzerland and the Netherlands. Boîte 18 on "La Travail a Domicile" additionally includes letters from Poland, while Boîte 23/Dossier 2 includes all the proceedings and reports from the 1919 Washington conference and the International Federation for Working Women (IFWW) that was subsequently established. Let us then trace this leitmotif to its beginning, Bouvier's experiences as a child worker in the silk factories of her home region, Le Dauphiné.

Bouvier's initiation into the hardships of industrial home work was a direct consequence of the financial disaster that befell her family due to a phylloxera infestation that made them sell everything and dislocated them to a nearby village, Saint-Symphorien-d'Orzon. It was there that Bouvier started working in a silk-throwing factory: "My parents, who until then had lived in relative comfort, were forced to sell everything: house, meadow, vineyard and even furniture and various belongings. [...] It was a disaster",[12] she wrote in her memoirs.

From the very beginning of her life as a silk worker Bouvier learnt that there were no laws to protect children at work, and even if there was some kind of

11 Paul Boyaval to Bouvier, 23 December 1920, BHVP/AMB/FJB/, Correspondance, Boite 17.2.

12 Bouvier, *Mes Mémoires*, pp. 55–56.

restrictive legislation, it was never applied. "A law had been passed in 1840 making it illegal to have children under the age of 12 work more than 8 hours, but it was never enforced. This is why I was working 13 hours", she wrote.[13] Her workday started at 5 in the morning; there was a break for *la soupe* at 8 a.m. and another break at midday for *le déjeuner*. Despite the five extra hours she was illegally made to work for, her wages were not enough to bring food to her family who were dependent on her, since her father had abandoned them very soon after their internal migration. "I was proud to bring my mother the fruits of my labour",[14] she wrote, but she also had to work at home to supplement their meagre income; despite her efforts bread was still scarce in the family:

> I remember one time amongst others when I went without eating for nearly two days. That evening when I came home from the factory, I started to work. My mother spent the night with me, shaking me whenever, in spite of myself, I began to fall asleep. She was telling me, "Don't fall asleep. You know very well that you mustn't sleep. Tomorrow we won't have any bread." I was making superhuman efforts to stay awake. It was very cold. Snow was falling against the windowpanes. Despite all this torture I continued to work until 4.30 in the morning, at which time I got ready to return to the factory.[15]

Bouvier's first job in the garment industry of Paris, where she moved in 1879, was at a milliner's atelier. She was happy there, in the company of so many fellow-workers. She picked up the milliner's skill easily and soon began to earn "a reasonable livelihood".[16] But her wage cycle followed the seasonal rhythms of the trade: "In the high season, my wages went from 30 to 40 francs a week, and sometimes up to 45, to drop back to 12 or 15 francs in the low season."[17] The fluctuations in her earnings, and particularly the need to save for the lean season, led her to take on additional sewing work at home: "I was able to make aprons, skirts, caracos and camisoles",[18] she wrote. It was not only the daily bread, but also the need to have a home of her own that made her take on extra home work: "I continued to live frugally and was still doing extra work to keep myself afloat. I wanted to move for I wanted a room with a fireplace.

13 Ibid., p. 57.
14 Ibid.
15 Ibid., p. 59.
16 Ibid., p. 81.
17 Ibid.
18 Ibid., p. 85.

Yes, I wanted to offer myself the luxury of a fireplace."[19] When she finally lost her job as a milliner due to the many crises that the Parisian garment industry went through at the turn of the century, industrial home work became a means of survival. Bouvier has vividly recounted her experience of sewing plackets on corsets, along with a neighbour-friend, in her *Mémoires*:

> We would get up early and sleep late. When the work was finished, we went to the employer to return it; he told us that he would pay us 11.50 francs for the work, but after the cost of the ribbon was deducted, only 4 francs remained for us! And we had worked for two days from 5 o'clock in the morning till 10 o'clock at night! Judging this work as very bad, we did not take it up again![20]

It is interesting that Bouvier's reminiscences of industrial home work conclude with a decision "not to take it up again". This was a choice not open to everyone. Bouvier's contemporary, Marguerite Audoux, who also had an ugly taste of industrial home work as a newcomer in the fashion metropolis at the turn of the twentieth century, wrote: "On my arrival in Paris, I had to earn my living at all costs, and I had to accept any kind of needlework that was offered."[21] Bouvier was not a newcomer in Paris when she took the decision to turn down industrial home work for its abject conditions. And yet, throughout her life, even after she had found a position in an atelier and become a successful dressmaker, she would always work at home to supplement her income and as a cushion for hard times:

> For some time, I had clients who would have me work at their homes during the lean season. I would thus escape the period of unemployment, which gave me a certain comfort. In this way, I never missed work. But during the high season, these clients brought me additional work. Apart from the days spent at the atelier, I always had some orders to do at home to satisfy my personal clientele. After my workday I therefore had to impose long late-night vigils on myself. My time was divided up like that: get up at 4 o'clock; work at home until 8; then get ready and have breakfast within half an hour; at 8.30 leave for the atelier, where I arrived at 9 o'clock and left only at 8 or 9 in the evening. I would rush home, eat

19 Ibid., p. 88.
20 Ibid., p. 86.
21 Marguerite Audoux, *Marie-Claire's Workshop*, trans. Frank. S. Flint (New York, 1920), p. 119.

> dinner in a hurry, and get back to work until midnight, when I finally went to bed, to sleep till 4 o'clock in the morning.[22]

What emerges from Bouvier's recollections of her solitary bio-labour rhythms, as forcefully recounted above, is that while in classical Marxist analysis the industrial conception of time is based on the requirement that "the worker relinquishes formal control over his or her labour time during the stipulated workday by exchanging it for pay",[23] things become much more complicated in the temporal organization of industrial home work. Historically, men have also worked at home-based sweatshops; but unlike women who have welcomed it as an opportunity, its drudgeries notwithstanding, men have always resisted work at home. As Joan Scott has noted in her influential study of the politics of work and family in Parisian trades of the nineteenth century, working at home was not a central issue or a problem *per se* for Parisian seamstresses.[24] Rather, they were concerned with seeking regulation of home-based work and especially higher wages, as arrangements of working from home not only enabled them to work and look after their family, but also safeguarded their professional identities as qualified seamstresses. Tailors, on the other hand, were very much against home-based work and fought for the right to do work only at workshops. In their context, it was shop-based work that protected their professional identity and not the level of wages. Nancy Green has further shown that such debates were carried on in the trade unions of the Parisian garment industry in the first half of the twentieth century, which nevertheless remained unregulated overall: "While workers, unions and the state sought greater protection and standards for labour conditions, the garment industry remained reticent to restrictive rules."[25] Moreover, home-based women needleworkers came to represent "the opposite of the atheist, materialist worker of the revolutionary committees"[26] in the socialist political discourse of their times.

There is a distinct gender issue here, which, as Scott has argued, has been largely ignored by labour historians: the way the home has been historically constituted as a desired workplace for women, and thus created the possibility of conflation of waged and unwaged labour for women, right up to the

22 Bouvier, *Mes Mémoires*, pp. 97–98.

23 Samuel Bowles and Herbert Gintis, *Schooling in Capitalist America* (London, 1976), p. 57.

24 Joan W. Scott, *Gender and the Politics of History* (New York, 1988).

25 Nancy Green, *Ready to Wear, Ready to Work: A Century of Industry Immigrants in Paris and New York* (Durham and London, 1997), p. 84.

26 Cited in Judith Coffin, *The Politics of Women's Work: The Parisian Garment Trades, 1750–1914* (Princeton, 1996), p. 175.

present day.[27] Women's memories of work bring this neglected dimension of the political economy of work to the surface and show that there is a marginalized genealogy of struggles, such as Bouvier's life-long passion for the regulation and protection of industrial home work—*le travail à domicile*—to which I now turn.

2 Bouvier's Agonistic Politics and Assemblage Theories

As Bouvier has recounted in her memoirs, it was through her conversations with enlightened bourgeois women that she learnt about trade unionism and feminism as options in her life of struggle:

> In 1897, a feminist journal was launched by Mme Marguerite Durand: *La Fronde,* a daily edition on feminist rights. [...] One of my clients, Mme Norat, was an ardent feminist. She became an assiduous reader of this journal and while I was trying her dresses, she would be talking to me about women's rights and the injustices of the law with regard to women. In this way, every fitting session was a lesson in feminism. [...] One day she told me: "I am surprised that an intelligent woman like you has not subscribed to the union of your trade. [...] There is a trade union for seamstresses, *lingères* and similar parties. I often see notifications of this union in *La Fronde.*" There was indeed a campaign in *La Fronde* for women workers to become union members. This invitation to unionize seemed to me extraordinary. Unionize? Me? Why? I confess, I did not understand anything. The very idea seemed strange to me. But the lady was tenacious and every time we met, she would ask me: "Well, Mademoiselle Jeanne, have you become a member of the union yet?"[28]

Bouvier's encounter with an enlightened middle-class feminist actively propagating syndicalism was not accidental. There was a lot of agitation and a number of rebellious strikes in the garment industry in the first decade of the twentieth century, where women needleworkers took centre stage.[29] In doing so, they followed a genealogical line of agonistic politics that went back to the July monarchy and the emergence of the first autonomous

27 Scott, *Gender and the Politics of History*, p. 93.
28 Bouvier, *Mes Mémoires*, p. 101.
29 See, amongst others, Green, *Ready to Wear, Ready to Work*; Tamboukou, *Gendering the Memory of Work*.

feminist movement in France, which was led by seamstresses.[30] Gender relations within the garment industry, as well as within the trade unions, were at the forefront of the confrontation and thus attracted a lot of attention from various feminist groups active in Paris at the time. Marguerite Durand and the group around *La Fronde* actively supported the women strikers, making connections with wider feminist demands. As Coffin has succinctly put it, "*La Fronde* saw the [1901] strike as a *feminine prise de parole,* a demonstration of women workers' seriousness of purpose and capacities for public action and speech."[31]

But these strikes were also the reason for Bouvier's initial resistance to the idea of joining the union. "The *Bourse du Travail* was not totally unknown to me", she wrote,[32] linking it to the revolutionary moments when workers had joined students at the barricades of the *Quartier Latin.* "These memories of the *Bourse du Travail* were not exactly a sufficient recommendation for my participation in the seamstresses' union", she boldly concluded.[33] Here again, Bouvier's aversion to syndicalism due to the dark memory of its riots had been recognized as a problem by the sociologists of her time. As Aline Valette, a feminist social reformer and factory inspector, wrote in *La Fronde* in 1898, women needleworkers were particularly difficult to unionize: "Their isolation makes them believe that they are totally and perpetually powerless, and they back off from any initiative."[34]

Despite her initial scepticism, however, Bouvier not only joined the union but soon rose in its hierarchy and became one of its few women leaders, not only in France but in the international workers' movement. Her papers include many letters from women trade unionists all over the world with whom she was in correspondence throughout her life, and some of whom she would meet in person when they happened to visit Paris. Below is a letter that Mary Anderson, Director of the Women's Bureau of the US Department of Labour, sent Bouvier on 20 May 1926, by way of introducing two friends, Amy G. Maher and Rachel Gallagher, who would be coming to Paris for the International Meeting of Women's Suffrage and who were interested in investigating the conditions of women workers in industry in France.

30 See Tamboukou, *Sewing, Fighting and Writing.*
31 Coffin, *The Politics of Women's Work,* p. 178.
32 Bouvier, *Mes Mémoires,* p. 101.
33 Ibid., p. 102.
34 Aline Valette, "Le Travail des femmes: Ouvrières et syndicats", *La Fronde,* 10 July 1898.

> My dear Mlle Bouvier:
>
> This letter will introduce you to Miss Amy G. Maher and Miss Rachel Gallacher, both from Toledo, Ohio. Miss Maher is the Chairman of the Ohio Council of Women and Children. This Council is composed of the different women's organizations in the State, together with the State Federation of Labour and their work, no doubt as Miss Maher will explain. Miss Gallacher is Miss Maher's very able assistant. They are both very anxious to see the labour movement of France and if there are any meetings which interested persons may attend, they may be allowed to do so.[35]

Not only did Bouvier meet the two women from Ohio, she also developed a life-long correspondence with Maher, who kept sending her personal letters and Christmas cards till the end of her life. They can now be found in the two boxes holding Bouvier's correspondence; the fact that she kept and filed them among her papers is a mark of their emotional importance in the solitude of her life.[36] For Bouvier, working with and developing personal friendships within a network of international women was amongst the pleasures of being a feminist and a trade- unionist. It was these friendships and connections that kept her going through difficult times with her comrades in France. "Thank you so much for your lovely New Year's Card. I was so pleased to get it and hear from you again. I know we have so much in common and are never able to express it to one another",[37] Anderson wrote to her on 15 January 1925.

It was indeed Bouvier's struggles for the regulation of home-based work that made her internationally famous. Her papers reveal how methodically and tirelessly she worked throughout her life, to put industrial home work on the agenda of French and international labour policies and politics. As already noted in the previous section, the phenomenon of industrial home work was deeply embedded in the traumatic memories and experiences of her own working life.

> I could not stay indifferent to these miseries, which reminded me of those I had suffered in my childhood, when there was no bread in my paternal home. Those sad memories of days without bread and without fire, when I was obliged to work late and sometimes throughout the night

35 Mary Anderson to Bouvier, 20 May 1926; there is an English version of this letter in Bouvier's papers, but with an earlier date, 18 April 1926. See BHDP/AMB/FJB, Correspondance, Boite 17.2.

36 BHDP/AMB/FJB, Correspondance, Boite 17.1.

37 Anderson to Bouvier, 15 January 1925, BHDP/AMB/FJB, Correspondance, Boite 17.2.

> so that my family could eat the following day; all these memories made me stand in solidarity with all the distressing reports I was reading in the newspapers.[38]

Memories of work here become a plane for sustaining class consciousness, and inspiring resistance and political action. It was from the position of an organic intellectual that Bouvier had intervened in the formation of discourses and policies around this major labour issue of her time. In doing so, she particularly referred to the first international conference on industrial home work held in Brussels in 1910, where the International Office for Industrial Home Work was founded.[39] She became a member of its French branch and represented France as an elected delegate at the second conference held in Zurich in 1912. It was this conference that largely prompted the 1915 law, which attempted to regulate unregulated spheres of work. While giving a concise and clear picture of the international efforts and debates, Bouvier also poignantly pointed to the failure of the syndicalist movement to understand and engage with the problem. "They were not interested in this important question. Their disinterest was carried to the point of completely ignoring the functions of the law and in effect becoming prejudiced against the interests of home-based workers", she wrote.[40]

Bouvier was absolutely furious with the consequences of such indifference, negligence and injustice; she knew from her own experience that industrial home work was a sphere that many women needleworkers would enter at some point in their lives, whether single, married or widowed, and whether or not they worked in workshops and ateliers. It is therefore not surprising that like many other women trade unionists, Bouvier fell out with the leadership of the Confederation General du Travail (CGT). Her *Mémoires* include a copy of a letter she received on 26 February 1923, through which, and without any prior consultation, her male comrades crudely announced their decision to remove her from the administrative committee of the Clothing Federation, although she was the only woman ever to have been elected to this position. They also asked her to step down from her position as the Vice-President for France of the International Federation for Working Women (IFWW): "I was undesirable on the national and international level", Bouvier bitterly noted.[41] Writing from London, the IFWW secretary Marion Phillips would express her deep

38 Bouvier, *Mes Mémoires*, p. 150.
39 Ibid., p. 151.
40 Ibid., p. 153.
41 Ibid., pp. 139–40.

regret, "fully shared by the Executive Board",[42] about the fact that she would no longer represent France. So deep was Bouvier's conflict with the CGT leadership that they even refused to cover her travelling expenses to attend the third International Women Workers' Congress (IWWC) held in Vienna in 1923, and it was this issue that Phillips' letter tried to resolve: "I am not sure what exactly the situation is about the expenses. I expect that since the CGT won't pay them, you will let me know the total sum so that the Federation can compensate you. It is our duty since you were acting in your role as our Vice-President."[43]

Although the details of Bouvier's friction with the CGT are not fully apparent in her *Mémoires*, the letters she exchanged with some of her ex-comrades are revealing. They also contain traces of a bitterness she wished to archive rather than write about. "I do not want to represent a Federation whose executive committee judged and condemned me without allowing me to defend myself", she wrote in response to a request to represent the Federation in the Conseil du Travail in April 1925.[44] It was at this time that Bouvier threw herself into the historical studies that made her a writer, the topic of the third part of her *Mémoires*. She bitterly noted, reflecting on her own experience of the French labour movement:

> Due to my estrangement from workers' organizations, I was able to work in tranquillity on historical questions which interested me and more particularly on women's work. In the silence of the library and the solitude of my home, I could see the state of inferiority women held within workers' organisations.[45]

Bouvier's multilayered experiences of industrial home work throughout her working life open up new avenues in feminist labour histories. My point here is that feminist analyses of women's work in its various modes and manifestations, classical, Marxist or otherwise, have been dominated by structuralist ideas, concepts and dualisms: waged/unwaged, paid/unpaid, production/reproduction, home/factory, local/global, to name but the obvious. A Hegelian either/or connects and separates these issues. And yet the phenomenon of industrial home work is much more complex and cannot really fit into any of the boxes or dualisms that have been deployed in attempts to analyse and understand it.

42 Marion Phillips to Bouvier, 13 September 1923, BHDP/AMB/FJB, Correspondance, Boite 17.2.

43 Ibid.

44 Bouvier to Camarade Manebus, 13 April 1925, ibid.

45 Bouvier, *Mes Mémoires*, pp. 145–46.

What I therefore want to suggest is that the notion of *assemblage*[46] can be a useful theoretical lens with which to grasp and analyse the multiplicities and complexities of industrial home work. But what is assemblage?

Unlike closed organisms, structural systems and fixed identities, assemblages do not have any organizing centre; they are rather networks of connections, always in flux, assembling and reassembling in different ways. Assemblages are thus emergent features of relationships and can only function as they connect with other assemblages in a constant process of becoming. Seen in this light, some of the components of the industrial home work *assemblage* would be labour power, fluctuating salaries and wages, domestic tasks, motherhood, gender relations, love, caring labour, state regulations, legal reforms and trade union politics, amongst others. Drawing on aspects of Deleuze and Guattari's analytics, Manuel DeLanda has further elaborated the theory of assemblages as a new philosophical understanding of social entities that "should account for the synthesis of the properties of a whole not reducible to its parts".[47] Conceived as a theory of "wholes whose properties emerge from the interactions between parts",[48] the assemblage approach offered by DeLanda particularly looks into the historically difficult problem of micro/macro relations, and therefore gives "a sense of the irreducible social complexity characterizing the contemporary world".[49]

As an assemblage of multiple problems and practices, roughly delineated above, *le travail à domicile* included capitalist and gender labour relations but was not reduced to these. There were also other issues to be considered. Boris has influentially mapped different sites and contexts of industrial home work conditions in the USA at the turn of the century.[50] In the context of the French garment industry, Judith Coffin has pointed to "subcontracting, piecework, artisanal autonomy and the regulation of the labour market";[51] I would add seasonal unemployment, lack of health insurance and pensions, the problems of widows and of unmarried women workers. To these economic, social, political and cultural components, we should also add emotions and affects, which are densely entangled in the assemblage of social inequality.

46 Gilles Deleuze and Felix Guattari, *A Thousand Plateaus: Capitalism and Schizophrenia*, trans. Brian Massumi (London, 1988 [1980]).

47 Manuel DeLanda, *A New Philosophy of Society: Assemblage Theory and Social Complexity* (London, 2006), p. 4.

48 Ibid., p. 5.

49 Ibid., p. 6.

50 Boris, *Home to work*.

51 Coffin, *The Politics of Women's Work*, p. 187.

Theorized within the framework of the assemblage, women's work emerges as a complex entanglement of some of the components already identified above, which make specific connections with other components within the assemblage, but also develop external relations with components of other assemblages: colonialism, migration, race relations, national and international economic crises, sex work, homelessness, family histories and moral panics, to name but the most striking. It is precisely the complexity of the phenomenon of industrial home work and its multifarious entanglements and connections with capitalism, colonialism and patriarchy that have historically rendered it such a difficult issue to grasp, understand and, most importantly resist. Boris's influential work[52] has already initiated the need for interdisciplinary conceptualizations of the home/work continuum, so I consider my suggestion of the assemblage as a contribution in continuation of such a line of thought in feminist labour histories.

What, then, are the implications of working with assemblage theories? A central task of the analysis would be to make specific cartographies of situated phenomena and problems, trace the connections they make in order to configure emerging new formations, but also follow their "lines of flight", since for Deleuze and Guattari, society is not so much defined by its molar formations and their dialectical oppositions but rather by what has escaped them, not the molar socio-cultural entities but the molecular counter-formations, the lines of flight.[53] It is by thus following "lines of flight" in the assemblage of industrial home work that I now consider Jean Bouvier's early theorization of the French lingerie industry as an exemplar of an assemblage *avant la lettre.*

3 Writing as a Modality of Resistance

In the last pages of her *Mémoires*, Bouvier wrote about the pleasures of intellectual work that she immersed herself in during the fifty-nine years of her long working life and after she had stepped down from her position in the CGT, in 1923. Bouvier's agonistic politics went hand in hand with hard work and intense intellectual activity, all beautifully recounted in her *Mémoires*, which was the last volume she published, in 1936, after a series of four historical studies on women's work, economics and politics, as already noted above.

52 Boris, *Home to work*.

53 Deleuze and Guattari, *A Thousand Plateaus*, p. 216.

What were the conditions that made it possible for such creative forces to be unleashed? As Bouvier wrote in her *Mémoires*, it was the law that regulated the work day to eight hours after the First World War that allowed workers time for intellectual activity.[54] It was also after the war that Georges Renard, professor of labour history at the Collège de France, took up the task of editing the 58-volume *La Bibliothèque sociale des metiers* [The Social Library of the Trades]. There were seven volumes on women in this collection: *La Lingerie* (by Jeanne Bouvier); *Fleurs, Plumes, Modes* (by Marguerite Boural); *La Dentelle* (by Mathilde Parat); *Les Gens de Maison* (by Mme Moll-Weiss); *L'Instutrice* (by Marguerite Bodin); *Tabac et Allumettes* (by Mme Claude Réal); and *Le Cinéma* (by Mme Germaine Dulac). The titles of these seven volumes commissioned to women are very interesting in terms of the gendered cultural politics of the first half of the twentieth century in France, but the mere fact that women were considered to be authors of studies in the history of work is, I think, important in the context of their environment and times. What is also worth noting is that Bouvier was the only woman worker who was asked to write a history of the *lingères*, an occupational group among French garment workers that was always at the bottom of the strict hierarchy of the trade.

Since the spirit behind Renard's edited collection was that all volumes were to be authored by field experts, the fact that Bouvier was chosen was not surprising. Although she had already become a skilled dressmaker by the time she was asked to write the history of the *lingères*, a *couturière* working in highly esteemed Parisian ateliers, she was also a militant activist in the *lingerie* trade union and a leading figure in the French federation of garment workers. She had served on the *Conseil Supérieur du Travail* in 1909, while in 1913 the Labour Minister asked her to carry out a comprehensive review of the conditions of industrial home work in France. Bouvier's status in the French labour aristocracy was thus the end-point of a long process that beautifully unfolds through the pages of her memoir. Yet, the invitation to write a book made her feel utterly out of her depth:

> When alone, I was thinking: "M. Georges Renard has been deluded about my value and my knowledge. No, it is not possible for me to accept to write a book, I have always suffered due to my ignorance. [...] How can I write the history of the *lingerie* and its workers?" It is true that in the course of my long career as a trade unionist I got to know the social questions for

54 Bouvier, *Mes Mémoires*, p. 213.

> better or for worse; but to translate them on paper and compose them in a book seemed an insurmountable task![55]

Despite the difficulty, however, Bouvier threw herself into the pleasures of research, and not only did she manage to write a history of *lingerie* and *lingères*, but when she had completed working on the manuscript and proudly took it to the editor, she actually found that she had to reduce its length as there was a page limit she had forgotten about. "I, who had thought myself incapable of writing a book because I didn't know how to put it together, had gone beyond the prescribed limit!"[56] she wrote in astonishment. The book comprises three parts. The first looks at the history of *lingerie* in terms of its antiquity, the sumptuary and protective laws, and the different pieces of *lingerie*. The second part is about the professional organization of *lingères* in the old regime up until the 1789 revolution, while the third part follows the journey of *lingerie* in the nineteenth and twentieth centuries. Since the initial manuscript as well as the author's notes have been kept among Bouvier's *Fonds*, today's researcher can see not only the amount of work that had to be removed from the final version, but also the fine character of Bouvier's final draft in terms of content as well as literary style.[57]

What is particularly interesting in the first part of the book is the meticulous way in which Bouvier presented the different historical phases of the trade, but also how carefully she traced the genealogy of various pieces of *lingerie*, highlighting their importance in the history of the garment industry. In tracing the micro-histories of garments, Bouvier used a variety of sources including archaeological evidence, such as mirror paintings and hieroglyphics. She also drew on literature, including theatrical playscripts and the Bible, as well as a wide range of archival sources that she studied at the French National Archives. Bouvier's meticulous research is thus an early contribution in the now bursting field of cultural studies, but it is more than that: in tracing the rich genealogy of her trade, she created an archive that would sustain and support women workers' awareness of their active contribution in the history of civilization. Also, it was not only the history of clothes and fashion in general, and *lingerie* in particular, that Bouvier was interested in. She also studied the economic history of the trade, focusing specifically on the emergence of laws regulating the fashion industry in terms of consumption. In doing so, she examined gender- and class-driven strategies and regulations, but also traced

55 Ibid.

56 Ibid., p. 216.

57 BHVP/AMB/FJB, *La lingerie et les lingères*, Manuscrit original, Boite 10.

early signs of biopolitics as well as the effects of an emerging global market on the lives of the working people.

Apart from the economics, technological changes and diversity of products in the *lingerie* industry, Bouvier also looked into the history of its women workers, the *lingères*. According to the guild records there were around 700 *lingères* mistresses in Paris before the revolution, but the total number of workers had never been calculated, Bouvier observed.[58] As Clare Crowston has noted in her history of the seamstresses' guild under the old regime, clandestine production was part of the labour economy in the clothing industry, but it went completely out of control after the dissolution of the guilds and the domination of free market forces.[59] Thus, the difficulty of knowing the exact number of *lingères* working in France in general, and in Paris in particular, was recorded as a recurrent problem in Bouvier's study of the history of the trade in the nineteenth and twentieth centuries. In support of her argument, she pointed to how *lingères* were absent from previous investigations, and particularly to discrepancies and inconsistencies in the national registers and records. For example, only 300 *lingères* were recorded across France in the period 1840–45, a ridiculous number especially when compared with the 10,110 *lingères* recorded in 1851 in Paris alone.[60]

It was not only the number of *lingères*, but also their wages and their social position that were obscured. It was thanks to some "fraternal spirits that their misery, that all their sufferings occasionally came to light", Bouvier noted.[61] She drew on Charles Dupin's[62] studies to highlight the fact that in the course of merely five years, between 1815 and 1820, the famous Salpêtrière had hospitalised 2,641 women for having lost their minds. Among them were 735 *lingères* and *couturières*, 104 embroiderers and 112 laundresses. There were also 247 workers from other trades and 4 women who were property owners.[63] These numbers showed the alarming effects of industrial home work on women needleworkers, and created the background for female labour to become the predominant social problem referred to in nineteenth-century discourses and practices.[64]

58 Bouvier, *La lingerie et les lingères*, p. 231.

59 Claire Haru Crowston, *Fabricating Women: The Seamstresses of Old Regime France, 1675–1791* (London and Durham, 2001).

60 Bouvier, *La lingerie et les lingères*, p. 238.

61 Ibid.

62 Charles Dupin was a moral economist, whose book, *Forces productives et commerciales de la France*, published in 1827, had made an impression in the first decades of the nineteenth century.

63 Bouvier, *La lingerie et les lingères*, p. 232.

64 See Jules Simon, *L'ouvrière* (Paris, 1862).

In trying to unearth the socio-historical, economic and political conditions that created such unbearable conditions for the *lingères*, Bouvier devoted a whole chapter to *travail à domicile,* carefully defining its nature, function and economics:

> The *travail à domicile* is work distributed to workers by an industrialist or a merchant, who then sell the manufactured objects. It is veritable industrial work. In opposition to work at the atelier, which is called centralized work or agglomerated industry, M. Georges Renard called the *travail à domicile* decentralized work or dispersed industry.[65]

In defining the term 'industrial home work', Bouvier further examined the gendered genealogy of this trade, tracing it back to the Middle Ages, when St Bernadier de Sienne had written: "Oh women, women! If one took one of your garments and *wrung* it, they would see the blood of God's creatures coming out of it."[66] But although the history of the trade goes well back in history, it was only in the middle of the nineteenth century, in 1858, that a comprehensive review of the conditions of *lingères* in Lille was conducted by M. Auvray. This study gives a full-fledged description of the *lingères*' actual labour process, which included pulling threads, fitting pattern pieces, matching seams and stitching them together.[67] Auvray's study also included an account of the *lingères*' daily activities, particularly emphasizing the intensity of their working hours: "The worker who dedicates 10 hours a day to her task earns 1.75 francs per day but she has to deduct a quarter of it for periods of unemployment or times of illness."[68] There was also an exact calculation of the time the workers needed to clean their homes, do their laundry, and make and mend the family's clothes. Finally, it had details of their daily meals as well as the overall organization of their household including room plans, furniture and home ware.

Apart from the biopolitics of this early study of the lingerie, what is striking about it is that home and work could not be separated from the very beginning of this trade: industrial home work was presented as an assemblage where waged and unwaged labour as well as productive and reproductive practices were tightly interwoven within the political economy of women's work, and has remained so till today as already noted in the previous section. There is a rich body of feminist literature around these issues, where Marxist analyses

65 Bouvier, *La lingerie et les lingères*, pp. 252–53.
66 Cited in ibid., p. 254.
67 Ibid., p. 264.
68 Ibid., p. 265.

have been influential in the way we make sense of the complexities of women's labour practices. Questions that still remain central in this area derive from different philosophical approaches to the concepts of work, reproduction and care, as well as the thorny relations between women's oppression, gendered labour and the class politics of the left.[69] In the context of this literature, Kathi Weeks has observed that "there is a lack of attention to the lived experiences and political textures of work within political theory".[70]

Bouvier's study addressed such omissions not just in political theory, but also in labour history, fighting against abstract representations of work in general and gendered labour in particular. As Katerina Kolozova has succinctly noted, abstraction lies at the heart of Marx's critique of capitalist exploitation in general and fetishization in particular.[71] When work loses the visceral elements of its reality, "the physical and sensuous" according to Marx,[72] it becomes a symbolic representation "more real that the real".[73] It was precisely this process that Marx criticized in his economic and political writings, seeking to protect the real from the speculations of fetishism, Kolozova has argued: "Marxism understood as a philosophical project aims to reclaim the real identified with matter and emancipate it from the dictate of the idea or of the speculative."[74]

The material reality of labour is at the heart of Bouvier's analysis in her history of *lingerie*, drawing on the lived experiences of *lingères* as well as her own memories of working as a *lingère*. The *lingères'* voices were thus crucial to Bouvier's project, particularly as they emerged from the documents she gathered during a four-year inquiry (1904–08) into the conditions of industrial home workers that she conducted as part of her research. This inquiry covered 24 administrative areas across the country and 2,300 respondents from all areas of the *lingerie* industry, including entrepreneurs, contractors,

69 Discussion of these issues goes well beyond the scope of this chapter and has been done elsewhere. See, amongst others, Kathy Weeks, *The Problem with Work: Feminism, Marxism, Antiwork Politics, and Postwork Imaginaries* (Durham, 2011); Silvia Federici, *Revolution at Point Zero: Housework, Reproduction and Feminist Struggle* (Oakland, 2012); Janet Newman, *Working the Spaces of Power: Activism, Neoliberalism and Gendered Labour* (London, 2012); Rafaella Sarti, Anna Bellavitis and Manuela Martini (eds), *What is Work? Gender at the Crossroads of Home, Family and Business from the Early Modern Era to the Present* (New York and London, 2018).

70 Weeks, *The Problem with Work*, p. 2.

71 Katerina Kolozova, *Towards a Radical Metaphysics of Socialism: Marx and Laruelle* (Brooklyn, 2015).

72 Karl Marx, "Theses on Feuerbach" [1845], in Karl Marx and Friedrich Engels, *The German Ideology*, trans. Roy Pascal (London, 1938).

73 Kolozova, *Towards a Radical Metaphysics of Socialism*, p. 2.

74 Ibid., p. 4.

subcontractors and workers. According to Bouvier, the results of this inquiry showed that the conditions of the *lingères* at the beginning of the twentieth century were actually worse than in 1858, thus highlighting the importance of understanding historical discontinuities and their effects while making sense of contemporary realities:

> Here are the results of research on the situation of some women workers. No. 60, Paris. The worker is a 35-year-old widow and has a little daughter. She has been working for some years. [...] She works between 15 and 18 hours per day. She has very little work during the summer months. [...] At the time of the research she was expecting to be evicted on the grounds of a small debt owed to the landlord. In the evening or on the next day she would find herself homeless. Her troubles prevented her from responding to certain questions posed by the researcher.[75]

Bouvier sketched pen-portraits of *lingères* whose life histories and work trajectories more or less followed similar paths: they were all between 30 and 40 years old, mostly widows or abandoned by their husbands and with children to look after. They all worked between 14 to 18 hours per day, were very poorly paid and went through long periods of unemployment.

> No. 189. Mme, R... has been a *lingère* since her childhood. She is a widow with two daughters; the youngest is 11 years old and is under her custody [...] she works until her forces abandon her. This excessive work combined with deprivation have so weakened her that at the time of the research she was found lying in bed, sewing. Her situation is so miserable that she cannot feed her daughter, who gets free breakfast at the canteen of the communal school. [...] She lives in a single room of an old house with narrow, filthy corridors.[76]

When asked about their working hours, most *lingères* would say that they worked "till my forces abandon me",[77] while they could not answer the question regarding how they organized their annual expenses: "This is not at all my way, sir [...] every day earns its bread".[78] In the case of younger *lingères*, the route of sex work would also emerge in their narrative: "With what one

75 Bouvier, *La lingerie et les lingères*, pp. 275–76.
76 Ibid., pp. 277–78.
77 Ibid., p. 299.
78 Ibid., p. 277.

can earn in Saint-Omer, many women who are not aided by a man, husband or lover cannot live without prostitution", said a 25-year-old *lingère* from Saint Omer who worked alongside her older sister 14 hours a day from March till October.[79] Bouvier compared her story with figures from a senior trade unionist which confirmed that 80 per cent of the young women and 30 per cent of the married *lingères* in Saint-Omer were involved in sex work to make ends meet, and that there was a high number of teenage mothers in the area.[80]

Apart from the voices of women workers that find expression in Bouvier's case studies, what is also staged in her analysis is the debate between atelier work and home-based work. "Why do some bosses prefer the atelier as a workplace?" she asks, listing five arguments in support of the atelier: (i) production is more regular and sure; (ii) the process is quicker; (iii) the output is of higher quality; (iv) the quantity of output is larger; (v) faults and errors are more efficiently fixed.[81] She then cites those who favour industrial home work, arguing that (i) it is more economic as there are no estate expenses and the wages are lower; (ii) there are no strikes or protective legislation to grapple with; (iii) the work is more regular and the articles are better made; (iv) it is beneficial for women as it allows them to combine work with running a household; (v) the working hours are more flexible.[82] According to Bouvier, then, the main arguments in favour of industrial home work were that it was totally unregulated and not subject to any social laws or labour legislation.[83] It was precisely the need for regulation and control that became the object of trade union interventions at the beginning of the twentieth century, and it was this history that Bouvier also looked at in her study.

Moreover, as part of her archival documents, Bouvier's *Fonds* at the Historical Library of the City of Paris include two important boxes (Boîtes 18 and 19) with over 1,200 folios comprising the genealogical *dispositif* of the *travail à domicile*, quite simply its grid of intelligibility. As Foucault has configured it, a *dispositif* is a system of relations that can be established between heterogeneous elements, "discourses, institutions, architectural arrangements, regulations, laws, administrative measures, scientific statements, philosophic propositions, morality, philanthropy [...] the said as well as the unsaid".[84] In

79 Ibid., p. 287.
80 Ibid.
81 Ibid., p. 297.
82 Ibid., p. 298.
83 Ibid., p. 299.
84 Michel Foucault, "The Confession of the Flesh" (a conversation), in *Power/Knowledge: Selected Interviews and Other Writings 1972–1977*, edited by Colin Gordon (London, 1980), pp. 194–228, p. 194.

this light, the *dispositif* of the *travail à domicile* that Bouvier carefully archived and organized consists of preparatory material for the 1915 law, its full content, parliamentary documents and ministerial decrees, and finally, projects for its future amendments. It also includes a detailed record of the activities of the French branch of the International Office for the *travail à domicile*, drafts of future international projects, Bouvier's personal notes and reflections on the problem, and an extended body of correspondence with national and international figures, institutions and agencies.

Besides the *dispositif* of the *travail à domicile*, whose genealogy has yet to be written, Bouvier's comprehensive archive of otherwise inaccessible and dispersed documents demonstrate the depth and seriousness of her involvement with this serious labour problem, not only on an intellectual level, but also in terms of minutiae at the legal and administrative level. As the editors of the 1983 publication of her *Mémoires* have noted, Bouvier was one of the originators of the 1915 law, the first international legislative attempt to regulate the *travail à domicile*, and nobody knew better than her how to catalogue and archive its multiple and complex files and documents.[85]

Bouvier chose to complete her study of the *lingères* with a genealogy of their struggles in a very Foucauldian way of writing the history of her present as a political activist in the *lingères'* syndicate, but also in a Deleuzian way of following "lines of flight". Choosing the 1789 French revolution as her genealogical *emergence*, the point when things erupted as events in the course of history,[86] Bouvier noted that the *lingères* were amongst the best organized trade bodies in Paris, and despite the admission of men workers, the union was totally managed by women only. The *lingères* reunited after the 1848 revolution to demand their own share in the right to work that was the rallying cry of the Second Republic. As I have elsewhere discussed at length, their leaders during the period of the July Monarchy (1830–48) included major figures of the first autonomous feminist movement in France, such as Désirée Véret-Gay, Marie-Reine Guindorf and Jeanne Deroin.[87] The brutal repression of the 1848 revolution and the political persecution of all workers' associations and their leaders delayed the professional organization of the *lingères*, and it was only after 1870, during the Third Republic, that they were able to unionize again in the Syndicat de la Chemiserie-Lingerie, founded in 1873.

Women workers' right to form a union was neither easy nor straightforward. Unsurprisingly, they were initially omitted from appeals to workers to form

85 Bouvier, *Mes Mémoires*, p. 273 n.41.
86 Foucault, "Nietzsche, Genealogy, History", p. 83.
87 See Tamboukou, *Sewing, Fighting and Writing*.

unions after the 1870 war. In her genealogy Bouvier has included a letter by Shaller, a proletarian woman, who wrote to "Citizen Barberet", the editor of the column *Bulletin du Travail* in the radical republican newspaper *Le Rappel*, on 29 October 1873: "How is it that you daily defend the workers' rights in *Le Rappel* with such authority and you have completely abandoned to this day one of the most interesting and exploited class, the women workers?"[88] Barberet swiftly responded that women were included in his appeals, and a wider movement for the organization of women workers was set in motion that ended in the founding of the Chambre Syndicale de lingères, couturières, brodeuses et confectionneuses, in May 1874.

What was particularly important in the foundation of this first Chambre Syndicale is that for the first time, women needleworkers surpassed intra-labour differences and by coming together they showed that women's work was always crossing the boundaries between specialities and hierarchies within their trade. Most importantly, they showed that the spatial division of women's labour was always blurred and that there could be no clear distinction between atelier work and home-based work. In uniting their forces, women workers fought for collective contracts that included regulation of their working hours as well as the stipulation of minimum wages and salaries. Such victories only became possible in the first decades of the twentieth century as a result of militant strikes in the garment industry, where the seamstresses took centre stage.

In writing the history of *lingerie* and *lingères*, Bouvier drew on facts and figures of previous investigations, but she carefully avoided the trap of pathologizing women's work and of victimizing the seamstress. There are thus four outstanding aspects of her study, as briefly presented above: (i) a careful mapping of the economics, structures and problems of the phenomenon of industrial home work, including its international context; (ii) close attention to the minutiae of the *lingères*' daily activities and labour practices; (iii) a genealogy of the *lingères*' trade union movement and its struggles; and (iv) a very early attempt to collect and archive case studies from the *lingères*' lived experiences of work.

I therefore suggest that, since many of the questions that were raised at the turn of the nineteenth century are both pertinent and unresolved even today, a genealogical investigation through the lens of assemblage theories can offer rich and useful insights in contemporary research and policies. To do this, however, we need to make cartographies of particular questions and issues within specific geopolitical contexts. The assemblage approach does not offer

88 Cited in Bouvier, *La lingerie et les lingères*, p. 349.

generic solutions and directions but rather encourages topological sensibilities and cartographies. What most importantly emerge from this approach are discernible traces of resistance and ultimately a deconstruction of the myth that women workers in the long history of industrial home work have been passive victims of oppression, rather than agents actively pursuing their right to life and to work. Bouvier's lived experiences, her agonistic politics and her careful historical studies on women's work are a sound counter-example of such mythologies, discourses and narratives.

CHAPTER 12

Industrial Home Work and Fordism in Western Europe

Women's Activism, Labour Legislation and Union's Mobilization in Golden Age Italy, 1945–75

Eloisa Betti

Industrial home work was the backbone of Italy's industrial system in the country's most important period of economic growth in the twentieth century, the boom years of 1945–75 known as the Golden Age. The home-based economy grew together with the expansion of Fordist large-scale factory manufacturing rooted mainly in the northern regions. The dualistic nature of Italy's economic structure[1] together with the dominance of medium-size industrial companies and workshops[2] laid the ground not only for the survival of industrial home work, which was thought to be a backward practice, but also for its renewed spread. In the 1970s, the crisis of the Fordist system led to a large expansion of home-based work,[3] revealing its persistence through and beyond the Golden Age of the twentieth century.

Industrial home work became increasingly feminized during these years. While young adult men entered the factories *en masse*, only a small proportion of young women did so. In the process of transition from agricultural to industrial dominance in the 1950s, an increasing number of rural women as well as former factory workers became industrial home workers. On the one hand, the employment structure of the boom years clearly revealed a gender pattern, by which women did not benefit in the same way as men from the economic

---

1 Vera Lutz, "The Growth Process in a Dual Economic System", *Banca Nazionale del lavoro Quarterly Review*, 9 (1958), pp. 279–324 ; Augusto Graziani, "Dualismo e sottosviluppo nell'economia italiana", *Nord e Sud*, 2 (1963), pp. 24–32; Lucio Cafagna, *Dualismo e sviluppo nella storia d'Italia* (Venice, 1989).

2 Micael Piore and Charles Sabel, *The second industrial divide: Possibilities for prosperity* (New York, 1984); Sebastiano Brusco, "The Emilian model: Productive decentralization and social integration", *Cambridge Journal of Economics*, 6 (1982), pp. 167–84; Andrea Colli and Michelangelo Vasta (eds), *Forms of Enterprise in 20th Century Italy: Boundaries, Structures and Strategies* (Cheltenham, 2010).

3 Luigi Frey (ed.), *Lavora domicilio e decentramento dell'attività produttiva nei settori tessile e dell'abbigliamento in Italia* (Milan, 1975).

© ELOISA BETTI, 2022 | DOI:10.1163/9789004499614_014
This is an open access chapter distributed under the terms of the CC BY-NC-ND 4.0 license.

growth.[4] On the other hand, adult women with family responsibilities faced workplace discrimination. Only in 1963 did parliament pass a law to stop the dismissal of women from jobs upon marriage. Moreover, due to a lack of publicly provided child care, they had little support in combining work and family duties.[5]

At the same time, a growing chorus demanded regulation of home-based work. Women's associations, women politicians and unionists played a major role in denouncing the conditions of such labour. Industrial home workers themselves mobilized in the 1960s–1970s, rallying in public spaces and debating their working and living conditions in informal gatherings as well as official conferences. In the social conflict and labour unrest that spread all over Italy from the late 1960s, home workers joined female factory workers in strikes. They too demonstrated to obtain better pay and proper labour contracts. The mobilization of home workers, along with the commitment of unionists and politicians, was crucial for creating the basis for regulation in the wake of 1968. The chronology of legal regulation in Italy, with action in 1958 and 1973, both reveals the pervasiveness of industrial home work in itself and the widespread perception of its significance well before the international discussion in the 1980s that led to ILO Convention No. 177 in 1996.[6]

The global expansion of industrial home work in the last three decades pushes us to come to terms with national and international historiographies, to understand the actual role of home-based work in different phases of industrial and post-industrial capitalism. Earlier studies by Eileen Boris, Elisabeth Prügl and Cynthia Daniels connected industrial capitalism of the nineteenth century and early twentieth century with the post-Fordist 1980s and 1990s.[7] During the latter phase, the diffusion of home work in the global South as well as in countries of the North, in particular among groups of Asian and Latin American migrants, generated new research questions concerning the role of industrial home work in the global economy in the long term.[8] The Italian case

4 Eloisa Betti, "Women's Working Conditions and Job Precariousness in Historical Perspective: The Case of Italian Industry during the Economic Boom (1958–1963)", in Isabella Agárdi, Berteke Waaldijk and Carla Salvaterra (eds), *Making Sense, Crafting History: Practices of Producing Historical Meaning* (Pisa, 2010), pp. 175–205.

5 Perry Wilson, *Women in 20th century Italy* (Basingstoke, 2009).

6 Eileen Boris' chapter in this volume, "From Industrial Evil to Decent Work: The ILO and Changing Perspectives towards Home-Based Labour".

7 Eileen Boris and Cynthia R. Daniels (eds), *Homework: Historical and contemporary perspectives on paid labor at home* (Urbana, 1989); Eileen Boris and Elisabeth Prügl (eds), *Homeworkers in global perspective: Invisible no more* (New York, 1996).

8 See Marlese van Broembsen and Jenna Harvey's chapter in this volume, "Realizing Rights for Home Workers: Participating in Global Supply Chains".

is of particular interest due to the important number of existing sources for the under-researched period of Fordism. Italian historiography almost exclusively has addressed the phenomenon during the first half of the twentieth century,[9] when it was considered to be complementary to the development of the modern industrial system.[10]

This chapter focuses on the various actors that debated home-based work and mobilized to regulate industrial home work. It begins with the first phase of the mobilization, revealing the role played by women unionists together with women parliamentarians and leaders of women's associations. It then conceptualizes the relationship between industrial home work, Fordism and economic development in post-war Italy. It turns to the years following the first protective law (1958), casting light on women's struggles, including strikes, to see the law enforced. It also considers women's mobilization against increasing job precarity in the mid-1960s. The fourth section frames the new mobilization for regulating industrial home work following the May 1968 upheaval in the years of the greatest social conflict of the twentieth century. The chapter concludes by looking at the new spread of industrial home work in the wake of the 1970s' economic crisis. With the 1973 oil shock, the Italian context becomes particularly illuminating of the relationship between post-Fordism and precarious labour.

1 Women's Agency, Parliamentary Enquiries and Labour Legislation in 1950s Italy

Industrial home work attracted wider institutional attention in the 1950s when the Italian parliament launched an official inquiry into workers' conditions, resulting in a regulatory law in 1958. The post-Second World War period saw the legacy of Fascism in cultural as well as juridical terms. Since industrial home-based work was legally defined as "autonomous" in 1924, industrial home workers were officially considered to be self-employed.[11] The perception of women's industrial home work as complementary work for housewives endured in spite

9 Barbara Curli, "Dalla Grande Guerra alla Grande crisi: I lavori delle donne", in Stefano Musso (ed.), *Storia del lavoro in Italia: Il lavoronell'etàindustriale* (Rome, 2015), pp. 201–51.

10 Germano Maifreda, *La disciplina del lavoro: operai, macchine e fabbriche nella storia italiana* (Milan, 2007).

11 Maria Vittoria Ballestrero, *Dalla tutela alla parità: La legislazione italiana sul lavoro delle donne* (Bologna, 1979).

of its increasing economic and social necessity.[12] In the 1950s, industrial home work underwent a process of transformation. In the first half of the decade, home-based work grew in several industrial areas, due to dismissals taking place in Italian factories.[13] A process of productive reconversion, accompanied by a downsizing of the workforce, eventually overlapped with the phenomenon of unfair dismissals targeting members of the labour movement as well as socialist and communist activists, including women belonging to the Union of Italian Women.[14]

Inquiries made by women's associations and the Italian Communist Party revealed that factory downsizing and closures led to a boom in industrial home work, often defined as a "social plague" because it involved whole families (including the young and the elderly).[15] *Noi Donne*, the magazine of the left-wing Union of Italian Women (UDI), reported on industrial home work in the Emilia-Romagna region, a key centre for home-based production in the 1950s and 1960s. It showed that men, after dismissal from factories, joined their wives in industrial home work.[16] Trade unionists and politicians knew about the extent of the practice. They started discussing the regulation of industrial home work in the early 1950s.

During the first half of the decade Giuseppe di Vittorio, general secretary of the Confederazione Generale Italiana del Lavoro (CGIL) and an MP from the ranks of the Communist Party, and Giulio Pastore, general secretary of the Confederazione Italiana Sindacati Lavoratori (CISL) and an MP from the ranks of Christian Democracy, presented two bills in parliament.[17] Both underscored the growth of industrial home work in the post-war period, and pointed to the absence of any protection for industrial home workers, as well as the high level

12 Eloisa Betti, "Lavoro a domicilio e relazioni di genere negli anni Cinquanta: appunti sul caso bolognese", in Ida Fazio, Aanna Badino and Fiorella Imprenti (eds), *Attraverso la città, Genesis*, 2 (2015), pp. 107–33.

13 Betti, *Lavoro a domicilio e relazioni di genere negli anni Cinquanta.*

14 Eloisa Betti, "Gendering political violence in early Cold War Italy: The case of Bologna in Pau Casanellas", in Anna Sofia Ferreira (ed.), *Violência política no século XX: Um balanço* (Lisbon, 2017).

15 Alessandro Skuk, "78 milioni di salario sottratti ogni mese ai lavoranti a domicilio della provincia: Nostra inchiesta sul lavoro a domicilio", *La voce dei lavoratori*, 9 October 1954; Rina Picolato, "La piaga sociale del lavoro a domicilio", *Rinascita*, 6 June 1957.

16 Remo Clementi, "Trappola a domicilio", *Noi donne*, 3 April 1955.

17 Camera dei Deputati, I Legislatura, Disegni di Legge e Relazioni, Documenti, Proposta di legge di iniziativa dei deputati Giuseppe Di Vittorio, Vittorio Santi *et al.*, Regolamentazione del lavoro a domicilio, annunziata il 7 marzo 1950; Camera dei Deputati, I Legislatura, Disegni di Legge e Relazioni, Documenti, Proposta di legge di iniziativa dei deputati Giulio Pastore, Luigi Morelli *et al.*, Tutela del lavoro a domicilio, annunziata il 28 aprile 1950.

of exploitation they experienced daily. The definition of an industrial home worker—as wage worker or self-employed—was a crucial aspect of the debate, together with the need to establish public commissions to oversee the possibility for employers to commission work to home-based workers. They proposed an employers' register to monitor and control the businesses employing home workers.

In spite of the Cold War dynamics, the Communists, Socialists and Christian Democrats within the Italian parliament fruitfully cooperated. A specific committee set up for the purpose drafted a joint text; it included women MPs belonging to different parties, like the Communist Adele Bei, the Socialist Elena Gatti Caporaso and the Christian Democrat Gigliola Valandro.[18] Women politicians, including key trade unionists like the general secretary of textile workers, Teresa Noce, played an important role in the talks. The Italian parliament and government considered protective regulations necessary. Italian MPs were not in favour of abolishing industrial home work because they realized that home-based work was the sole source of income for thousands of marginal workers, especially women. They began to distinguish between traditional home-based work, related to handicraft manufacturing, and industrial home work, a substitute for factory work. Trade unionists within the parliament proposed to contribute to the definition of piece-rates as well as to establish a Central Commission for industrial home work within the Ministry of Labour.[19]

The Parliamentary Commission of Inquiry into Workers' Conditions in Italy, established in 1955, collected information on the dynamics of industrial home work. The parliament relied on its report to finalize the law on industrial home work.[20] The Labour Commission of the Lower House nearly unanimously passed a single draft law, which encompassed the previously introduced bills and the Commission's suggestions, in 1957.[21] The Labour Commission of the

18 Camera dei Deputati, II Legislatura, Commissioni in sede legislativa, XI Commissione, Seduta del 20 aprile 1955, pp. 557–62.

19 Camera dei Deputati, II Legislatura, Commissioni in sede legislativa, XI Commissione, Seduta del 21 novembre 1956, pp. 916–25; Camera dei Deputati, II Legislatura, Commissioni in sede legislativa, XI Commissione, Seduta del 25 gennaio 1957, pp. 1002–08; Camera dei Deputati, II Legislatura, Commissioni in sede legislativa, XI Commissione, Sedute del 30 gennaio 1957, 1 febbraio 1957, 13 febbraio 1957, 15 febbraio 1957, 22 febbraio 1957, 22 marzo 1957.

20 Camera dei Deputati, II Legislatura, Commissioni in sedelegislativa, XI Commissione, Seduta del 25 gennaio 1957, p. 1000.

21 Camera dei Deputati, II Legislatura, Commissioni in sede legislativa, Seduta del 27 marzo 1957, pp. 1111–22.

Senate however watered down the draft. Defined as "traditional", home work failed to qualify for unemployment benefits; also reduced were the guarantees demanded of entrepreneurs to join the provincial register of employers. The shared aim of the MPs to make home work more costly, putting it on par with factory work, fell through. The MPs were not in favour of the draft issued by the Labour Commission of the Senate which substantially altered the originally proposed law.

The 1958 law, "Safeguards for home work", excluded workers registered as artisans, a restriction that would be the basis for the extremely limited implementation of the measure, leading to its review in 1973.[22] There were gains in the 1958 law: the prohibition of entrepreneurial use of intermediaries/subcontractors; the creation of registers at the Provincial Office for Labour, both for home workers and entrepreneurs/employers; the creation of provincial commissions to assess the registrations of the entrepreneurs and to carefully monitor industrial home work; and the establishment of a Central Commission for control at the Ministry for Labour. The law also created a "payroll register" for the entrepreneurs which had to be checked by the Labour Inspectorate, and an employment card for home workers where they had to note down their job description and the related wages. Wage rates in collective bargaining or agreements through provincial commissions were set, based on the highest prevailing piece work rates at the time. Workers registered in the records could apply for the main forms of social insurance (disability, old age, maternity and sickness), but not for unemployment subsidy. The law also introduced a daily fine for any infringement, ranging between 5,000 and 20,000 lire.[23]

The debate in parliament was not the only one in the second half of the 1950s. The UDI played a crucial role in denouncing home workers' conditions; it published comprehensive reports in *Noi Donne* during the years of the economic boom.[24] Shortly before the passage of the 1958 law, the association initiated a National Congress on Home Workers in Florence on 23 February,[25] which was accompanied by local meetings in numerous other cities including Bologna. These events led to greater awareness not only of women home

22 Decreto del Presidente della Repubblica, Approvazione del regolamento concernente l'applicazione della legge 13 marzo 1958, n. 264, sulla tutela del lavoro a domicilio, approvato il 16 dicembre 1959, pubblicato sulla Gazzetta Ufficiale n. 35 dell'11 febbraio 1960.

23 Ivi, art.2-15.

24 Luisa Melograni, "Prigioniere nella propria casa", *Noi Donne*, 23 February 1958; Luisa Melograni, "Il ricatto a domicilio", *Noi Donne*, 12 July 1958; Luisa Melograni, "Voci della città", *Noi donne*, 8 March 1959.

25 "Il convegno dell'UDI sul lavoro a domicilio", *Noi Donne*, 8 March 1958; UDI, *Convegno nazionale sulle lavoranti a domicilio* (Florence, 23 February 1958).

workers' conditions but also of their numbers, which ranged between 800,000 and 1 million, according to estimates provided by the association.[26] Home workers gathered at the Congress in large numbers to raise their voices in protest against their working conditions, revealing the pervasive nature of industrial home work across Italy.

2 Industrial Home Work, Fordism and Economic Development

> Who are these male or female workers? Generally speaking, they are women who, owing to the continuous dismissals that have been taking place in the past few years in industry, were made redundant with no prospect of stable work in an industrial or commercial company. Given the great demands of the families, they have become home workers. Others, and mostly women from the countryside who, having work for just two or three months a year, for the remaining period become home workers. Others still are the same workers employed in the factories who, to round up their wages that very often are below the standard rates, as the employment contracts are not respected, take work to be done at home, in the evening and on public holidays, to support the other family members. This can be seen in particular in the printing sector and that of the papermakers. Others are the women who, albeit being classified as housewives, and not managing to make ends meet with the sole income of their husbands [...] have no chance of leaving the home, either because the children are too small or because there is a lack of essential services like nurseries, and become home workers.[27]

Industrial home work, according to the estimates made by the Parliamentary Commission of Inquiry into Workers' Conditions in Italy, involved between 600,000 and 700,000 workers towards the end of the 1950s, most of them women. The high feminization of industrial home work was the reason why it was treated as an almost exclusively female issue.[28] Home-based work seemed to be widespread across the whole country, especially the cities of southern Italy (Palermo, Naples, Salerno) and those of the north-east (Venice, Vicenza).

26 Melograni, *Prigioniere nella propria casa.*

27 Archive of the Union of Italian Women of Bologna (hereafter AUDIBO), b. 2 "Anni '50", f. "Convegno sul lavoro a domicilio"(Bologna, October 1958).

28 Ibid.

The crisis that swept across Italy's textile industry in the early 1950s does not seem to have effected a reduction in home-based work, as the rapid growth of the garment industry (knitwear, in particular) offered new opportunities to home workers both in rural and urban areas.

In the late 1950s, a broad range of jobs were done at home. Urban areas benefited from geographical proximity to factories. Home work appeared not only in the textile and garment sectors, but also in ceramics, chemicals (pharmaceutical and cosmetics), paper-making and food industries. Even the machine tool industry put out some of its work processes.[29] In the surroundings of a single factory, Benfenati, for example, there were "fifty-five female workers who perform the most various types of work, from trousers to shoes, from leather goods to toys, from sweet wrapping to doll packaging".[30]

At the dawn of the economic boom, the nexus between industrial home work, Fordism and economic development reflected the precarity of women's labour. The 1958 Bolognese Congress highlighted the heterogeneity of social conditions (i.e. farmer, worker, housewife) and the different contexts of membership (i.e. city, countryside) that accompanied high feminization of labour. The reports of the unions and UDI inquiries show how more and more rural women (sharecroppers and labourers) responded to the decline in traditional rural activities by taking on industrial home work, which was expanding. This was hardly surprising as rural women suffered from chronic underemployment; they were the ones who most lacked farm work in the countryside.[31] In 1957, researchers Diana Sabbi and Tilde Bolzani claimed that "the definitive abandonment of work in the fields for badly paid and exploitative home working"[32] was a generalized trend due to the lack of alternatives.

The structural conditions of the labour market, characterized by high rates of unemployment during the 1950s[33] and by a very large supply of male and female manpower, facilitated processes of expulsion of labour from the factories; many former female factory workers were forced to be re-employed

29 Commissione parlamentare d'inchiesta sulle condizioni dei lavoratori in Italia, Relazioni della Commissione parlamentare di inchiesta; Nella Prandi, "Lotta Unitaria alla Zucchelli", *La voce dei lavoratori*, 5 April 1953.

30 AUDIBO, b. 2 "Anni '50", f. "Convegnosullavoro a domicilio".

31 Maurizio Parasassi and Giorgio Ruffolo, *La disoccupazione in Italia: relazione sintetica delle indagini e degli studi promossi dalla Commissione parlamentare d'inchiesta sulla disoccupazione* (Bologna, 1954).

32 AUDIBO, b. 2 "Anni '50", fasc. "1956", Comunicazione presentata dall'Assessore all'Amm.ne Provinciale Sabbi Diana e dal Consigliere Tilde Bolzani su "I diritti delle donne contadine e la difesa del lavoro femminile nelle campagne".

33 Parasassi and Ruffolo, *La disoccupazione in Italia*.

as home workers simply in order to have an income.[34] The Parliamentary Commission of Inquiry into Workers' Conditions in Italy highlighted the social consequences of the expansion of industrial home work in various regions of Italy, casting light on the impoverishment of local economies in small and medium-sized urban centres that relied on a limited number of companies. Of particular interest was the point of view of entrepreneurial organizations like the Association of Industrial Employers of Vicenza, expressing concern that the expansion of home work could lead to the contraction or even closure of a whole industrial plant.[35]

The inquiry exposed conditions that made home work the most precarious form of work. It showed in great detail how the closure of factory units corresponded to the installation in homes of former factory workers' looms, previously situated in industrial plants. After being dismissed, the workers were forced to lease or purchase machines simply to be able to continue to work. The inquiry documented the absence of contracts, the lack of worker safeguards in case of sickness, pregnancy, termination or reduction in work, and the instability of wages from piece-work—in short, the exploitation stemming from such a situation.[36] The pressure to pay in instalments for the purchase of machines along with the very low piece-work rates forced women home workers to extend their working hours beyond the limits of physical endurance, reaching an average of 12 to even 14 hours per day.[37] In the garment sector, the wage of a specialized factory "machinist" was 1,238.32 lire for 8 hours' work, while that of a home worker doing the same job was at most 1,040 lire.[38]

> Generally speaking, the machinist needs two-and-a-quarter hours to two-and-a-half hours per piece, provided that she does not leave the machine. Thus, the wool spindles had to be ready to pick up those ladders that can happen here and there during the work, and so she must add from 20 to 30 minutes per piece, coming to 3 hours each. If we consider that they are paid 430 lire a piece, reaching an average of 130 lire per hour, [...] if she works 8 hours as the worker does in the factory, she would reach a daily wage of 1,040 lire.[39]

34 Betti, *Lavoro a domicilio e relazioni di genere negli anni Cinquanta.*

35 Commissione parlamentare d'inchiesta sulle condizioni dei lavoratori in Italia, *Relazioni della Commissione parlamentare di inchiesta.*

36 Ibid.

37 Ibid.

38 "l dibattito del Comitato Cittadino : Ducati e lavoro a domicilio", *La lotta*, 3 March 1960.

39 Ibid.

3 Industrial Home Workers' Strikes and Women's Mobilization against Job Precarity in 1960s Italy

The competitive nature of industrial home work during subsequent industrial growth led to slower and less successful implementation of the 1958 law than expected. The persistence of very high levels of exploitation and the expansion of home work in the years of the economic boom precipitated the first significant struggles. In March 1960, over 1,200 home workers living in the rural municipalities of the eastern Bolognese plains (San Giovanni in Persiceto, Crevalcore, Sant'Agata, Anzola dell'Emilia and Sala Bolognese) went on strike with the combined support of the unions. They marched on the streets of their respective town centres. The striking workers demanded increased rates of pay, continuity of work and enforcement of the 1958 law.[40]

Just weeks earlier, on 11 February 1960, the President of the Republic had signed the "Safeguards for Home Work" regulation to enforce the law passed two years earlier, which threatened employer profits. Therefore, to evade the obligations imposed by the new law, employers started blackmailing the home workers, urging them to become artisans if they did not want to lose their jobs. This strategy fostered the development of artisanal companies paying very low wages, often lower than that of a "third level" shop floor worker.[41] The employers' blackmailing strategy meant a further worsening of working conditions. Once the home workers became artisans, they were forced to bear all the costs related to their status, in addition to the cost of purchasing or leasing the machines they needed to do their work. Being registered as artisans was incompatible with the working conditions of the home workers. They lost all the benefits the law gave them as home workers, including, first and foremost, contributions from the "employer" relating to health care and pensions.[42]

This was the context that generated the first important forms of protest initiated by the home workers themselves. The strike that took place on 2 March 1960 represented a break with the past. There had been few previous occasions when home workers made their voices heard as a group. The fear of appearing in public was widespread, since the risk of losing their jobs was particularly high due to the informal character of industrial home work. Notwithstanding its widespread nature in the province of Bologna, home work had remained

40 "Ha rivelato un quadro impressionante lo sciopero dei lavoranti a domicilio", *l'Unità, Cronaca di Bologna*, 6 March 1960.

41 Remo Cappelli, "La tessera del pane per le lavoranti a domicilio?", *La lotta*, 10 March 1960.

42 Ballestrero, *Dalla tutela alla parità*.

until then an "invisible" form of work. A City Committee was set up to support the organization of the strike. A meeting laid out some of the priorities, especially the need to break down the wall of isolation behind which the women workers lived, with a view to help them to come together. Besides the 2 March strike, home workers initiated other forms of collaboration. In the municipalities of Sant'Agata, Sala Bolognese and San Giovanni in Persiceto, groups of knitwear workers established autonomous groups with the support of the union, moving towards the creation of full-fledged cooperatives.[43]

Women home workers were a subject of renewed attention from left-wing political and union organizations, first and foremost the PCI (Partito Comunista Italiana/Italian Communist Party) and the CGIL, and then the UDI. The PCI leadership judged home work negatively because it took women away from participation in public life, reducing their potential unionization and politicization.[44] The rank-and-file of the party, on the contrary, saw in home work the right balance between the fulfilment of the family's economic needs and the carrying out of care responsibilities. In the early 1960s, home work was at the centre of discussions within the women's commission of the Bolognese PCI, which stressed the difficulty of "organizing" home workers: only 250 home workers had been "organized" in Bologna, spread across the main working-class neighbourhoods and the central area of the city.[45] The UDI indeed played an important role in promoting the socialization and organization of home workers through the so-called "riunioni di caseggiato", which pushed home workers to step out of their houses and discuss their problems in informal gatherings.[46] Some of the leaflets of 1960 urged home workers to emerge from their invisibility and achieve their legal rights.[47] The emphasis was once again on the isolation that women workers had to endure: the UDI promised not to

43 Cappelli, "La tessera del pane per le lavoranti a domicilio?".

44 Fondazione Gramsci Emilia-Romagna (hearafter FGER), Archivio del Partito Comunista Italiana (PCI)—Federazione Provinciale di Bologna (hearafter APCIBO), Section "Commissioni, Sezioni di lavoro e Dipartimenti", Sub-section "Commissione femminile", f. 2 "Problemi della politica del PCI verso le donne 1953–1959", dattiloscritto (Tilde Bolzani 1953).

45 FGER, APCIBO, Section "Commissioni, Sezioni di lavoro e Dipartimenti", Sub-section "Commissione femminile", f. 3 "Posizione partiti sulla condizione femminile 1953–1960", Risoluzione della sezione femminile e lavoro di massa della direzione PCI (5 dicembre 1959), Sviluppo dell'azione per la tutela del lavoro a domicilio (Marzo 1960).

46 Numerous ways at reaching out to home workers were attempted by the UDI, particularly evident in the association's leaflets: AUDIBO, b. 1 "Storia GDD e UDI 1944–1964", f. "Volantini e stampa di archivio", 1958, [Ricamatrice, Confezionista, Magliaia, Pantalonaia, Guantaia].

47 AUDIBO, busta n. 3, "1960–1963", fascicolo cat. III.

leave the home workers alone, guaranteeing them support and a help-desk at the association's offices.

A few years later, during the 1963–64 economic crisis following the economic boom, about 300,000 Italian women lost paid work. Once they were ousted from the production cycle, especially if employed in industry, women could no longer find regular work and were relegated to the informal economy, once again swelling the ranks of home workers. Between 1963 and 1965, the UDI published numerous studies on the effects of the crisis on female workers.[48] The aim was to understand how women reacted to the "great fear of unemployment", and their conditions of life and work during the crisis. The UDI's main slogan became, "We are not going home"; a recurring question it posed was, "Where is the miracle?"[49] Italian women workers and their associations demanded job stability along with an end to job precarity. In 1965, the UDI held a national conference in Milan followed by a large demonstration of more than 4,000 women. The title of the conference, which became the demonstration's major slogan, was "Women's right to stable and qualified work", testifying to the UDI's innovative approach.[50]

4 Industrial Home Workers as Wage Workers: The Struggle for Recognition, 1968–73

> Today home work is no longer just a complementary activity to round up household income and, as such, entrusted to the housewife, the pensioner, the farmer's wife or the worker dismissed from the crisis-hit textile company. Instead it is based on a multitude of young workers searching for their first job, female workers marginalized from the factory in the years of economic recession and in unfavourable phases, who did in fact all work within a decentralized organization but with industrial machines. The result of which is a cut in the labour costs achieved by means of the payment of

48 "A casa non si torna", *Noi Donne*, 5 Dicember 1964; "300 giorni perduti", *Noi Donne*, 28 November 1964.

49 "A casa non si torna".

50 National Archive of the Union of Italian Women (hearafter NAUDI), chronological section, 1965, b. 112, f. 894, Per il diritto delle donne al lavoro stabile e qualificato, Atti della conferenza nazionale (Milan, 12–13 giugno 1965).

> lower wages to the contractual workers and bypassing of the obligations stemming from social legislation.[51]

The continuous increase in home-based work in the mid-1960s led to renewed parliamentary discussions in the wake of the May 1968 upheaval, the greatest social conflict of the twentieth century. The 1973 law, "New norms for safeguarding home work", followed the Statute of Workers' Rights, which represented the most important Italian labour law of the twentieth century.[52] Women MPs played a pivotal role in passing the 1973 law on industrial home work. They were the first signatories of the bills presented by different political parties, supporting the struggle of industrial home workers to be recognized as wage workers. The parliamentary process that led to the new law on industrial home work was shorter than the one that ended in 1958.[53] The first proposal was presented just prior to the so-called "hot autumn" of 1969 and followed the national conference on female employment of February 1968, which provided relevant elements for an understanding of the evolution of home-based work.[54]

The first bill, presented in December 1969, was signed by the Communist MP Luciana Sgarbi, followed by NildeIotti, Nives Gessi and many other politicians belonging to the same party.[55] An accompanying report outlined the failed enforcement of the 1958 law. This negative assessment was shared by the Under-Secretary to the Ministry for Labour and by the main unions, CGIL (Confederazione Generale Italiana del Lavoro/Italian General Confederation of Labour), CISL (Confederazione Italiana Sindacati Lavoratori/ Italian Confederation of Workers' Trade Unions) and UIL (Unione Italiana del Lavoro/Italian Labour Union).[56] According to the latter, the most critical aspect

51 Camera dei Deputati, VI Legislatura, Disegni di Legge e Relazioni, Documenti, Disegno di legge presentato dal Ministro del Lavoro e della Previdenza Sociale Dionigi Coppo, di concerto con il Ministro di Grazia e Giustizia, Guido Gonnella e il Ministro dell'Industria, Commercio e Artigianato Mauro Ferri, Nuove norme per il lavoro a domicilio, presentato alla Presidenza il 16 aprile 1973.

52 Paolo Mattera, "Legislazione sociale e welfare", in Musso (ed.), *Il Novecento, 1945–2000*, pp. 378–415.

53 Marcello De Cristofaro, *Il lavoro a domicilio* (Padua, 1978).

54 Ministero del bilancio e della programmazione, Conferenza sull'occupazione femminile (Rome, 1968).

55 Camera dei deputati, V Legislatura, Disegni di Legge e Relazioni, Documenti, Proposta di legge di iniziativa dei deputati Luciana Sgarbi, Nilde Iotti *et al.*, Modifiche alla legge 13 marzo 1958, n. 264, concernente la tutela del lavoro a domicilio, annunziata il 19 dicembre 1969, p. 3.

56 Ivi, p. 1.

was the large number of home workers registering as artisans, often blackmailed by employers who threatened them with denial of any more work. In 1968, it was estimated that there were between 1 million and 1.5 million home workers, as compared to just 24,000 formally registered as such. The growth of home work as the last productive unit of the Italian industrial system coincided with a major decline in female employment, of around 1,200,000 workers. Hence, the bill aimed to increase the cost of home-based work, pushing entrepreneurs to make greater investments and re-absorb the external workforce. As a safeguard, the juridical redefinition of the home worker as a subordinate worker was considered essential, along with the extension of all the social benefits granted to factory workers.

In January 1973, the Socialist lawyer and MP Maria Magnani Noya presented a new bill.[57] Its short accompanying report highlighted the abuses and violations made possible by the omissions and the ambiguities of the 1958 law. Redefining the figure of the home worker, making explicit her subordination, and clarifying the distinction between home-based work and entrepreneurial activities, became the focal aspects. In March 1973, Tina Anselmi,[58] who had worked for long as a unionist for CISL and was appointed as Minister for Labour only a few years later, was the first signatory of a Christian Democrat bill. This draft reviewed the definition of home worker in line with previous proposals, specifying that workers who leased machines and equipment from a company were to be considered employees of the latter. It introduced a clause aimed at tighter regulation of the use of home work in company restructuring: it forbade companies affected by dismissals and lay-offs to outsource work. Anselmi's proposal also addressed problems of hygiene and health, forbidding the implementation of processes[59] that involved the use of substances harmful to the well-being of the workers and their families at home. After these bills of law came the government's draft law, "New norms for home working".

Tina Anselmi led a committee to draft a joint bill. She highlighted the great attention that the issue of home work had attracted in the press and in public opinion, as well as among local institutions, trade unions, women's associations

57 Camera dei Deputati, VI Legislatura, Disegni di Legge e Relazioni, Documenti, Proposta di legge di iniziativa dei deputati Magnani Noya Maria, Alfredo Giovanardi *et al.*, Modifiche alla legge 13 marzo 1958, n. 264, recante norme per la tutela del lavoro domicilio, annunziata il 27 gennaio 1973.

58 Camera dei Deputati, VI Legislatura, Disegni di Legge e Relazioni, Documenti, Proposta di legge di iniziativa dei deputati Anselmi Tina, Vincenzo Mancini *et al.*, Modifica della legge 13 marzo 1958, n. 264, per la tutela del lavoro domicilio, annunziata il 14 febbraio 1973.

59 The proposal put forward the drafting of a table of harmful processes by the Ministry for Labour, acting in synergy with the Ministry of Health.

and, of course, among the workers themselves, most of them women.[60] MPs sought to define home work more precisely to safeguard it against illegality and to better safeguard the workers, as well as reduce the causes of its abnormal and distorted spread. Luciana Sgarbi Bompani and Magnani Noya Maria highlighted the intersection between the decline in female employment and the expansion of home work as the sole source of income for many women.[61] However, opinions on the role (positive or negative) of industrial home work varied, showing the persistence of the housewife model, especially within certain parts of the Catholic milieu. The Christian Democrat Ines Boffardi underlined that "when home work does not degenerate into irregular situations and thus illegal acts of exploitation, it always represents a qualifying and dignified means to allow the female worker to perform a profitable activity without abandoning her home and her family".[62]

In December 1973, the new law on home work was enacted, whereby home workers were recognized as equal to factory workers.[63] There was now the possibility to bargain with employers over piece-rates, through the unions. Thousands of home workers, once legalized, would at last be able to enjoy all the social guarantees available to the factory workers related to illness, maternity leave and redundancy. The law also did away with the incompatibility between enrolment in the artisans' registers and the registers of home workers. It forbade the use of home work for harmful processes, and after restructuring or conversions leading to layoffs or dismissals.

5 The Explosion of Home-based Work in the Wake of the Fordist Crisis: Critiques and Mobilization of Unions and Women

As shown by Tania Toffanin, the decentralization of production in the 1970s produced a fresh rise in home-based work in all areas of the country.[64] The 1973 law created an opportunity to improve and stabilize home workers' conditions, defining them as subordinate workers and ensuring that they had access

60 Camera dei Deputati, VI Legislatura, XIII Commissione, sedute del 4 ottobre 1973, pp. 242–47.

61 Ibid., pp. 247–50.

62 Camera dei Deputati, VI Legislatura, XIII Commissione, sedute del 10 ottobre 1973, pp. 264.

63 Legge n. 877, Nuove norme per la tutela del lavoro a domicilio, approvata il 18 dicembre 1973 e pubblicata sulla Gazzetta ufficiale n. 5 del 5 gennaio 1974.

64 Tania Toffanin, *Fabbriche invisibili: storie di donne, lavoranti a domicilio* (Verona, 2016).

to the main social guarantees connected to work. It was unable, however, to slow the growth of industrial home work, although it set limits to its use in the case of restructuring that involved cuts in employment.[65] The possibility to reduce labour costs as well as the entrepreneurial desire to achieve the "greatest possible flexibility in the use of workforce" lay behind the (new) increase of industrial home work, which was accompanied by a parallel growth of small firms. The textiles–garments sector was at the centre of numerous studies in the 1970s, initiated by both economists and sociologists, also in collaboration with trade unions.[66]

The most important of these, conducted by Luigi Frey,[67] studied the relationship between production decentralization and home work expansion in textiles–garments. Italy responded to the crisis of Fordism by decentralizing industrial production, which became more and more evident in the second half of the 1970s after the oil shock. Researchers considered home work to be the last unit of production in the decentralized factory, which they analysed alongside small companies and artisanal businesses. Decentralization appeared to be stronger where there was a concentration of unemployed or underemployed personnel willing to accept lower wages, especially women, youth and elderly people.[68] Women accounted for 90 per cent of home workers due to a lack of alternatives. Often classified as housewives in the official statistics, many home workers came from backgrounds of rural underemployment, marked by a prevalence of female and youth unemployment.[69]

Specific studies were conducted on the conditions of female industrial home workers. Among these, *Operaie senza fabbrica* (1977) by Maria Rosa Cutrufelli, offered in its very title a full-fledged conceptual category that informed subsequent debate. Cutrufelli highlighted the worsening of female job precarity since the late 1960s, "the expulsion of a substantial number of female workers from the market of stable work" to "the area of *marginal* and precarious work".[70] Female workers were the true protagonists of the process of industrial restructuring that had developed outside the factory. The situation of the labour market, together with women's family responsibilities, were the chief

65 Luigi Mariucci, *Il lavoro decentrato : Discipline legislative e contrattuali* (Milan, 1979).

66 Sandro Del Giudice and Galvano Pizzol (eds), *Ristrutturazione produttiva e lavoro a domicilio : Indagine sul decentramento produttivodell'industriatessile, dell'abbigliamento e delle calzature in provincia di Treviso* (Verona, 1975).

67 Frey, *Lavora domicilio e decentramento dell'attività produttiva.*

68 Ibid.

69 Ibid.

70 Maria Rosa Cutrufelli, *Operaie senza fabbrica* (Rome, 1977), p. 16.

causes of diminished stability and greater precarity among female workers. Married women with children appeared to be over-represented in industrial home work and in undocumented work at large, owing to the impossibility of finding jobs that might allow them to combine productive and reproductive work.[71] According to Cutrufelli, behind the high rates of female workers' turnover in factories was the unresolved question of household management.

The explosion of industrial home work in the 1970s led to a new mobilization, which saw the involvement of trade unions and women's associations influenced by a second-wave feminism. With the worsening of that decade's economic crisis, precarity, marginalization and disqualification increased significantly, especially among younger women, due to the exponential growth in home-based work and undocumented labour following the process of industrial restructuring. The expansion of industrial home work and the rise in female unemployment produced a renewed elaboration and mobilization on the part of the UDI, as its political strategy closely linked the right to paid work and social progress. In February 1976, the association led a national demonstration dedicated to female employment, protesting the "secondary", "peripheral" economy of which women increasingly tended to be the protagonists during the crisis years.[72]

UDI's critique was directed towards both the organization of workplaces and women's role in society and in the family. It rejected the concept of being "a housewife" as a "fate" not chosen by women, for obscuring female unemployment and underemployment and weakening women's claims to fair compensation and other rights. Alongside the trade unions, the association conducted numerous studies on home-based work in various parts of the country. A new generation of women unionists directed their actions towards home workers, above all in the regions that were most affected such as Emilia-Romagna.[73] They organized numerous rallies and conferences to inform home workers of the new law. They undertook several inquiries into home workers' conditions, alongside bargaining for better piece-rates.[74] The fact that these actions were not always effective paved the way for self-organization, such as the "unitary league for home work" of Naples set up in 1975.[75]

71 Ibid.

72 NAUDI, Thematic Section, Diritto Al Lavoro, b. 26, f. 161, Manifestazione Nazionale Dell'unione Donne Italiane 11 Febbraio 1976 (Conclusioni Margherita Repetto).

73 Leonardo Tommasetta, *Il lavoro a domicilio nell'Emilia-Romagna* (Bologna, 1977); Renato Zangheri, "Caratteri dell'economia emiliano-romagnola", in *Atti dell'Accademia delle scienze dell'istituto di Bologna, Rendiconti*, LXVI (1978).

74 "Il lavoro a domicilio", in *Quaderni di Rassegna sindacale*, 44–45, September–Dicember 1973.

75 Toffanin, *Fabbriche invisibili*.

6 Conclusions

Industrial home work coexisted and spread along with the Fordist factory system, contributing to a "dual" labour market. It was a crucial element in the massive industrial growth of twentieth-century Italy, especially in textiles and garments where it became the backbone of industrial production. Industrial home work did not undergo any crisis in the Golden Age period of the twentieth century, even as its function was partially reshaped by the changes taking place in the industrial system. Home-based work was supported by factory owners, who often directly subcontracted a part of their production to home workers. The competitive character of industrial home work, together with the lack of other employment opportunities, especially for women, created the basis for its pervasiveness. During the economic crisis experienced by Italy in 1963/64, industrial home work grew significantly due to its low cost and flexibility. Again, during the crisis of the Fordist system, home-based work saw renewed and massive expansion.

Although difficult to enforce, legislation on industrial home work, conceived and established during the Fordist period, showed a political commitment towards improving the conditions of industrial home workers. Women played a crucial role in advancing industrial home work regulation as well as in exposing the conditions of industrial home workers. Women's agency was an important aspect of Italian discussion and mobilization in the sphere of industrial home work, while the actions of unionists within parliament were also crucial. Abolishing industrial home work was never part of the Italian debate in the Golden Age, as it was considered a necessary source of employment despite its negative characteristics. Only in the early 1970s, in the wake of the Fordist crisis, were concrete attempts made to balance the relationship between factory work and industrial home work.

Industrial home work in Italy was a continuous phenomenon over the twentieth century, going beyond established periodization. The importance of understanding industrial home work as part of the national industrial structure clearly emerges in the Italian context. Moreover, it underscores the significant role played by women, as unionists and politicians, in regulating industrial home work, which also happened elsewhere, as other chapters in this volume indicate.

CHAPTER 13

Refusing Invisibility

Women Workers in Subcontracted Work in a South Indian City

K. Kalpana

This chapter explores the relationship between capital accumulation and women's labour, using the case of women's paid work in a food-making industry carried out in homes and neighbourhood-based workspaces in a South Indian city.* The chapter discusses the creation of an informal and feminized workforce and its links to export revenue-earning companies that have pursued subcontracting strategies since the early 1980s. Women's work experience in the food production units is shaped by the intersecting dynamics of household and community patriarchies, the profit-maximizing ends of private capital, as well as the women's survival imperatives and their quest for financial independence. Resisting the "invisibility" that their principal employers seek to impose on them, the women workers have participated in strike action and registered themselves with the state government's informal workers' welfare board. In doing this, they have staked claims to their rights as workers vis-à-vis private employers and as citizens vis-à-vis the state.

Feminist theorists argue that the current epoch (the era of neoliberal capitalism) is an important moment in history to understand the relationship between capital accumulation and women's labour, and that accumulation strategies are built on women's labour in this period in global history perhaps more than in any other.[1] The chapter seeks to explore this relationship in the context of women's economic activity in a food-making industry carried out in homes and community spaces in select neighbourhoods of Chennai city, the capital of the South Indian state of Tamil Nadu. It explores the making

* The field work for this chapter was carried out as part of a research project titled "Changing Contours of State Welfarism and Emerging Citizenship: A Comparative Study of Tamil Nadu and Kerala", sponsored by the Indian Council of Social Science Research (ICSSR), New Delhi. I thank Archanaa Seker and D. Manjula for their enthusiastic assistance with primary data collection.

1 Nancy Hartsock, "Globalization and Primitive Accumulation: The Contribution of David Harvey's Dialectical Marxism", in Noel Castrée and Derek Gregory (eds), *David Harvey: A Critical Reader* (Oxford, 2006), pp. 167–90.

© K. KALPANA, 2022 | DOI:10.1163/9789004499614_015
This is an open access chapter distributed under the terms of the CC BY-NC-ND 4.0 license.

of an informal and overwhelmingly feminized workforce, and discusses how the industry in question thrives on concealed and yet secure links between home and neighbourhood-based food production units, on the one hand, and well-established private sector companies, on the other. These export revenue-earning companies rely on a feminized and "invisible" workforce and subcontracted production chains as the prime strategies of capital accumulation. The chapter fleshes out the ways in which women's ties to the family, their socially defined roles as primary providers of household care work and their circumscribed mobility, or, in other words, their unfreedom, acts as a resource that facilitates capital accumulation in the food-manufacturing industry located in the study area.

The chapter aims to show how women's work experience in the food production units is shaped by the intersecting dynamics of household and community-based patriarchies, the profit-maximizing ends of private capital, as well as women's survival imperatives and their quest for dignity and financial independence. It also discusses women's involvement in collective bargaining activities and their efforts to resist the "invisibility" that their principal employers seek to impose on them. Scholars of labour movements note that the growing informalization of the workforce in many parts of the world has presented traditional trade unions with multiple challenges, such as a dispersed workforce hidden within homes and neighbourhoods; production processes that are geographically mobile and can shift elsewhere at short notice; the mobility of workers who may themselves move from one workshop to another, making it difficult for unions to locate them; and the blurring of the employer–employee divide in hybrid work arrangements. Research from other parts of the world (such as Brazil and South Africa) shows that even when industries subcontract work assignments through small workshops or home-based work, it has been possible to monitor work conditions and protect workers' rights if local government actors and trade union organizers work synergistically.[2]

However, national, regional and local contexts vary enormously, and such synergies are not present in many cases. How do informally employed workers defend their rights in such instances? This case study in South India attempts to answer the question by showing how home- and neighbourhood-based women workers of a subcontracted industry managed to successfully defend their rights even when government agencies remained unmoved by the representational claims of trade unions and their workers. Drawing on theorization

2 Chris Tilly, Rina Agarwala, Sarah Mosoetsa, Pun Ngai, Carlos Salas and Hina Sheikh, *Informal Worker Organizing as a Strategy for Improving Subcontracted Work in the Textile and Apparel Industries of Brazil, South Africa, India and China* (Los Angeles, 2013), pp. 7–52.

of resistance and claims-making by informal workers in non-standard employment,[3] the chapter discusses diverse forms of collective action by workers including *en masse* work stoppage and strike action, addressing wage-related demands to private employers and social protection-related claims to the state. The chapter argues that a particular conjuncture of circumstances has allowed the women workers to defend their rights as workers vis-à-vis the principal employers and citizens vis-à-vis the state, without privileging one set of demands over another.

1 Study Setting and Methods

The chapter draws on an immersive ethnographic study of tiny production units that make *appalams* or *papads*,[4] clustered in the working class and industrial belt of North Chennai. It is estimated that about 1,500–2,000 workers (mostly women) are currently employed in the *appalam* industry in North Chennai. In the neighbourhood of Otteri, where this study was conducted, 75 *appalam*-making units employ on average between five and twenty workers per unit. Unlike most other trades that were transient and often disappeared from neighbourhoods due to vagaries of the market, *appalam*-making is well established and has a long history in the neighbourhood. The primary data collection for the study, carried out between January and March 2015, included observation of the *appalam*-making process in the neighbourhood units, structured and in-depth interviews with a total of 60 women workers, focus group discussions (FGDs) with the workers of two units, and semi-structured interviews with the owner-manager of two units and the key trade union representative in charge of organizing the women workers. Interviews with trade union organizers continued until mid-2016. Of the 60 women workers interviewed in Otteri, 51 worked in neighbourhood units close to their residence and 9 worked out of their own homes.[5]

3 Rina Agarwala, "From Work to Welfare: A New Class Movement in India", *Critical Asian Studies*, 38 (2006), pp. 419–44; Rina Agarwala, "Resistance and Compliance in the Age of Globalization: Indian Women and Labour Organizations", *Annals of the American Academy of Political and Social Science*, 610 (2007), pp. 143–59.

4 *Appalam, papad* or *papadum* is a thin, crisp, disc-shaped food made from seasoned dough usually of black-gram flour. It is consumed as a snack or an accompaniment to a meal.

5 The grassroots organizers of a prominent trade union (the Centre for Indian Trade Unions, CITU) facilitated the initial contact between the research team and the unit owners and workers. Women were selected for interview on the basis of the unit owners' willingness to allow the research team access to the units and the women workers' readiness to participate

In the following sections of the chapter, I discuss the emergence of subcontracted production in the *appalam* industry and the corresponding feminization of the workforce; the organization of production relations; the somewhat ambivalent position of the unit owner in the production chain; the reasons that have led women to choose this form of employment rather than any other; the women workers' and trade union's actions to secure wage hikes; the centrality of women's earnings to the survival of their households, and their efforts to seek legitimacy and acknowledgement as workers in the eye of the state. In the concluding section, I discuss the key findings and lessons from this case study in the light of scholarly literature on the changing nature of capital–labour relations in contemporary times, workers' resistance and organization in informal work settings, and trade union strategies of mobilization of informal (subcontracted) workers from other parts of the world.

2 The Origins: The Making of an Informal and Female Workforce

In the 1950s, several entrepreneurs from Kerala (a state neighbouring Tamil Nadu) started the *appalam* business in North Chennai with the help of their extended families, and supplied the product to local retail shops. With the rise of branding and marketing over the last few decades, big companies like Bindu, Ambika, Maan Mark and Popular Appalam, who export the food item and earn foreign exchange, have established themselves as principal market players. The established big players or "trademark companies", as they are called in local parlance, employed male workers who were paid monthly wages and directly owned and managed production units from the 1950s to the early 1980s. The monthly wage was Rs 800–900, provided the worker made 2,000 *appalams* a day. A radical change took place in the year 1981, following a strike led by The Centre for Indian Trade Unions (CITU)[6] demanding higher wages. The companies decided to switch to piece-rates and to employ women workers as a strategy to evade labour legislation and demands for wage hikes.[7]

in the study. The interviews were held in the women's place of work based on their preference in this matter.

6 The Centre for Indian Trade Unions (CITU) is a well-known national trade union in India. The leadership of the union is affiliated to the Communist Party of India (Marxist), CPI(M).

7 This account of the history of the *appalam* industry in North Chennai is sourced from the author's interviews with trade union organizers of the CITU (conducted in January–March 2015 and a second round of interviews in April 2016).

From 1981–82, the *appalam* companies began to put up sign boards asking for women to apply for jobs and advertising the presence of an *appalam* unit. Formerly, even a large company employing thirty to forty workers or so would not have a name board advertising its presence. Sacks, flour scattered everywhere and the style of the house were the only identity markers that signalled *appalam*-making in particular homes in the neighbourhood. Women first entered the trade as "helpers" who would make a premature version of the large-sized *pandi appalams*. The male employees acknowledged their presence as subordinate workers who earned a much smaller amount as helpers. As the women acquired the skills to make *pandi appalams* and graduated from being helpers to *appalam* makers themselves, they began to enter the trade in large numbers, in response to the companies' selective recruitment of women workers.[8] The entry of women and the introduction of a piece-rate system of wage payment proceeded in tandem with the exit of men, who sought higher-paid employment elsewhere, and the emergence of unit owners, who formed an intermediary level between the company and the worker.

3 The Process and Chain of Subcontracted Production

The lowest unit in the production chain is the woman worker who works either in her own home or a neighbourhood production unit. The majority of women work in neighbourhood units. The distinct types of *appalam* piece-rate workers include those who knead the dough, the cutters who cut the dough into small pieces, the helpers who flatten the cut pieces into tiny round shapes, and the *appalam* makers who enlarge the pieces, mix them with rice flour and dry them.[9] Women sometimes take along their daughters or younger siblings as their "helpers" to the unit. No more than 15–20 per cent of the *appalam*-making workforce in Otteri is home-based. Work in neighbourhood-based *appalam* units is generally higher paid as it is here

8 Information on women's entry into the trade is sourced from interviews with older women workers in the *appalam* trade and interviews with the Appalam Workers' Union secretary, Selvaraj.

9 The terms "cutter", "helper" and "maker" are used in local parlance. In the year 2016, for every 100 *appalams* made, the payment was Rs 15 (USD 0.21) and usually shared between the helper who was paid Rs 3.50 (USD 0.05) and the *appalam* maker who was paid Rs 11.50 (USD 0.16). Those who kneaded the dough and those who cut it into small pieces earned Rs 27.50 (USD 0.38) and Rs 20.50 (USD 0.28) respectively for every 5 kilograms of dough they worked on.

that women make the large-sized *pandi appalams* that require skill gained through practice and training in the units. Home-based *appalam* workers obtain the flour in the morning from neighbourhood units close to their homes and deliver the stipulated number of *appalams* to the supplier units by the end of the day.[10] In the last stage of production, the *appalams* are laid out to dry for several hours. The requirement of physical space – usually an attached terrace – makes it impossible for women who live in smaller tenements to make *pandi appalams*. Home-based workers usually make smaller-sized *appalam* "chips" that require less space for drying. Making the chips is deemed easier and low-skilled work and is therefore paid less. Home-based workers are likely to be women who are unable to leave their homes for paid work even for a few hours a day owing to domestic care work-related responsibilities. Women also migrate from home- to unit-based work over the course of their working lives, depending on shifting domestic responsibilities.[11]

While the workers are overwhelmingly women, the unit owners are mostly men or, in some cases, married couples. The unit owner is the person who receives the raw material (sacks of flour) from the *appalam* company. He rents a house (also the owner's living quarters), recruits women from the neighbourhood, manages the unit's affairs and oversees production activities. The unit owners work alongside the workers and pay themselves wages on a piece-rate basis. They must ensure that their homes have the required space (to dry the *pandi appalams*) and that they have the permission of the house owner, if the house is rented, to run an *appalam* unit.[12] We found that the *appalam* industry in Otteri has optimally used neighbourhood residential spaces (larger homes with terraces attached as well as smaller tenements) and women's life cycle-related constraints in strategic ways and to its advantage.

10 Source: Research team's first-hand observation of the *appalam* industry in Otteri, North Chennai.

11 Source: Interviews conducted with a sample of women workers. The structured interviews included questions on women's entry into and exit from the industry in the course of their working lives.

12 Source: Direct observation of the *appalam*-making units and interviews with two *appalam* unit owners conducted as part of the field work for the study.

4 Why Do Women Choose Appalam Work?

The popularity of *appalam*-making among women in the Otteri area may be attributed to the familial nature of the neighbourhood unit workspace.[13] It was not uncommon for women to be working in units owned by their female kin. Two of the respondents were working in their sisters' units, while one was working in her mother's unit. The degree of comfort the women felt was reflected in their choice of attire: 30 per cent of them said they wore nighties to work regularly, while 8.3 per cent alternated between wearing nighties and saris.[14] We noted that women never wore nighties when they moved out of their neighbourhood to work. When asked why they had chosen *appalam* work, almost all the respondents mentioned the advantage of combining the responsibilities of social reproduction and domestic care work. Apart from the proximity of the workspace and its convenient location in the neighbourhood, work in the units offered flexibility of timing in terms of coming to work late, leaving early and taking leave when required: 81.7 per cent of the women interviewed reported that their workspaces offered this flexibility. As a woman is paid for the work she does, she cannot be pressured to report for work at a fixed time every day.

Amongst the 60 respondents was a young mother who left her infant at home and came to work in a neighbourhood unit for approximately three hours a day. When her child grew a little older, she was confident that she could bring the child with her as she worked in her mother's unit. Children came to the units from school and spent time waiting for their mothers to finish work. Units sometimes doubled up as *de facto* crèches or nurseries, without any of the associated infrastructure. Table 13.1 shows the age break-up of the 60 women workers interviewed. The data indicate that *appalam* work in the units permitted women to manage household tasks and childcare alongside paid work. As Table 13.1 shows, women in the age group 20–35 years, who are more likely to have younger children including infants and toddlers, constituted close to 42 per cent of all respondents.

The women workers' preference for *appalam* work also derived from a pragmatic assessment of other employment opportunities available in and around

13 All the material in this section is drawn from the testimonials of 60 women *appalam* workers interviewed for the study, and the research team's observation of the *appalam*-making units.

14 The nightie is a loose, flowing garment that is often worn by women in Chennai (and other Indian cities as well) in and around their residential spaces, as a more comfortable alternative to the sari.

TABLE 13.1 Age profile of sample respondents (Otteri, North Chennai)

	Age (years)	Frequency	Percentage
1	20–35	25	41.6
2	35–50	26	43.3
3	50–65	8	13.3
4	65–75	1	1.6
	Total	60	100

SOURCE: FIELD DATA, JANUARY–MARCH 2015.

their neighbourhoods. As they saw it, most of the alternative opportunities were dismal and involved drudgery. Besides, the same income or even more could be earned from *appalam* work in the units, where a woman could push herself to work harder and longer and earn the money she required on a particular day. Some women expressed relief that they were spared the sexual harassment that women routinely face on the streets when using public transport in the city, and the discomfort and expense of a daily commute to work. A few also cited the absence of men in the workplace as a blessing. Besides the problems (of harassment) that male co-workers might pose, an all-woman workspace had other advantages. As one woman said, "My husband will not send me for domestic work [in other homes] or anywhere else. He suspects me [of infidelity] all the time." Another respondent stated that she was worried that "others" (neighbours and relatives) would disapprove if she went far from the home and neighbourhood to work. A third woman mentioned that the proximate location of her workplace allowed her to keep an eye on her teenage daughter at home. The need to protect girls' reputations and watch out for "undesirable" relationships that might lead to cross-caste elopement was a concern often expressed by the mothers of young daughters.

Of the 60 respondents, ten were from the Scheduled Castes (SCs). The rest were from the poorer sections of Other Backward Classes (OBCs) and Other Castes (OCs).[15] The social norms of female domesticity are stronger among

15 The Indian government classifies caste groups as Scheduled Castes, Other Backward Classes and Other Castes in decreasing order of social oppression and deprivation. The SCs include the historically disadvantaged population of India that has endured the most severe forms of social discrimination and poverty. The term OBCs designates those castes that are deemed socially and educationally disadvantaged by the Indian government.

these two groups and circumscribe women's choices with respect to paid work. As compared to SC women, OBC and OC women are more likely to face caste and social status-related barriers to working outside the home and the neighbourhood. We also noted that the caste life-worlds the women inhabit mark certain types of paid work as socially acceptable and certain other types as less so. Caste-specific ideologies make it difficult for women from socially advantaged and dominant castes to countenance certain types of employment, such as housekeeping in shops and offices and domestic work in others' homes, because of involvement in sanitary work (the requirement of cleaning toilets and bathrooms), which is considered to be socially menial. *Appalam* work, on the other hand, involves food preparation in workspaces situated within the neighbourhood, enhancing its perceived status as a "respectable" occupation.

The chapter has discussed, thus far, how the flexibility of *appalam* work, its all-women composition, its neighbourhood location and the crisscrossing of familial and kin-based social ties and relationships in the units facilitated women's negotiations with household and community patriarchies, enabling them to secure and sustain access to paid employment. We turn next to the question of the position of the unit owner within the subcontracted production chain.

5 The Unit Owner: "Self-Made' Entrepreneur or a Cog in the Wheel of Subcontracted Production?

While the unit owners received flour from the company, they invested their own money to buy other raw materials such as coconut oil, water and lime water. For 100 kilograms of flour received from the company, the unit owner was expected to deliver 120 kilograms of *appalam* and was paid Rs 8,200 (USD 113.75) by the company. If the quantity delivered fell short even by a kilogram or two, the loss had to be borne by the unit owner. After wage payment to workers and deducting the costs of raw material purchased, it was estimated that the unit owner generally earned between Rs 500 and Rs 1,000 (USD 6.9 and 13.9) for every 100 kilograms of *appalam* supplied to the company. The size of the unit (in terms of the number of workers) determined the production capacity and earnings of the unit owner.[16]

While the SCs and the OBCs are covered by affirmative action policies, the Other Castes (OCs) are not, since they constitute the socially advantaged and privileged sections of the population.

16 All the material in this section is sourced from interviews with two owners managing *appalam*-making units in the study area.

Unit owner Swarna's account of how she graduated from being a daily wager in an *appalam* unit to starting her own unit illustrates the challenges involved in making the transition. Now aged 53 years, Swarna had begun to work full-time in *appalam* units from the age of thirteen. She started her own unit twenty years ago along with her husband, in order to create a more flexible work environment for herself, her mother and her six sisters; all of them currently work in Swarna's unit. Lacking the capital required to start a unit, she decided to approach the popular Tamil actor, "Superstar" Rajinikant, who has a reputation as a philanthropist. Accompanied by her sisters, she showed up at the home of the actor and pleaded their case successfully. Swarna and her sisters were given Rs 1,000 (USD 13.9) as well as a few sacks of flour, rice and oil to kickstart the business. Swarna spoke with pride of the initiative she had taken to approach the actor and seek his assistance.

Apart from workers' wages, the unit owners need to generate sufficient income to pay the rent for the premises (also their home) where the production takes place. A house that doubled up as an *appalam*-making unit was large-sized and therefore more expensive. The case of Sarala discussed here clarifies the position of a unit owner in the subcontracted production chain of the *appalam* industry. Sarala entered the *appalam* trade as her sister's helper, when she was sixteen years old. At the time of our study, Sarala ran a twenty-worker unit in a large-sized house whose monthly rental value was Rs 14,100 (USD 195.6). Sarala had paid the *appalam* company a (refundable) deposit of Rs 100,000 (USD 1,387) and the women workers in her unit an advance of Rs 100,000 that will be repaid when they leave the unit. Sarala claimed that the costs of running the unit have ruined her financially, pushing her into debt amounting to Rs 200,000 (USD 2,774). The particular company she transacted with paid less for the *appalams* as compared to other companies, but did not impose too many conditions regarding the terms of delivery.

According to Sarala, a unit owner has to keep lending small amounts of money to the workers, ranging from Rs 50 (USD 0.7) to Rs 100 (USD 1.4), in order to incentivize them to come on time and be regular at work. This was something she was unable to do, given her low cash reserves. When workers were tardy or took leave, it took the unit fifteen days to deliver *appalams* that ought to be made in a week. Sarala estimated that if her unit made 300 kilograms of *appalam* a day it would allow her to pay the house rent out of the profits. But her unit made only 150 kilograms a day and so she ended up paying the rent out of her own (piece-rate) wages for doing *appalam* work. Sarala was clear that she was a coolie worker like the other women workers in her unit. In her words: "I have the status or the 'name' of an owner (*'owner amma'*), but nothing more than that." She maintained that the *appalam* trade can be a profit-making business for an "entrepreneur-owner" only if s/he is able to buy the flour directly from the market, establish contact with and procure orders from a large number of retail shops, and sell the *appalams* to a range of buyers (both shops and *appalam* companies), choosing higher prices wherever available. Being a single woman of limited financial means, the mobility, social and business networks and capital investment required to run a successful *appalam*-making business were out of the question for her.

6 Naming the "Hidden" Employer and Exposing the "Dummy" Union

As part of a deliberately cultivated strategy to distance themselves from the workers, the *appalam* companies insisted that every unit owner legally register the unit as an independent entity in his/her name. The companies supplied flour to the units and established a regular relationship with them only after they were formally registered. Once a unit was registered, all transactions were conducted in the name of the unit's owner.[17] In the year 2013, the CITU-led Appalam Workers' Union filed a case in the labour court asking that the companies be held directly accountable to *appalam* workers for employee benefits, and that they acknowledge their subcontracted relationship to the units that receive the flour and supply *appalams* to them. The companies filed responses in turn, claiming that they were merely wholesale traders who buy from small traders or the "real" manufacturers – the unit owners. Therefore, the companies argued, they could not be held responsible for employee benefits. While the case has stagnated after a few hearings, the CITU continues to maintain its position (argued in the labour court) that the supplier of the raw material was the real employer and cannot abdicate responsibility for the welfare of the workers. The only units that the *appalam* companies directly own and manage are the godowns/sheds where the storing and packaging of the *appalams* take place. The majority of workers in these units were also women, who, unlike the *appalam* workers in the units, received benefits like Provident Fund (PF) and Employees State Insurance (ESI) that the companies contribute to.[18]

Although a union does exist for the owners of the *appalam* units, it is generally acknowledged that it is a "dummy" union managed by the *appalam* companies, with no real power to increase wages or offer benefits to workers. As the secretary of the CITU-led Appalam Workers' Union put it, "We look at all

17 Source: Interviews with two unit owners and the CITU's Appalam Workers' Union secretary, Selvaraj.

18 Source: Interview with CITU's Appalam Workers' Union secretary, Selvaraj.

unit owners as workers, even if they think they are above the workers." When deposing before the Labour Commission in 2013, the CITU union secretary declared before the commissioner that the office-bearers of the unit owners' union (also present at the meeting) were employees "like us" and could not take any autonomous decisions. All the office bearers present reportedly concurred, knowing that if they protested his statement, they would be in trouble when they returned to their neighbourhood.

7 Strike Action and Wage Bargaining

The CITU-led trade union has played a central role in securing yearly wage increases for the *appalam* workers. The Appalam Workers' Union formally presented a petition at the start of every year to the "dummy" union representing the unit owners, with the implicit understanding that a strike would follow if the proposed increase was not accepted.[19] The years in which big work strikes had taken place were 1981, 2013 and 2014. The strike action in 2014 was noticeable for the arrests of women workers. Around 75–90 per cent of the women workers usually participated in strike calls, excepting those who could not survive without the daily wages earned from *appalam* work.[20] Sit-in and *gherao* protests (involving encirclement of buildings) were organized outside the packing and supply depots and godowns of the big *appalam* companies (not the homes of the office-bearers of the "dummy" union) in order to foreground the responsibility of the companies towards the workforce. The unit owners did not directly participate in the strike, but some of them sent their workers whenever collective action was planned. The unit owners, who were also workers in their own units, stood to gain if the wages rose.[21]

In January 2016, the wage increase was accepted as soon as the Workers' Union submitted the petition and without any form of action on the part of the workers. Interestingly, it was the smaller companies that decided upon and initiated the wage increase, forcing the hand of the trademark companies in this matter. The small companies reportedly feared a strike more as they would lose their market (retail and other shops) to the trademark companies. With

19 Each year, the wage increase demanded (and obtained) was approximately Rs 1.50 (USD 0.021) for every 5 kilograms for those who knead the dough, Re. 1 (USD 0.014) for every 5 kilograms of dough for the cutters, and 50 paise (USD 0.007) per 100 *appalams* for the *appalam* makers.

20 Source: Interview with the CITU Appalam Workers' Union secretary, Selvaraj.

21 Source: Interviews with *appalam* women workers and two unit owners.

tonnes of stock in their godowns, the big companies could deliver to the shops even during a period of strike. At the end of each strike, the small companies found that they had lost their regular buyers to the trademark companies.[22] The competition between small and large players worked to the advantage of the *appalam* workforce in terms of providing the workers and their union some leverage with respect to wage negotiations. While the trade union could not prevent the transition from monthly wages to piece-rates (in the early 1980s), they continued to organize the workforce through the 1990s and the 2000s, securing some wage relief for the workers. In the next section, we turn to the question of what employment in the *appalam* industry meant for its women workers.

8 Women's Earnings and Household Survival

Several women workers described *appalam* work in neighbourhood units as a means for destitute women to survive with dignity.[23] It is noteworthy that many other types of home-based and piece-rated work in the Otteri area only allowed the workers to earn a supplementary or secondary income, whereas *appalam* work allowed its workers to be the primary earners of their families, if their household circumstances warranted it. Table 13.2 shows the marital status of the 60 respondents of our study.

TABLE 13.2 Marital status of sample respondents (Otteri, North Chennai)

Marital status	Frequency	Percentage
Married	41	68.3
Unmarried	2	3.3
Divorced/separated	13	21.7
Widowed	4	6.7
Total	60	100

SOURCE: FIELD DATA, JANUARY–MARCH 2015.

22 Source: Interview with the CITU Appalam Workers' Union secretary, Selvaraj.

23 All the material in this section is sourced from interviews held with the sample of 60 women *appalam* workers.

In Table 13.2, the two unmarried women (aged 25 years each) were part of their natal households consisting of their parents and siblings. We might therefore regard the households of the 17 (13+4) divorced/separated and widowed women as the potential female-headed households in this sample. Of these seventeen, six were sole earners, whereas one other income earner co-supported the households of the others. Of the seventeen, the households of eleven women depended exclusively on earnings from *appalam* work, with the other income earner in the family also employed in the *appalam* industry. All six women who were sole earners were part of *de jure* female-headed families, where the husband was dead or permanently absent. Four of the six women lived alone and supported themselves. Two of them had two dependent children each. Table 13.3 shows women's earnings from *appalam* work (calculated for a month) for all 60 respondents.

Table 13.3 shows that 40 per cent of the women interviewed earned between Rs 2,000 (USD 27.7) and Rs 4,000 (USD 55.5) a month. The eight women who earned upward of Rs 6,000 (USD 83.2) a month included those whose economic need was dire as well as those who could work more hours a day as they were free of child-care responsibilities. It was found that women's earnings primarily financed the welfare-enhancing consumption expenditure of their households and also enabled them to meet the self-consumption needs that they prioritized. The women identified food and house rent as the most common end-uses of their incomes, followed by children-oriented expenses

TABLE 13.3 Monthly earnings of sample respondents from *appalam* work (Otteri, North Chennai)

Women's monthly earnings (in Rs)	Frequency	Percentage
<1000	2	3.3
1000 < 2000	16	26.7
2000 < 4000	24	40
4000 < 6000	10	16.7
6000 < 8000	4	6.7
8000 < 10,000	4	6.7
Total	60	100

SOURCE: FIELD DATA, JANUARY–MARCH 2015.

(such as clothing and snack food), their own needs, health care and children's education-related expenses, and the repayment of debt of household members.

Almost all the women interviewed asserted the identity of "working woman" with pride, in response to a question probing the dimension of self-identification. As their responses indicated, the (self and family) recognition that they made a significant contribution to family incomes was a critical factor here. "Yes of course, I am a working woman, I brought up my sisters with this money", "I was able to take care of my son" and "I stand on my own feet" were some of the responses. One woman informed us that she had separated from her husband who had sought to control her. Resisting his domineering ways, she left him and supported her children with wages from *appalam* work. Women's status as income-earners enabled a measure of dignity within marriage, even if the wages they earned were not critical to family survival. Married to a government employee who earned well, a home-based worker made *appalams* from home despite her husband's unconcealed irritation at the sight of the flour and her work.

Three women testified to how work at the neighbourhood unit served as a welcome break for those who craved a few hours of "escape" from home. One woman commented on the relaxing work atmosphere of the unit, which is an "outlet for all the sorrows at home". Another asserted that she was happy only when she was working. For the most part, the respondents' families recognized and respected the women's financial contribution, motivated as it was by the economic needs of the households. In a telling response to our question on what her family thought of her employment, a woman replied bluntly, "There's nothing to think. There's a need and there's no choice." In the course of a focus group discussion held in an *appalam* unit, a woman emphatically said, "Nowadays men don't want women to sit at home. They don't mind us working anywhere as long as the money comes on time. 'Don't ask me for money, you earn', is what they say." Her co-workers enthusiastically endorsed her response as an accurate commentary on a changing and lamentable state of affairs, marked by men's readiness to renounce their role as primary family providers.

9 Citizenship Claims vis-à-vis the State

While the *appalam*-making women were absolutely certain that they were workers who added value to their families and society, claiming their entitlements as workers from the state was a different matter. The state government of Tamil Nadu has in place a Tamil Nadu Manual Workers Welfare Board, set up in March 1999 in order to implement the provisions of the Tamil Nadu Manual Workers (Regulation of Employment and Conditions of Work) Act, 1982. Significantly, this was the first Act to cover all workers irrespective of the employer–employee relationship; in all previous laws, a permanent relationship with employers had to be demonstrated. Currently, the Manual Workers Welfare Board administers the state government's social security and welfare schemes for workers of both sexes, which include compensation for accidental death or disability; funeral expenses; pension benefit when the worker completes 60 years of age; disability pension; education scholarships and marriage assistance for the children of workers; maternity benefits for women workers for two pregnancies, and assistance for miscarriage or medical termination of pregnancy.[24]

The Appalam Workers' Union secretary estimated that the CITU-led union had facilitated the registration of close to 50 per cent of *appalam* workers in the neighbourhood of Otteri with the Manual Workers Board, and that it had been a struggle to accomplish this. The workers were required to directly visit the Welfare Board to enrol as members, for renewal of membership, to obtain subsidies and other welfare and relief measures, and so on. As the union secretary put it, workers who have to sacrifice wages of Rs 1,000 in order to get a benefit of the same amount or a little more were hardly likely to consider it a worthwhile pursuit. Whatever the shortcomings of the state's administrative procedures, the women *appalam* workers interviewed were forthcoming and emphatic on what they expected from the government and/or their employers that could enhance their work experience. One of them said, "I have been working for thirty years and when I stop I will have nothing to show for it unless the government decides to give me a pension." Another told us, "So many of us are single women who depend on the *appalam* money for our next meal. There should be a special welfare scheme for women like us."

With respect to their rights as workers, quite a few women asked that the current piece-rates be converted to monthly wages with provision for periodic wage revisions. While the wage did rise when the union announced protest actions, the strikes took a toll on the women and their families. As one woman described it, "We sat on strike for a whole month to get an increase of 50 paise [for every 100 *appalams* made]. How hard it was and how much our families suffered that month!" One worker said in strident tones, "During festivals, a bonus. And when we fall ill, we want leave and our wages too!" Significantly,

24 Tamil Nadu Manual Workers Welfare Board and 13 Other Boards, "Information Handbook under 'Right to Information Act 2005' "; available at www.tn.gov.in, last accessed 8 December 2019.

the women's demands and expectations displayed a clear understanding of the precise measures and interventions required (both on the part of the state government and the "real" employers – the *appalam* companies) to formalize their employment status, to improve the conditions of work, to guarantee minimum wages and to extend the full gamut of social security provisions to them.

10 Discussion and Conclusion

Home-based work remains entrenched in many countries, as part of a growing informalization of the labour force. Such informalization has gained momentum as a consequence of neoliberal policies of economic restructuring adopted in India since the 1990s, and in other countries since the 1980s.[25] In a global climate wherein capital, pursuing cost-cutting competitiveness, seeks out a "flexible" and cheap labour force that can be hired and fired at will, home-based workers appear to be an optimal workforce for companies that can subcontract and hire contingent or contractual rather than regular workers. Women employed as home-based workers in such a system have subsidized capital accumulation by constituting a low-waged labour pool, providing and paying for infrastructure and other input costs as well as completely taking over the costs of labour reproduction.[26] Given this larger canvas, this chapter closely examines the case of home- and neighbourhood-based women *appalam* makers in Chennai city labouring in the lower rungs of the informal sector in an industry that, in a calculated manner, informalized its workforce at the same time as it feminized it.

In the chapter, I heed feminist researchers who emphasize that women's work, be it unpaid, subsistence-oriented or low-paid, is integral to capitalist

25 Jan Breman, "An Informalized Labour System: End of Labour Market Dualism", *Economic and Political Weekly*, 36 (December 2001–January 2002), pp. 4804–21; Agarwala, "Resistance and Compliance in the Age of Globalization", pp. 143–59; Ravi Srivastava, "Changing Employment Conditions of the Indian Workforce and Implications for Decent Work", *Global Labour Journal*, 3 (2012), pp. 63–90; Guy Standing, "Global Feminization through Flexible Labour: A Theme Revisited", *World Development*, 27 (1999), pp. 583–602.

26 Jayati Ghosh, "Globalization, Export-oriented Employment for Women and Social Policy: A Case Study of India", *Social Scientist*, 30 (2002), pp. 17–60; Jayati Ghosh, "Informalization and Women's Workforce Participation: A Consideration of Recent Trends in Asia", in Shahra Razavi (ed.), *The Gendered Impacts of Liberalization: Towards "Embedded Liberalism?"* (New York, 2009), pp. 1–36; Elisabeth Prugl, "Home-based Workers: A Comparative Exploration of Mies's Theory of Housewifization", *Frontiers: A Journal of Women Studies*, 17 (1996), pp. 114–35.

accumulation.[27] However, as has been pointed out, there is need to flesh out theoretically and empirically "the manner in which capitalist relations of production operate on the ground to keep large masses of people perennially informal".[28] Thus, it is important to provide a fine-grained and ethnographically informed account of how women's work in different capacities as subcontracted workers, self-employed, petty commodity producers, service providers or in their reproductive capacities, is linked to the process of capitalist accumulation and expansion. In the *appalam* industry in North Chennai, the entry of women in large numbers since the early 1980s, the introduction of piece-rated wages and the creation of an intermediary level of unit owners were interlinked developments that drastically changed capital–labour relations. Even as men moved out of the industry seeking higher paid employment elsewhere, women emerged as a disciplined workforce willing and eager to accept the piece-rated wages on offer.

As feminist researchers note,[29] women whose identities are ideologically constructed in ways that tie them to the family, household and subsistence production do not own their full labour power and do not therefore become free wage workers, in so far as their wage-earning opportunities are constrained by ideological constructions and material realities. This study of the *appalam* industry in North Chennai reveals how patriarchal and possibly also caste-mediated ideologies have made available a feminized workforce for exploitation by export revenue-earning companies that pursue subcontracting and labour law-evading strategies of growth. The chapter thus lays bare the modalities by which capital accumulation in a food preparation industry in Chennai city is "at its very core" a gendered set of processes, constituting a moment that cannot be understood without central attention to the differential situations of women and men.[30]

---

27 Nandita Gandhi and Nandita Shah, "Women Workers and Industrial Restructuring in Two Industries in Mumbai", in Bharati Ray (ed.), *Women of India: Colonial and Post-Colonial Periods* (New Delhi, 2005), pp. 320–50; Maria Mies, "Capitalist Development and Subsistence Reproduction: Rural Women in India", *Bulletin of Concerned Asian Scholars*, 12 (1980), pp. 2–14; Maria Mies, "Dynamics of Sexual Division of Labour and Capital Accumulation: Women Lace Workers of Narsapur", *Economic and Political Weekly*, 16 (1981), pp. 487–500; Prugl, "Home-Based Workers", pp. 114–35.

28 Padmini Swaminathan, "Introduction", in Padmini Swaminathan (ed.), *Women and Work: Essays from Economic and Political Weekly* (Hyderabad, 2012), pp. 1–17, p. 15.

29 Elisabeth Prugl and Irene Tinker, "Microentrepreneurs and Homeworkers: Convergent Categories", *World Development*, 25 (1997), pp. 1471–82; Mies, "Dynamics of Sexual Division of Labour", pp. 487–500.

30 Hartsock, "Globalization and Primitive Accumulation", in Castrée and Gregory, *David Harvey: A Critical Reader*, pp. 167–90, p. 183.

The chapter maps the processes by which women workers acquired a political consciousness of their subordinate relation to capital, and gained the voice and visibility required to make claims vis-à-vis their employers and state actors. In this case, a crucial component of trade union mobilization of workers (both women workers and unit owners) was to *foreground and politicize their identities as "dependent workers"* in a triangular relationship (of *appalam* company, unit owner and worker), where power lay with the principal employers who gave out work orders, supplied the raw materials, checked for quality and adherence to production standards, and made payment to unit owners. Notwithstanding the trademark companies' efforts to pass off the unit owners as the real producers or independent manufacturers, the owners clearly knew that they were disguised wage workers, not self-employed or own-account entrepreneurs. The women who owned and managed *appalam*-making units interviewed for this study, no doubt, displayed a spirit of enterprise and risk-taking in making the transition from working in others' units to setting up their own units, besides investing considerable reserves of working capital. Nonetheless, they had no direct relationship with the market, lacked control over raw materials, products and deadlines, and were paid piece-rates themselves.

While discussing the organizing strategies of traditional trade unions versus new kinds of unions working among informal sector workers (mostly women workers in highly precarious employment situations) in India, scholars have observed that the latter tend to target the state rather than employers and to demand welfare benefits for workers rather than workers' rights. The paradigm of "worker versus employer" is seen as having given way to "citizen versus state", with demands too being shifted from workplace benefits to family-related social welfare benefits. In contrast, the traditional trade unions make workplace-related demands of the employer, such as minimum wages, permanent contracts for all workers, eradication of subcontractors and so on.[31] In the case of the *appalam* industry of North Chennai, the trade union put forward both wage- and employment status-related demands to the employers and social welfare demands to the state, without emphasizing one at the expense of the other. To understand better how this was possible, it might be instructive to compare this case with that of trade union strategies and struggles in other parts of the world, especially where they involve irregularly employed workers in non-standard employment.

31 Agarwala, "From Work to Welfare", pp. 419–44; Agarwala, "Resistance and Compliance in the Age of Globalization", pp. 143–59.

Experiences of labour organization among informally employed workers in other parts of the world reveal that collaborative action between trade union organizers and government officials and institutions opened up spaces that enabled the protection of workers' rights and well-being. For instance, when the garment industry in Sao Paulo city of Brazil restructured in the 1990s and increased subcontracting through small workshops and home-based work, the Ibitinga Needle Workers Union was set up to help the largely female workforce improve labour conditions and register with the Ministry of Labour in order to get labour cards. In 2001, the union mobilized support from the labour courts in order to push local employers to sign a collective bargaining agreement so that home-based workers would be granted labour cards, and unions would have the right to oversee and inspect conditions in all workplaces. The Ibitinga Union, the Seamstresses' Union of São Paulo and Osasco, and the National Confederation of Apparel Workers (CNTV) of Brazil used a comprehensive strategy of educating home-based workers (on their rights as workers), pressure on government officials to intervene and direct negotiation with employers at the top of the supply chain in the garment industry. Significantly, trade unions active in the (increasingly subcontracted) garment industry forged alliances with government agencies and inspectors to pressure principal employers to conform to labour laws by fining offenders and referring cases to labour courts, where 90 per cent of complaints had decisions favourable to workers.[32]

In South Africa, the South African Clothing and Textiles Union (SACTWU) sought to register all workers (including home-based workers) by bringing them under the scrutiny of regional Bargaining Councils, key institutions that resolved labour disputes and enforced laws. Like in Brazil, unions in South Africa worked collaboratively with government inspectors to initiate proceedings against employers for not complying with labour standards. Unions have persuaded the Bargaining Councils to extend their agreements to cover wages and working conditions of workers in informal sectors, including home-based workers.[33] The synergistic action between trade unions and government agencies in South Africa and Brazil stands in contrast to our case in India, where the state government was least interested in protecting the employment status of workers, responding to their demand for wage hikes or censuring the companies, despite the abundant evidence furnished by the CITU-led union with respect to the identity of the "real" employers in the *appalam* industry. Following the stagnation of the case in the labour court, the union organizer

32 Tilly, Agarwala, Mosoetsa, Ngai, Salas and Sheikh, "Informal Worker Organizing as a Strategy", pp. 7–52.

33 Ibid.

admitted (to me) that the union had neither the funds nor the time to fight exhausting court battles and feared that a legal route would simply destroy their case. In such a situation, a strategy of petitioning the companies and inviting them to conciliation talks while continuing to work in the *appalam* units would have demoralized the workers. And therefore, strikes and agitation were seen as the only way forward.

If government pressure and intervention on their behalf was not forthcoming, the workers' interests were inadvertently served by the market heterogeneity that prevailed with respect to the buyers of their product – the *appalam* companies. The struggle of small companies to survive vis-à-vis the large trademark companies had made them the allies, albeit unintended, of the *appalam* workforce, given the part they played in initiating the sought-after wage increase. Commenting on the bargaining power of the Appalam Workers' Union, its secretary Selvaraj said with some pride, "No other union, of either domestic workers, petty vendors, street hawkers or other informal workers, has the power to merely put forward a petition and get a wage raise." However, this state of affairs cannot be generalized elsewhere. In other districts in Tamil Nadu, including those close to Chennai, the prevailing wage in the *appalam* industry was 70 per cent less as compared to Chennai, and annual wage hikes did not take place as the union secretary confirmed.

It is important to note that a particular conjuncture of circumstances, including the strong base established by the trade union in North Chennai since the 1950s and market competition among the buyers of the product, has made possible successful collective action on the part of the women *appalam* workers. It was this conjuncture of circumstances that allowed the trade union to defend home-based women workers' rights as workers vis-à-vis their "hidden" employers and their rights as citizens vis-à-vis the state government's Manual Workers Welfare Board. And therefore, as the chapter has shown, the relationship between women's unprotected, low-paid labour and capital accumulation is mediated by state policies extending social protection to informal manual workers, trade union strategies of mobilization, market competition among the product buyers and the women's aspirations for a better life for themselves.

The women workers' struggles, however, are far from over, and their gains, hard-won as they are, remain fragile and tenuous. During the period of this field study (April–June 2016), a threefold increase in the price of the primary raw material (*urad dhal* or black gram) hit the *appalam* trade severely. The inflation impacted sales and reduced the demand for *appalams*. This in turn considerably decreased the production orders received by unit owners from the companies to which they remain attached, adversely affecting the generation of employment in this sector. Registration with the Manual Workers Welfare Board and securing benefits through the assorted welfare schemes of the Board remain a bureaucratic nightmare for the women workers. We might, however, draw hope from the fact that the women *appalam* workers of North Chennai have consistently refused to remain invisible and fiercely contested the efforts of private capital to invisibilize them. Their experience of organizing as home- and neighbourhood-based workers located in the last rung of a subcontracted production chain highlights the strategies by which women workers and their trade union allies have sought to counter the organized power of private capital and wrest concessions from an increasingly indifferent state.

CHAPTER 14

Home-based Workers

Organizing from Local to Global

Chris Bonner

This chapter briefly traces the history of home-based workers' organizing over the past forty years. It then provides a snapshot of how some home-based workers are currently organizing in different countries and regions, including the size and status of the regional networks, the forms that grassroots organizations take and how different characteristics require a range of organizational strategies. In Stockholm, in May 2018, prior to the Conference on "Long-term Perspectives on Home-based Industrial Work", representatives of home-based workers from five regions, together with *Women in Informal Employment: Globalizing and Organizing* (WIEGO), met, discussed and took a decision to work towards the formation of an international network of home-based workers. This chapter provides information on the process and plans for the launch of HomeNet International, originally scheduled for 2020 but rescheduled as a virtual event in early 2021, due to COVID-19. The chapter is based on the personal experiences of the author, and draws on information and writings of others active in supporting organizations of home-based workers.

1 Organizing: A Long Journey

In the early 1970s, the Self Employed Women's Association (SEWA) began organizing informal workers in India. Women workers who "stitched garments in their homes for contractors but were seen only as 'housewives' "[1] started approaching SEWA. "We realized that many 'housewives' are workers, but are invisible – even for their husbands", said Renana Jhabvala, president of SEWA

1 Chris Bonner, Pat Horn and Renana Jhabvala, "Informal Women Workers Open ILO Doors through Transnational Organizing, 1980s to 2010s", in Eileen Boris, Dorothea Hoehtker and Susan Zimmermann (eds), *Women's ILO: Transnational Networks, Global Labour Standards and Gender Equality* (Leiden, 2018), pp. 176–201, p. 180.

© CHRIS BONNER, 2022 | DOI:10.1163/9789004499614_016
This is an open access chapter distributed under the terms of the CC BY-NC-ND 4.0 license.

Bharat and HomeNet South Asia, and former national coordinator of SEWA. This led SEWA to coin the term "home-based workers".[2]

In the 1980s, groups of home-based workers who were organizing in both developing and developed countries began forging links. During this period, SEWA in particular put pressure on trade unions and the International Labour Organization (ILO) to recognize home-based workers. This gathered momentum in the late 1980s, and in 1990 the ILO agreed to convene an Expert Meeting to discuss the conditions of home workers. In 1991 the home-based worker groups, together with allies, met and discussed the idea of forming an international network. And in 1994, at a meeting held at the headquarters of the International Confederation of Free Trade Unions (ICFTU) in Brussels, home-based worker representatives from India, Canada, Netherlands, South Africa and the UK, together with representatives from unions, ICFTU, ILO, the International Union of Food, Agricultural, Hotel, Restaurant, Catering, Tobacco and Allied Workers' Associations (IUF) and the International Textiles, Garments and Leather Workers Federation (ITGLWF) established an international coordinating body. This was registered in the Netherlands as a formal trust known as HomeNet. By then the Governing Body of the ILO had agreed to put home work on the agenda for a discussion on an international standard at the 1995–96 International Labour Conferences (ILC). In 1996, after tense negotiations, the Home Work Convention (C177) and accompanying Resolution (R184) were adopted.[3] This victory led to moves to extend the membership of HomeNet and to put in place a democratic structure and constitution. This did not succeed, however, and a split took place. One group formed Home Workers World Wide (HWWW), based in the UK, and later, in 2006, the Federation of Home Workers Worldwide (FHWW).[4] The focus of SEWA and its allies, especially WIEGO, shifted to helping build and strengthen regional networks in South and Southeast Asia, namely, HomeNet South East Asia (HNSEA), formed

2 Renana Jhabvala, "History of this Movement", opening address at the Conference of Home-based Workers, New Delhi, India, February 2015; available at www.wiego.org, last accessed 28 May 2020.

3 See accounts in IUF, "Organizing Home-based Workers", *Women at Work*, Winter 1994–95; Renana Jhabvala and Jane Tate, "Out of the Shadows: Home-based Workers Organize for International Recognition", *SEEDS, No. 18* (New York, 1996); Bonner, Horn and Jhabvala, "Informal Women Workers", pp. 182–85. For a detailed account of the processes towards and during the ILC discussion on home work, see Eileen Boris's chapter in this volume, "From Industrial Evil to Decent Work: The ILO and Changing Perspectives towards Home-Based Labour".

4 For more information on Home Workers World Wide, see www.homeworkersww.org.uk, last accessed 2 June 2020.

in 1997, and HomeNet South Asia (HNSA), formed in 2000 and formally launched in 2007.

From 2008, organizing in South and Southeast Asia intensified, aided by an injection of funds and support from WIEGO including research, statistics and capacity-building. Organizations grew, became stronger and made some remarkable gains. HomeNet Thailand, an affiliate of HNSEA, succeeded in gaining a law for home-based workers. In 2010, the Thai parliament passed the Home Workers Protection Act. As Poonsap Tulaphan, coordinator of HomeNet Thailand, noted: "Over the past ten years, we have dedicated our efforts, energy and resources to push for the passage of this law. So its enactment brought us such pride and joy". In 2011, in another victory for HomeNet Thailand and its allies, the Thai government introduced a policy to pay about 30 per cent as contributor's fee towards a social security fund for informal workers, making social security accessible to home-based and other informal workers.[5] In 2008, SEWA and HNSA launched the South Asian Association for Regional Cooperation (SAARC) Business Association of Home-based Workers (SABAH) in several South Asian countries, supported by the SAARC Development Fund. As the majority of home-based workers in South Asian countries are self-employed, gaining access to markets through SABAH was a major achievement for them. Sheel Kant Sharma, General Secretary of SAARC, acknowledged this in a speech at the Conference of Home-based Workers in Delhi in 2015: "This is a flagship that focuses on increasing employment – collective marketing and selling of products, learning from each other are some of the aims of the project".[6]

While the existing regional networks continued their organizing activities, WIEGO began to reach out to home-based workers in other regions: Eastern Europe, Africa and Latin America. In Eastern Europe, led by the Association of Home-based Workers in Bulgaria, HomeNet Eastern Europe was formed in 2013, which later extended its reach to Central Asia to become HomeNet Eastern Europe and Central Asia (HNEE-CA) in 2018. In Latin America and Africa, identifying organizations of, or working with, home-based workers proved challenging. While some home-based workers were organized into collectives of various kinds, most were not organized as home-based workers. They were organized instead in self-help savings groups, women's groups, fair trade producer groups, artisan cooperatives or street vendor associations, among others. As Norma Sanchís from Argentina, who conducted a mapping exercise

5 WIEGO, "Winning Legal Rights for Thailand's Homeworkers", leaflet, available at www.wiego.org, last accessed 1 June 2020.

6 See www.wiego.org, last accessed 28 May 2020.

in Buenos Aires, commented, "It was very difficult to begin […] because there were no people who identified as home-based workers. We could find people that could be identified as home-based workers but they had other names such as own account workers, independent workers".[7]

However, with careful contact-building, networking and capacity-building, the basis was established for convening the first global conference of home-based workers. This conference, organized jointly by HNSA and WIEGO, was held in Delhi in February 2015 with home-based worker representatives from five regions of the world, together with supporting organizations. The conference adopted the "Delhi Declaration of Home-based Workers", which documents the needs and demands of home-based workers. It also adopted a five-year action plan, which includes a vision for a global network of home-based workers as well as plans for building organizations from the grassroots up.[8]

Acting on this plan was the next major challenge. While the home-based workers coming from many different countries were surprised to find they had so much in common with one another, they also noted considerable differences in organizational development and approaches across the different regions. Much more work had to be done on the ground if they wanted to build global unity.

2 On the Ground and in the Regions

From 2012, WIEGO had taken responsibility for supporting organizing and network-building in Africa, Latin America and Eastern Europe.[9] In these regions an important first step was reaching out and identifying organizations organizing or working with home-based workers in selected countries. Bringing them together in country and regional meetings to share experiences, build an identity as home-based workers and plan activities followed. In some countries, home-based workers formed working groups to steer things forward, supported by WIEGO, and all engaged in grassroots-organizing

7 Kendra Hughes, "Strengthening the Movement of Home-based Workers", Case Study, WIEGO, 2016, p. 17, available at www.wiego.org, last accessed 30 May 2020.

8 "Delhi Declaration of Home-based Workers", adopted at the Conference of Home-based Workers, New Delhi, India, February 2015, available at www.wiego.org, last accessed 30 May 2020.

9 For a detailed account of activities during the 2012–15 period, under the Funding Leadership Opportunities for Women (FLOW) project, see Hughes, "Strengthening the Movement of Home-based Workers".

TABLE 14.1 Regional networks of home-based workers and members

Region	Regional organization or network	"Affiliates" and their membership
Africa	Africa Regional Platform: five countries	140 groups with 6,700 members
Eastern Europe and Central Asia	HomeNet Eastern Europe-Central Asia: thirteen countries	Thirteen organizations with 46,000 members
Latin America	COTRADO-ALAC: six countries	Six organizations with 3,400 members
South Asia	HomeNet South Asia: eight countries	60 organizations with 900,000 members
Southeast Asia	HomeNet South East Asia: six countries	Six country networks with 78,000 members

and capacity-building activities. As noted above, Eastern Europe established HomeNet Eastern Europe in 2013, but Latin America and Africa moved more slowly. In 2017, with the support of WIEGO, the Latin American organizations established an informal coordinating body with representatives from six countries, COTRADO-ALAC, while in Africa they established a Regional Platform, consolidated in 2019, with representatives from five countries. All these organizing processes are ongoing, with numerous challenges along the way.

Table 14.1 and the information that follows[10] gives a snapshot of the regional organizations or networks, their affiliates, and approximate membership in the five different regions associated with the movement.

HNEE-CA, HNSA and HNSEA are all established regional organizations, while the nascent networks in Africa and Latin America are still informal. The newest of the regional networks to be established, HomeNet Eastern Europe and Central Asia, is a registered body with thirteen affiliates. HomeNet Eastern Europe held its first Congress in 2014 (prior to the addition of Central Asia). The affiliates are a mix of associations, producer companies, unions and

10 This information was collected by the author, and in particular draws on WIEGO, "Report and Minutes, HNI Working Group Meeting, 2–4 October 2019, Western Cape, South Africa".

cooperatives. Most are made up of self-employed workers producing crafts and clothing, but some comprise subcontracted piece-rate workers linked to global brands of garments and shoe-making. Some are registered as non-governmental organizations (NGOs), but operate as democratic, membership-based organizations (MBOs). Most are small, except for the Bulgarian Association of Home-based Workers, which is also a part of the trade union UNITY. This Association was established in 2002 and has more than 40,000 members.

HomeNet South Asia is the largest of the established networks. Formed in 2000, registered in 2006 and formally launched in 2007, HNSA is a well-established regional organization with sixty affiliates in eight countries. It consists of MBOs including trade unions, cooperatives, worker-owned producer companies and networks, as well as NGOs with home-based worker members or beneficiaries. Members of affiliates make a range of products, including garments, food, crafts and jewellery, either as self-employed workers or as workers at the bottom end of domestic and global supply chains. HomeNet South East Asia, established in 1997 after the adoption of the Home Work Convention, is the oldest of the HomeNets. Its affiliates are six country networks, each of which is made up of a variety of MBOs such as national or local associations, small producer groups and cooperatives. Self-employed workers and those producing for global and domestic supply chains make a rich variety of products, from fishing nets in Thailand to rattan furniture in Indonesia.

WIEGO provides support for the two nascent regional networks. The Africa Regional Platform coordinates activities in East and South Africa and has representatives from five countries together with WIEGO. The approximately 140 grassroots groups involved are mainly small self-help groups, cooperatives, and women's or community-based groups. Most of these produce crafts and, especially in Kenya and Uganda, are linked to the fair trade movement. As yet, there are no national networks or organizations. However, the groups are forming area clusters and working towards forming national networks. In Latin America, COTRADO-ALAC (Coordinadora Regional de Organizaciones de Trabajadoras/res en Domicilio en América Latina y el Caribe) is an informal regional coordination body, formed in 2017 during a regional workshop convened by WIEGO. It is working towards establishing a more formal regional network and is developing its statutes or constitution. The six organizations from six different countries are a mix of unions of informal workers (single and multi-sector), cooperatives and networks, many producing garments.

As Table 14.1 and the information above demonstrate, organizations from and within different regions display different characteristics, and need a range of organizational strategies. This is not uncommon amongst workers in the

FIGURE 14.1 Discussing the home-based workers group in Tanzania called UWAKE at an Africa Regional Workshop with participants from five countries, organized with support from WIEGO
PHOTO: CHRIS BONNER

informal economy from different sectors,[11] but amongst home-based workers that WIEGO and home based worker networks are working with, it is more pronounced. Employment arrangements (subcontracted or self-employed), products, culture, history and maturity, organizing traditions and ideologies, all play a part, as do the economic opportunities prevailing in their countries and their relationship to global supply chains. For example, in Latin America, the primary form of organization amongst home-based workers we work with is a union, with some unions being made up of cooperatives of home-based workers. This non-traditional union format requires an approach of both economic development and political organizing. The notion of the solidarity or popular economy is a strong feature, associated with a pronounced political consciousness. In East and South Africa, organizations in our constituency

11 See *Françoise Carré*, "Defining and Categorizing Organizations of Informal Workers in Developed and Developing Countries", WIEGO Organizing Brief, No 8, September 2013, available at www.wiego.org, last accessed 1 June 2020.

are more commonly small self-help groups, community-based organizations or cooperatives producing crafts, traditional garments, conference bags and other items for local and export markets. The focus so far has been on economic development and livelihoods, with organizing for collective recognition and rights now emerging as an important driver.

Being poor and invisible, lacking recognition as workers (by self and others) without legal or social protection, and being subjected as women to gender stereotyping and patriarchy means that home-based workers are often dependent on the support of NGOs, fair trade organizations and non worker-owned social enterprises (profit and non-profit) for access to markets, training and welfare activities. This leads to a variety of "hybrid" organizational forms. " 'Hybrids' [are organizations] with some elements of MBOs and other parts more akin to non-governmental organizations (NGOs)".[12] We see this in South Asia, where large NGOs with a focus on identities such as being poor or a woman, work with home-based workers as a group of beneficiaries, and also support their organizing into groups or cooperatives. In Ethiopia, an NGO supports women to form and sustain Savings and Credit Cooperative Societies (SACCOS), with most of the women members being home-based workers.

Cutting through all this are common issues that make organizing in and across countries and regions both necessary and possible. Having regular work is perhaps the most important issue they all share, whether as self-employed workers or as workers on piece-rates at the bottom end of domestic or global supply chains. Having access to markets is critical for everyone, for without markets there is no work. Other crucial issues faced by all home-based workers are recognition and rights as workers, as well as legal and social protection. In all these cases, organizing into collectives, and from there into bigger networks or associations, can provide a vehicle for livelihood support and development (sharing knowledge, skills, resources and accessing markets) and for political mobilization (recognition and rights), through increasing their knowledge and power to bargain with firms or brands, with local and national governments or on international platforms (for example, the ILO).

3 Reviving HomeNet International

In Stockholm, Sweden, in May 2018, two days prior to the Conference on "Long-term Perspectives on Home-based Industrial Work", representatives from

12 *Carré*, "Defining and Categorizing Organizations", p. 2.

Africa and Latin America, HNEE-CA, HNSA, HNSEA and WIEGO met to discuss the formation of a global network of home-based workers. This was the culmination of many years of prevarication as to if and how such a global network should be formed. The limited grassroots organizational bases in Africa and Latin America, and the ongoing challenge of building and sustaining democratic, accountable, membership-based organizations and networks in the established regions, had made it difficult to answer those questions. Renana Jhabvala, president of HNSA, explained, "There are two views: one is that everyone continues to organize in our place, as Latin America and Africa have not developed, perhaps it is better to wait. The other view is that if we form a global network we will get more visibility and help other organizations develop. This is the right time".

At the end of two days of intense discussions on the need, purpose and vision for a global network, the second view prevailed. The meeting unanimously agreed to forge ahead with mobilizing towards the founding of a home-based workers' international network in 2020, subject to confirmation by the affiliates. With a collective sigh of relief and excitement they set up a Working Group to lead the process, with a representative and alternate from each of the five regions, and with support from WIEGO. Violeta Zlateva, president of HNEE-CA, expressed a commonly shared sentiment when she said, "Now is the moment to move forward. Globalization into HomeNet International is a great idea". And Firoza Mehrotra from HNSA added, "We are all together in solidarity". Importantly, they came away with a draft purpose and vision for the network, and a commitment to a careful and participatory process of organization-building. Patricia Coñoman from Chile, a long-time trade unionist and political activist, and, as we later found out, a poet, penned a poem to celebrate the moment.

At the time of writing this, the Working Group had met regularly (mostly virtually) and developed a detailed plan of action towards a founding Congress; painstakingly developed a draft constitution; including agreement on the thorny issues of membership criteria and representation; set up a system for recruitment of affiliates; and agreed on unifying issues as a basis for the initial work of HomeNet International (the name decided upon). An important part of the process has been deepening the understanding of differences and similarities across regions, building shared perspectives and a sense of solidarity.

At the same time, work in the different regions and countries, with both established and nascent organizations, is continuing. Recognizing that there is no global without local, building the leadership capacities and increasing membership participation are high priorities. New communication tools are being developed to effect global visibility, on the one hand, and on the other, to support information flow and decision-making at the grassroots.

4 Conclusion

As we know, work content and work arrangements are rapidly changing, and this is expected to accelerate following the COVID-19 pandemic. The home-based workers in this constituency, namely (mainly) poor working women in the informal economy, are in an even more precarious position than before. New struggles will be required to find and retain work, improve conditions and adapt to new demands; older or ongoing struggles will require to be intensified for recognition and rights. Organizing at local, national, regional and global levels, and building alliances, will become even more imperative.

5 Postscript

On 24th February 2021 HomeNet International became a reality. Recognizing that global solidarity and visibility were even more important during the COVID-19 pandemic, HBW representatives were determined to press ahead and form their global network. They decided to launch HNI virtually. Despite the many challenges posed by using such a platform, 80 delegates from 36 affiliates in 20 countries participated in the virtual congress. They were joined by over 200 HBWs from affiliates and emerging affiliates, with another 200 or more allies from trade unions, NGOs, funding organizations and many more. Over two days and five hours they adopted the HNI constitution, appointed a transitional leadership (International Working Committee) and an International Coordinator, and identified key activities for HNI. HNI is now focusing on building solidarity amongst affiliates and advocating for social protection for home-based workers together with other organizations of informal workers.

Saludo A Las Mujeres Trabajadoras

Con orgullo y entusiasmo, con semillas de amistad
Conocí a mujeres del mundo entero, que nos ayudan a soñar.
Son las mujeres de WIEGO que nos instan a,
Sembrar ilusiones de justicia social
No te hinques de rodillas, no te pongas a llorar,
Une tu mano a mi mano que la lucha hay que globalizar
Une tu mano a mi mano y para defender nuestra dignidad
Une tu voz a la mía, para gritar al mundo entero el valor de la igualdad
Unamos las manos, unamos las voces, para romper el silencio, de la invisibilidad
Con palabras e ideas, con firmeza, con valor. Las mujeres trabajadoras
por los derechos humanos levantamos nuestra voz.
Somos las invisibilizadas del mundo entero, que nos atrevemos a soñar con unidad y solidaridad, para cambiar este modelo, que nos impide avanzar.
A ti mujer consiente te quiero saludar

Greeting to All Working Women

With pride and enthusiasm, and seeds of friendship
I met women from all over the world, who help us dream.
These are women in WIEGO who urge us to,
Sow illusions of social justice
Do not kneel down, do not cry,
Join your hand to mine, as the struggle we must globalize
Join your hand to mine, to defend our dignity and
Join your voice to mine, so that we can shout to the whole world the value of equality
Let us join hands, let us join voices, to break the silence, of invisibility
With words and ideas, with strength and courage.
Women working for human rights must raise our voice.
We are the ones who are invisible in the world, who dare to dream of unity and solidarity,
to change this model, which prevents us from moving forth.
It is you concious woman, to whom I want to salute.

PATYLU

© PATRICIA COÑOMAN CARRILLO, 2022 | DOI:10.1163/9789004499614_017
This is an open access chapter distributed under the terms of the CC BY-NC-ND 4.0 license.

PART 4

CHAPTER 15

Introduction Perspectives on Contemporary Home-based Work

Indrani Mazumdar

Approaches towards home-based work have seen significant shifts over the two decades preceding the adoption of the ILO Convention on Home Work (1996) and the more than two decades that followed. It was in this period that the situation of women home-based workers in "third world" countries came to the forefront. Their concerns were backed by women's movements in several countries, and became integrated with the gathering momentum of the permeable concept of informality in work relations in the informal sector and/or the informal economy, which continues to provide the typical frame for home-based work in contemporary times.

By the 1980s, home-based work had emerged as emblematic of the invisibility and lack of recognition of several forms of women's productive work, and of an expanding informal workforce. The conceptualization of home-based work in developing countries moved beyond the confines of self-employment in "traditional" or "household" industries to include piece-rated wage work, outsourced by modern industries to women in their homes. Following the ILO Convention, such industrial out-workers were globally designated as home workers, although the larger category of home-based workers continued to include the self-employed.[1]

From another vantage point, theorization around home workers was propelled by debates among feminists in developed capitalist countries regarding the nature and value of domestic labour (house work) as well as women's work for wages. Some argued that these debates did not take into account the "subsistence production" of women in the "third world". Carrying forward such questioning to third world locations, an influential study of export-oriented lace workers of Narsapur in India theorized that the introduction of capitalist farming led to "housewifization", followed by the integration of such

1 Indrani Mazumdar, Approach paper: Vulnerabilities of women home based workers. (New Delhi, 2005); Santosh K. Mehrotra and Mario Biggeri, 'A cross-country analysis of industrial outwork in Asia' in Mehrotra Santosh K. and Mario Biggeri, *Asian Informal Workers: Global risks, local protection* (Abingdon, 2007).

© INDRANI MAZUMDAR, 2022 | DOI:10.1163/9789004499614_018
This is an open access chapter distributed under the terms of the CC BY-NC-ND 4.0 license.

housewives into a world market-oriented production system.[2] Underlying such analysis, of course, was the phenomenon of labour-intensive manufacturing that was being exported by corporate conglomerates of western countries to third world countries, which led to the conception of a new international division of labour (NIDL). But it was a combination of gender ideologies *and* export-oriented production that became increasingly central to approaches towards home-based work in developing countries.

Meanwhile historians of women's work and family life in industrializing Europe suggested that the reproductive strategies and family organization that influenced women's productive work or dependent situation had not been directly altered by industrialization and changes in the mode of production.[3] Research on home-based work in the US pointed out that it was inevitably linked to the problems of working mothers; that its existence, and indeed persistence, denied the division between home and work, private and public. Evidence of the centrality of home-based work in the debates around state intervention in the labour contract and the gendering of such state action was added to the discussions.[4] Across the world, feminists agreed that behind industrial home work lay the sexual division of labour that assigned child care and household maintenance to women, albeit redefined by capitalist industrialization that promoted ideologies of male breadwinner/worker, female housewife and homebound motherhood.

Such discussions remained largely outside the older institutionalized trade union frame that had premised itself on the waning of home-based work, and tended to have a more limited, and perhaps limiting, perspective on gender. Expanding numbers of women home-based workers actually emerged from "out of the shadows" through a combination of activism by organizations of informal women workers in the developing world (see for example Figure 15.1 depicting homebased worker members of such an organization of informal women workers in India); feminist debates around women's work in Europe, the US and "third world" countries; as well as a new strategic focus on women in government policy that developed around the UN's Decade for Women (1975–85). Further, as country after country restructured their economies towards neoliberal globalization, and as scholars, workers' organizations and

2 Maria Mies, 'Dynamics of Sexual Division of Labour and Capital Accumulation: Women Lace Workers of Narsapur, *Economic and Political Weekly*, 16:10/12 (1981), and Maria Mies, *The Lace Makers of Narsapur: Indian Housewives Produce for the World Market* (London, 1982).

3 Louise A Tilly and Joan W, Scott, *Women, Work, and Family* (New York, 1978).

4 Eileen Boris, *Home to Work: Motherhood and the politics of industrial homework in the United States*, (New York, 1994).

women's movements grappled with increasingly integrated global markets and production systems, and complex informal labour relations, research on women home-based workers acquired particular salience.

From the 1990s, as neoliberalism and globalization became more universal, theorization around global commodity chains (GCCs) and then global value chains (GVCs) became influential in discourses and methods of analysis of home-based work. Although rooted in world systems theories that had historically defined capitalism through trade and markets, the GCC approach redefined itself, on the premise that transnational corporations-driven internationalization of production in this period, and increasing integration in globalized coordination and governance – buyer or producer-driven, were qualitatively new.[5] As GCC approaches combined with value-added chain analysis developed by business scholars, approaches towards home-based work began to focus even more on export orientation in home work in the developing world, or home work linked to global markets. Integration with international markets and globalization was seen by some as an opportunity for home workers to move from the margins to the centre stage, alongside a thesis that flexibilization of labour led to feminization. In the wake of the Asian financial crisis (1997) and its spill-over in Latin American countries, when "defeminization" began to be talked about, a reformulated view of informality that encompassed the range of "flexibilized" labour relations gained greater currency, with some commentators suggesting that women workers in export-oriented manufacturing were the early "winners" in the globalization process, but later began to lose out.[6]

At another level, developments in information technology, accelerated communications and fragmentation of production systems including of services were generating conditions for the development of home work in what was called the "new economy". From extravagant futuristic predictions of the death of industrialism and the rise of a new civilization where millions of jobs in factories and offices would be swept back into the home and its "living room" as an "electronic cottage",[7] through the actualities of the "digital revolution" with development of the internet, the submarine fibre-optic cable and the communications satellite in the 1990s, and related expectations of IT-enabled home

5 Gary Gereffi, "Commodity Chains and Regional Divisions of Labor in East Asia", *Journal of Asian Business*, 12:1 (1996) pp. 75–112.

6 Marilyn Carr and Martha Chen, 'Globalization, Social Exclusion and Work: With Special Reference to Informal Employment and Gender', Working Paper no. 20, World Commission on the Social Dimension of Globalization, International Labour Office (Geneva, 2004).

7 Alvin Toffler, *The third wave* (New York, 1980).

FIGURE 15.1 Ahmedabad, India: Rookmani Ram Naryan (left) and her daughter, Kavita Harshiresh Yemul, spend many hours each day on the floor of their small home hand rolling Indian-style cigarettes called bidi. Home-based workers such as Rookmani and Kavita, both members of the Self Employed Women's Association (SEWA), a trade union for poor, self-employed women in the informal sector, are vulnerable to exploitation by middlemen and suppliers. As SEWA members, they have more bargaining power and visibility for their hard-earned income.
PHOTO: PAULA BRONSTEIN/GETTY IMAGES REPORTAGE

work sweeping across the world, additional dimensions have indeed been brought into the discussions on home work.

From the perspective of a broader interest in home-based work in the contemporary age, the question is whether these new forms of home work are gender-indifferent, as conceived by Toffler; gender-friendly, as conceived by those who saw the developments as opening up more employment opportunities for women in developing countries; or reflective of a gendered construction of a low-wage, flexible reserve of home workers, to whom the risks of endemic volatilities inherent in the rising frequency of short booms followed by busts that characterized the era of untethered globalized finance could be transferred. For home workers' movements, the questions are more specific to the conditions of work and the possibilities of their regulation, and whether the new and more educated home-based workers in the digital service production economy can indeed relate to the poorer classes of home-based workers and vice versa. Bringing in research on some of the current processes at work in new and older forms of home-based work of the twenty-first century, the chapters in this section update, add fresh insights and indeed pose new challenges to the framing of issues and contexts of contemporary home-based work.

The section begins with Janine Berg's account of the conditions of home-based workers who are crowd-sourced through intermediary web-based platforms – a twenty-first-century form of digital home work. While sharing features akin to other home-based workers in terms of falling in the grey area between independence and dependency and invisibility, she points to differentiations among digital home-based workers by gradations in skills as well as nature of tasks and modes of payment. Specialized higher skilled professionals crowd-sourced by "macro-task" platforms are paid by project or by hours through a bargaining process. More clerical-type work from "micro-task" platforms, on the other hand, is paid for at rates set by clients or platforms without negotiation. The chapter draws on an ILO survey of 3,600 micro-task workers drawn from 75 countries in 2015 and 2017 by five leading digital platforms, to draw out the characteristics of the home-based worker. It points out that while work is searched for by, rather than reached to, home workers, intermediation is through an automated process with opaque systems of selection, rejection and constant rating by means of an algorithm. Workers' experiences and difficulties in contesting unfair practices, including wage theft, are discussed. Interestingly, Berg shows that significant amounts of unpaid labour time are expended by workers in the search and selection processes, as well as in work that may be rejected but are still used by employer/clients. The chapter brings out how a significant proportion of home workers receive payments below statutory minimum wages, and the common refrain of shortage of work availability. It presents the educational levels of workers, variations in gender composition across countries, and gender differences among those who combine home work with other jobs. It also suggests regulatory possibilities, using the same centralized data-based monitoring and surveillance technologies that are used for supervision of workers.

Archana Prasad's analysis of contemporary restructuring in internationalized garment production and its implications for home workers suggests that centralized accumulation, through increasing the share of unpaid labour time in production, has led to greater emphasis on sweatshop factories, where the flexibility associated with home work is achieved through the use of temporary workers in sweatshops, and where greater discipline and control over labour time is possible than in home work. Contesting suggestions that the bargaining power of home workers in global apparel value chains can be enhanced through skill augmentation, she argues that the contemporary reorganization in global apparel production is geared to discipline and social control of labour productivity in high-speed volume production that limits/marginalizes the use of home workers. Drawing on the findings of a survey of home-based workers by a trade union in India, Prasad shows that export-oriented home-based work for textiles and garments has only a small proportion of workers, with a more concentrated share only among embroidery workers. She suggests that while in an earlier phase, production for global markets indeed spawned home work in ready-made garments in India, at present it is domestic market-oriented production of ready-mades that is more significant, where the emphasis is on driving down costs in order to compete with the influx of low-priced international brands.

Srabani Maitra enters the field of contemporary home-based work from a different angle, through the increased share of the self-employed among home-based workers in Canada. Her study of South Asian immigrant "women entrepreneurs" shows how women from highly educated backgrounds were forced into home-based work as a consequence of gendered racism and exclusionary hiring in the Canadian labour market. Her findings are based on interviews with a range of women educated in their countries of origin – Pakistan, India, Bangladesh, Sri Lanka – who were selected as "qualified" immigrants based on criteria including education, work experience, age and language proficiency, with expectations of finding jobs suited to their qualifications. On their road to self-employment, she recounts stories of journeys through immigration processes, the search for jobs, and the final turn to home-based work in sewing, designing and stitching, and cooking, networking with kin and community in order to set up business and find markets for their products. Maitra reports that the women workers found satisfaction in creating and the appreciation they received for their products, and that they loved their work even though it involved long hours of laborious effort. She suggests that love, community ties and familial relations in the creation of relationships of mutual support can also be markers of entrepreneurial success, and that their small businesses should be included as part of the Canadian economy.

With reference to India, Sona Mitra argues that the current process of integration of women home-based workers into globalized production reflects a strategy of capital that focuses on taking advantage of locally created systems of home-based manufacture by women rather than generating it, and that home-based work has to be seen in the larger context of women's employment in manufacturing. Her analysis is located in the macroeconomic setting of slow rates of growth in manufacturing and overall employment, within the speculative finance-driven acceleration of India's growth rate since the 1990s. Using national employment survey data, Mitra presents a subsectoral analysis of women's employment that shows a falling share of manufacturing, within which women were concentrated in traditional activities that catered mostly to domestic demand, and also in apparel, which is driven by a mix of both domestic and global demand with jewellery and some specific processed food products being solely export-driven. She concludes that domestic demand patterns influenced employment in rural home-based work in manufacturing, while urban home-based work was influenced by both local and global factors. She argues that home-based work in India was never exclusively driven by globalization.

CHAPTER 16

Contemporary Digital Home Work

Old Challenges, Different Solutions?

Janine Berg

Digital labour platforms provide the technical infrastructure for businesses and individuals to access a large number of potential workers across the globe – "the crowd" – who can perform a myriad of tasks in a relatively short time, with the business having no further obligation to those workers.[1] These "crowd-working" platforms mediate the work between clients and workers. They offer workers a centralized location for identifying tasks from many different requesters, a method for submitting work products, and the technical and financial infrastructure to receive payment for work completed.

Crowd work resembles many long-standing work arrangements, but with a digital tool serving as intermediary. The strategies of crowd work that centre on breaking down tasks into small units assignable to unskilled workers are "a throwback to the de-skilled industrial processes associated with Taylor, but without the loyalty and job security".[2] Yet the payment structure by task rather than time and the home-based location of the workers means that crowd work can be considered a form of contemporary digital home work. Indeed, it is subject to many of the concerns of labour exploitation common to industrial home work. Currently, workers on crowd-working platforms are not covered by labour protection, and workers have little control over when they will have work or their working conditions. They also have limited options for recourse in cases of unfair treatment.

This paper draws on findings from original surveys of micro-task workers of five leading micro-task platforms, covering 3,600 workers from 75 countries, conducted by the International Labour Organization (ILO) in 2015 and 2017.[3]

1 The views expressed in this paper are my own and do not necessarily reflect the views of the ILO.

2 Miriam A. Cherry, "Beyond Misclassification: The Digital Transformation of Work", *Comparative Labor Law and Policy Journal*, 37 (2016), pp. 578.

3 For more details on the survey and its results, see Janine Berg, "Income security in the on-demand economy: Findings and policy lessons from a survey of crowd workers", *Comparative Labor Law and Policy Journal*, 37 (2016), pp. 543–76, and Janine Berg *et al.*, *Digital Labour Platforms and the Future of Work: Towards Decent Work in the Online World* (Geneva, 2018).

© JANINE BERG, 2022 | DOI:10.1163/9789004499614_019
This is an open access chapter distributed under the terms of the CC BY-NC-ND 4.0 license.

The findings provide information on the socio-demographic characteristics of the workers, their reasons for entering crowd work, their financial situation, their working conditions, as well as the different work experiences of women and men crowd workers. Based on the survey, I draw some parallels between the experiences of crowd workers and that of industrial home workers, but also distinguish between the two when discussing possible regulatory options.

1 Crowd Work: Digital Home Work in the Twenty-first Century

Amazon launched its first crowd-sourcing platform in the mid-2000s internally when it realized that its computer programmes could not correctly classify the products in its growing online catalogues. Originally conceived as something for Amazon employees to do in their "spare time", the company soon realized that it could outsource the tasks to a crowd of workers across the globe,[4] as well as provide a platform for other companies to post tasks. Ironically, it was the failure of artificial intelligence that spurred the need for human input, and which continues to fuel demand for an array of activities needed for the smooth functioning of the internet and the wider digital economy.

On web-based crowd-working platforms, work is posted online and a worker located in any part of the world, so long as she has a reliable internet connection, can access the work, perform it, submit it and receive payment.[5] There are a range of crowd-working platforms, from higher skilled, macro-task platforms where workers offer their services as graphic designers, computer programmers, statisticians, translators and so on, to micro-task platforms which typically involve clerical tasks that can be completed quickly and require less specialized skills. Common tasks on micro-task platforms include copywriting and other forms of content creation for websites; visiting websites or downloading apps to increase traffic and for search optimization ("content access"); product categorization; verifying and validating data (e.g., verifying if a Twitter account is for a real person); content moderation (removal of pornography or violent images before they are uploaded on social media accounts); writing (fake) reviews; text or audio transcription; and filling out surveys, for either market research or academic purposes.[6]

---

4 Lilly Irani, "Difference and Dependence among Digital Workers: The Case of Amazon Mechanical Turk", *South Atlantic Quarterly*, 114 (2015), pp. 225–34.

5 The study does not consider workers on local, app-based digital labour platforms, such as Uber, Deliveroo or TaskRabbit, as this work is not performed in the home.

6 Berg *et al.*, *Digital Labour Platforms and the Future of Work.*

Well-known macro-task platforms include Upwork, Freelancer.com and Jovoto, though there are scores more operating in different languages and markets, and specializing in particular fields. Most of these platforms are designed so that workers set up individual profiles, indicate their expertise and their rate, with the final price for their work set via a bargaining process with the clients. Clients can pay per project or on an hourly basis; if hourly, the platform facilitates monitoring of the work through special software that counts keystrokes and takes random screenshots using the worker's webcam. The platform charges a fee, typically ranging from 10 to 25 per cent depending on the platform; this is charged to either the worker or the client.[7]

Micro-task platforms are more one-sided. Clients post tasks on the platform, either directly using an application programming interface (API), or through the platform company which breaks up the work into micro-tasks and then uploads it. Workers see the tasks posted and as long as they have the right qualifications (usually a minimum threshold for their rating and experience, though they may also be required to pass unpaid qualification tests), they can access the job, complete it and submit it. Prices are set by the client or platform, and there is no negotiation. Fees are charged to the client and not the worker.

Like traditional home-based workers, crowd workers fall in a "grey intermediate zone" between independence and dependency.[8] While macro-task workers exercise much greater independence than micro-task workers, and are more akin to self-employed home-based workers, they are still subject to control and dependency on the platforms and an unequal bargaining position with the client. Like self-employed home-based workers, they have limited access to capital, limited control in commercial transactions, and are acutely aware of the global competition from workers with similar skill-sets. However, the monitoring of their work through the platform's software suggests a degree of control that is greater than amongst self-employed home-based workers in traditional industries.

Micro-task workers have many similarities with subcontracted home-based workers, also commonly referred to as industrial outworkers or home workers. Like their sisters in traditional home work, they absorb many of the costs and risks of production, including paying for their computers, internet connection and electricity, and are also subject to control by the client and the platform,

7 Mariya Aleksynska *et al.*, Work on Digital Labour Platforms in Ukraine: Issues and Policy Perspectives (Geneva, 2018).

8 Martha Alter Chen, *Informal Economy Monitoring Study Sector Report: Home-Based Workers* (Cambridge, MA, 2014).

possibly to a greater extent than in traditional home work. They are paid by piece (or 'task'), and they bear the risk of fluctuations in demand as well as other inefficiencies in the organization of work.

2 Exercising Control in Crowd Work: Management through Algorithm

A critical difference between traditional and digital home work is its management. While both forms of home work rely on an intermediary who offers the tasks, controls quality and ensures payment, on digital platforms most of these functions are automated.[9] The process of posting tasks, evaluating results and paying workers can be automated through algorithmic programmes.[10]

Following the worker's selection of task(s) on the platform, the work is in many instances "supervised" by an algorithm that controls the work process, the worker's submission and the worker's payment. Relegating the supervision to an algorithm may result in instances of unfair treatment. For example, when three workers perform a particular task and if the result of one of the workers is different from that of the other two, then the algorithm may be set up to automatically reject the work of the one response that is different, even if it is correct. Thus, having an algorithm review the work runs the risk of rejecting work that has been completed well. Also, workers often do not know why the work was rejected, either because they do not receive an answer or because the answer is unclear. As one large-scale requester on Amazon Mechanical Turk explained, "You cannot spend time exchanging e-mail. The time you spend looking at the e-mail costs more than what you paid them. This has to function on autopilot as an algorithmic system … and integrated with your business processes" (personal communication with L. Irani).[11]

---

9 Berg *et al.*, *Digital Labour Platforms and the Future of Work*; Min Kyung Lee *et al.*, "Working with Machines: The Impact of Algorithmic and Data-Driven Management on Human Workers", *CHI 2015: Proceedings of the 33rd Annual ACM Conference on Human Factors in Computing Systems* (Seoul, 2015).

10 Management through algorithms concerns not just the web-based micro-task crowdsourcing platforms studied in this report, but also "location-based" digital labour platforms that direct workers to deliver local services, such as Uber or Deliveroo. See Lee *et al.*, *Working with Machines*, and Alex Rosenblat and Luke Stark, "Algorithmic Labor and Information Asymmetries: A Case Study of Uber's Drivers", *International Journal of Communication*, 10 (2016), pp. 3758–84, for a discussion of the algorithmic management used by Uber.

11 Irani, "Difference and Dependence among Digital Workers", p. 228.

This approach is unfair to the worker for the following reasons. First, because the worker is often not given feedback for the rejection, and thus misses the opportunity to learn from his or her mistake and improve future performance. Second, it is possible that the work is actually still useful to the requester, in which case non-payment constitutes wage theft. In addition, rejections can affect the workers' ability to get new tasks or even lead to workers being deactivated (in essence, fired) from the platform automatically when a certain threshold of rejections is reached. For example, on AMT a standard criterion used to attribute work on the platform is an approval rating of at least 95 per cent. On the platform, Microworkers, workers whose approval rating ("temporary success rate") falls below 75 per cent are prevented from performing jobs for the next thirty days. On the platform, CrowdFlower, "Individual customers/clients have the power to accept or reject any submission by a CrowdFlower worker, as well as to 'flag' the account of workers in such a way as to prevent workers from receiving future work".[12] More troubling is the fact that there are no mechanisms through which the worker can contest the decision.

3 Insufficient Work, Low Earnings and Inefficiencies Borne by the Worker[13]

Like traditional home work, micro-task workers work when work is available, and are paid by piece for the work they perform. The ILO survey included a detailed question on working time, which revealed that there was a considerable amount of down-time or unpaid working time associated with micro-task work. Indeed, the survey found that for every hour of paid work, workers averaged eighteen minutes of unpaid work. This was time spent looking for the tasks, reading reviews about the requester to ensure they are fair and honest, and taking unpaid qualification tests.

An overwhelming majority (88 per cent) of the micro-task workers surveyed by the ILO responded that they would like to do more work. On average, these individuals wished to do 11.6 more hours of crowd work per week. The willingness to do more crowd work was similar among both men (86 per cent) and women (90 per cent). Across regions, it was especially high in Africa (98 per

12 http://faircrowd.work/platform/crowdflower/, accessed 5 January 2018.

13 This section draws from Berg *et al.*, *Digital Labour Platforms and the Future of Work*. I would like to thank my colleagues, Uma Rani and Marianne Furrer, as well as Six Silberman and Ellie Harmon, for their collaboration on the report.

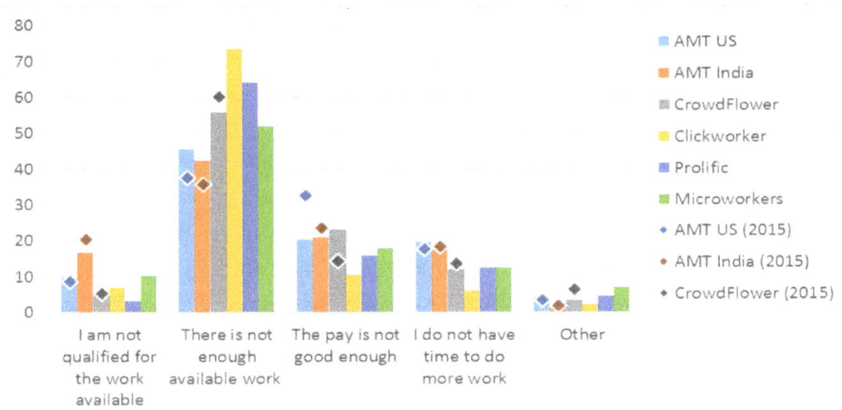

GRAPH 16.1 Reasons for not doing more crowd work currently (percentage by category)

cent), Central East Europe (96 per cent) and Asia (91 per cent); 80 per cent of North Americans expressed a desire for more work.

Sixty per cent of workers on all platforms except American workers on AMT (46 per cent) indicated that they would like to do more work that is not crowd work. When asked why they were not currently doing more crowd work, 58 per cent replied that the availability of tasks was insufficient and an additional 17 per cent did not find enough well-paid tasks (Graph 16.1). A higher proportion of workers in Europe (68 per cent) mentioned that they did not find enough work as compared to workers in Asia (48 per cent). As some workers explained:

> The toughest part of turking[14] for a living is actually finding the jobs; for every hour I spend working I most likely spend two hours monitoring the various scripts I have running to see what jobs show up. – AMT worker

> I would like to change how hard it is to find the jobs to work on. I often have some time to do a task, but cannot find anything to work on. – AMT worker

> You cannot expect people to spend time on "test questions" and then not give them paid work when they have finished – yet this happens every day, the forums are full of complaints. If there is no work left on a job, the job should be removed from the task list. This does not happen. – CrowdFlower worker

14 "Turking" is slang for working on the Amazon Mechanical Turk platform.

Indeed, the pressure to remain online to find work appears to erode the flexibility that is so coveted in the job. As one AMT worker stated in response to what they would change about crowd work if they could, "I would want to know when tasks are up so I can plan my day".

Ironically, crowd work appears to provide less employment stability than traditional home-based work. Home-based workers employed as weavers, embroiderers or *beedi* rollers are usually provided with sufficient work to last several days. In crowd work, the search for work is continuous. This unpaid and excessive search time exacerbates underemployment and feelings of insecurity, besides affecting the earnings of the workers.

The ILO survey found that on average, in 2017, a worker earned US$ 4.50 per hour if only paid work was considered, and if total paid and unpaid hours were considered, then the average earning reduced to $3.40 per hour. If we take only time spent on paid work, then, depending upon the platform and country of the worker, workers earned between $2.70 (CrowdFlower) and $8.60 (AMT US) per hour. The average earnings reduced to between $2.00 (CrowdFlower) and $6.60 (AMT US) when accounting for unpaid work.

A substantial proportion of the workers earn below their local minimum wage. For instance, in 2017, about 48 per cent of American workers on the AMT platform earned less than the federal minimum wage of $7.25 when only paid work was considered, and this proportion increased to 64 per cent when unpaid work was taken into account. A recent data-driven study which involved a plug-in that tracked worker log data of approximately 2,500 workers over two years on AMT, found that taking into account unpaid work, the median hourly wage was around $2 per hour and the mean wages of workers amounted to $3.13 per hour. The study further found that only 4 per cent of workers earned above $7.25 per hour, raising concerns about below minimum wage earnings.[15] The German-based platform Clickworker advertises an average earning of $9 per hour.[16] This roughly corresponded to the German minimum wage of €8.84 per hour as of 1 January 2017. However, the average wage on Clickworker was $4.6 per hour of paid work, and among the survey respondents, only 11 per cent of workers on Clickworker reported earning $9 or more per hour of paid work; this reduced to 7 per cent if both paid and unpaid work were taken into account.

15 Kotaro Hara *et al.*, "A data-driven analysis of workers' earning on AMT", *CHI 2018: Proceedings of the annual Conference on Human Factors in Computing Systems* (Montreal, 2018).

16 "Depending on qualifications, speed, practice and concentration you can earn well over $10.00 per hour. On average, we expect that a Clickworker earns $9.00 per hour", https://www.clickworker.com/clickworker-job/, last accessed 18 January 2018.

Graph 16.2 presents the distribution of hourly paid and unpaid work across the five platforms. The distribution of hourly paid work is skewed towards the left for all the platforms, and becomes even more skewed when unpaid work is taken into consideration. As a result, a high proportion of workers are remunerated below the average wage per hour: 59 per cent of American workers on AMT; 61 per cent on Prolific; and around 70 per cent of workers on CrowdFlower, Clickworker and Microworkers and Indian workers on AMT. The "typical" (median) worker earns much less than the platform average, namely $2.16 across all platforms, and as little as $1.01 per hour for paid and unpaid work on Microworkers. This means that half the workers earn less than $2.16 per hour of the total time (of paid and unpaid work) that they invest into crowd work.

The organization of crowd work at present requires very little investment by the platforms. With the exception of the set-up and maintenance of the server there are no fixed costs; labour costs are tied to sales and not covered directly by the platform, and are therefore entirely variable. According to Silberman and Irani,[17] only eight workers are employed by Amazon to maintain and administer the Amazon Mechanical Turk platform. Yet, because the workers are paid by piece, and bear the burden or cost of tasks that are not clearly explained or of downtime from searching for work, there is no incentive for the platforms to organize the work in a manner that would be more efficient for the workers.

4 Who Are Crowd Workers? Why Do They Perform Crowd Work?

Crowd workers are well-educated and digitally skilled, and live in households with computers and internet connection. Many combine crowd work with other paid employment activities, while others perform crowd work because of a need or preference to work from home. Although their work is invisible, unlike traditional home workers, they are not, generally, from marginalized communities, nor do they represent the poorest of the poor. Nevertheless their involvement in the work, given the conditions described in the previous section, points to an extension of the restructuring that led to an increase in home work in manufacturing industries in industrialized countries in the 1980s,[18]

17 M. Six Silberman and Lilly Irani, "Operating an employer reputation system: Lessons from Turkopticon, 2008–2015", *Comparative Labor Law and Policy Journal*, 37 (2016), pp. 505–41.

18 Mireia Baylina and Michaela Schier, "Home work in Germany and Spain: Industrial restructuring and the meaning of home work for women", *Geo Journal*, 56 (2002), pp. 295–304.

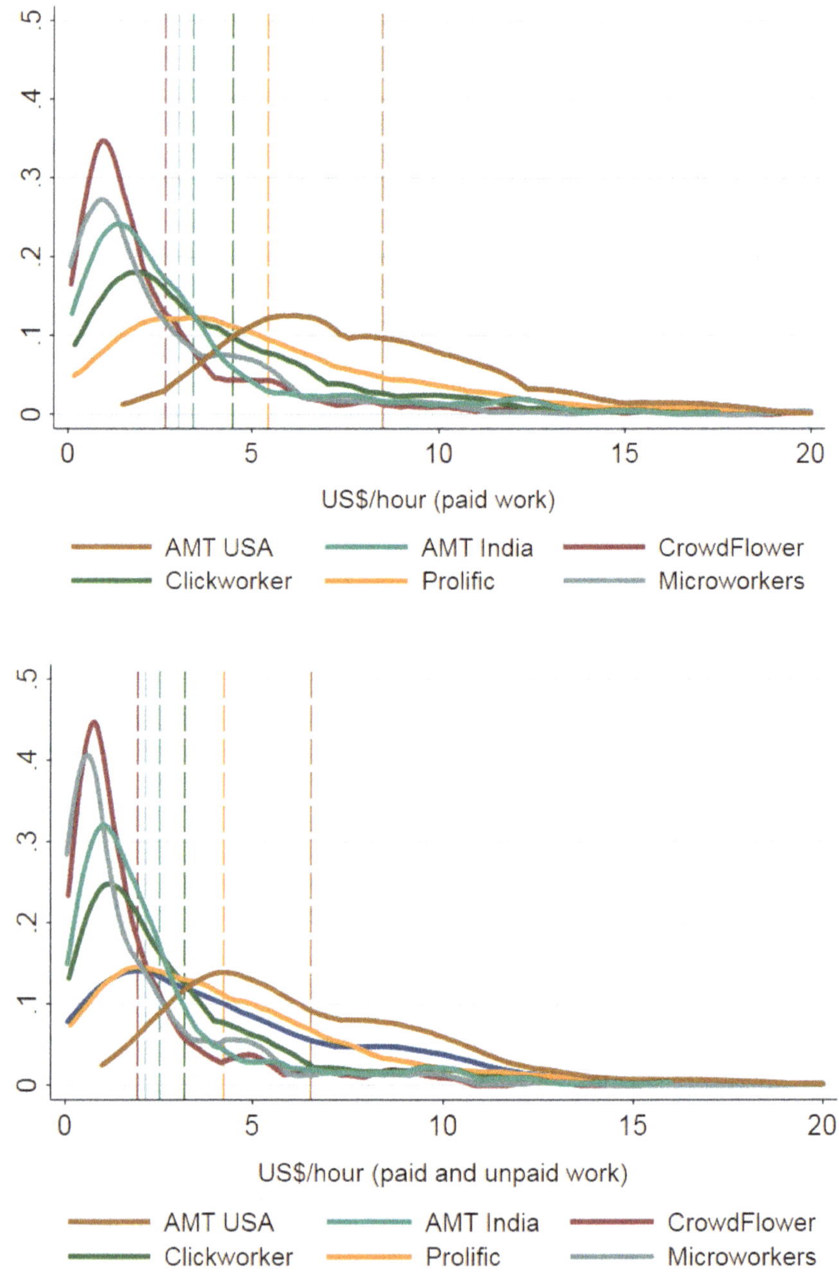

GRAPH 16.2 Distribution of hourly paid and unpaid work among workers by platform, 2017 (in US$)

as well as the outsourcing of business process activities in the 1990s to back-offices in developing countries. It therefore appears that with crowd work we are seeing an extension of work restructuring that affects higher skilled workers in the service sector, made possible by the growth of digital technologies.

One of the important differences between crowd workers and traditional home workers is the gender composition, which, though not uniform across countries, reveals a greater predominance of men, especially in developing countries (see Graph 16.3). In the United States, where the work is considered to be low-paid, there was near gender balance in 2015, and a slight lowering in 2017. In developing countries, however, men outnumbered women on the micro-task platforms surveyed by the ILO in 2017 by a ratio of five to one. While still a low-paid job, with earnings of around $3 per hour, the wage compares more favourably with local earnings. But perhaps more important than the relative wage levels, many of the workers had an educational background in the field of science and technology that is otherwise dominated by men, which possibly contributed to their interest in engaging in micro-task crowd work.

The average age of crowd workers was 33.2 years in 2017, slightly lower than the 34.7 years in 2015 (Graph 16.4), though the range differed across platforms. Workers on the platform, Prolific, were on average younger, at 30.3 years, as compared to American workers performing tasks on AMT, at 35.8 years, in 2017. Most crowd workers were aged 25 to 40 years; 10 per cent of them were above the age of 50 years.

Crowd workers are well educated, with more than 80 per cent having done post-secondary school studies. About one-third of the workers have a technical

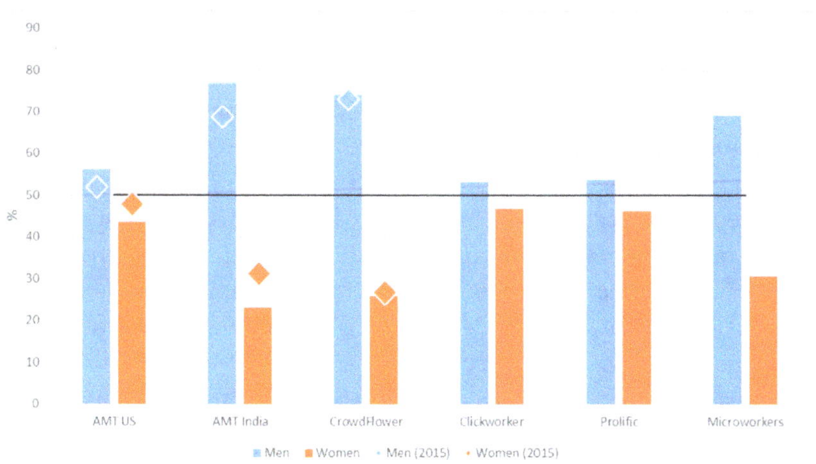

GRAPH 16.3 Distribution of crowd workers, by platform and gender

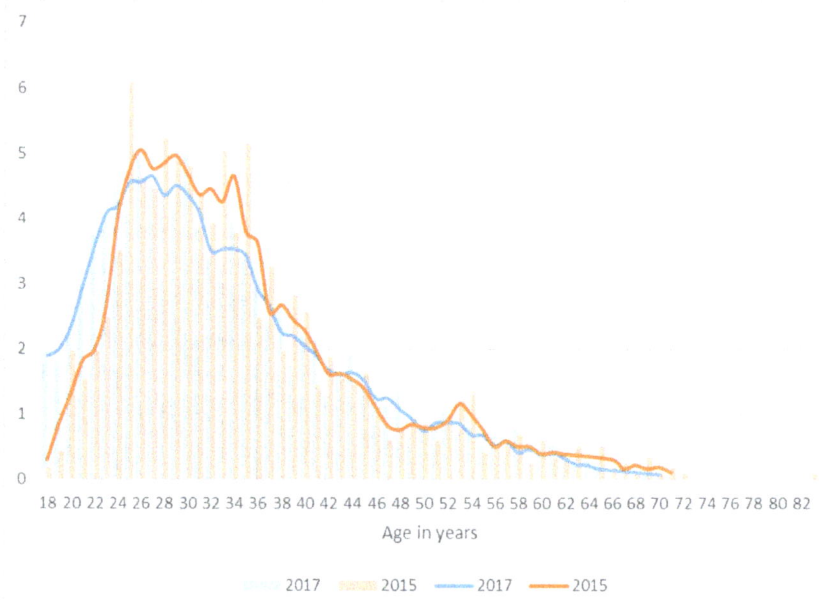

GRAPH 16.4 Age distribution of crowd workers, all platforms

certificate or have completed some university courses, 37 per cent have a college (Bachelor's) degree, and 20 per cent have a postgraduate (Master's) degree (Graph 16.5). These proportions are similar for both the 2015 and 2017 surveys. Education levels are high in Asia with 80 per cent of the workers having a college degree as compared to Africa, where it is the lowest at 47 per cent. Across platforms, a high proportion of Indian workers on AMT have college degrees (57 per cent) or postgraduate degrees (35 per cent), compared to 48 per cent of Microworkers respondents and 44 per cent of American workers on AMT in 2017. One-fifth of crowd workers are currently pursuing a university degree, ranging from 17 per cent in North America to 40 per cent in Africa.

Crowd workers are almost equally divided between those who are single (48 per cent) and those who are married or co-habiting (47 per cent). Workers in developing countries live in larger households; very few live alone. Among AMT workers, 27 per cent of American workers lived alone as compared to just 1 percent of Indian workers.

For the sample as a whole, about 43 per cent of the respondents had children living in their households in 2017, which was slightly higher than in 2015 (41 per cent); 80 per cent and 86 per cent workers in 2017 and 2015, respectively, reported that these were their own children. Among respondents with children, more than 50 per cent had children under the age of six years (56

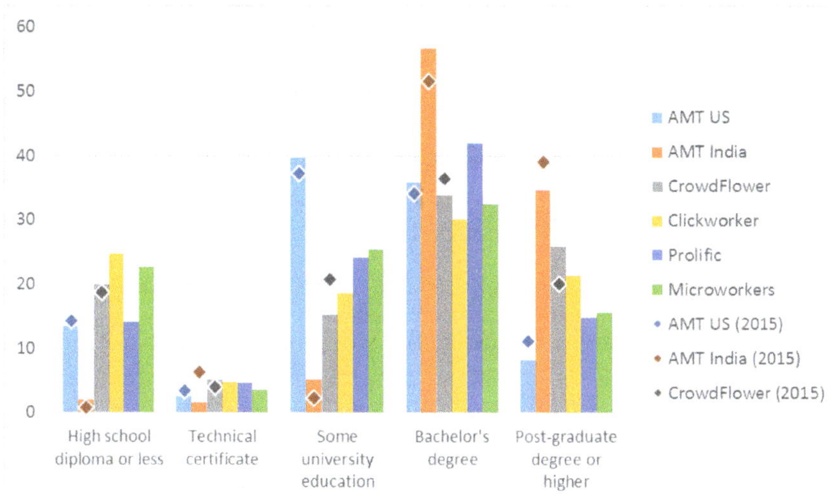

GRAPH 16.5 Educational levels of crowd workers (percentage by category)

per cent in 2017 and 61 per cent in 2015). In 2015, a higher proportion of Indian workers on AMT had children under the age of six (37 per cent) as compared to American AMT workers (16 per cent); these proportions were similar in 2017.

5 Reasons for Crowd-working

The survey asked workers about their reasons for undertaking crowd work and if they responded with several reasons, they were asked to identify the most important one. In 2017, for about 22 per cent of workers the most important reason for performing crowd work was that they "prefer to work from home", and for 32 per cent it was "to complement pay from other jobs". These proportions were 20 per cent and 36 per cent in 2015 (Graph 16.6). There were important differences across platforms; for example, "to complement pay from other jobs" was more important for workers on Prolific and American workers on AMT (around 44 per cent). These two reasons were also the most important in all the regions. In addition, 22 per cent of workers in Latin America (with strong representation from Venezuela and Brazil) and 9 per cent of Indian workers on AMT preferred crowd work because the "pay is better than for other jobs available". Respondents on other platforms or regions did not share this view. There were strong differences by gender for those who could "only work from home", with 15 per cent of women workers giving this reason as compared to 5 per cent of men. Across platforms this perception was quite high among Indian female workers on AMT (20.7 per cent), compared to Indian male workers on AMT (10 per cent). The other reason cited for undertaking crowd work was that "they enjoyed it" (9.5 per cent), a view shared in particular by Indian workers on AMT (14.7 per cent) and workers on Prolific and Microworkers (10 per cent).

The qualitative information provided by the respondents also brought out the care responsibilities (caring for children, disabled or elderly adults) that many of them had, which restricted them from undertaking work outside their homes.

> I am unable to work, because I take care of my ill mother and being a crowd worker gives me the flexibility and means to make some money while I am confined to home. – Respondent on AMT, USA

> I can only work from home because I can't leave my Mom who is sick. – Respondent on Microworkers, Philippines

> I have a sick child [autism and cancer] and he needs all-day care. – Respondent on CrowdFlower, Republic of Serbia

> I really like that it gives me the freedom to be home with my kids but make a little income when I can. – Respondent on Microworkers, USA

Health problems were also mentioned as one of the reasons why the respondents preferred to work from home or could only work from home. Sixteen per

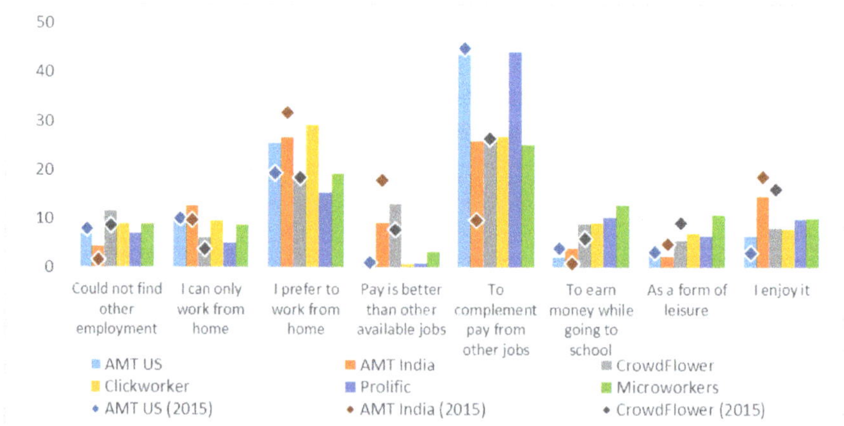

GRAPH 16.6 Most important reason for doing crowd work, by platform (percentage by category)

cent of respondents described their health as fair; 4 per cent described it as poor or very poor. About 19 per cent of respondents reported current physical or mental health conditions or illnesses lasting or expected to last 12 months or more. For more than half of these individuals (54 per cent), these health problems affect the kind of paid work they can do. For about 18 per cent of them, the health conditions or illnesses affect their ability to carry out day-to-day activities, and crowd work seems to provide an alternative way of continuing to work and earn some income.

6 A Closer Look at Care Responsibilities among American AMT Workers[19]

Looking more closely at the samples, there were key differences regarding the structure of households and care responsibilities between male and female crowd workers. Among American AMT workers, 47 per cent of women as compared to 24 per cent men had children at the time of the survey, a huge 23 percentage point gap (see Graph 16.7). American women also lived in larger households; the average household size for female crowd workers was 2.86 compared to 2.39 for male crowd workers. Many more women come to crowd work from care roles, and have care responsibilities while crowd-working.

Male crowd workers have a slightly greater attachment to the offline labour market and are more likely to be working in a technical occupation. While the proportion of the sample working in the "offline" economy is large (59 per cent women and 67 per cent men), men are 9 per cent more likely than women to hold additional jobs besides crowd work (see Graph 16.8). Amongst those not engaged in crowd work, men work more hours in paid work (between 30 to 36 hours per week) and have significantly higher average earnings (typically, between $400 to $700 per week). While the majority of men with offline jobs work in professional and technical occupations, a larger proportion of women work in support and clerical occupations.

The motivation for entering into crowd work differs by gender. Extra pay is the most important factor influencing the decision to crowd work. While this is also important for a sizeable proportion of women (39 per cent), women are 11 percentage points more likely to report that their most important reason for doing crowd work is because it is difficult for them to work outside

19 This section draws from Abi Adams-Prassl and Janine Berg, *When Home Affects Pay: An Analysis of the Gender Pay Gap among Crowdworkers* (2017), available at SSRN: www.ssrn.com or www.dx.doi.org last accessed 2 June 2021.

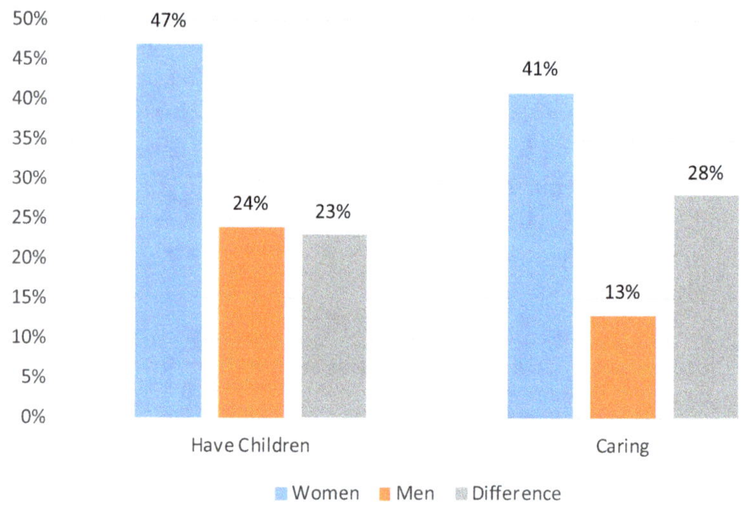

GRAPH 16.7 Gender differences in care responsibilities

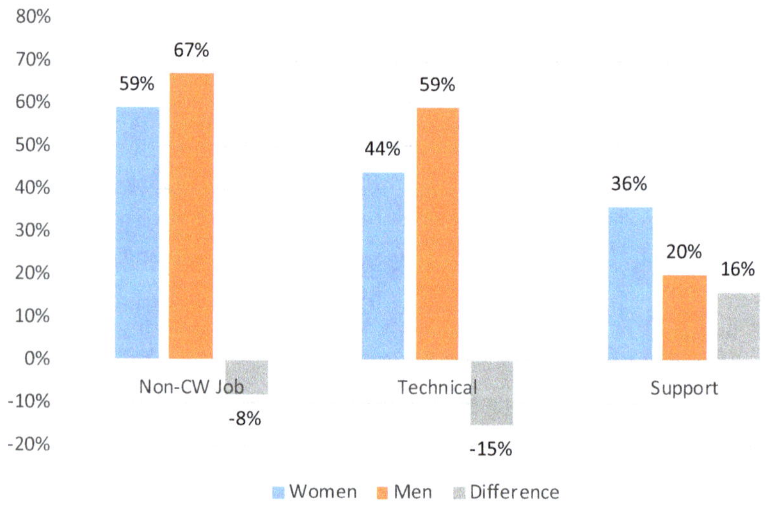

GRAPH 16.8 Gender differences in offline labour market activity

the home(24 per cent for women compared with 35 per cent for men) . There was also an important share of the sample (14 per cent overall) that reported health problems which interfere with their ability to complete day-to-day tasks. Among women, 18 per cent reported a health problem that affects the kind of paid work they might do; 10 per cent of men reported similar health problems (see Graph 16.9).

Not surprisingly, women are more likely to report juggling crowd work and care duties in the home at the same time. In their qualitative responses to the survey, approximately 11 per cent of women explicitly mentioned that they do domestic work and crowd work simultaneously; only 2 per cent of men mentioned this.

For these women, the reliance on crowd work is analogous to the experience of industrial home workers in traditional industries. They work from home because it is not possible for them to participate in paid employment outside the home, either because of their domestic responsibilities or because of a lack of income-earning opportunities outside the home. Like home workers across the world, they are paid by the piece, experience great uncertainty in whether they will continue to have work and are at the mercy of agents who control the flow of work for their payment.

Yet there are two main differences: the women (and men) performing crowd work are more educated, and have digital literacy skills that allow them to communicate with other crowd workers at online fora. In addition, the technology on which the work is based offers the potential for more effectively regulating the work to ensure compliance with labour protection.

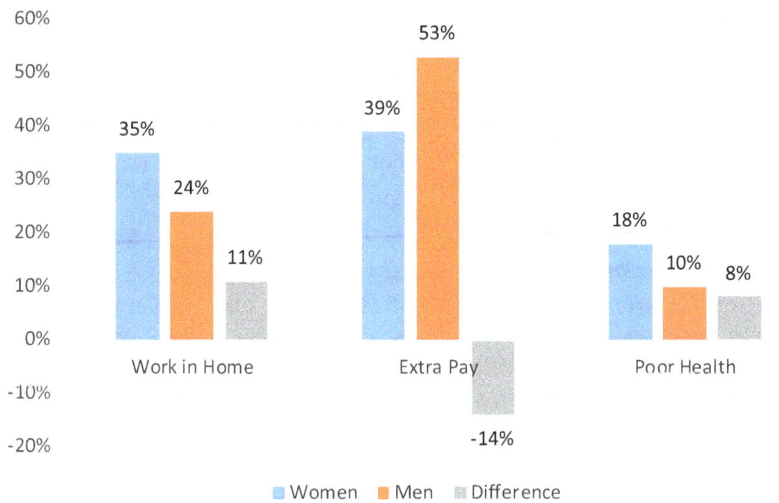

GRAPH 16.9 Gender differences in reasons for crowd-working

7 Regulating Crowd Work: Technological Tools for Ensuring Effective Protection

While home work has always been difficult to regulate because of its invisibility, the situation of crowd work differs in two fundamental aspects: (1) the work is dispersed among workers located throughout the world; and (2) the technology that mediates the platforms offers potential for regulating the working conditions, thus making the invisible visible. In this section, I discuss the implications of these two attributes of crowd work for its possible regulation in the future.

At present, there is no government regulation of crowd work, with the platforms self-governed through unilaterally established "terms of service". Work on digital labour platforms is not unregulated – rather, it is "platform-regulated". The platforms decide how information is collected and displayed, how and in what contexts participants are exposed to each other, who can work on the platform and the status they will have, as well as whether or not to intervene and mediate disputes.[20] Clients and platforms use the data they gather on the work that is done to refine learning algorithms used by them for governance and management purposes. Workers do not have access to the data that they are generating through their work and activity on the platform, nor do they have information about the algorithms used to govern task dispersion (particularly relevant for macro-task platforms and locally-based "apps"). Workers have to establish and maintain a good reputation to continue working on the platform, but the criteria used to determine their rating are not always made available and are difficult to contest. In addition, reputation systems create a lock-in effect for workers given the high costs, both in terms of time and in unpaid qualifications and jobs that are done to establish one's reputation, further undermining the workers' bargaining position vis-à-vis the platform.[21]

Any change to the current conditions of crowd-working platforms will not occur on its own. It requires governments to step in and regulate. The main difficulty that faces government regulation is that the platforms are global. While a platform may be operating from California or Germany, it has clients and workers spread throughout the world. The 2017 ILO survey revealed workers

20 Ajay Agrawal et al., Digitization and the Contract Labor Market: A Research Agenda, NBER Working Paper No. 19525 (2013).

21 Sangeet Paul Choudary, The Architecture of Digital Labour Platforms: Policy Recommendations on Platform Design for Worker Well-Being, ILO Future of Work Working Paper Series (2018).

located in 75 countries.[22] Given that a worker is covered by the labour laws of his or her place of residence, this would mean applying and enforcing laws of a vast number of countries. Applying local labour laws from scores of jurisdictions complicates the application of the law, as well as creates differences in standards among workers despite performing the same work, perpetuating labour arbitrage. The other more politically difficult and thus unlikely option would be to institute an international governance system for crowd work that sets and requires platforms (and their clients) to abide by universal minimum standards, as is done with the Maritime Labour Convention, 2006 (MLC, 2006). Though crowd workers do not work in foreign countries as in seafaring, the workforce is international and the platforms and clients, in many cases, reside in foreign countries. Unlike seafaring, however, crowd work is invisible, and the denial of entry into ports that is critical for the effective enforcement of MLC, 2006, is not evident with crowd work. Moreover, deciding on appropriate minimum standards would be difficult, particularly with respect to pay, though such a system could facilitate guidance on occupational safety and health for the psychologically damaging tasks of content moderation (the removal of pornography or violent images before they are uploaded on social media accounts), and could facilitate the creation of contributory social security accounts for the workers.

Nevertheless, the data and the tracking inherent in digital labour platforms do provide important means for monitoring working conditions, once such standards – whether local or international – are established. These data would need to be made available to the regulatory authority, much like enterprise activities can be monitored by labour inspectors. Moreover, if workers are tracked through keystrokes and screen shots, then it seems that they should be given access to this information on their performance, should they need to contest it. Workers should also have access to their work activities and histories in order to prove their employment, should they choose to pursue other professional activities. If given access to their work data, workers would be in a position to turn over the data to a union, which could then use this information in negotiations with platforms.[23]

Regardless of the prevailing laws, if crowd workers are recognized as part of an employment relationship or if other forms of labour protection are extended to crowd workers, the workers could continue to be compensated at piece-rates and the piece-rates could be set up to comply with the established

22 Given that the ILO only surveyed English-speaking platforms, this already extensive global representation is understated.

23 Choudary, *The Architecture of Digital Labour Platforms.*

minimum wages. Technology would facilitate setting this rate, which could be based on average completion time for a task. Technology could also facilitate the monitoring of working hours to ensure that the workers receive paid breaks (as required by many laws governing piece-work).[24] Having to comply with minimum standards on wages and working hours would put pressure on the employer to ensure that the work is organized in advance and limit the amount of downtime. Time spent looking for work, reading reviews about the requesters to ensure they are fair and honest and taking unpaid qualification tests would thus be eliminated. The productivity gains for workers would be significant. Other aspects of the work would have to be reorganized. For example, a general rule in establishing effective piece-rate systems is to hire fewer employees to ensure that there is sufficient work.[25] Moreover, an important part of ensuring quality in piece-work is noting the precise reasons for making a rejection as well as establishing a quality control system with a validated scoring system, so that workers can learn from their mistakes. Regulating crowd work would likely force some restructuring in the organization of the work, which would not only be beneficial to the workers, but to the clients and platforms as well.

8 Conclusion

Micro-task crowd work shares many similarities with industrial home work. It is invisible work broken up into small tasks and dispersed to multiple workers for piece-rate pay. There is a middleman who disperses the work – in this case, a platform – and who takes a fee for this service. The workers are isolated with little contact with other workers and no bargaining power. There is also uncertainty as to whether the worker is an independent contractor or if the person should be classified as an employee, subject to the same labour protection as other workers in an employment relationship. Many women take up this work because of the lack of possibility or constraints on working outside the home, and because home work, digital and traditional, provides a way of combining paid work with domestic responsibilities.

24 See Kamala Sankaran, "Piece-Rated Minimum Wages" (unpublished manuscript), for a discussion of piece-rate legislation in different countries of the world. Many countries issue guidelines on how to calculate piece- rates and how to factor in rest-times.

25 Gregorio Billikopf, *Labor Management in Agriculture: Cultivating Personnel Productivity* (California, 2003).

But despite the many similarities between industrial home work and crowd work, the data-centred focus of the latter creates the potential for its effective regulation. However, a first step in improving working conditions would be to establish the standards – whether it should be subject to local laws of the worker's place of residence, or whether a universal standard is needed, given its global nature. Crowd work is emblematic of the challenges inherent in an ever-more globalized and technologically driven world of work. More effort is needed to understand how technology can be used to more effectively regulate and improve working conditions.

CHAPTER 17

Dynamics of Contemporary Capitalist Accumulation and the Prospects for Home Work in the Indian Garment Industry

Archana Prasad

1 Introduction

This essay explores the interface between the structural transformations in capitalism and home work by women in the specific context of the internationalization of garment production and retail following the Agreement on Textile and Clothing (ATC) of the WTO (World Trade Organization), and with special focus on its implications for home workers in India. It shows that the position and prospects of home work in global apparel production systems are structured by the gendered character of the industrial reserve army. As we know, home workers are paid at piece-rates with an aim to depress the wages of regularly employed workers and increase productivity. In this sense, home workers constitute a part of a floating active army of labour, as they depend on and are required to work in accordance with the demand in the market. This condition not only pertains to the garment industry but also prevails in other sectors like electronics, cosmetics and automobiles, in jobs where women have "traditional skills". The perception of the employers is that the tasks performed by home workers do not require much creativity or innovation, and are "low-skill" and "repetitive" jobs that can be managed without much monitoring and control. This basic logic underlies the offshoring of jobs in the apparel industry throughout the world, and home workers are part of a larger structural transformation in global apparel production which also has an immense impact on domestic production and markets. Therefore, India's place in the world's apparel industry will also determine the position of home workers in the production chain, largely because the domestic market is also moulded by this factor.

Another important marker of the position of home workers is that they only perform given tasks, and therefore their hourly productivity is not the main concern of the employer or the contractor. The value extracted out of them is not merely through low piece-rates, but also through checks on quality, which reduce the number of pieces they are paid for. In addition, the subsidies

© ARCHANA PRASAD, 2022 | DOI:10.1163/9789004499614_020
This is an open access chapter distributed under the terms of the CC BY-NC-ND 4.0 license.

provided by women workers includes unpaid transport allowances to fetch raw materials and get payments, and non-payment of rent and other basic amenities that an employer is required to provide in the workspace. These subsidies constitute an important portion of the rate of exploitation and the value extracted from home workers. However, as this essay shows, this method of extraction of value has limits which arise out of the constraints to accumulation within merchant capitalism itself. Perhaps it is for this reason that corporations prefer to locate their production in factories (which get converted into sweatshops), where the employer is able to extract both absolute and relative surplus value, and therefore able to increase the rate of accumulation. This process involves two different methods of control: on the one hand, relative surplus value is extracted by increasing targets and introducing new technologies; on the other hand, absolute surplus value is enhanced by prolonging the working day beyond the socially necessary time needed by labour power to reproduce itself. This simple distinction in the forms of extraction of surplus value can only be maintained through a closely monitored system of floor management, which is possible in a sweatshop and not within the system of home work. It is therefore not surprising that slave-like conditions have appeared in different developing countries where transnational corporations and brands have offshored production.

So the question is, how does a firm decide whether to employ home workers or not? The answer to this, once again, is to be traced in systemic changes within the capitalist system. The decentering of production by apparel giants is a result of the integration of global markets through supranational arrangements, and, through these, the creation of wage hierarchies structures the current employment pattern. However, the rise in the rate of accumulation is only possible if social control over the workers and their working day is maintained through processes of management and discipline. This is not possible within the framework of home work, and therefore it is not surprising that export-oriented corporations prefer sweatshops to home work. On the other hand, the use of home workers by domestic industry is largely motivated by the need to drive down costs and deal with the influx of low-priced branded apparel products. It is obvious that the cost of production of branded transnational firms is brought down by the sheer volume of production, and the domestic players attempt to stay alive in this competition through outsourcing so that their products are cheaper.

In both cases, the forms of oppression and conditions of social reproduction differ. In the case of home workers, the conditions of reproduction of piece-rate work are almost collapsed with social reproduction processes within the household. But the existence of home work is a result of the conditions of reproduction of the international apparel industry, which spawned home-based work in India's ready-made garment sector in the first place and then, more recently, drove the shift in emphasis to sweatshops, in the run-up to and after the ATC phase. Domestic regulatory structures, when seen in conjunction with the integration of global markets, not only define the "worker", but also influence the way in which they are integrated into the larger apparel market and its labour processes after supranational and bilateral agreements influenced changes in the organization of production. Prior to the dominance of multinational supply chains, large apparel exporters from developing countries sought markets elsewhere in the world and therefore benefited from the integration of the global apparel market. But in the post-ATC period, the removal of restrictions over imports within the Indian market not only increased their competition, but also restructured the apparel export industry through the dominance of finance capital. Such an arrangement compelled changes in the labour processes. One of the markers of this phase was that apparel supply chains considered flexibility as a key principle of their operation,[1] and therefore the ease of hire-and-fire was extended beyond home workers to other workers as well. For example, the apparel sector was the first to implement fixed-term employment in India, and many of the non-supervisory staff in sweatshops were also hired on contractual arrangements and under fixed-term subcontracts that do not allow for permanent work. Hence, there is a tendency to create temporary workers who work under indecent working conditions (for instance, the Sumangali scheme in India, which is elaborated in a later section of this essay). In other words, the idea that the presence of home workers provides greater flexibility to firms and contractors,[2] is probably an overstatement. Flexibility plus disciplining and control are possible in a sweatshop to a greater extent than in the case of home work. This is largely because flexibility in home work is not a result of the actions of the corporate management, but a consequence of the need of women home workers to subordinate their paid work to the function of social reproduction, which is considered their primary responsibility.

In all, the themes indicated above – management, disciplining and social control – are key to the maintenance of competition within the apparel sector. This essay highlights some of these by focusing, not on an assessment of

1 Indrani Mazumdar, *Women Workers and Globalization: Emergent Contradictions in India* (Kolkata, 2007); S. Satyaki Roy, *Garments Industry in India: A study of two clusters* (New Delhi, 2009).

2 For instance, see KimV. Eyck, "Flexibilizing Employment: An Overview", *SEED* Working Paper 41 (Geneva, 2003).

profitability but on the tendency of international corporations to centralize control over workers right down to local shopfloor arrangements through what mainstream literature has termed as "global value chains" or "global production networks". The essay elaborates its argument in the context of the emerging critique of the "value chain" and "production network" paradigm, which shows that the decentering and reorganization of production are a product of the concentration of capital, and require the disciplining and social control of labour.[3]

As is well-known amongst Marxist political economists, the existence of both paid and unpaid labour within a commodity is a necessary condition for the expansion of capitalism through the creation of additional capital. However, the creation of additional capital itself requires the additional recruitment of paid labour. This means that the rate of surplus extraction can only be maintained by recruiting more paid workers who produce both paid and unpaid labour. As the total cost of paid labour rises, the capacity of the capitalist to create additional capital decreases. This creates a crisis within capitalism and propels the productive system into making adjustments – both the deployment of capital and the deployment of labour – in order to come out of this crisis. Alternatively, greater extraction of unpaid labour can also be achieved through stricter disciplining and control of workers, which increases their productivity without increasing their wages. This is only possible through minimizing the well-being of workers and maintaining a surplus supply of labour or the industrial reserve army. Even today, the labour reserve consists of floating workers who are in and out of the labour force, a latent labour force that is continuously formed through processes of primitive accumulation, and paupers who are largely at the margins of the labour force.

Home workers may be located as part of a floating labour force whose presence results in a lowering of the reservation wage. This is done by restructuring

3 This is also indicated by Karl Marx in *Capital*, Volume 1, where he wrote that the "Production of surplus-value is the absolute law of this mode of production. Labour-power is only saleable so far as it preserves the means of production in their capacity of capital, reproduces its own value as capital, and yields in unpaid labour a source of additional capital. The conditions of its sale, whether more or less favourable to the labourer, include therefore the necessity of its constant re-selling, and the constantly extended reproduction of all wealth in the shape of capital". See K. Marx, *Capital Volume One: A Critical Analysis of Capitalist Production* (Delhi, 2018 [1887]), p. 436. For more recent work, see Praveen Jha, "Global Production Networks: What's Labour Got To Do With It?", in Achim Truger *et al*, (eds), *Monetary Markets, Labour and Development Festschrift for Hansjörg Herr* (Marburg, 2016); Praveen Jha and Paris Yeros, "Global Agricultural Value Systems in the South: Some Critical Issues at the Current Juncture", *Agrarian South: Journal of Political Economy*, 8 (January–April 2019), pp. 1–16.

the global system of production through investments by transnational corporations. The continuous replenishment and renewal of the industrial reserve army takes place through new forms of accumulation born out of processes of appropriation and expropriation that are undertaken by different nation-states under the influence of supranational agreements like the ATC. Thus, the so-called "value chains" represent, not a sharing of profits or a redistribution of wealth, but a redeployment of capital in a manner that remoulds the contours of the working class itself. Such a restructuring starts with the family, and requires the remoulding of institutions regulating both production and social reproduction. The appearance of home work is also embedded in such an intensifying accumulation process. As this essay shows, the tendency of capitalism to control and discipline labour limits the prospects for the development of home work, whose future will be determined by labour processes that are external to the immediate subjective context of such work. Therefore, the arguments for improving the bargaining power of home workers through skill augmentation and improved organization have their limits, as home work only serves a limited purpose for the global apparel industry.

2 Identifying Home Workers in the Circuit of Production

In its Convention on Home Work (Convention No. 177, 1996), the International Labour Organization (ILO) described a home worker as a person who carried out work (i) in his or her home or in other premises of his or her choice, other than the workplace of the employer; (ii) for remuneration; (iii) which results in a product or service as specified by the employer, irrespective of who provides the equipment, materials or other inputs used. The Convention made it quite clear that home workers could not be considered as "independent workers" because they did not have the "autonomy" or "economic independence" to be given the status of workers. Thereafter the ILO set up different City Groups in 1997, of which one was the Delhi Group, with the aim of harmonizing the statistics on informal employment of the member countries. This independent group of statisticians reviewed the categories that were used by the National Sample Survey Organization (NSSO). In the pre-2007 period such workers were clubbed under self-employed workers since they did not work in a relationship of direct wage employment. However, the Delhi Group did not entirely agree with this classification. In its Report of 2007, the Delhi Group recommended to the Ministry of Statistics and Programme Implementation that home workers be classified not only according to the "place of work" but also according to the nature of the contracts they had with the contractor/employer. It recognized home work as a variant of wage employment as the workers worked according to "particular specifications" on piece-rated work. Such a recommendation should have led to the classification of home workers as wage workers rather than as "self-employed workers". But the government did not agree with this because the official statisticians argued that:

> Like the other self-employed, these workers have to meet certain costs, like actual or imputed rent on the buildings in which they work, costs incurred for heating, lighting and power, storage or transportation, etc. That means, they have some tangible or intangible means of production. Note that employees are not required to provide such inputs for production.[4]

In the wake of such reasoning, home workers continued to be classified as "self-employed" even when they worked in relationships of disguised wage employment.

It is because of such a classification that policy-makers have largely used the "autonomy" argument to deny the status of workers to home workers and deny them rights even though the nature of their work is largely disguised wage labour. This problem persists in the recommendation of the 20th International Conference of Labour Statisticians, which classified home workers as "dependent contractors". Dependent contractors were defined as follows:

> ... workers who have contractual arrangements of a commercial nature (but not a contract of employment) to provide goods or services for or through another economic unit. They are not employees of that economic unit, but are dependent on that unit for organization and execution of the work, income, or for access to the market. They are workers employed for profit, who are dependent on another entity that exercises control over their productive activities and directly benefits from the work performed by them.[5]

Significantly, piece-rated workers have also been classified as dependent contractors in this resolution. This directly contradicts the understanding that piece-rate is one of the most exploitative forms of labour because the wage

4 Ministry of Statistics and Programme Implementation (MoSPI), *Report of Independent Group on Home Based Work* (Delhi, 2008), p. 12.

5 International Labour Organization (ILO), *Resolution Concerning Statistics on Work Relationships*, 20th International Conference of Labour Statisticians (Geneva, 2018), p. 7.

rate is used as a controlling mechanism to devalue labour time. The autonomy and independence of the home worker is illusionary, as suggested by many,[6] thereby implying that home workers ought not to be classified as people who have taken up work of their own volition, as the nomenclature of dependent contractor suggests.

The question, then, is that if home workers are tied within the circuit of production, where are they placed in relation to the others as far as the export market is concerned? The actual extent of export-oriented home work in the apparel industry is virtually unknown because of the lack of consistent data. The evidence of home workers in export-oriented supply chains is also anecdotal, with several media and non-governmental organizations report the use of home workers by international brands. However, there are no conclusive data to show how much of the production for export is actually done by home workers or the proportion of apparel home workers in the export segment. In fact, there are significant arguments to show that the increase in home work in apparel manufacture in India is largely due to the expansion of the domestic industry and market. Estimates point out that the number of home workers in the apparel sector increased from 0.41 million in 1999–2000 to 2.99 million in 2011–12, constituting about 85.5 per cent of the entire female workforce in the apparel industry. However, this increase cannot be attributed to the expansion of the export market, but to the spurt in clothing consumption within the domestic market.[7] Studies show that as far as export markets are concerned, they largely looked for embellishment work for outworkers, but there was a shift in operations from the home to the sweatshop in countries where penetration of transnational capital has increased rapidly.

Scanty data from a recent study show that there are multiple employment relationships within the export-oriented industry. This includes ready-made garment units with both regular and contract labour, as well as jobbers who take out raw materials and give them to outworkers. There is not much information about who these jobbers are and how many workers they have at their command. Table 17.1 gives some rudimentary estimates.

It is quite evident from the table that the relations of production in the apparel sector do not clearly demarcate between domestic and export

6 Martha Chen, *Informal Economy Monitoring Study Sector Report: Home Based Workers* (Cambridge, MA, 2014); International Labour Organization (ILO), "The Future of Work in Textile, Clothing, Leather and Footwear", Working Paper 326 (Geneva, 2019).

7 Indrani Mazumdar, *Home-based Work in 21st Century India* (Delhi, 2018); Govindan Raveendran, Ratna Sudarshan and Joann Vanek, *Home Based Workers in India: Statistics and Trends* (Cambridge, MA, 2013).

TABLE 17.1 Number of units across key clusters, 2009

Cluster	Number of units	Remarks
Kolkata	12,291	Knitting 7,291 + woven **cloth units** 5,000
Mumbai	6,000	Manufacturer + jobbers (unspecified)
Tiruppur	2,500	Jobbers 1,500 + domestic cum exporters 500 + exporters 500
Ludhiana	2,500	
Indore	2,000	Manufacturer cum exporters 20–25 + manufacturer for domestic market 450–475 + jobbers 1,500
Bellary	1,305	Big manufacturers 5 + trader manufacturer 450 + jobbers 850
Jaipur	950	Garment manufacturing units 250 + fabricators 700
Bangalore	850	Garment manufacturing units 350 + jobbers 500 + exporters 50
Chennai	650	Exporters 100 + job worker 400 + garment manufacturers for exports 150 units, + domestic players 150 units] + jobbers 500
NOIDA	750	Export units 550 + domestic units 200
Gurgaon	675	Export units 600 + domestic units 75
Okhla	250	All manufacturer exporters excluding fabricators and embroiderers)
Total	**30,721**	

SOURCE: A. MEZZADRI AND R. SRIVASTAVA, *LABOUR REGIMES IN THE INDIAN GARMENT SECTOR: CAPITAL–LABOUR RELATIONS, SOCIAL REPRODUCTION AND LABOUR STANDARDS IN THE NATIONAL CAPITAL REGION*, REPORT OF THE ESRC–DFID RESEARCH PROJECT "LABOUR STANDARDS AND THE WORKING POOR IN CHINA AND INDIA" (LONDON, 2015), P. 20.

production. However, surveys by different unions and agencies highlight that embroidery work constitutes the bulk of home work that is connected to export networks. A Centre of Indian Trade Unions (CITU) survey showed that embroidery accounted for about 13.6 per cent of home workers in the garment sector.[8] Only half of this 13.6 per cent were working solely for export. In all, about 12 per cent of all home work was linked to the export market. Handwork and machine tailoring constituted about 42 per cent of the entire work, of which less than 1 per cent was linked to the export market. The same was true for handloom, which comprised about 38.2 per cent of home workers; here only 14 per cent of the work was linked to the export market.[9]

These estimates show that there is limited recording of home workers, largely because of their invisibility as argued by a plethora of studies. But this argument could be extended beyond the question of mere recognition; invisibility could be emblematic of the relatively weak social control of corporate houses over home workers. After all the existing data show that the paid working time of home workers is far lower than that of factory workers, even though the wages set on a piece-rated basis may be lower in such labour relations. For example, a pan-India CITU survey showed that a majority of the home workers in embroidery and other garment-related work earned below Rs 1,000 per month and worked five to seven hours a day. This was similar to the results of an earlier survey done by the Janwadi Mahila Samiti in the National Capital Region (NCR),[10] which showed that on average women home workers worked for approximately seven hours a day. However, the percentage of women working for this average time had declined from approximately 54 per cent to 30 per cent. Even this work was irregular in nature as only 39 per cent of the studied sample received work for the whole year.[11] Further, most home workers were not confined to just garment work but may also be working in other sectors as and when work came their way. Hence, though home workers work long hours, they still constitute a floating labour force whose existence depresses the wages of shopfloor workers.

It should also be noted that offshoring of work has structural limits. First, most of the home workers are women who perform unpaid work in their households and also attempt to manage their work at the same time. In most cases the task of paid production is subordinated to the task of social reproduction. Second, distance from the principal employer does not enable control of quality or speed of production. Therefore the only way to extract surplus is by setting the piece-rate through an underestimation of productivity, i.e. through the setting of lower wages. In other words, surplus value is usually

8 Centre for Indian Trade Unions (CITU), *Findings from Survey on Home-based Workers* (Delhi, 2013).

9 Ibid., p. 40.

10 Janwadi Mahila Samiti (JMS), *Survey of Home-based Workers in Delhi* (Delhi, 2008).

11 CITU, *Findings from Survey on Home-based Workers.*

extracted through depression of wages and through the unpaid work of supporting workers (including children). Despite all this, the capacity of home workers to contribute to the expansion of capital itself is quite limited. In this sense, perhaps the main function of the home workers is twofold: (i) to provide specialized skilled work in traditional and unmechanized niche areas like *zari*, *zardozi*[12] and other such embroidery jobs,[13] in which women are trained because of their socialization; and (ii) to provide a supplementary reserve workforce whose presence reduces the cost of labour in tasks that are not required to produce large volumes of goods. For example, the price charged by a master craftsman for *zardozi* work may be much higher than the cost of labour time of the home worker, which was about Rs 32 to Rs 35 per hour in 2012–13.[14]

Seen in this context, the coexistence of piece-rates with time-rated wages is essential for maintaining the basic structure and high volume of the entire garment sector. The wage hierarchy created by this coexistence also ensures that the industry catering to domestic demand remains competitive in a market that is increasingly dominated by international brands and imported garments from countries like China and Bangladesh.[15] The cheapness of the branded products is due to their volumes and the scale of productive activities within highly controlled labour processes. On the other hand, the survival and competitiveness of those who produce for the domestic market are maintained through their penetration into local and rural markets where the big brands have not had the same intensity of penetration. Evidence of this is seen in the fact that the size of the domestic apparel market was about USD 59 billion in 2015, whereas the size of the export apparel market was only USD 17 billion, i.e. about 22 per cent of the entire production.[16] Nevertheless, the presence of home workers in the domestic market is a feature that is largely structured by the level of integration of the apparel market into the global system.

---

12 *Zardozi* is heavy embroidery with silver or gold metallic threads on silk or satin cloth. *Zari* is fine gold or silver thread used in traditional garments, largely in South Asia and the Middle East.

13 Mazumdar, *Home-based Work in 21st Century India.*

14 CITU, *Findings from Survey on Home-based Workers.*

15 Mazumdar, *Home-based Work in 21st Century India*; Technopak, *Study on "Garment Sector to Understand Their Requirement for Capacity Building"* (Delhi, 2018).

16 Wazir Advisors, *Existing FTAs and Their Impact on Indian Textile Exports* (Delhi, 2016).

3 Why Home Workers Are Marginal to Export-oriented Production

The integration of the apparel markets and production regimes following supranational and regional arrangements has influenced labour regimes in the export-oriented industry. Increased productivity and efficiency are seen as key for maintaining an edge within the highly competitive scenario. The place of a particular country's apparel exporters within the entire garment supply chains is dependent on the way in which brands develop supply chains, especially in relation to existing competence, labour surpluses and conditions of production. The main indicators of these are the comparative wages, labour regulations and the areas of product specialization. These factors influence the place of a country in the global apparel export market. The discussion below shows how social control on the shopfloor is a crucial aspect for remaining competitive in the export market, and therefore marginalizes home work in export-oriented production.

The structure of the global apparel trade was dominated by West Europe, North America and East Asia, which together with South America and Southeast Asia produced 85 per cent of the value added in the apparel sector. Production was largely domestic or regionally oriented, and at least 80 per cent of value added derived from the production of final outputs within the region. By 2011 the relative importance of North America and West Europe declined as far as apparel production was concerned. The decrease in value added in these regions was compensated by an increase in the shares of East Asia, South and Southeast Asia, and South America. This pointed to an increase in the number of regions integrated into the global value chains in apparel. The destinations of intermediate goods supplied by the region were diversified. By 2011, Asia had become the key region of global textile and apparel production. East Asia's value added share in the world increased from 24 per cent in 1990 to 33 per cent in 2011, while South Asia and Southeast Asia's share increased from 6 per cent to 10.5 per cent. Production links between the developed and developing countries were strengthened and expanded after 2011.[17]

The post-crisis phase of 2008–09 saw a contraction in the size of the wearing apparel global market. Between 2008 and 2010 the annual growth rate of exported final apparel products in the world market was –1.8 per cent, whereas the demand for exported intermediate apparel products remained somewhat unchanged. This meant that countries, especially in South America, that exported fabrics and textiles faced a recession in apparel exports since there

17 World Trade Organization (WTO), *World Textile and Apparel Trade in 2016* (2017).

was no demand in the world market. Thereafter, the market recovered a little between 2011 and 2015, when the annual growth rate was about 4.8 per cent for final apparel products; but this was still about 1 per cent lower than the pre-crisis level. For intermediate products too, the annual growth rate slowed down from 12.5 per cent in the pre-crisis period to 2.7 per cent in the post-crisis period. In this period, the highest percentage increase as a share of all exports was in the South Asian region, with Bangladesh, Sri Lanka and Pakistan registering significant increases in wearing apparel exports from their own countries. In comparison, apparel exports from India rose at a much slower place. Overall, we can conclude from Table 17.2 that long-term trends in the apparel export market have seen significant shifts in the regional basis of apparel production, with India, China and Bangladesh forming an important part of the supply chains in South Asia.

Long-term trends in the apparel export market show that there has been a steady decline in growth rates of apparel production, and this has had an impact on the nature of labour relations. It is obvious that corporations in the apparel export business would find ways of cutting costs to manage competition. This forms the context of the development of global value chains in the sector which is based on offshoring of production activities. Long-term trajectories of change have been seen in the offshoring of activities in the textile

TABLE 17.2 Growth rates within apparel value chains (CAGR) in select countries

Country	Final apparel		Intermediate apparel	
	2000–09	2010–15	2000–09	2010–15
World	5.97	4.8	12.5	2.7
Mexico	−7.88	0.33	−9.43	1.03
Thailand	1.23	−3.9	3.62	−2.68
China	12.73	5.97	12.93	7.98
Vietnam	18.49	16.1	25.84	13.61
Bangladesh	12.82	12.37	12	2.2
India	8.02	10.11	4.4	6.24
Peru	9.77	−5.25	6.62	0.78
Philippines	−5.43	6.02	−8.7	0.68
Indonesia	2.24	2.29	2.33	1.03

SOURCE: CALCULATED FROM WORLD BANK, *WORLD INTEGRATED TRADE SOLUTIONS* (WASHINGTON, 2016)

and clothing sector by the developed countries. Though offshoring started as early as the 1970s, it became a dominant and generalized trend in world textile and apparel trade between 1990 and 2015. Table 17.2 shows that the size of the global market for exports of wearing apparel contracted by about 1.10 per cent between 2000 and 2015. However, the period between 2010 and 2015 saw some recovery with the expansion of the market by 0.40 per cent. This small growth can be largely attributed to the rising trend of apparel exports in South Asia, as well as in the East Asia and Pacific regions.

However, India's largest competitor for exports emerged within the South Asia region where competition was structured through regional agreements like the South Asian Free Trade Area (SAFTA). For example, in terms of supply of intermediary products, India is the largest producer of yarn and cotton after China. It supplies yarn and cotton to Bangladesh, which has a much higher productivity of export-oriented final products in the apparel sector, especially after its greater integration into supply chains after through free trade agreements (FTAs). A recent assessment of the Ministry of Textiles, Government of India, shows that China is the only country with the capability to dominate the entire chain of international apparel production. It is the largest producer of cotton, and the second largest producer of silk, wool and man-made fibre after India. Vietnam and Bangladesh import cotton and fabric from India and China, but after China they are the overall lead exporters of finished apparel goods along with Cambodia. In fact, Indian markets are also flooded with cheap Chinese and Bangladeshi apparels, giving stiff competition to India's domestic suppliers.[18]

The existence of labour reserves is the main structural factor that makes South Asia an attractive destination for export houses to offshore production. The most important disciplining force in factory work is the control of the working day through labour regulations that have been liberalized under the influence of big business over the last one-and-a-half decades. The process of deregulation is designed to make developing countries like India more competitive in the international market and attract investment. The reformed labour laws provide a degree of flexibility and control to the employer, as in the case of the hiring of temporary workers (or *badli* workers) in Bangladesh. Such workers have fixed-term employment and often work on a piece-rated system. As a recent study notes, from 2005 to 2012 the percentage of *badli* workers in Bangladesh increased from almost 0 to 5 per cent, whereas in India the

18 Wazir Advisors, *Existing FTAs and Their Impact on Indian Textile Exports*, p. 48.

corresponding rise was from 8 to 10 per cent.[19] The labour laws of Bangladesh and China provided for an indefinite temporary workforce, whereas India only recently introduced fixed-term contracts in the apparel sector.[20] Hence the introduction of flexibility in hiring and firing seems to be one of the major factors that structures the availability of labour reserves. The second factor is the control over the working day and regulation of hours of work, including overtime. While the ILO Convention typically mandates a 40-hour working week, India, Bangladesh and Vietnam permit 48 hours a week, and China permits 44 hours a week. However, what is important is that the working week does not conform to a normal five to six-day week, and the schedule of leave permitted is oppressive. In Bangladesh, workers are allowed one day of paid leave for every 18 days of work or about 17 paid holidays annually; in India, workers get 12 paid days of leave annually. Overtime is legal everywhere with most countries permitting one to two hours of overtime at 150 to 200 per cent of the hourly wage. Another factor that comes into play in extending the working day is the "night shift". Bangladesh, Vietnam and India do not provide for premium wages on night shifts, whereas China provides a premium of 130 per cent of the hourly wage for the night shift.[21]

Whatever the legal framework, the working day of a garment worker in almost all these factories extends far beyond the legal limit. A recent study showed that Bangladesh women workers (constituting about 80 per cent of the workforce) work from 14 to 16 hours a day, seven days a week.[22] This means that instead of 48 hours, the women actually worked for 98 hours a week. Similarly, a multi-country study of the ILO concluded that in Vietnam and Pakistan, two out of three workers worked for more than 48 hours a week, that too without receiving the stipulated overtime payment.[23] The situation was similar in India: surveying about 500 workers, the study concluded that for 80 per cent of current workers a six-day working week was the norm, while 20 per cent of workers reported working seven days a week. Three-fourths of the

19 World Bank, *Stitches to Riches: Apparel Employment, Trade and Economic Development in South Asia* (Washington, 2016) or World Bank.

20 Technopak, *Study on "Garment Sector to Understand Their Requirement for Capacity Building"*, p. 40.

21 Ibid., p. 41.

22 Sarpong (2018), 'Sweatshops and the Duty of Care: To What Extent? The Case of Bangladesh in Shahka Seifi and David Crowther eds, *Stakeholders, Governance and Responsibility*, 14 (2018), pp. 229–47.

23 Phu Huynh, *Employment, Wages and Productivity in Asia's Garment sector: Finding New Drivers of Competitiveness*, Working Paper Series, ILO Regional Office for Asia and Pacific (Bangkok, 2015), pp. 11–13.

workers usually worked 8 hours a day but the remaining 25 per cent worked more than 10 hours, including more than 12 per cent who reported working 12 hours or more.[24] However such results are very region-specific and do not cover many clusters like Coimbatore and Tirupur in the south of India, where working hours are much more oppressive and young girls were forced to work overtime without pay. The normal working day consisted of 14 to 16 hours, or 24 hours in three shifts, in export-oriented spinning factories.[25]

Oppressive control over the working day is possible because of the persistence of global labour arbitrage, which forms the context of the emergence of the global apparel producing and trading corporation that exploits cheap labour across the globe. As a Report of the Workers Consortium shows, between 2001 and 2011, real wages in the apparel sector fell in nine out of ten top apparel-exporting countries.[26] Competition between developing countries to attract global apparel business creates wage hierarchies within the South Asian region and within the industry itself, as seen in Table 17.3.

The data show that of all the top apparel-exporting countries, Bangladesh and Cambodia (considered India's main competitors, apart from China) have declining wages, whereas China has increased its wages more than twofold. However, China's complete product range, and technological and infrastructural advantage are seen as having made up for the rising labour costs. Hence, perhaps low wages are not the only factor structuring labour practices as, despite rising wages, China continues to dominate the world market. This is seen if we compare the unit costs of production of the most popular items for export.

Table 17.4 clearly indicates that labour intensity is not the only factor contributing to domination of the world export market. The variety and technology of production also play an important role in structuring the competition. Thus, though China has a higher average cost of production as compared to India and Bangladesh in several items like coats, sweaters and sweatshirts, it still dominates the market because of the quality and breadth of its variety. This is a result of public investment in knowledge and research infrastructure, which is lacking in the other countries. Rather, countries like India and Bangladesh use labour-intensive production systems which are competitive primarily because

24 Fundamentals, *Insights into the Working Conditions in India's Garment Industry* (Geneva, 2015).

25 SOMO and ICN, *Maid in India: Young Dalit Girls Continue to Suffer Exploitation in India's Garment Industry* (Amsterdam, 2012).

26 Workers Rights Consortium, *Global Wage Trends for Apparel Workers, 2001–2011* (Washington, D.C., 2013), p. 7.

TABLE 17.3 Monthly real wages in 15 of the top 21 apparel exporters to the United States, in 2001 currency

	Monthly real wage				Per cent change
	2001		2011		
	LCU	USD, PPP	LCU	USD, PPP	
Bangladesh	2,083.00	$93.67	2,033.60	$91.45	–2.37%
Cambodia*	51.00	$161.89	39.78	$126.26	–22.01%
China	480.00	$144.86	1,076.57	$324.90	+124.29%
Dominican Republic	2,698.00	$293.52	2,057.45	$223.83	–23.74%
El Salvador*	162.00	$332.44	143.34	$294.14	–11.52%
Guatemala	1,414.66	$397.62	1,230.10	$345.75	–13.05%
Haiti	1,014.00	$104.42	1,502.99	$154.78	+48.22%
Honduras	2,514.83	$359.47	2,294.53	$327.98	–8.76%
India	2,019.55	$150.20	2,281.27	$169.67	+12.96%
Indonesia	421,958.00	$134.90	583,786.75	$186.64	+38.35%
Mexico	4,766.00	$755.14	3,386.54	$536.57	–28.94%
Mexico	1,258.00	$199.32	1,297.31	$205.55	+3.12%
Peru	487.50	$335.93	570.94	$393.43	+17.12%
Philippines	4,979.00	$249.25	4,662.19	$233.39	–6.36%
Thailand	5,748.50	$360.33	5,378.25	$337.12	–6.44%
Vietnam	730,167.00	$182.43	1,019,766.50	$254.78	+39.66%

SOURCE: WORKERS RIGHTS CONSORTIUM, GLOBAL WAGE TRENDS FOR APPAREL WORKERS, 2001–2011, P. 11.

of low wage structures. Hence low wages and their relationship with productivity targets become the main methods of control over workers.

Another important way of disciplining the workforce on the shopfloor is through quality control which takes place through wage cuts if targets are not met and there are too many rejects. An increasing tendency to make unrealistic targets is evident and is achieved by squeezing intervals between batches through mechanization or reducing the mandated time available to workers for rest; this leads to stricter disciplining and greater oppression of garment workers. A study commissioned by the Ministry of Textiles, Government of

TABLE 17.4 Estimated unit cost of production of selected items, 2013

Country	Number of items produced/Average unit cost in USD						Product-wise world export rank					
	Trousers	Sweater/ sweatshirt	Knit shirt	Coats	Woven shirts	Dresses/ skirts	Trousers	Sweater/ sweatshirt	Knit shirt	Coats	Woven shirts	Dresses/ skirts
China	4/6.5	8/7.7	5/4.1	7/17.4	4/7.2	7/8.5	1	1	1	1	1	1
Bangladesh	3/6.3	6/6.2	2/2.9	3/13.3	2/6.2	1/5.0	3	3	3	4	4	9
India	5/6.9	4/5.2	3/3.8	4/16.0	7/7.8	8/8.6	11	8	5	13	3	3
Pakistan	8/8.2	3/4.8	1/2.8	1/7.8	3/6.7	3/6.1	9	11	14	14	29	33
Sri Lanka	7/7.5	7/6.3	7/4.6	5/16.7	8/9.2	6/8.4	13	17	15	24	10	12
Vietnam	6/7.0	1/4.6	8/4.6	8/20.5	5/7.2	4/6.8	5	4	6	3	7	5
Cambodia	2/6.3	5/5.5	4/3.9	2/10.9	1/6.2	2/5.3	7	6	9	8	11	10
Indonesia	1/6.0	2/4.6	6/4.2	6/16.9	6/7.6	5/6.9	6	7	8	5	6	6
World	**7.8**	**7.0**	**3.9**	**19.8**	**8.3**	**9.7**						

SOURCE: WORLD BANK, *STITCHES TO RICHES* P. 64.

India, shows that Bangladesh and Vietnam had the least number of rejects in production. Their order to shipment ratio was also much higher than that of India. In low technology systems this is only possible when tight controls are maintained over labour time.[27] This is especially the case with Bangladesh, which follows many more manual processes in designing, checking, etc., than even India and Vietnam. The Chinese industry is comparatively more automated and semi-automated in some functions, but the important point to note is that most of its machinery is self-made or of Chinese origin, whereas big export houses in India import machines from China, Japan and Germany whose cost has to be recovered from production.[28] This can only be done through increases in volumes, and therefore it is not surprising that India's Ministry of Textiles is constantly demanding changes in the labour laws to enable multiple shifts (through an increase in night work) for raising production. What is important to note is that the value added by an Indian worker (measured through the lens of neoliberal economics) is only one-third the value added by a Chinese worker.[29] Hence, unless there is greater investment in worker-enabled and worker-oriented technology, the social cost of which is borne by the government (as it is in China), the tendency of capital to set up a management system of daily physical control of the worker is much higher, and this cannot be done in a production organization that depends too much on home work.

These multiple features of the control of labour create conditions of production that subordinate the process of social reproduction to capitalist production processes. The rate of accumulation is largely maintained through working conditions that effectively reproduce relations of forced and unfree labour. But this unfreedom is not merely in terms of extracting unpaid labour time, but also in terms of lack of access to safe and habitable working conditions. The contemporary literature on Bangladesh and of forced work camps for young girls in the Delhi region, Tirupur and other parts of India is too vast to detail in this paper.[30] But it is possible to generalize that if women workers want to make a survival wage (as most do not even get a minimum wage), they will have to work overtime and sacrifice their family life in a situation where

27 Technopak, *Study on "Garment Sector to Understand Their Requirement for Capacity Building"*, p. 43.

28 Ibid., pp. 23–24.

29 World Bank, *Stitches to Riches*, p. 65.

30 SOMO and ICN, *Maid in India*; ILO. (December 2015); International Labour Organization (ILO), *Minimum Wages in the Global Garment Industry*, International Labour Organization Research Note (Geneva, 2015).

social wages are minimal. Further, the discounting of the woman's role in social reproduction is also done through recruitment practices and composition of the workforce. The highest demand is for women workers between the ages of 12 and 29 years, i.e. young workers whose burden to perform functions of social reproduction is somewhat lower than that of older women. But employment in these age groups also ensures the perpetuation of certain patriarchal values wherein older women with double burdens are considered a liability for the workplace. This can be illustrated through the example of the Sumangali scheme of Tamil Nadu, where contracts are signed with the parents of the girl worker for payment of a specified amount over a period of three to five years, money that can be saved as dowry for their daughter. The girl worker is made to live in a dormitory under abysmal conditions and overworked. A part of her wages is withheld till the contract period is over. These young girls supply labour to big garment manufacturers that service the European and American markets.[31] Such a scheme not only reproduces the supply of cheap labour, but also perpetuates and strengthens patriarchy within the family. However, the reproduction of patriarchy is a secondary objective, the primary aim being to ensure a perpetual supply of cheap labour which functions in slave-like conditions because of the oppressive character of sweatshop management, needed to maintain a competitive advantage. Further, the intensification of super-profiteering and rate of accumulation within the apparel sector cannot be maintained in the long term without direct and repressive control over the labour process. This is only possible if the organization of production is done at centralized workplaces, and this underlying tendency limits the prospects for the growth of home work within the export-oriented industry.

4 Conclusion

This essay focuses on the dynamics of labour processes within the export-oriented garment sector, and their implications for the present and future prospects of home work. It uses Marx's General Law of Capitalist Accumulation to show that there is an increasing tendency within capitalism to have centralized social control over labour processes in order to cope with the high competition that emerges from the internationalization of capital. This pattern is evident in the global apparel industry, where sweatshop management is emblematic of the way in which the workforce is disciplined through a mix of coercive

31 SOMO and ICN, *Maid in India.*

and non-coercive processes, which subordinate the function of social reproduction to the larger accumulation strategy. The analysis shows that this is not possible if there is a preponderance of home work within the export chain. Therefore, home work plays a limited role in ensuring that wages in the production of certain niche products such as embroidered clothing remain low. However, as is also evident from the analysis, home workers have a greater role in enabling the survival and viability of domestic businesses that are struggling to cope with increasing international competition in the period after 2005. It must be noted that decentred networks of domestic production, where home work plays an important role, may have emerged as the result of a restructured export orientation of Indian apparel industry, but competition from international brands in the post-ATC period also places constraints on the expansion of domestic production. This in itself can be a constraining factor in the future prospects of home work in the apparel sector.

It is important to debate the future of home workers in the context of the structural transformations and tendencies in the global apparel sector under contemporary capitalism. This may be done by a cursory consideration of some important contentions which argue that skill augmentation and social dialogue with multinational corporations can result in a brighter future for home workers.[32] However, as this essay shows, such a contention is of limited value and can only help the workers to overcome short- and medium-term crises of survival. Such measures will not challenge the basic structural constraints which limit the growth of home work because of the dominant tendencies within capitalism itself. This is largely because women need to be freed of their care and family responsibilities if their participation through home work is to become meaningful. Since the unpaid work of women subsidizes costs of production in contemporary capitalism, home workers have to be recognized as "workers" both within the network of industrial production and at home. The analysis in this essay shows that the recent categorization of home workers as "dependent contractors" in the recommendations of the 20th Conference of the International Conference of Labour Statisticians is therefore counterproductive, even from the limited objective of improving the working conditions of home workers.

Finally, from the perspective advanced in this essay, home work can only be emancipatory for women if it enables them to unleash their creative abilities without the burden of a bulk of the tasks associated with social reproduction.

32 ILO, "The Future of Work in Textile, Clothing, Leather and Footwear"; Chen, *Informal Economy Monitoring Study Sector Report.*

It is obvious that neoliberal capitalism is incapable of achieving this objective because it has an inherent tendency to privatize, not socialize, social reproduction. This is possible, therefore, only by challenging the very basis of the capitalist system. In this light, it is important to consider whether home work has any relevance outside the system of capitalism, especially where social reproduction itself is socialized and does not require women to stay at home. Since this is a distant dream, the ongoing partial struggle for recognizing women as legitimate "workers" must continue and be intensified.

CHAPTER 18

Are We Not Being Entrepreneurial? Exploring the Home/Work Negotiation of South Asian Immigrant Women Entrepreneurs in Canada

Srabani Maitra

On a warm Sunday afternoon, I walk towards a buzzing neighbourhood in Toronto to meet Rehana, one of my research participants, who runs a small, informal sewing business from home within her own ethnic community. An ex-school teacher who immigrated to Canada with her husband from Pakistan in 2005, Rehana and her husband now live in Toronto with their two sons. They live in a predominantly Pakistani neighbourhood, in the Thorncliff area of Toronto. Rehana's husband Hamid is a former bank officer who now works full-time in a drug store as an assistant manager. He earns a little more than the minimum pay on an hourly basis. As I enter her building and walk towards the elevator, a typed red flyer on the notice board catches my attention: "Newly arrived *salwar kameez*[1] and dress materials from Pakistan at an affordable price. Stitching and fitting also done. Contact Rehana at …". Rehana, along with other women whom I interviewed at various periods during my field work, run small businesses like that of sewing, catering or babysitting from home, almost always in those areas of Toronto with a high concentration of South Asians. Their businesses are specifically geared to function within their own communities. For example, women running garment businesses mainly sell *salwar kameez, sari*[2] and other dress materials either stitched by them in Canada or brought over from their home countries. Many of them also do sewing, embroidery, crochet work, or stitch baby clothes, trousers, skirts, dresses and household items like curtains, pillow covers and cushion covers. For those involved in catering, most of the food items exclusively relate to South Asian cuisines, although a number of women also advertise their skills in preparing "western" dishes like various kinds of sandwiches, pies, pastries, etc. They usually cater for small functions and family events within their own communities.

1 Dress commonly worn by South Asian women.

2 Traditional dress in India and Bangladesh, also worn by women in Pakistan and Sri Lanka.

© SRABANI MAITRA, 2022 | DOI:10.1163/9789004499614_021
This is an open access chapter distributed under the terms of the CC BY-NC-ND 4.0 license.

It is necessary to clarify here that the appellation South Asian does not constitute a homogeneous group but differs in terms of religion, language, diet, cultural habits, caste or class status, as well as national identities. In North America, the diversity of people collectively described as South Asian includes those coming from India, Bangladesh, Pakistan, Sri Lanka, Nepal and Bhutan. Highly educated with university degrees and professional experience, these women immigrants, whom I had a chance to interact with, came to Canada along with their spouses in expectation of an improved quality of life and socio-economic opportunities.[3] However, given the gendered and racialized nature of the labour market that exists in Canada,[4] none of the women could get into a job that was commensurate with their previous educational or professional backgrounds. Home-based entrepreneurship was often a last resort to economically survive in Canada after multiple failures to enter into the mainstream labour market.

The focus on home-based work in Canada is vital for two reasons. First, since the 1990s, women's work in Canada has undergone increased "informalization" as well as "domestication" due to the trade liberalization and economic recessions characterizing the global world.[5] While "informalization" refers to non-regulated work, both paid and unpaid,[6] "domestication" has ushered in a "shift in the locations and sites of paid work from formal workplaces to domestic premises".[7] According to Statistics Canada, while the number of employees working from home increased from 1.4 million in 2000 to 1.7 million in 2008, the number of self-employed increased more substantially. Their participation rate climbed from 54 per cent in 2006 to 60 per cent in 2008, for a total of 1.8 million workers.[8] This is in a context where, while 15 per cent of all workers in Canada are self-employed, they still account for about half of those who work from home.[9] Statistics Canada further points out that the percentage of self-employed women working from home is higher than that of men (67 per

3 Statistics Canada, *Women in Canada: A Gender-based Statistical Report* (Ottawa, 2015).

4 Tania. Das Gupta et al, *Race and Racialization: Essential Readings*, second edn (Toronto, 2018); Jeffrey G. Reitz, "Tapping immigrants' skills: New directions for Canadian immigration policy in the knowledge economy", *Choices*, 11 (2005), pp. 1–18.

5 Annie Delaney *et al.*, *Homeworking Women: A Gender Justice Perspective* (London, 2019); Wenona Giles and Valery Preston, "The Domestication of Women's Work: A Comparison of Chinese and Portuguese Immigrant Women Homeworkers", *Studies in Political Economy*, 51 (1996), pp. 147–81.

6 Giles and Preston, "The Domestication of Women's Work", p. 147.

7 Ibid.

8 Statistics Canada, *Working from Home: An Update* (Ottawa, 2016).

9 Ibid.

cent and 56 per cent, respectively) because of the various family responsibilities and child care that women have to engage in.[10] While it is evident from the above that there can be a variety of home-based work ranging from paid work to businesses that are often gendered, what is still lacking in the analysis is a focus on how the creation of such work arrangements has disproportionately affected not just women but especially immigrant women of colour, who are over-represented in the informal, low-paid, precarious types of home work.[11]

Second, home work challenges any boundary existing between the private and the public by making it malleable. By dint of being located at home, the space ideologically constructed as "women's place", home work "brings wage into the place where 'love', 'duty', and 'need' … compel labour".[12] Within the limited literature that exists on immigrant women's home-based work in Canada, most studies concentrate on the gendered division of labour and the invisibility that home-based work shares with domestic work.[13] In this context, scholars mainly argue that home-based work exacerbates women's dual responsibilities of household work and child care. Moreover, as the separation between home and work becomes quite blurry, home-based work often loses its "professional legitimacy not only at the macro level in the hierarchy of professions but also in the perception of other family members".[14] Such underestimation is exacerbated when home work is undertaken by immigrant women of colour, who are often assumed to be docile and domesticated.[15] Consequently, despite earning at home, the social organization of the women's lives remains rooted in gender/race hierarchies and an ideology of motherhood.[16]

While the literature discussed above is important in identifying how racial and gendered processes affect women's (self) employment trajectories within homes, I argue that by depicting immigrant women of colour as merely a cheap labour force, these studies significantly undermine any resourcefulness

10 Martin Turcotte, *Working at home: An update* (Ottawa, 2010).

11 Giles and Preston, "The Domestication of Women's Work", p. 151.

12 Elisabeth Prügl and Eileen Boris, "Introduction", in Eileen Boris and Elisabeth. Prügl (eds), *Home workers in global perspective: Invisible no more* (New York and London, 1996), pp. 3–18, p. 7.

13 Alice Rangel de Paiva Abreu and Bila. Sorj, "Good Housewives: Seamstresses in the Brazilian Garment Industry", in Eileen Boris and Elisabeth Prügl (eds), *Home workers in Global Perspective*, pp. 93–110, pp. 101–07; Jinghzou Liu, "The Precarious Nature of Work in the Context of Canadian Immigration: An Intersectional Analysis", *Canadian Ethnic Studies*, 51 (2019), pp. 169–85.

14 Abreu and Sorj, "Good Housewives", p. 101; Delaney *et al.*, *Homeworking Women.*

15 Lalaie Ameeriar, "Pedagogies of Affect: Docility and Deference in the Making of Immigrant Women Subjects", *Signs: Journal of Women in Culture and Society*, 40 (2015), pp. 467–86.

16 Abreu and Sorj, "Good Housewives", pp. 101–02; Delaney *et al.*, *Homeworking Women.*

or initiatives that these women might articulate while coping with the various exclusionary practices they experience in the host country where they have migrated with skills, education and credentials.[17] Only a few studies address women's negotiations and struggles while engaged in home-based work.[18] Despite pointing out the disadvantages that immigrant women—especially immigrant women of colour—experience, these studies underscore the importance of understanding the strategic bargaining that women often engage in, thereby challenging those arguments that primarily describe women within home enterprises as a subservient and unpaid labour force.

Drawing on the above lines of argumentation, this paper, based on qualitative interviews with twenty-five South Asian home-based women entrepreneurs in Canada, examines the various exclusionary experiences of "living in a gender/race stratified society that force South Asian immigrant women to enter home-based work after migration and how they weather their diminished status from being full-time professionals in their home countries to part-time, low-income precarious business owners".[19] In a country and society where gendered racism is deeply embedded, and Eurocentric ideals, values and norms dominate, South Asian women experienced difficulty in finding their bearings. The constraints were particularly evident when they tried to enter the labour market. Various institutionalized barriers such as the need for Canadian work experience, coupled with the discriminatory attitude of employers, systematically devalued and deskilled their previous education, knowledge or expertise, and pushed them to unemployment and eventual poverty. Marginalized and excluded from the labour market, these women found themselves facing a dilemma. On the one hand, there was the neoliberal thrust to remain

17 Srabani Maitra, "Points of Entry: Examining the Conditions of South Asian Immigrant Women's Entry into Enclave Entrepreneurship in Toronto", *South Asian Diaspora*, 5 (2013), pp. 123–37.

18 Arlene Dallalfar, "Iranian Women as Immigrant Entrepreneurs", *Gender and Society*, 8 (1994), pp. 541–61; Maitra, "Points of Entry"; Srabani Maitra, "Perspectives on Work and Family Lives: Exploring the Lived Experiences of South Asian Immigrant Mothers Working from Home in Toronto", in J. Sangha and T. Gonsalves (eds), *South Asian Mothering: Negotiating Culture, Family and Selfhood* (Toronto, 2013), pp. 149–64; Edwina Pio, "Ethnic Minority Migrant Women Entrepreneurs and the Imperial Imprimatur", *Women in Management Review*, 22 (2007), pp. 631–49; Margaret Walton-Roberts and Daniel Hiebert, "Immigration, Entrepreneurship, and the Family: Indo-Canadian Enterprise in the Construction Industry of Greater Vancouver", *Canadian Journal of Regional Science*, 20 (1997), pp. 119–40; Margaret Walton-Roberts and Geraldine Pratt, "Mobile Modernities: A South Asian Family Negotiates Immigration, Gender and Class in Canada", *Gender Place and Culture*, 12 (2005), pp. 173–95.

19 Maitra, "Points of Entry", p. 126.

productive, self-sufficient and responsible citizen-subjects; on the other hand, there was the inability to enter their own professional fields, despite having the skills and education to be successfully employed in the Canadian labour market. These social realities constituted the everyday experiences of these women, and it is critical to address these issues when analysing their participation in home-based entrepreneurship. At the same time, it is also important to emphasize how women, despite being forced into low-end businesses at home, try different avenues to remain productive. Going

> beyond notions of profit or economic competitiveness, such productivity entailed broader considerations about love, creativity and passion in their work. They actively refashioned their positions within their households, extending their love and support for the family members and also mobilizing ties with other women within the community, thereby challenging their stereotypical depiction as a silent, invisible, and extractable labour force.[20]

This paper therefore makes an important contribution to the literature on home-based work by highlighting how, far from the self-absorbed, profit-oriented neoliberal enterprising self, these women, by evoking kin networks and by valuing their family lives and relationships, presented new forms of agential worker-subjects who actively negotiated various exploitative ideologies and barriers "for their own ends in the daily struggles".[21] By providing new significance and meaning to their relationships with their families and with other women in the community, these home-based women workers also challenged the stereotypical assumptions of oppressed and isolated women reeling under family pressure within home-based economies. Negotiating their presence on the peripheries of the Canadian market economy that offered nothing more than precariousness, these women demonstrated how alternative crafting of an "enterprising self" was possible by "offering collaborative, meaningful work and relationships".[22]

20 Ibid.

21 Ngai Pun, *Women Factory Workers in a Global Workspace* (Durham and London, 2005), p. 61.

22 Tara J. Fenwick, "Transgressive Desires: New Enterprising Selves in the New Capitalism", *Work, Employment and Society*, 16 (2002), pp. 703–23, p. 717.

1 Being Enterprising

In Canada's neoliberal economy, where individuals are expected to choose their own path to economic growth and pursue "self-defined goals",[23] starting a business as an entrepreneur is seen as an important initiative by immigrants for "penetrating" a totally foreign country, in which, often, economic choices and opportunities for them are severely constrained by the dominant groups of the host country.[24] The idyllic portrayal of the neoliberal "enterprising self" can perhaps be best examined in the context of immigrant entrepreneurship, which is often promoted as a form of work that entails empowerment and agency for individuals willing to be flexible, risk-taking and determined to achieve success and professional development. Indeed, the emerging image of an entrepreneur is that of a self-made individual (read: white, middle-class man), daring and decided, driven by a sense of power and independence, characterized by such words as innovation, risk-taking, opportunity recognition and economic growth.[25] These values associated with entrepreneurship are in sync with the "dominant western enterprise development models emphasizing competitive edge in a globalized market to attract investors and secure wealth".[26] Within this context, the agency of the individual is defined in terms of an empowered and autonomous individual who can successfully establish the business against all odds. Closely tied to the neoliberal ideals of "pulling oneself up by one's bootstrap" and a "can do attitude", entrepreneurship thus evokes an image of empowerment where women and men are seen as developing their capabilities to improve their sense of individuality and confidence. Concurrently, this empowerment is seen as leading to the autonomy and agency that they can exercise to live a better life and subsequently assimilate into the mainstream community.[27] Entrepreneurship then seems to portray a

23 Naila Kabeer, *Reversed Realities: Gender Hierarchies in Development Thought* (London and New York, 1994), p. 14.

24 Feiwel Kupferberg, "The Established and the Newcomers: What Makes Immigrant and Women Entrepreneurs so Special?", *International Review of Sociology*, 13 (2003), pp. 89–104.

25 Monica Boyd, "Family and Personal Networks in International Migration: Recent Developments and New Agendas", *International Migration Review*, 23 (1989), pp. 638–70.

26 Fenwick, "Transgressive Desires", p. 718.

27 Robert L. Bach, Jennifer B. Bach and Timothy Triplett, "The Flotilla Entrants: Latest and most controversial", *Cuban Studies*, 11 (1981), pp. 29–48; Alejandro Portes, "Modes of Structural Incorporation and Present Theories of Immigration", in Mary M. Kritz, Charles B. Keely and Silvano M. Tomasi (eds), *Global Trends in Migration* (New York, 1981), pp. 279–97; Alejandro Portes and Robert L. Bach, "Immigrant Earnings: Cuban and Mexican Immigrants in the United States", *International Migration Review*, 14 (1980), pp. 315–41;

classic example of neoliberal enterprising citizens who, amidst labour market insecurity and barriers, can create their own success through ingenuity, hard work and zeal. Those unable to do so, the "unenterprising" ones, tend to end up in the precariousness of the secondary labour market.

While entrepreneurship is usually depicted as a panacea for immigrants, especially unemployment or underemployment among immigrants of colour, South Asian women's home-operated businesses present a different dynamic. Being excluded from the white collar job market, they not only for the first time utilized the skills "they have learned in carrying out their domestic, maternal and family responsibilities" for economic purposes,[28] but also reconfigured the home space, traditionally held as a space of leisure, freedom and privacy[29] and ideologically held as distinct from the work space or that of the public sphere.[30] Moreover, their businesses were small, low-income, with no benefits, and in most cases unaccounted for. These kinds of businesses are technically defined as own-account or solo self-employment—that is, where there are no paid employees[31]—and are considered to be in an even more precarious position than self-employed employers.[32]

In the following sections, I will discuss the ways in which South Asian women negotiate neoliberal ideologies associated with economic productivity and success. First, despite being engaged in a precarious form of work, they demonstrate their love and passion for their work, challenging the notion of an abstract, highly individualized and competitive entrepreneur. Second, by cultivating ethnic ties with other community members, they foster collaborative relationships and reinvigorate "relational values".[33]

Alejandro Portes and Robert L. Bach, "The Latin Journey: Cuban and Mexican Immigrants in the United States" (Berkeley, CA, 1985).

28 Dallalfar, "Iranian Women as Immigrant Entrepreneurs", p. 549.

29 Graham Crow and Graham Allan, "Constructing the Domestic Sphere: The Emergence of the Modern Home in Post-war Britain", in H. Corr and L. Jamieson (eds), *Politics of Everyday Life: Continuity and Change in Work and the Family* (Basingstoke, 1990), pp. 11–36; Jon Dart, "Home-based Work and Leisure Spaces: Settee or Work-Station?", *Leisure Studies*, 25 (2006), pp. 313–28.

30 Dart, "Home-based Work and Leisure Spaces"; Prügl and Boris, "Introduction".

31 Cynthia L. Cranford, Leah F Vosko and Nancy Zukewich "The gender of precarious employment in Canada", *Relations Industrielles/Industrial Relations,* 58:3 (2003), pp. 454–82.

32 ibid.

33 Fenwick, "Transgressive Desires".

2 Research Findings

Exploring the complexities of the Canadian labour market

> The whole application process took us … one year … I think … and then we had to wait for four years after submitting the application, when we finally heard from the consulate. I remember we had to put in details of our education, work experience, language tests to get the required number of points to become eligible. Although I was the principal applicant, me and also my husband had to put all our qualification details. We went and got our educational certificates, letters from our past employers … my god … the amount of documents and information that we had to put in was huge. But we were determined to come here, we wanted a good life. So when we finally got accepted we were so happy.

The above quotation is from one my interviewees, Leena, who came to Canada in 2002 with her husband. A former kindergarten teacher in India, Leena, during the interview, shared with me the documentation that is involved in the application process for Canadian immigration. According to her, the process was not merely handing in a bunch of papers, but involved matching their qualifications with the NOC[34] list, putting in the details of their work experience, education, and then waiting for four long years before they finally heard about their application. Education, work experience and language skills are some of the important determinants for getting selected for Canadian immigration, and the amount of documentation that Leena and her husband had to hand in makes clear the rigorous and time-consuming selection process that exists for choosing some of the "best and brightest" immigrants considered suitable for settling down in Canada.

Canada has an active immigration programme that invites individuals to apply to enter the country and contribute her/his skills, education and experience to the social, cultural and economic growth of Canada's national life. Immigrants are thus considered "assets" to this nation and only those who are held to be substantially qualified to enter Canada are inducted into the migration process.[35] The selection of "qualified" immigrants is based on criteria

---

34 The National Occupational Classification (NOC) is a "nationally accepted reference on occupations in Canada", available at HRSDC, www5.hrsdc.gc.ca, last accessed 2 June 2021, to understand the jobs available in Canada's labour market and to find out their eligibility to those job requirements.

35 Daniel Hiebert, "Economic Associations of Immigrant Self-Employment in Canada", *International Journal of Entrepreneurial Behaviour and Research*, 8 (2002), pp. 93–112.

like education, work experience, age, English/French language proficiency, arranged employment in Canada and adaptability, so that only those are chosen who can enrich Canada not only demographically but also economically by contributing to its labour market and maintaining its status as a globally competitive knowledge economy. No wonder, the other interviewees also had to experience rigorous screening like Leena in terms of their application for immigration. Despite not being the principal applicants in most cases,[36] the participants (including those sponsored by their husbands) still had to submit their educational and work-related certificates as these were vital for successful acceptance of their applications.

During the interviews, most of the respondents also expressed how happy and excited they were to be in what they felt was a "land of opportunity". Repeatedly, the women reiterated how they thought of immigration as an opportunity to enhance their career, earn copiously, and ensure a secure future for themselves and their children. Neeta, who had worked in a non-governmental organization (NGO) in Bangladesh before coming to Canada in 2004, described how the very thought of migrating to Canada brought happiness not only to her but also to her whole family: "Coming to Canada was the dream come true. We were all very happy including my family back in Bangladesh. For the entire family it was like a dream come true".

Neeta had planned to work in a community organization or NGO after migration as she was confident that her five years of experience working with women's issues in Bangladesh would be useful in getting her the desired job. Many other women also mentioned such reasons as "better opportunities", "better future" and "good life" as dominant reasons for migration. Overall, a majority of the women expressed their happiness at being able to come to Canada. As Shazia, a computer data entry operator from Pakistan explained, "We had a very high expectation about Canada. I was very happy that I was coming to abroad, you know people back home think a lot about foreign life".

Thus an enmeshment of desires and expectations pervaded the initial stage of women's migration to Canada, and their decision to look for a job also came out of such a desire to be settled in the labour market as soon as possible. Although the majority of the women were not principal applicants, being highly educated and having worked before, they were very keen on entering the labour market as quickly as possible.

36 Amongst the women interviewed only Saadiya, Neeta and Leena applied as principal applicants while in the rest of the cases the women were co-applicants. Their spouses were the principal applicants.

The keenness of these women to work after immigration corresponds to the research findings of scholars such as Das Gupta and Jamal,[37] who indicate a strong tendency on the part of most South Asian immigrant women to work. Prompted by eagerness to develop their careers as well as contribute to the fast-depleting reserve money, the respondents in my study also wanted to start earning as early as possible. Their fervour to find gainful employment was also driven by the zeal to be self-sufficient and earning members of the Canadian society. Laxmi had been working in an administrative position in Sri Lanka and did not want to depend on her husband after immigration. Similarly Sabitha, who had been working as a teller in a bank in India, did not want to remain without work: "After settling down in Toronto, my first intention was to find a job. I have worked for so many years and never had to depend on anyone for money. I wanted to support myself here too". A common theme that seemed to emerge from our conversations was the confidence these women had regarding their qualifications. While their desire to migrate to Canada may have been induced by global capitalism and Canada's proactive immigration system, as far as their abilities were concerned, none of the interviewees looked upon themselves as deficient or lacking in any way, such that their prospects of becoming successful members of mainstream Canadian society and its economy might be hindered.

Perhaps the interviewees' first introduction to the notion that their past experience and education might be perceived as inadequate or deficient by the Canadian system was when they started applying for jobs and going out to meet job counsellors and recruiters. They would then start wondering why they were not getting any response from the employers or the recruiters, and whether there was something wrong with their application or job-seeking procedures. All but three of the respondents pointed out how, even after applying for several positions, they were not asked to an interview. The women expressed their anguish at the existing system not recognizing their previous experience, rendering them jobless, and pushing them towards re-training and re-learning. Mita, a university graduate from India with experience in administrative work, expressed her despair at the situation she was in:

> I have worked for five years in India and when I came here I used to apply for various administrative jobs. But so far nothing. A couple of places

37 Tania Das Gupta, "Political Economy of Gender, Race, and Class: Looking at South Asian Immigrant Women in Canada", *Canadian Ethnic Studies*, 26 (1994), pp. 59–73; Amina Jamal, "Situating South Asian Immigrant Women in the Canadian/Global Economy", *Canadian Woman Studies*, 18 (1998), pp. 26–33.

> called me for interview but never hired me. Later a friend told me that unless I do some course here on administration nobody will hire me. I need to specialize because I am an immigrant. Can you imagine? I was so shocked that all my education has gone down the drain.

Experiences such as the above-mentioned, where women were identified as lacking in Canadian work experience, reflect the "discriminatory bias" towards foreign credentials existing in Canada.[38] As there is no uniform or consistent system to evaluate and assess immigrants' skills and education, the devaluation process remains largely ambiguous and hazy with no definitive answers as to why their previous education of many years are negated or underestimated. Devaluation of foreign education/work experience is also part of the systemic forms of discrimination or racism based on the assumed ethnic inferiority of certain foreign-born women and the assumed inferior quality of educational systems in their country of origin, thereby perpetuating exploitation of and disadvantage for immigrants of colour.[39] South Asian women's entry into home-based businesses was therefore driven by their need to survive economically and supplement family incomes after arriving in Canada. Home-based entrepreneurship was often their last resort after multiple failed attempts at entering the mainstream labour market. Similar findings have been reported by other scholars studying immigrant women of colour and their labour market experiences in Canada.[40] These scholars

> have also posited that the predominant siphoning of immigrant women of colour into these unstable, low-paid, contingent job sectors elucidate how the highly racialized and gendered neoliberal, post-Fordist Canadian labour market deskills them and turns them into a captive labour force who are essential yet remain disposable in the capitalist labour market.[41]

38 K.D. Sadiq, "Race, Ethnicity and Immigration in the Workplace: Visible Minority Experiences and Workplace Diversity Initiatives", *Canadian Issues: Immigration and the Intersections of Diversity*, Spring (2005), pp. 61–66, p. 63.

39 C. Khan, "The closed door: credentialized society and immigrant experiences", *Canadian Issues: Foreign Credential Recognition*, Spring (2007), pp. 63–6.

40 Kiran Mirchandani, *et al.*, "The Paradox of Training and Learning in a Culture of Contingency", in David W. Livingstone, Kiran Mirchandani and Peter Harrold. Sawchuk (eds), *The Future of Lifelong Learning and Work: Critical Perspectives* (Rotterdam, 2008), pp. 171–84.

41 Maitra, "Points of Entry", p. 130.

Apart from institutionalized barriers, patriarchal control and gendered divisions of household work also forced many women to work from home. Many studies have pointed out how South Asian women often have to take up most of the responsibilities when it comes to child care and house work.[42] In the absence of full-time job opportunities,

> such responsibilities were further exacerbated for interviewees who were forced to spend a considerable amount of time within their homes. Many women worked exceptionally long days. They usually got up early in the morning and worked throughout the day preparing meals, cleaning the house, or sending the children to school. Women who also had part-time paid work outside the home not only worked long hours, but also had to put more effort into managing their domestic responsibilities.[43]

Thaya, for example, mentioned to me that stitching a whole *lehenga*[44] required at least three days of continuous sewing, and if clients wanted additional embroidery, an extra day or two. I remember visiting Thaya on a Monday afternoon, when she was extremely busy with her sewing. It was just before *Diwali*[45] and she had to stitch fifteen *lehenga*s for a group of girls who were to perform in a community hall. She did most of her stitching in the living room of her house (a common practice among most of my interviewees), where we sat down for the interview. As she spoke to me, I noticed how fast she was at sewing the buttons. The *lehenga*s she had stitched were extremely intricate and artistic. She said that she had hardly slept the past week as she had several orders to handle. Often sewing while cooking or doing laundry while preparing meals for catering, women had to do a lot of juggling of tasks and felt overwhelmed at times. When women like Sheila or Priya had to cater for small parties, they not only had to deal with a large amount of cooking, but also washing and cleaning. Priya mentioned how every weekend, once she was done with making *chappati*s, she would be too tired to do any of her other house work. Although their husbands would pitch in sometimes, the majority of family responsibilities still rested with the women.

In the next part I highlight the various negotiations that women undertook to make their lives and work more meaningful in contexts where various social

42 See ibid.; Maitra, "Perspectives on Work and Family Lives".

43 Maitra, "Points of Entry", p. 130.

44 A type of long skirt with intricate designs.

45 A South Asian festival, often described as the Festival of Lights. People buy new clothes and exchange food, sweets and gifts with each other on this occasion.

processes and forms of stratification impede their acceptability into mainstream Canadian society.

3 Challenging Neoliberal Ideologies of Success

While discussing with my respondents the various factors that motivated them to continue with their small businesses, a common response I received from the majority of the women was that stitching or cooking was more a passion or a hobby that they had never planned to practise as a form of business.

For example, a bit hesitant at first, Priya did not know what she could do from home. She had neither the money nor the experience to start a big business. It was then that her husband suggested that she could try her hand at catering. Priya knew that in her building, there were many South Asian families where both the wife and the husband went out to work, and a few of them she knew were always complaining about all the cooking and cleaning they had to do on their own. She decided to take a chance and put up a flyer in her building. She intentionally kept her charges affordable so that families would get interested. She considered herself lucky when, within a couple of days, she got a response from a member of her building who inquired if she could supply only *chappatis*[46] for them. Priya readily agreed not only because she had got her first client, but also because generally, within her family, she had a reputation for "rolling out really soft and tasty *chappatis*". This was something she had learned from her mother and she was excited that her very first customer had asked her for what she was good at. Since then, as part of her business, Priya makes around 300 *chapattis* every weekend, and supplies them to various friends and families. Apart from that, she also delivers home-cooked food regularly to a few families. Another interviewee, Shabana, who knew stitching from before, decided to utilize this skill from home when she felt the lack of any other "proper" employment: "I love stitching. That's my passion, so I thought why not do something from home. I mean, I have friends who do that. And if I can't go out and work, what do I do? This is my work now".

There were many others like Shabana who really enjoyed sewing or cooking but had never thought of earning out of it. Shashi was a financial analyst before, and at the time of the interview she ran a catering business from her home in Brampton. While she had never dreamt of pursuing catering in Canada and had always wanted to work in her own field, unemployment forced her to start

46 Wheat bread.

this business. She had learned cooking as a little girl but never had to cook while in India. It was after coming to Canada that she started cooking again and eventually took it up as a business. She had a number of clients, mostly young single men and a few families, who regularly picked up food from her on weekends. Moreover, she also cooked for small functions and get-togethers within the community, and sometimes helped a friend who ran a small sweet shop in Malton.

Since all these women had been professionals before, I was interested to understand how they perceived their transition from white-collar professionals to home-based entrepreneurs. Coming from highly educated, middle-class families, how did they view their present work from home? One of the first comments the women made was about how the unemployment they experienced after migrating to Canada led them to the decision to utilize their past "feminized" skills for economic survival. But then, there was still the fact that cooking or sewing was not something any of the women had done on a regular basis when they were in their home countries. So how did they negotiate this change in their lives? While women like Shabana, Jyoti and Priya mentioned how much they loved to cook or stitch, at the same time they also pointed out how there was a sense of despair and frustration that remained associated with the fact that they were not able to enter their own professions. Often, they would compare their previous status with their present work and family life. Priya said to me, "I often thought, oh God, look at me, I used to be in an office and now I am cooking to earn a living". It was not that the women devalued the work itself, as many of them loved to cook for their friends and family members or would do occasional sewing for themselves. What they felt depressed about was the monotony of the work along with the isolation they experienced while doing home-based work.

However, during our conversations, it was most important to note the way in which the women described their home-based work. Despite all the desperation and frustration, they had started to love and enjoy the work. Priya, for instance, pointed out to me, "Although I never had to do so much cooking before, I have started liking it now. I think one of the main reasons is the appreciation you get from people. That makes a difference".

Jyoti, who worked as a fashion designer, also referred to how much she enjoyed her work and really loved it when people praised her for the work:

> In my building there are few young girls and they always come to me whenever they need new clothes to be stitched. Every time I come up with new styles and they love it. I too enjoy seeing them wear the clothes I have stitched. That's my reward.

Appreciation from clients and family members seemed to play an important role in how women viewed their home-based work. They mentioned that their work not only gave them a sense of satisfaction when clients praised their cooking or stitching, but also instilled in them a sense of responsibility and an urge to do their work more professionally. Ghazala was one among a few women who had decided to take up garments as her profession, and at the time of the interview she was busy setting up her own store where she wanted to sell home-stitched items as well as garments brought from Pakistan. Through these efforts that the women made to initiate a business, often something they had not done before, what comes across as part of their agential self is the creativity and innovativeness they demonstrated by being able to market skills that they learned as a part of their growing up. At the same time, in their use of such a language of love, enjoyment and passion, the women actively negotiated the neoliberal ideology of "bodiless, abstract versions of knowledge and work, and models of enterprise that distance the owner-manager from the business activity".[47] While not necessarily successful or productive in the neoliberal sense, the women underscored their own definition of productivity and success that remained entwined with love and enjoyment, rather than with mere financial stability. The bulk of the literature on home-based entrepreneurship that construct immigrant women's business endeavours within homes as too small, informal and unproductive fails to recognize the kind of resourcefulness at work behind such endeavours.

4 Mobilizing Ethnic/Community Ties

In order to set up their businesses, the women showed their "power and creativity in making and remaking their familial and kin networks".[48] These networks provided them with information about how to start a business. Although these micro-businesses were quite informal, for many there were "lots of things" they needed to know. For example, "finding clients" and "spreading the word" were two vital aspects the women needed assistance with. Sabitha spoke about the issue in detail:

> I had decided to start a garment business but I had never done it before. I was worrying what to do but then there are many women from our

47 Fenwick, "Transgressive Desires", p. 711.
48 Pun, "Women Factory Workers in a Global Workspace", p. 50.

> countries who do this kind of work. I knew some of them and decided to talk to them. They were very helpful. They gave me the idea that putting up flyers will be useful. Also the grocery stores, you know, that's also my friend's idea. Three of us visited quite a few grocery stores to put up flyers. We decided to put up one flyer and then share the earning if any. … Yes, yes we got good response. I would also let people know when I met them in the elevator. I don't mind mixing with or talking to people I don't know (laughs). A friend of mine has advertised in Bengali and Hindi newspapers, she told me yesterday. I think I'll also do that.

One of the primary ways in which women networked and built resources in order to successfully continue with their work was by creating what can be defined as "relationships" with other women within the community. Many of them also spoke about the different ways they would continue their community links. Saadiya, for instance, was a volunteer in a local community centre where she helped other less educated women prepare their résumés or type out job applications. She also shared some of her own soft-skills training with low-income and low-skilled women with the hope of assisting them to enter the labour market. Rehana offered a free English conversation course from home and gave free Quran lessons to girls. Jennifer often babysat for free if someone was facing financial difficulties. Mita gave computer lessons to South Asian women who could not afford paid training.

Elyachar, in her ethnographic study of micro-entrepreneurs in Cairo, has argued that in light of the various "conditions of structural adjustments where jobs and futures were no longer being provided by the state", the Egyptian "worker masters" would often rely on various exchanges that, although not "exchange of money", yet were "essential to the master's success in the market".[49] Similar to these Egyptian workers, the South Asian immigrant women also depended on a number of practices that, by valorizing certain cultural practices, mobilized ethnic ties and kinship amongst the home workers. This valorization or reinvigoration of cultural practices was important to the women not only for "keeping and acquiring customers",[50] but also effective in creating "sisterhood networks"[51] amongst themselves.

Such sisterhood networks were evident in how women often cooked and shared food to remain attached to a communal feeling. Meals occupied an

49 Julia Elyachar, *Markets of Dispossession: NGOs' Economic Development, and the State in Cairo* (Durham, NC, 2005), pp. 26, 42.

50 Ibid., p. 140.

51 Pun, "Women Factory Workers in a Global Workspace", p. 61.

important place in the lives of the South Asian women. When I visited them for interviews, I was often offered snacks and sweets, and many of them would ask me to stay for lunch or dinner. The few times that I did stay, the meals were lavish, consisting of meat dishes, kebabs, *pulav*, *biryani*, *daal*, *chappatis*, vegetables, and *kheer* or *gulab jamun*. Sharing meals and cooking was a way for women to maintain their ties with each other. These get-togethers over food not only forged friendships, but also provided opportunities to share information, exchange social skills and break out of isolation. The culinary activities thus functioned as a "technique of nearness",[52] a form of sociability and a collective, as opposed to individualistic, competitive neoliberal work processes. The women also wore similar ethnic clothing within their homes or when going out for grocery shopping, spoke in their vernacular, and spent time together in long sessions of *adda*—"long, informal, and unrigorous conversations" that formed a vital idiom of social interaction among them.[53] Apart "from fostering a semblance of community life, these informal networks of communication that women establish with each other, therefore, also become vital nodal points for exchanging possibilities of finding work and economically productive activities".[54]

5 Conclusions

In this chapter, I have highlighted how South Asian immigrant women, despite adopting home-based entrepreneurship that is considered as one of the most effective means by which immigrants can avoid labour market constraints and create opportunities for themselves, challenge the ideologies of productivity and success that remain associated with the notion of entrepreneurial self. While, within a neoliberal economy, success and productivity are measured in terms of economics, these women through their work provide an alternative. By underscoring love, community ties and familial relations, they highlight how the creation of relationships, love and mutual support can also be markers of entrepreneurial success. Despite being located in an individualized, competitive and racialized market economy, these women, rather than pursuing the ideas of a neoliberal worker-subject, redefined the notion of enterprising

52 Keya Ganguly, *States of Exception: Everyday Life and Postcolonial identity* (Minneapolis, 2001), p. 136.

53 Dipesh Chakrabarty, "Adda, Calcutta: Dwelling in Modernity", *Public Culture*, 11 (1999), pp. 109–45, p. 110.

54 Maitra, "Perspectives on Work and Family Lives", p. 160.

selves to encompass collaboration, love and creativity. These are women whose endeavours not only need to be recognized, but also their businesses counted as an important part of the Canadian economy.

Going beyond the discourse of any static definition of productivity or self-sufficiency, these efforts on the part of the women are important in delineating how immigrant women of colour can actively refashion their own course to "success", "taking a multiple front, criss-crossing individual and collective levels, and negotiating not only with" racial and gendered factors but cultural experiences as well.[55] In recognizing their tremendous, effort-filled abilities to sustain and survive in Canada, I conclude this chapter with a quotation from one of my interviewees, Sheila, who aptly sums up the significance of their work for the Canadian society and its labour market:

> Because we do not have big businesses we are not taken seriously. But there are so many women doing this, and they want to expand and be taken seriously. I mean, even for me my earning is important for my family. ... I am doing important work, and it takes a lot of my time, energy and resource. I want the society to recognize that. Do not look down upon me just because I am South Asian.

Unless we acknowledge that creativity, originality and passion play an important role in the business efforts of these women, we will lose sight of the agency that remains embedded within their initiatives to determine an opportunity for themselves within the precariousness and uncertainty they experience in their everyday lives in Canada.

55 Pun, "Women Factory Workers in a Global Workspace", p. 196.

CHAPTER 19

Home-based Manufacturing Work for Women in India

Drivers and Dimensions

Sona Mitra

Understanding home-based work in the context of contemporary capitalism based on an overdrive for global integration has been a core research theme for economists and other social scientists engaged with questions of the structure of labour and its impact on labour relations. Home-based work has also been explored extensively by researchers studying altered forms of labour relations vis-à-vis women workers, related to the question of emerging feminization of a certain type of work due to altered production processes, fuelled by a rapid rise in globalization. There are several dimensions to home-based work. While it is a statistical fact that a large part of such work has witnessed an increase under outsourced, subcontracted and informalized structures that are a part of global supply chains, and thus engages a large proportion of women workers, evidence also suggests that the existence of home-based work among women is not new to capitalism. Such forms of work existed even in pre-capitalist societies, albeit in differing forms of organization of production—not to ignore the fact that the oldest forms of organization of work rested on workers at home. Thus the current system of capitalist production via global integration reorganizing itself into home-based processes of production can be seen as a continuation of the process of reorganization of production according to the needs of accumulation of capital, marked by various elements of change.

This paper challenges the existing claims of the emergence of home-based manufacturing work among women in India. It highlights that a large part of home-based women's work in India has been driven by local factors that have driven the overall demand for manufacturing employment among women. It argues that women's manufacturing work in India has had a large component of home-based organization of work that was utilized by the global value chains, and not the other way around. The paper attempts to substantiate that the existence of home work pre-dates the process of global integration, and questions the claims that newer forms of homebased work for women were generated by such integration.

© SONA MITRA, 2022 | DOI:10.1163/9789004499614_022
This is an open access chapter distributed under the terms of the CC BY-NC-ND 4.0 license.

In addition, the paper cites extensive data from secondary sources that capture the essence of women's home-based work. All such work is categorized under self-employment, which is clearly problematic given the current organization of production processes for home-based work. The paper is structured to include a brief review of the existing forms of home-based manufacturing/industrial work among women, and provides an overview of the magnitude and dimensions of the existing forms. Examining secondary evidence provided by the Government of India's Employment–Unemployment Surveys, the paper explains how the data have been interpreted, and the issues associated with enumerating and recording home-based work of women in India. Two sections focus on manufacturing sector output and employment patterns, and how this affected women's manufacturing work. The final section of the paper underlines the overall manufacturing growth trajectory and the important role played by women's home-based work, to establish the argument that global value chains were not the most important drivers of women's home-based manufacturing work in India. The paper concludes by discussing important questions around women's home-based work in India's manufacturing sector as enumerated in existing data systems, towards a potentially better understanding of such work for women.

1 A Longer View on the Existence of Home-based Work: A Brief Review

The literature on a longer view of home-based workers has provided enough evidence of the existence of home-based work even in pre-capitalist societies, the putting-out form of production being an example. However, even after the industrial revolution and the evolution of factory-based forms of production in the mid-nineteenth century, home-based work was not obliterated completely. Scholars have provided evidence to show that a form of home-based work evolved that was connected with industry, commonly referred to as "industrial home work".[1]

While the early phase of capitalism required the factory-based systems of production to be established as the most important form of surplus appropriation, the advance of capitalism, especially in the twentieth century and thereafter, essentialized the necessities of expanding the process of production to

1 Eileen Boris and Elisabeth Prügl (eds), *Homeworkers in global perspective: Invisible no more* (New York and London, 1996); Elisabeth Prügl, *The global construction of gender: Home-based work in the political economy of 20th century* (London, 1999).

countries with ready availability of a reserve labour force, accessible at much lower rates. This albeit was accompanied by massive alteration in the organization of production, which led to the development of global value chains and supply networks. Such changes in the forms of production were absolutely compatible with the requirements of rapid global integration of the already transformed capitalist economies of the global North with the less developed and transition economies of the global South, as they not only provided access to large markets for the global corporations in those regions, but also simultaneously provided access to cheap and flexible labour reserves, especially that of women, to expand the process of surplus accumulation. Thus, the current form of globalization has not only ushered in a process of capital accumulation based on the re-emergence of free markets, removal of tariff barriers and ushering in of free trade agreements, it has also led to an overwhelming increase of women workers in the manufacturing sector across all Asian countries as the organization of production kept altering its forms. The process of restructuring of global labour markets and the emergence of the new industrial division of labour were a consequence of such altered production processes.

However, this kind of "feminization" of employment in labour-intensive manufacturing in Asia's export processing zones or special economic zones (with women accounting for between 70 to 90 per cent of the workforce) peaked and eventually went into decline post the economic crisis in the developing South, especially in the developing Americas, in the early and mid-1990s, and the Southeast Asian crisis of 1997–98.[2] It also led to increased defeminization of factory-based women's work in manufacturing, and also informalization of overall labour markets, especially that of women's work.[3]

Such a process was a testimony to the arguments provided by feminist scholars regarding the use of "women as reserve army". It has been historically argued with substantial supporting evidence that the usefulness of women workers lay in the fact that not only could they be drawn in and thrown out of wage labour at different points of the development of capitalism, but they were perceived to be "more tractable and subservient to managerial authority, less prone to organize into unions, more willing to accept lower wages because

2 William Milberg and M. Amengual, *Economic development and working conditions in export processing zones: A survey of trends* (Geneva, 2008); Ingeborg Wick, *Women Working in the Shadows: The Informal Economy and Export Processing Zones* (Munich, 2010); Sheba Tejani and William Milberg, "Global Defeminization? Industrial Upgrading and Manufacturing Employment in Developing Countries", *Feminist Economics*, 22:2 (2016), pp. 24–54.

3 Tejani and Milberg, "Global Defeminization"; Jayati Ghosh, *Never Done and Poorly Paid: Women's Work in Globalizing India*, Feminist Fineprint (Delhi, 2009).

of their own lower reservation and aspiration wages, and easier to dismiss using life-cycle criteria such as marriage and childbirth".[4]

In the newer forms of accumulation, especially in the late twentieth century and the twenty-first century, where the production process is marked by fragmented, subcontracted, outsourced mechanisms and complex networks of global value chains, especially in the production of specific export commodities, the inherent tractability, adaptability and flexibility associated with women workers also facilitated such processes by transforming the households themselves into sites of production for exchange-values in addition to being sites for consumption, as per the needs of contemporary capitalism.[5] The literature on the existence of such work organizations thus makes a connection between home-based work and current patterns of production processes. It presents this kind of home-based worker as an integral part of the supply chains under current forms of globalized production, which in turn have been replicated by the domestic/more localized value chains in developing countries. Therefore, while such trends of increased home-based work may substantially be linked to greater economic integration and have constituted a large part of the evidence on globalization and its impact on women's work in developing and low-income countries, it is also required that the discourse on home-based work is integrated with the larger context of women's manufacturing work.

2 Dimensions and Organization of Home-based Work in Developing Regions

The ILO report on *Women and Men in the Informal economy* (2013) provided macro evidence of a concentration of women in home-based work in most developing regions of the world. It showed that among home-based workers, 62 per cent in South Africa, 70 per cent in Brazil and 88 per cent in Ghana were women. The majority of home-based workers remained informally employed, as in the case of 60 per cent in Buenos Aires and 75 per cent in South Africa. The report clearly mentioned that a significant proportion of home-based workers was to be found in manufacturing and trade. In South Africa, 24 per

4 UNESCAP, *Sustainable Social Development in a Period of Rapid Globalization: Challenges, Opportunities and Policy Options* (Bangkok, 2002).

5 Guy Standing, "Global Feminization through Flexible Labor: A Theme Revisited", *World Development*, 27:3 (1999), pp. 583–602; Milberg and Amengual, *Economic development and working conditions in export processing zones.*

cent of all home-based workers were involved in manufacturing. The report also cited evidence of subcontracted home-based work among brick-makers, stone masons, construction workers and hand-packers. Further, in Buenos Aires, 33 per cent of all home-based workers were in manufacturing and 42 per cent of women home-based workers were in manufacturing. Home-based work for women also accounted for self-employment in women workers and this formed a bulk of women's work in South Asia.[6]

The ILO report suggested that there were at least 41 million home-based workers outside agriculture in South Asia alone, representing 15 per cent of total non-agricultural employment (and 31 per cent of female non-agricultural employment) in India, and as much as 40 per cent of total non-agricultural employment (and 48 per cent of female non-agricultural employment) in Nepal. In India, the number of home-based workers was 37.4 million in 2011–12, the last available figure from a large and detailed sample survey conducted to estimate the situation of employment and unemployment in India at the time of writing. The data also suggest that subcontracted workers represent between 14 per cent (Bangladesh) to 33 per cent (India and Pakistan) of all home-based workers; and as high as 45 per cent (India) to 60 per cent (Pakistan) of women home-based workers.[7] In India, home-based manufacturing work for women accounted for almost 70 per cent of total female manufacturing work in 2011–12. More than one million women in the manufacturing sector in India were home-based workers. Apart from the current organization of home-based work noted above, much of this work came in the form of a wide range of activities.

Many of the female activities within manufacturing, were commonly the more traditionally "feminized" ones (being "light" as they did not use heavy equipment or machinery, but no less arduous in terms of the long hours of work and the nature of repetitive, mechanical tasks involved) and thus underlined the importance of such work for women in manufacturing. These activities were also well-adjusted within the arrangements of organization of work under home-based production systems. Under these arrangements,

> workers produce goods and services for both global and domestic supply chains from within and around their homes. By the several accounts provided by WIEGO, the most common sub-contracting arrangements involve home workers providing the workplace, pay for utilities, buy/rent

6 International Labour Organization (ILO), *Women and Men in the Informal Economy: A Statistical Picture*, second edition (Geneva, 2013).

7 Ibid.

> and maintain their own equipment. The contractors provide the work orders and raw materials, specify the products to be made, and supply firms further up the chain with the finished goods. In a few cases, the home worker may herself be a sub-contractor who splits the order and raw materials that she receives among other women in her "group" in which they work together.[8]

Whatever the arrangements, the access to the market for home workers remains limited due to their limited exposure within supply chains. In addition, following the perception of home-based work being subordinate to factory work as well as women's subordinate status in the labour market, in most of these arrangements, women are paid piece-rates—which are much lower on average than what factory workers in the same supply chains are paid—without any non-wage benefits. The payments also do not refurbish any depreciation costs on equipment or reimburse transport costs associated with delivery of finished goods or acquiring raw materials incurred by the home-based workers.

Thus, towards the end of the twentieth century and thereafter, home-based work emerged mostly as a part of global production networks, either as subcontracted or outsourced work by large multinational corporations (MNCs). The alteration in the organization of production from singular to fragmented processes, not only divided by stages of production but also located across different regions in different countries and also in different locations within the countries, witnessed a surge of such work being performed within households, mainly using the principles of comparative advantage in the cost of labour realized under such organization of work.[9] And within such a process, women workers working out of their homes were at the bottom of such labour-intensive global supply chains, particularly in those that are relatively more globally integrated in terms of production. They received the worst remuneration, and worked under poor conditions.[10]

In most of the emerging and transition economies that were adapting export-oriented strategies for the growth of output in the manufacturing sector in the latter part of the twentieth century, the bulk of the women were

---

8 Govindan Raveendran, Ratna M. Sudarshan and Joann Vanek, "Home-Based Workers in India: Statistics and Trends", *WIEGO Statistical Brief No. 10* (2013), pp. 1–9.

9 Jeemol Unni and Suma Scaria, "Government Structure and Labour Market Outcomes in Garment Embellishment Chains", Working Papers id: 3061, eSocialSciences (2010).

10 Marilyn Carr, Martha Alter Chen and Jane Tate, "Globalization and Homebased Workers", *Feminist Economics*, 6:3 (2000); Renana Jhabvala, "Informal Workers and the Economy", *Indian Journal of Industrial Relations*, 48:3 (2013).

located within informal employment, often employed as casual and temporary workers who served as a "buffer workforce" for product chains, both global and local. The objectives of such employment were mostly to accommodate just-in-time ordering, fluctuations in orders and prices, and stiff competition among suppliers. This in turn influenced the nature of activities that women performed within the sector, which, coupled with the social constructs around women's physical abilities, often ascribed "light work" to them in manufacturing. These were the precise factors for a relatively greater concentration of women workers in specific manufacturing sectors, such as textiles, garments, leather and footwear, and electronics, and even within specific buyer-driven food-processing industries, which also happen to be the export-oriented production sectors. Much of such work also happens to involve "light equipment and tools" and the use of simple technology that does not always require elaborate factory set-ups. Finally, the predispositions vis-à-vis the preferences of women workers to work from home in order to be able to both participate in paid activities as well as manage unpaid and care commitments do have a role to play even in specific manufacturing employment, which can be performed from home. Such preconceived notions attached to women's abilities have encouraged the participation of a large number of women in such home-based work. Further, these notions have played a role in evolving the current organization of home-based manufacturing work, which has become an effective tool for the process of capital accumulation that exploits the cheapest and most easily accessible form of labour.

While the above formulation of globalization-driven home-based work, especially for women, holds true for most countries that embarked upon the path of globalized export-oriented growth strategies, for example, countries in East and Southeast Asia, Bangladesh, Sri Lanka in South Asia, and some others such as Turkey, Mexico, Brazil and Peru, the case of India stands apart. In India, globalization and economic integration followed a different path, which did not necessarily involve globalization of the manufacturing sector, i.e. there was no export thrust to the manufacturing sector as in other countries. As a result, home-based work, even as it existed in large measure for women in manufacturing, was not driven by the above factors. The drivers of home-based work in India were different in character as compared to the experiences of other developing countries. Such differences emerged primarily due to the unique features of India's high growth trajectory in general amidst stagnation of the manufacturing sector in particular. The repercussions of such stagnation—both in terms of the volume of work and the conditions of work—were felt in all forms of women's home-based work.

The above argument is backed by secondary sources of information on women's home-based work in India. This paper uses the Employment and Unemployment estimates provided by the National Sample Survey Organization (NSSO) of the Government of India in its major rounds since 1993–94, which cover the period of neoliberal economic reforms in India. The study is restricted to employment estimates up to 2011–12, as those are the latest available figures from a comparable data source.[11] Output growth figures are used from the National Accounts Statistics provided by the Central Statistical Organization (CSO), Government of India.

3 The Indian Growth Story: Setting the Context

The Indian growth story has often been cited as one of the success stories of globalization. However, the trajectory of the Indian growth process has been unique among the experiences of developing countries. India has sustained a relatively high rate of growth over several decades, which saw acceleration since 2002 and marginal lowering since 2009 for some years.

The proponents of globalization attributed the transition to this higher growth path to the economic reforms of 1991. An analysis of the growth strategies reveals clear shifts in the policies pursued: from a regime of increased fiscal stimulus provided by public expenditure in the 1980s to one of market-driven growth since the 1990s. Broadly, the macroeconomic strategy pursued to achieve high rates of growth in the 1990s and after was largely dependent upon (i) greater reliance on exports, especially of services, and (ii) increased

11 The data on home-based work in India's labour force statistics (LFS) are bound by a caveat. While the ILO defines two specific categories within home-based work, the LFS in India do not provide such distinctions. The two categories of home-based work are: (i) independent self-employed workers who take entrepreneurial risks; and (ii) other home-based workers dependent on a firm or its contractors for work orders, supply of raw materials and sale of finished goods. This second category of home-based workers is referred to as subcontracted workers/home workers. Since they are not directly supervised by an employer and provide their own workspace and equipment, they are routinely classified as self-employed by the LFS in India. The ILO's basis of distinction stems from the conceptual differences in categorizing home-based work into self-employed and wage-employed categories, as the latter, being dependent on a firm or its contractor for work orders, raw materials and sale of finished goods, should be conceptually classified as wage work. The Indian data system does not allow for such a distinction and hence the bulk of home-based workers in India are classified in the category of self-employed. This may limit the analysis to a small extent but the larger arguments get substantiated in the following discussion.

dependence on capital inflows, primarily of the short-term variety. The policies not only included removal of several tariff restrictions for facilitating international trade in goods and services, but also easing of rules for cross-border capital flows with the aim of attracting foreign investment. Thus, apart from trade liberalization, some of the other policies included a series of concessions to reform the structure of tax policies, and deregulation of financial markets including partial removal of restrictions on capital mobility. The latter policy was meant to attract foreign investment and make India one of the world's most favoured destinations for international capital so as to boost investment ratios. Such theorization became more dominant in the 2000s. While it is a statistical fact that post-2002–03 the GDP growth of India rose rapidly, whether this was a consequence of increased investment or due to the concessions provided to the financial markets has been widely debated.

An important feature of the Indian growth story was the slowing down of the manufacturing sector, despite the open market strategies, the tax concessions, and the trade liberalization policies followed aggressively by the Indian state. Studies on India's earnings from exports and on the nature of foreign capital entering India clearly reveal two important factors. First, the high rates of growth in India were not driven by foreign direct investments (FDI), as shown in a comprehensive study indicating that despite concessions, India failed to attract the desired quantum of foreign investments in the manufacturing sector.[12] This finding gets further corroborated by the second factor. An analysis of capital inflows clearly indicate that the above-mentioned concessions which facilitated large increases in the flow of capital into India were mainly in the form of external commercial borrowings, portfolio investments and short-term credit, rather than due to India's prowess in merchandise export earnings.[13]

Another important factor responsible for driving growth over the period was internal financial liberalization and banking reforms, which resulted in a process of institutional change in which the role played by state-owned financial institutions and banks was substantially altered. These changes led the banks to adopt a newer strategy of credit allocation, which further led to huge increases in the bank credit to GDP ratio from 2005 onwards. These changes were not driven by increased credit to the productive sectors of the economy.

12 K S Chalapati Rao and Biswajit Dhar (2014). *FDI into India's Manufacturing Sector via M&As: Trends and Composition*, Working Paper #161, Institute for Studies in Industrial Development, New Delhi.

13 C.P. Chandrasekhar, 2008. *Financial Liberalization and the New Dynamics of Growth in India*, Third World Network, Global Economy Series #13; also available at www.twn.my, last accessed 2 June 2021.

Instead, retail loans became the prime drivers of credit growth. The result was a sharp increase in the retail exposure of the banking system, with overall personal loans increasing from slightly more than 8 per cent of total non-food credit in 2004 to close to 25 per cent by 2008. This of course resulted in a boom in retail credit consumption by the upper deciles of the population, especially in the urban areas. Of the components of retail credit, the growth in housing loans was the highest in most years.[14]

Thus, the surge in growth could be attributed to greater global integration associated with increased speculative activities around the financial, housing and real estate sectors. This resulted in fuelling private consumption of the elite and burgeoning middle classes, which emerged as the main driver of the high rates of growth. It needs to be highlighted that the earlier emphasis on public spending as the principal stimulus for growth was gradually substituted with speculative financialization, which unfortunately had a range of repercussions for the sectoral performance of the Indian economy. The Indian economy over the period has been marked by uneven sectoral performance, with all other sectors except services facing low growth or stagnation. Manufacturing especially had had a volatile performance since the 1990s, despite aggressive neoliberal policies.

4 Manufacturing Output and Employment Growth in the Period of Globalization

A closer look at the sectoral composition of growth confirms the fact that the high rate of GDP growth was not contributed by the manufacturing sector, much to the dismay of the proponents of neoliberal policies. The manufacturing sector growth rate in the 1990s averaged 5–6 per cent per annum and increased to 9 per cent during the high growth period, declining thereafter post-2010 (Graph 19.1). While the growth rate of the sector showed fluctuations, the sectoral contribution of manufacturing to GDP stagnated at around 16 per cent, implying reduced importance of the sector in the overall growth story of India (Graph 19.2). Thus, an important feature of the Indian trajectory of growth has been not a transition from agriculture to industry but a direct transition from agriculture to services, in terms of shifts in the sectoral contribution to GDP. Such transitions have had direct implications for non-agricultural

14 C.P. Chandrasekhar and Jayati Ghosh, "Growth, Employment Patterns and Inequality in Asia: A Case Study of India", ILO Asia-Pacific Working Paper Series (Bangkok, 2014).

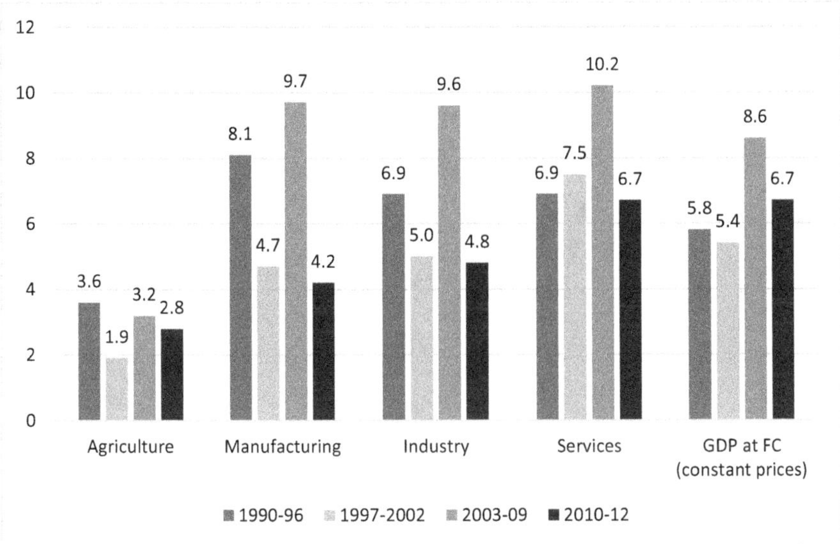

GRAPH 19.1 Average annual rate of growth of output by sectors, 1990–2012 (%)
SOURCE: COMPILED FROM NATIONAL ACCOUNTS STATISTICS, CSO, GOVERNMENT OF INDIA

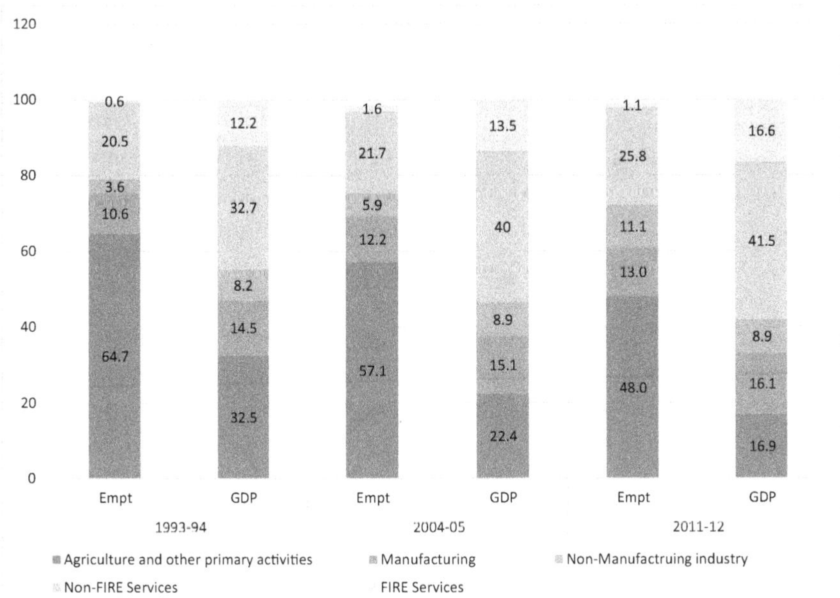

GRAPH 19.2 Sectoral contributions to employment and GDP, 1993 to 2012 (%)
SOURCE: COMPILED FROM NATIONAL ACCOUNTS STATISTICS, CSO AND EUS, NSSO, GOVERNMENT OF INDIA, VARIOUS YEARS

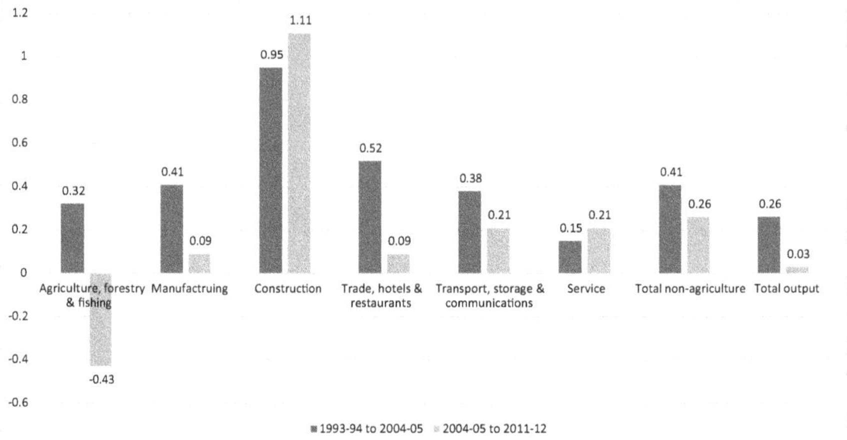

GRAPH 19.3 Output elasticity of employment by sector, 1993–94 to 2011–12
SOURCE: CALCULATED FROM ESTIMATES PROVIDED BY NAS AND EUS OF NSSO, GOVERNMENT OF INDIA, VARIOUS YEARS

employment in general and manufacturing employment in particular. The share of manufacturing employment to total employment showed stagnation at 12–13 per cent over the period, indicating a lack of labour-absorptive capacity of the sector over the period.

The overall output elasticity of employment at 0.03 shows that over the high growth period, there was an employment generation problem. Within that, substantially low elasticity in the traditionally labour-intensive manufacturing, one of the largest declines in the high growth period among the non-agricultural sectors, confirmed the reduced capacity of the sector to create additional employment with increases in output (Graph 19.3).

The trend of a slowdown in manufacturing employment was clearly a result of the policies followed by the government, which somewhat neglected the productive capacities of labour-intensive sectors such as manufacturing and so the overall growth was unable to create employment commensurate with the rate of growth of GDP. The unevenness of sectoral growth patterns also indicate that while the drivers of economic growth remained confined to the financial sectors, employment generation suffered in the traditionally labour-intensive sectors, especially manufacturing.

5 Women Workers in the Manufacturing Sector

The above process directly impacted the lives of women workers, especially those in the non-agricultural sectors, as the manufacturing sector played a

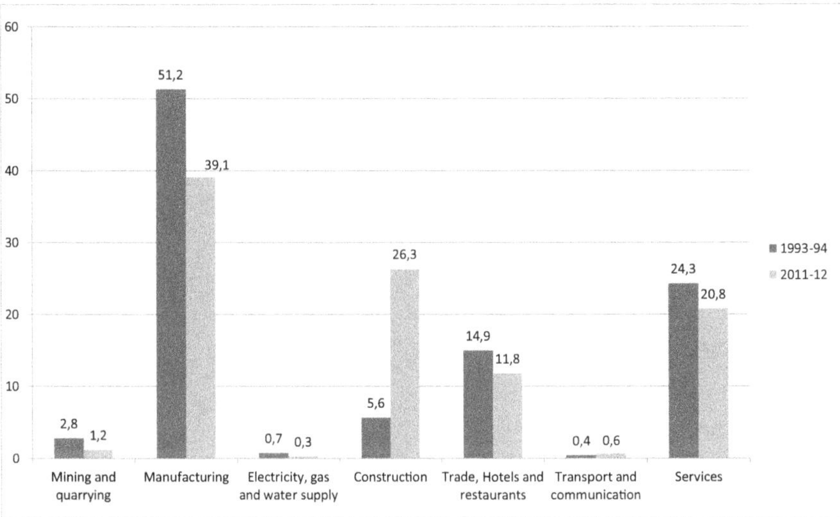

GRAPH 19.4 Distribution of usual status rural non-farm women workers
SOURCE: CALCULATED FROM UNIT-LEVEL ESTIMATES OF EUS, DATA CDS FROM NSSO, VARIOUS YEARS

significant role as an employer of a large section of non-agricultural women workers, both in rural and urban areas. Graphs 19.4 and 19.5 show the distribution of women workers in non-agricultural sectors by broad industrial classification, and the changes over the period for rural and urban women workers. While the figures show large-scale concentration of non-agricultural women workers within manufacturing, they also reveal the sector's declining importance in more recent years, especially in urban areas. In rural areas, manufacturing continued to be the largest employer of women engaged in non-agriculture. In this section, we look at rural and urban women's manufacturing work separately in order to understand the importance of such work among women.

6 Rural

In the rural areas, women workers employed in manufacturing constituted around 9.2 million out of the total of 94 million rural women workers. Despite the fact that the sector accounted for almost 40 per cent of all non-agricultural women workers in rural areas, the rate of growth of manufacturing employment for women in rural areas was only 2.1 per cent over the long period of 1993–94 to 2011–12, one of the lowest employment growth rates registered for women workers in the non-agricultural sectors. In absolute terms, there was

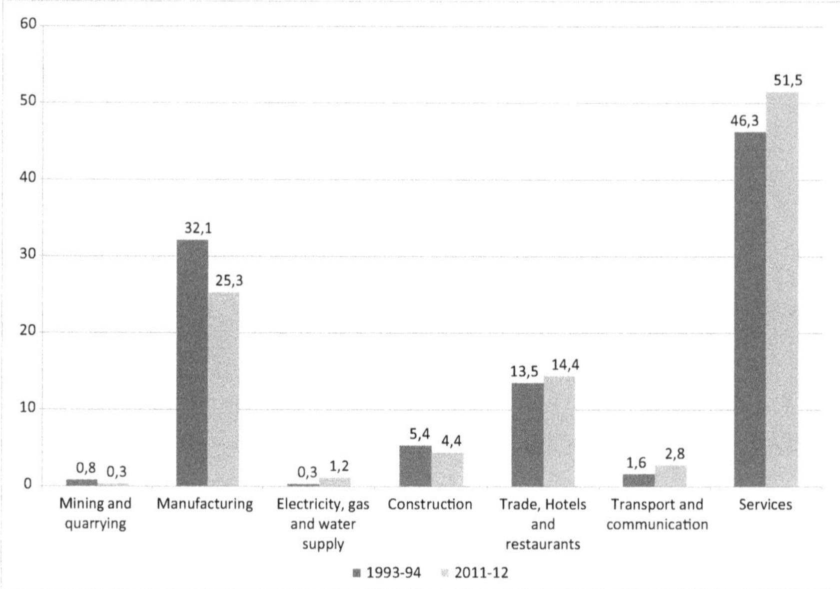

GRAPH 19.5 Distribution of usual status urban non-farm women workers
SOURCE: CALCULATED FROM UNIT-LEVEL ESTIMATES OF EUS, DATA CDS FROM NSSO, VARIOUS YEARS

an addition of 2.6 million women workers to the manufacturing sector over this period.

The distribution of rural women workers within the manufacturing sector reveals an overwhelming presence of *bidi* workers, at 36 per cent. This was followed by garments and related activities, food processing, wood, cane, rattan, reed, bamboo products, spinning, weaving and finishing of textiles, and the manufacture of refractory and structural clay products, in that order (Graph 19.6). It is evident that employment was confined mostly to the traditional sectors. Among these, traditional manufacturing activities such as food processing, spinning and weaving of textiles, pottery and related activities showed declines in their shares. Spinning and weaving activities especially showed a phenomenal decline in employment. One possible explanation for this decline is the replacement of handloom by powerloom production, which displaced a large section of women workers. Several studies have shown such trends.

Disaggregating manufacturing sector employment to the lowest digit of industrial classification and comparing them across the years shows that major increases in manufacturing employment for rural women took place in: processing and preservation of marine products, manufacturing of bakery and farinaceous products, and processing of edible nuts within food processing;

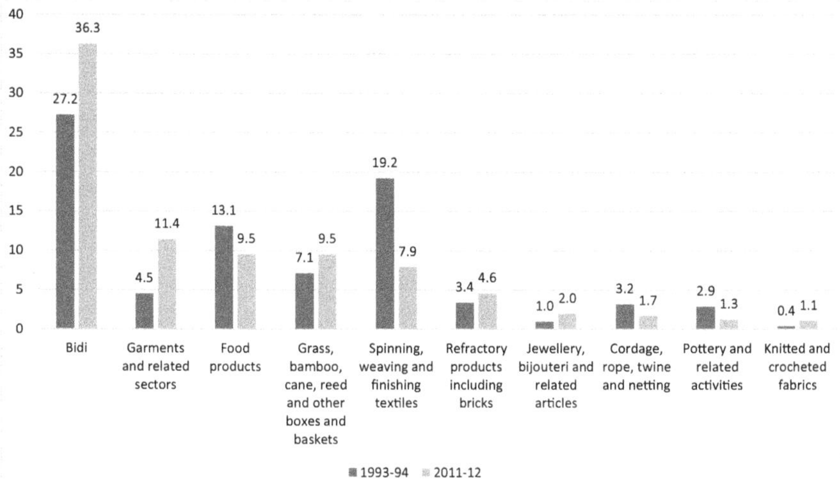

GRAPH 19.6 Distribution of rural women workers in manufacturing employment, 1993–94 and 2011–12

SOURCE: CALCULATED FROM UNIT-LEVEL EUS DATA FOR 1993–94 AND 2011–12, NSSO, GOVERNMENT OF INDIA

embroidery work, *zari* work, and making of laces, fringes and ornamental trimmings within garments; manufacture of knitted and crocheted fabrics; manufacture of artificial jewellery; and manufacture of soap, detergents, incense sticks, wood and cane products, refractory and clay products (mainly bricks) among others (Table 19.1). Table 19.1 reveals the absolute decline in traditional manufacturing, namely spinning, weaving and finishing of textiles, pottery and related activities, and manufacture of rope, netting, etc. Among these, spinning, weaving and finishing of textiles was a major employer of both men and women in 1993–94, which saw considerable depletion by 2011–12. The table also suggests that although *bidi* was the largest employer of women workers in rural manufacturing, it increased by a little more than 56 per cent, which was much lower compared to some others, namely garments and related sectors. With a 198 per cent increase in rural women's employment in garments and related sectors, it was the second most important group of manufacturing activities after *bidi*.

These figures suggest a slowdown in women's engagement in traditional activities without much increase in newer manufacturing activities. However, manufacturing of refractory products, which includes manufacturing of bricks, emerged as a large employer of women in rural and urban areas. In the rural areas, it constituted 3.4 per cent of total women's manufacturing work and featured as one of the top five activities in the manufacturing sector in 2011–12.

TABLE 19.1 Change in employment in select rural manufacturing sectors, 1993–94 to 2011–12

Sector details	Rural female absolute difference	Rural female % change
Major manufacture of food products of which:	**−124288**	**−14.4**
Processing and preserving of fruit and vegetables (includes jams, pickles, etc.)	3284	12.6
Processing and preserving of fish, crustaceans and molluscs and products	54754	397.9
Grain-milling and other related products	9794	5.0
Manufacture of bakery products (includes manufacture of farinaceous products like pasta, macaroni, noodles, etc.)	23298	250.9
Manufacture of cocoa, chocolate and sugar confectionery	2029	7.0
Processing of edible nuts	100286	128.8
Manufacture of food products n.e.c. (includes grinding and processing of spices, manufacture of *papads*, *appalams* and similar food products)	−169497	−72.6
Spinning, weaving and finishing of textiles of which:	**−649853**	**−51.5**
Preparation and spinning, weaving, manufacture and finishing of cotton and blended cotton textiles	−406696	−51.8
Preparation and spinning, weaving, manufacture and finishing of other textiles (includes silks, wool, blended)	−243156	−51.0
Major garments and related sectors of which:	**586747**	**197.5**
Embroidery work, *zari* work and making of laces, fringes and ornamental trimmings	576523	339.9
Manufacture of all types of textile garments and clothing accessories	2918	3.4
Manufacture of made-up textile articles, except apparel	7306	17.7
Other manufacturing	**1418697**	**46.2**

TABLE 19.1 Change in employment in select rural manufacturing sectors (*cont.*)

Sector details	**Rural female absolute difference**	**Rural female % change**
of which:		
Bidi	1014738	56.7
Knitted and crocheted fabrics	58646	253.3
Cordage, rope, twine and netting	−79995	−37.9
Wooden and cane boxes, crates, drums, barrels, baskets and other wares made entirely or mainly of cane, rattan, reed, bamboo, willow, fibres, leaves and grass	263745	56.1
Soap and detergents, cleaning and polishing preparations, perfumes and toilet preparations and *agarbatti* (incense sticks)	27395	96.2
Refractory products and structural clay products	127756	56.7
Articles of porcelain or china, earthenware, imitation porcelain or common pottery, including earthen statues	−91150	−47.9
Cutting, shaping and finishing of stone	9500	14.5
Jewellery, bijouterie and related articles	88062	135.7
A. Total select manufacturing	1217415	22.1
B. Total manufacturing employment	1157363	17.6
C. Total non-primary employment	10871856	87.5

SOURCE: UNIT-LEVEL EUS DATA FOR 1993–94 AND 2011–12, NSSO, GOVERNMENT OF INDIA.

Apart from the above, some interesting findings emerge from Table 19.1 regarding food processing work for women. The decline in overall food processing in absolute terms—led by grain- and flour-milling activities, manufacture of *papads and appalams*, and grinding of spices—clearly occurred due to a change in the production process, which became more mechanized and less labour-intensive, thus moving into factory-based production and leading to a decline in women's participation in these activities. The activities within food processing that showed increased participation were the processing of marine products and edible nuts, which used traditional methods and constituted much of the home-based work. In addition, the concentration of women in *bidi*, embroidery and *zari* work, lace-making and so on show the predominance of manufacturing work among women that is home-based rather than factory-based.

The trends thus confirm that women workers in manufacturing, though diminishing in an overall sense, remained trapped within less productive manufacturing activities, where women were mostly concentrated in home-based set-ups rather than factory-based processes. While some of the traditional home-based production processes such as milling and spinning/weaving shifted to factory-based mechanized processes, others such as *bidi*, rolling of incense sticks, processing edible nuts and so on continued to prevail within home-based set-ups. In addition, some other activities emerged within home-based work, such as the processing of marine products, embroidery and other garment-related manufacturing activities.

7 Urban

In the urban areas, the rate of growth of women's employment over the period 1993–94 to 2011–12 was a mere 2.4 per cent, one of the lowest rates of growth of employment when compared to all other non-agricultural sectors. It also implies an addition of a mere 1.5 million women workers to the sector over a period of almost two decades, although the sector employed a substantial section of urban women workers (almost 5 million, or a quarter of all non-agricultural women workers) and was the second largest employer of women workers in urban areas.

The distribution of urban women workers within manufacturing employment showed that a few traditional manufacturing occupations, such as food processing, *bidi* manufacture, preparing wooden and cane articles, spinning, weaving and finishing of textiles, exhibited either absolute decline or a degree of stagnation. On the other hand, there were large increases in certain non-traditional units, especially manufacture of bakery products, manufacture of apparels made of fur and leather, manufacture of costume jewellery, and a phenomenal increase in embroidery, *zari* and lace work, and manufacture of textile articles other than apparels, the last two belonging to garments and related manufacturing activities (Graph 19.7).

It also showed that unlike in the rural areas, food processing witnessed substantial increases, led by manufacture of bakery (including farinaceous) products and marine processing. Garments and related sectors showed major increases in *zari* and embroidery-related activities, and some amount

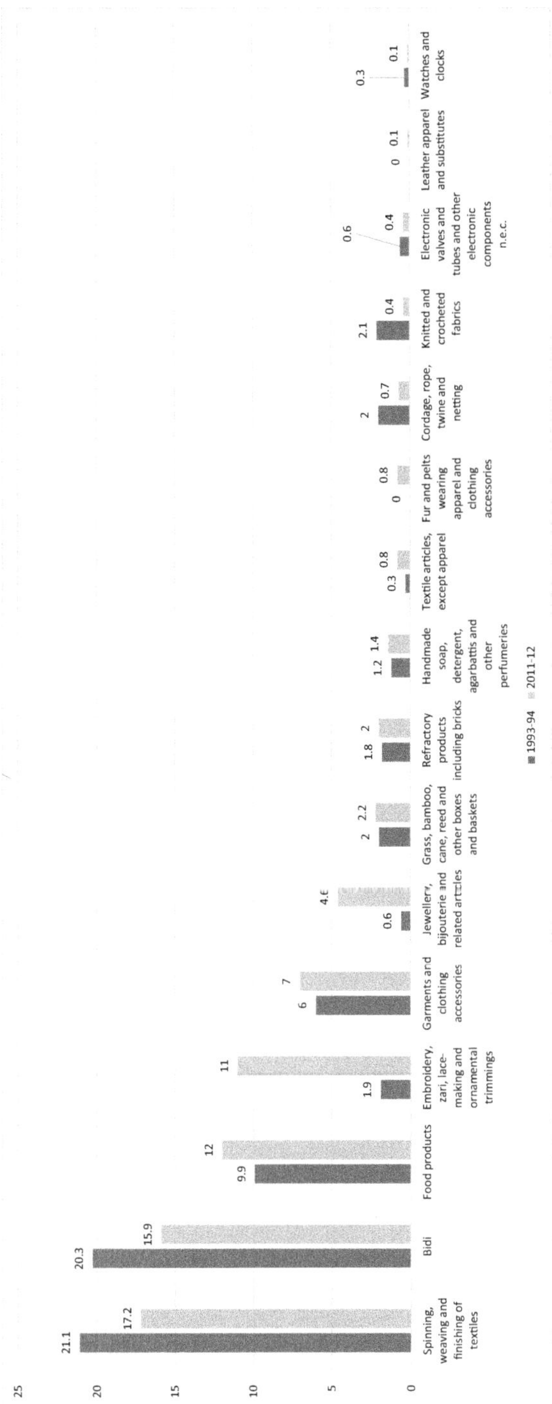

GRAPH 19.7 Distribution of urban women workers in manufacturing employment, 1993–94 and 2011–12

SOURCE: CALCULATED FROM UNIT-LEVEL EUS DATA FOR 1993–94 AND 2011–12, NSSO, GOVERNMENT OF INDIA

of increase in textile articles other than garments and non-textile garments. However, despite their declining shares, traditional industries, namely *bidi* manufacture, and spinning and weaving, continued to be the largest employers within manufacturing (Table 19.2). Both Table 19.2 and Graph 19.7 clearly show that among manufacturing activities, the sectors that emerged as important were *bidi*, food processing, embroidery and *zari* work, spinning and weaving, manufacture of textile articles and non-textile apparels, and manufacture of costume jewellery.

The trends in Table 19.2 indicate that there were specific changes within manufacturing subsectors, which are not captured when we look at the manufacturing sector as a whole. These suggest that the relatively low increase in manufacturing employment for women workers was due to stagnant or depleted traditional activities. The trends in general also confirm that while some processes moved to factories, newer products emerged using home-based organization of work and engaging women workers within these set-ups. However, it is also clear that the magnitude of such activities was not enough to counter the loss of or slowdown in employment in traditional activities that created an overall dearth of manufacturing work for women, exhibited by the low employment growth rate of the sector.

8 What Drove Manufacturing Work for Women in India?

The drivers of such changes in employment patterns within the manufacturing sector can be traced to the emerging patterns of consumption of food and non-food items both globally and locally.

Considering the changes in urban food processing industries, the increases led by processed and packaged food mainly can be traced to globalization. Some studies reported that increased nuclearization of families in a period of rapid globalization induced changes in the domestic consumption and dietary patterns of a section of the population, mainly urban.[15] Urban consumption baskets have started to include a high proportion of readymade snacks, semi-cooked and semi-processed condiments and spices, packaged and processed food and beverages, and so on. Such changes in consumption patterns also

15 Prabhu Pingali, "Westernization of Asian Diets and the Transformation of Food Systems: Implications for Research and Policy", *Food Policy*, 32:3 (2007), pp. 281–98; S. Mahendra Dev and N.C. Rao, "Food Processing and Contract Farming in Andhra Pradesh: A Small Farmer Perspective", *Economic and Political Weekly*, 40:26 (2005), pp. 2705–13.

TABLE 19.2 Change in employment in select urban manufacturing sectors, 1993–94 to 2011–12

Sector details	Urban female absolute difference	Urban female % change
Food products	**255979**	**75.8**
of which:		
Processing and preserving of fruit and vegetables (includes jams, pickles, etc.)	3614	68.2
Processing and preserving of fish, crustaceans and molluscs and products	47957	766.3
Bakery products (includes manufacture of farinaceous products like pasta, macaroni, noodles, etc.)	138966	2357.8
Cocoa, chocolate and sugar confectionery	24904	72.6
Processing of edible nuts	7506	22
Grinding and processing of spices, manufacture of *papads*, *appalams* and similar food products	−3248	−2.2
Bidi	99933	14.5
Spinning, weaving and finishing of textiles	**135386**	**18.9**
of which:	0	
Preparation and spinning, weaving, manufacture and finishing of cotton and blended cotton textiles	−12081	−2.5
Preparation and spinning, weaving, manufacture and finishing of other textiles (includes silks, wool, blended)	147467	64.3
Knitted and crocheted fabrics	−53833	−75.1
Cordage, rope, twine and netting	−34579	−50.7
Garments and other related sectors	**699118**	**250.6**
of which:		
Embroidery work, *zari* work and making of laces, fringes and ornamental trimmings	483798	767.4
All types of textile garments and clothing accessories	140862	68.9
Made-up textile articles, except apparel	30790	303.8

TABLE 19.2 Change in employment in select urban manufacturing sectors (*cont.*)

Sector details	Urban female absolute difference	Urban female % change
Wearing apparel made of leather and substitutes of leather	5526	395.6
Wearing apparel and clothing accessories made of fur and pelts	38142	–
Wooden, cane rattan, reed, bamboo, willow, fibres, leaves and grass articles	40097	58.8
Soap and detergents, cleaning and polishing preparations, perfumes and toilet preparations and incense sticks	31697	79.8
Refractory products and structural clay products	38399	62.5
Electronic valves and tubes and other electronic components n.e.c.	−2465	−11.9
Watches and clocks	−4830	−54.2
Jewellery, bijouterie and related articles	207969	990.1
A. Total select manufacturing	**1464509**	**61.5**
B. Total manufacturing employment	**1560152**	**45.9**
C. Total non-primary employment	**9059623**	**86**

SOURCE: UNIT-LEVEL EUS DATA FOR 1993–94 AND 2011–12, NSSO, GOVERNMENT OF INDIA.

led to an increase in the demand for packaged and processed food, extensively available at big and middle-level retail outlets spread across urban areas, which in turn was the primary reason for altering the nature of women's work in food processing. It triggered a shift in women's employment from traditional food processing activities to newer forms of processing, especially within packaged food. While such changes were prevalent in urban areas, rural areas that remained relatively less integrated with global factors did not experience similar increases in food processing employment within manufacturing.

It has also been pointed out that many of the activities in food processing are low-productivity activities and occur within an informal set-up, pointing towards an increasing tendency towards home-based work among such activities. The processing of nuts, marine processing, cooperative bakery production and so on are some of the examples. A study by Rao and Dasgupta[16] revealed a high degree of gender segregation of activities within the sector in terms of higher incidence of low-end and non-factory opportunities for women workers.

In the non-food segment, the particular increase of women in garment, electronics and jewellery was driven by increases in global demand patterns. Within garments and related sectors as a whole, the predominance of women was partly a result of increased global integration into global value chains. However, the development of a large domestic market for garments over the last decade also created domestic value chains, which too included a large number of women workers. While readymade garment (RMG) exports increased their share in total exports steadily in the 2000s (except for the period of the global financial crisis in 2008–09), domestic demand for RMG exports also grew by more than 10 per cent from 2004–05.[17] this increased demand was generated locally. So both global and local demand played a major role in driving employment within the garments sector. However, it is interesting to note that even within garments, if the sector is divided into home workers and factory workers, factory-based employment was dominated by men while women constituted the bulk of home-based workers (discussed in the following section). This held true for women manufacturing workers in both rural and urban areas.

The other important and emerging sector in the last decade which contributed to women's manufacturing employment in urban areas especially was the manufacture of artificial jewellery. The growth of employment in this sector was clearly driven by export-driven production processes, as captured in a study by Sumangala Damodaran.[18]

On the basis of the above analysis of the manufacturing sector over the last two decades, it can be argued that both global and local demand patterns played important roles in driving output growth for the sector, thus impacting women's employment. In addition, the analysis points towards two important findings. It clearly shows a slowdown in manufacturing employment for

16 N.C. Rao and Sukti Dasgupta, "Nature of Employment in Food Processing Sector", *Economic and Political Weekly*, 44:17 (2009), pp. 109–15.

17 National Council of Applied Economic Research (NCAER), *Report on Assessing the Prospects for India's Textile and Clothing Sector*, for Ministry of Textiles, Government of India and Confederation of Indian Textile Industry (2009); also available at www.texmin.nic.in, last accessed 2 June 2021.

18 Sumangala Damodaran, "Global Production, Employment Conditions and Decent Work: Evidence from India's Informal Sector", ILO Working Paper (New Delhi, 2010).

women, where sectors showing bulk employment of women workers also revealed declining employment growth. It also shows a clear depletion of traditional manufacturing employment in both rural and urban areas, and an emergence of newer manufacturing work for women only in urban areas.

Simultaneously, it reveals that rural manufacturing employment for women was driven mainly by domestic demand patterns, with rural areas remaining more or less excluded from the financialized economic growth process in India (as discussed earlier). However, in urban areas, the driving force of manufacturing employment comprised both domestic and global factors. While employment in traditional activities such as spinning, weaving, *bidi* manufacture, etc., which had the bulk of women manufacturing workers, catered mostly to domestic demands, garments and apparels were driven by a mix of both, and a few others such as jewellery and some processed food products were solely export-driven. Given this trend in the manufacturing sector, home-based women's work in manufacturing reveals several interesting patterns in recent years.

9 Dimensions of Home-based Manufacturing Work of Women

Despite the slowdown in manufacturing employment for women in India, it is interesting to note that women's home-based work expanded across several sectors. There were clear extensions of women's home-based work in manufacturing towards food and beverages, apparel and other manufactured products, alongside the existence of home-based work for women within tobacco, wood products, and spinning and weaving. By 2011–12 official statistics on Employment–Unemployment produced by the Government of India, showed that the share of women home-based workers in the manufacturing sector is more than 70 per cent, with a preponderance of home-based work among women in rural areas (Table 19.3). It reconfirms the incidence of home-based work among women being much higher as compared to men.

The distribution of women workers in rural and urban areas by 2011–12 provides a picture of the female clusters of home-based work in manufacturing. While the analysis of rural manufacturing employment among women showed the prevalence of traditional activities, despite a visible decline, 86 per cent of these rural women manufacturing workers were operating within home-based processes of production. The distribution of women workers across sectors showed a predominance of home-based manufacturing work in mostly the traditional sectors, dominated by the rolling of indigenous cigarettes or *bidi*, followed by garments and textile-related activities under tailoring, embroidery

TABLE 19.3 Share of home-based manufacturing work in India, 2011–12[a]

	Rural male	Urban male	Rural female	Urban female
Total home-based manufacturing work (HBMW)	4209419	2470109	6629741	4163443
Total manufacturing employment	15620226	19960206	7733771	6334622
Share of HBMW to total manufacturing	26.9	12.4	85.7	65.7

a Comparability across years in the incidence of home-based work is difficult as the information on the location of workplace for usual status workers is provided by EUS 2011–12; EUS 1993–94 does not contain such information.

SOURCE: CALCULATED FROM UNIT-LEVEL EUS DATA FOR 2011–12, NSSO, GOVERNMENT OF INDIA.

and *zari* work, and the manufacture of wood and cane products (Graph 19.8). Home-based work within manufacture of jewellery and porcelain and pottery work showed a significantly low presence.

In the urban areas, while the disaggregated distribution of women workers in home-based manufacturing work apparently showed a greater variety of sectors indicating that newer forms of home-based work existed within urban areas, if we aggregate the subsectors in urban areas, it shows that home-based work is dominated by garments and related activities, *bidi* and food processing. There are also a certain number of workers in manufacture of artificial jewellery, and in leather, fur and pelts (Graph 19.9). It is to be noted that while *bidi* is not the most important home-based work in urban areas, unlike in rural areas, garments-related work (including tailoring) dominates women's home-based work in the urban context. This should be seen in tandem with the findings of women's work in the urban manufacturing sector, which also highlighted food processing as an important employer of women in manufacturing. "Others", which accounts for a substantial share (20 per cent) of women workers within home-based work, constitutes a range of activities such as manufacture of incense sticks, broomsticks, common pottery, porcelain articles, knitted and crocheted wearing apparels, manufacture of integrated circuits in electrical and electronic equipments, cane products, sports goods, dolls, stuffed toys and

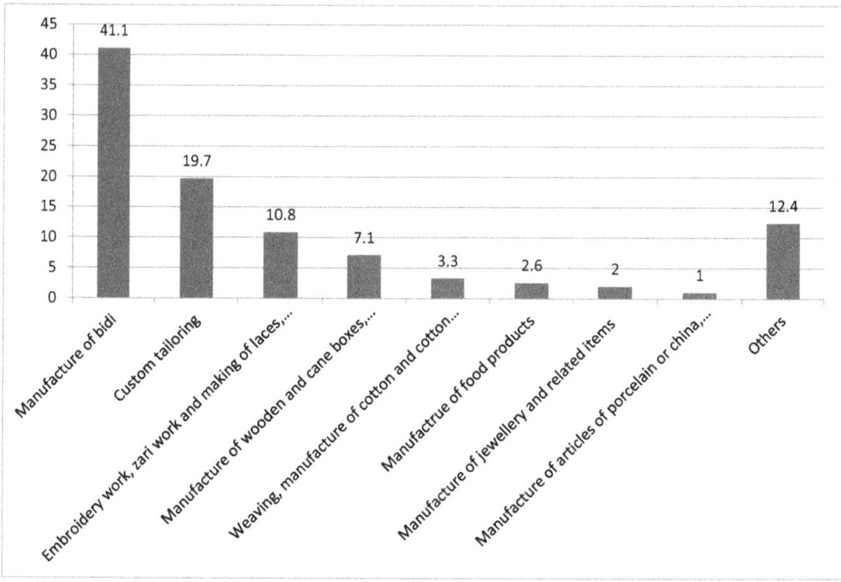

GRAPH 19.8 Distribution of rural women workers in home-based work in manufacturing, 2011–12

SOURCE: CALCULATED FROM UNIT-LEVEL EUS DATA FOR 2011–12, NSSO, GOVERNMENT OF INDIA

animals, and so on. While some of these activities are visible in rural areas, a large number of urban activities spread across different manufacturing sectors among home-based workers are exclusive to urban locations.

Given this distribution of home-based work among women workers in manufacturing in rural and urban areas, it is interesting to look at the incidence of women's home-based work in select sectors. Tables 19.4 and 19.5 clearly show that sectors in which home-based work for women dominates are also the ones that display almost the entire organization of work within the set-up of the home. For example, in rural areas, 97 per cent of all women *bidi* workers work from home. Similarly, more than 90 per cent of all women workers in embroidery, *zari*, tailoring activities and imitation jewellery work under home-based organization of production. These proportions reduce a bit in other sectors such as manufacture of wood, cane products and porcelain products, but remain significantly above 50 per cent (Table 19.4).

In urban areas similarly, home-based work dominates sectors such as *bidi*, embroidery, ornamental trimming and tailoring, specific food processing and so on. Sectors like jewellery, food processing, etc., reveal almost 50 per cent of work as home-based. However, manufacture of garments and clothing

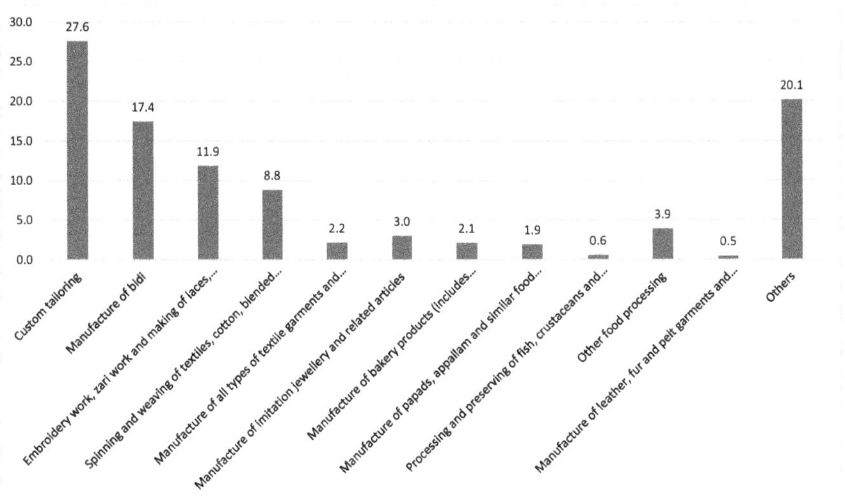

GRAPH 19.9 Distribution of urban women workers in home-based work in manufacturing, 2011–12
SOURCE: CALCULATED FROM UNIT-LEVEL EUS DATA FOR 2011–12, NSSO, GOVERNMENT OF INDIA

accessories show only 26 per cent incidence of home-based work by women. This indicates a significant presence of factory-based production work for women in this sector. It is also important to note that a few new sectors, such as marine processing and manufacture of leather and pelt items, show 43 per cent incidence of home-based work among women in urban areas (Table 19.5).

10 Drivers of Home-Based Manufacturing Work of Women in Brief

The distribution and dimension of home-based women workers across some important sectors provide significant insights. In rural areas, the distribution of home-based work reveals that women were mainly spread across traditional manufacturing sectors such as *bidi*, wood, cane, rattan products, common pottery and so on, even as these were on the decline. While this definitely highlights the overall crisis of manufacturing employment for women in rural areas, such that women have not been able to find newer employment within manufacturing and have stuck to such low-productivity activities, it should also be noted that these kinds of home-based work are certainly not an outcome of India's drive for economic integration as they existed even prior to the 1990s, albeit within a decline in the volume of such manufacturing work post 1990s.

TABLE 19.4 Rural women workers in select home-based manufacturing industries, 2011–12

S. No.	Sector details	Total female employment (TFi)	Home-based female employment (HBFWi)	HBFWi/ TFi
1	Manufacture of *bidi*	2805947	2725580	97.1
2	Custom tailoring	1479258	1307621	88.4
3	Embroidery work, *zari* work and making of laces, fringes and ornamental trimmings	746114	717045	96.1
4	Manufacture of wooden and cane boxes, creates, drums, barrels and other containers, baskets and other wares made entirely or mainly of cane, rattan, reed, bamboo, willow, fibres, leaves and grass	733486	473692	64.6
5	Weaving, manufacture of cotton and cotton mixture fabrics.	378526	219451	58.0
6	Manufacture of jewellery and related items	152962	129409	84.6
7	Manufacture of articles of porcelain or china, earthenware, imitation porcelain or common pottery, including earthen statues	99292	63024	63.5
	Total	7733771	6629741	85.7

SOURCE: CALCULATED FROM UNIT-LEVEL EUS DATA FOR 2011–12, NSSO, GOVERNMENT OF INDIA.

TABLE 19.5 Urban women workers in select home-based manufacturing industries, 2011–12

S. No.	Sector details	Total female employment (TFi)	Home-based female employment (HBFWi)	HBFWi/ TFi
1	Custom tailoring	1372785	1148898	83.7
2	Manufacture of *bidi*	790045	726428	91.9
3	Embroidery work, *zari* work and making of laces, fringes and ornamental trimmings	546840	493471	90.2
5	Spinning and weaving of textiles, cotton, blended cotton, silk, silk mixtures	851947	368437	43.2
8	Manufacture of all types of textile garments and clothing accessories	345227	89900	26.0
9	Manufacture of imitation jewellery and related articles	127886	84623	66.2
10	Manufacture of bakery products	144860	87620	60.5
11	Manufacture of *papads*, *appalams* and similar food products	104326	79886	76.6
12	Processing and preserving of fish, crustaceans and molluscs and products	54215	23508	43.4
13	Manufacture of leather, fur and pelt garments and accessories	45065	19667	43.6
	Total manufacturing	6334622	4163443	65.7

SOURCE: UNIT-LEVEL ESTIMATES FOR 2011–12, EUS, NSSO, GOVERNMENT OF INDIA.

Urban areas reveal a slightly different picture. The number of sectors across which women are spread in home-based manufacturing work in urban areas is higher as compared to rural areas. This is in tandem with the relatively greater diversity of activities within urban manufacturing. The analysis also reveals: (i) that there has been some form of employment creation for women in urban areas apart from the declining traditional work; and (ii) that while home-based work is important for women's manufacturing activities, the incidence of factory-based organization of work is not insignificant, unlike in rural areas (Table 19.5). It therefore follows that the prevalence of home-based work is greater in areas with a dominance of traditional work patterns. As regards new employment creation within manufacturing, except for embroidery, *zari* and other such ornamental and finishing work related to garments, it has been comparatively higher within factories.

Embroidery, *zari* and ornamental and finishing work related to garments that emerged post-1990s had a high incidence of home-based work by women in both rural and urban areas. While in the rural areas the addition of women workers to such work over the last two decades was almost 0.58 million, the percentage increase in such employment in urban areas was higher as compared to rural areas (approximately 770 per cent; Tables 19.1 and 19.2). This clearly implies that in urban areas, over this period, a large number of women entered into such activities, while in rural areas, women were already involved in such work from earlier. The increase in such work in urban areas coincided with the period of globalization and thus can be directly associated with subcontracted/outsourced work by large manufacturers, which may have global linkages. However, the pre-existence of substantial similar work in rural areas prior to globalization indicates that demand for such work existed previously and thus may have been a domestic phenomenon, even if the organization of work may have been different than the current forms of subcontracting.

It therefore follows from the earlier discussion of drivers of manufacturing employment that while domestic demand patterns influenced employment in rural home-based work in manufacturing, urban home-based work was influenced by both local and global factors. The discussion on manufacturing employment clearly noted that the bulk of the increased demand for apparels was not led by export manufacturing but was mainly driven by domestic demand, which in turn drove employment in home-based activities in garments. Other sectors of home-based manufacturing employment, such as processed and packaged food, jewellery, bijouterie, etc., were also influenced by both global and local demand.

11 Concluding Comments

The above discussion and data clearly shows the wide range of activities that women engage in the form of home-based work. These include stitching garments and weaving textiles; embroidery; beading necklace and making bangles; stitching shoe uppers and footballs; producing craft products; processing and preparing food items; rolling incense sticks, *bidi*, cigarettes and cigars; assembling or packaging electronics, automobile parts and pharmaceutical products mainly within manufacturing sectors such as garments and textiles (especially embellishments and finishing of factory-made garments), handicrafts, leather, toys and sporting goods (e.g., footballs, rackets, nets), jewellery, furniture, carpets and mats, shoes and other footwear, tobacco, incense sticks and flower garlands, processed and cooked food items, electronics, automobiles, pharmaceuticals; manufacturing paper bags and envelopes and so on. Clearly, such forms of work were not driven by global demand and substantial local factors acted as drivers of these activities for women.

It could be argued that home-based work in India was never exclusively driven by globalization as was evident in other Asian countries which experienced a 'feminization' of manufacturing employment. This was mainly due to the strategies of economic integration followed in India, which encouraged a financialized, urban-centric economic growth, rather than growth led by a labour-intensive, export-oriented manufacturing process. Such a strategy culminated in years of "jobless growth" in India starting from the mid-2000s, the repercussions of which are evident in low and declining female work participation rates. This holds true especially in rural areas, which remained excluded from the benefits of the growth process and thus trapped in forms of traditional, low-productive, home-based activities for women within manufacturing, driven mainly by domestic demand patterns.

While home-based work for women thrives on such conditions of work, two further arguments can be made following the above analysis. First, globalization may not be directly driving home-based work for women in manufacturing in India, but it has an indirect impact via altering the domestic consumption patterns of a section of the urban population (discussed in the first section), which in turn drives a substantial part of the home-based manufacturing employment via the typical multiplier effects operating within an economy.

In addition, although manufacturing was not leading the growth process in India and thus remained caught in low-productive activities, the forms of work that evolved under these circumstances were a simple replication of the altered forms of global organization of work. In the altered regime of production organization, home-based work for women across the developing countries got a fillip via subcontracting/outsourcing, through the evolution of global production networks and elaborate supply value chains. Several studies have pointed to the worsened conditions of work under such arrangements of work. However, despite the fact that the Indian economy was never an integral part of global export-manufacturing networks, the domestic organization of home-based work also altered following the globalized patterns of organization of work that could accumulate surplus at a relatively faster pace, with greater exploitation and increased vulnerabilities of the workers. This particular observation may be a bit too stretched for the analysis presented in the paper, but can be left open for further explorations.

PART 5

CHAPTER 20

Artwork

Frida Hållander and Åsa Norman

Sewing Factory Sisters!

Öxabäck IF – Without You No Tomorrow

Sewing Factory Sisters! Öxabäck IF – Without you no tomorrow was an exhibition held at The Labour Movement's Archives and Library by Åsa Norman, textile artist and Frida Hållander, Ph.D., craft artist, during the conference Long term perspectives on home-based work.

The exhibition had its origins in a common interest in how struggles have been formulated by and through women in textile rooms, with a focus on the textile industry and sewing factories, as well as in women in industrial homework in Sjuhäradsbygden, a rural textile area in the southwest of Sweden. The exhibition consisted of three textile stories that originate from three different places and from three different times.

The exhibition began with archival documents from the Swedish Textile Workers Union depicting the struggles of workers. The agitation pamphlets *Textilarbetare! = Ut till frihet! Fram för frihet* [Textile Workers! = Go out for freedom! Get ahead for freedom] from 1910, reads: "If we do not put our own interests first, and if we do not see ourselves in them, we are and will remain the bottom line of the working class".[1] Among the archival materials there were also two agitation poems that describe the union struggles: *Vi väva, vi väva och Vi spinna, vi spinna* [We weave, we weave and we spin, we spin] from the early 20th century. The archive tells us about the difficulties for textile workers had in organizing themselves. In the memorial publication from The Textile Workers Union's from 1923 we can read that "more than anyone else, the textile workers have fallen to resignation and powerlessness".[2] It was a work-force, including

1 Translated by Norman & Hållander from: *Textilarbetare! = Ut till frihet! Fram för frihet* (Norrköping, 1910) 1904–1924. Archive: Sv. Textilarbetarförbundet box: 2769/1/169 The Swedish Labour Movement's Archives and Library.

2 Translated by Norman & Hållander from: Gustaf Janzén, *Svenska textilarbetareförbundet: Minnesskrift 1898–1923*, Norrköpings boktryckeri (Norrköping, 1923) p. 13.

© FRIDA HÅLLANDER AND ÅSA NORMAN, 2022 | DOI:10.1163/9789004499614_023
This is an open access chapter distributed under the terms of the CC BY-NC-ND 4.0 license.

FIGURE 20.1 Exhibition at The Labour Movement's Archives and Library, in Stockholm: Sewing Factory Sisters! Öxabäck IF – Without you no tomorrow, by Åsa Norman and Frida Hållander, 2018
PHOTO FRIDA HÅLLANDER, 2018

homeworkers, that consisted mostly of women, and that endured long working hours and low wages. The book *Svenska textilarbetareförbundet 1949–1971* [Swedish Textile Workers Union 1949–1971] published in 1991 describes how textile workers have always been the proletarians of the proletariat; poorer and sicker than everyone else.[3]

One of the central works of the exhibition is based on women who worked in a sewing factory in Sjuhäradsbygden, during the 1960s and 1970s. It tells of how these women organized themselves by starting a football team: Öxabäck IF. The team was formed in 1966 in the village Öxabäck in Sjuhäradsbygden – a region in which the textile industry and industrial homework existed since the seventeenth century. Thanks to Öxabäcks IF's constant pressure on the Swedish Football Association, first official series in women's football in Sweden was founded in 1968. The women in the team met in Öxabäck Sewing Factory. At the factory they sewed their own shorts and shirts to play in. The team also recruited new players from southwestern Sweden by giving them work in the sewing factory. Norman's and Hållander's art work *Öxabäck IF – Without you no*

3 Majgull Axelsson, *Svenska textilarbetareförbundet 1949–1971* (Stockholm, 1991) p. 12.

FIGURE 20.2 Öxabäck IF, Courtesy of the Öxabäck IF museum. Photo Sigge Bengtsson, 1968. Reproduction: Frida Hållander och Åsa Norman 2016

tomorrow underscored the influence of the team Öxabäck IF's on the Swedish women's football, and also re-activated a text *On banners and banner making* from 1909 by the British suffragette and the artist Mary Lowndes (1856–1929).[4] The work examines the processes of textile making in different times and spaces revealing that making can be understood as embodied experience and knowledge, conditioned, but not always bounded, by societal structures.[5]

The exhibition also showed two other works. Hållander showed a pair of jeans she sewed herself, with the title *The broken line: Jeans – I sew the best I could* (2018). It was based on her experience of growing up in a textile village in Sjuhäradsbygden. It is a work that reflects the lives of her relatives who worked in the industrial homework and in the sewing factories from the beginning of

4 Mary Lowndes, "Banners and Banner-Making" in Lisa Tickner, *The Spectacle of Women: Imagery of the Suffrage Campaign,* 1907–1914 (Chicago, 1988), p. 262–264.

5 Frida Hållander, *Vems hand är det som gör? En systertext om konst/hantverk, klass, feminism och om viljan att ta strid* [Whose Hand is Making? A Sister-Text about Craft, Class, Feminism and the Will to Contest], (Stockholm, 2019) p. 191–232.

the 20th century to the end of 1980s. The story-telling narratives came from her own experiences and from the stories of her relatives, as well from archives. The "broken line" refers to the textile industry's restructuring process, a process that affected the textile and clothing industries in Sjuhäradsbygden. The crisis, which began in the 1950s, ultimately resulted in a large proportion of textile production being decommissioned around 1980. The work explored how knowledge about sewing a pair of jeans cannot be found in Hållanders craft skills; she doesn't know how to sew or how to make a pair of jeans – a story of a broken line.

The third place visited in the exhibition was Manchester's silk industry in the early part of the 20th century. In the art work *Bombyx Mori, well fitted for women?* Norman examines how the resistance to wage cuts and other exploitative practices was formulated and organized by the many women who worked with silk at home. In her artwork Norman also addressed the question of how working with an exclusive material influenced the image of the women who worked in the silk industry, in contrast to the image of the women who worked in the cotton industry. The women silk workers made many different textile accessories: socks, buttons, bands and fringes. Accessories that surround, frame, highlight and visualize, but which could be described as being on the periphery, and easily manufactured at home. The art work consists of a silk banner with pearl embroidery.

Hållander and Norman's works addressed issues such as how the textile material and textile making intersect over the question of women's subordination. The order between the sexes is present in all dimensions of doing. These reasons have led Hållander and Norman to questions about what it means to be a sister from a feminist perspective?

Factory Sisters! is one of Hållander and Norman's borrowed concepts.[6] Being a factory sister was a profession in women-dominated industries around 1900. The factory sisters, who were employed by the factory, helped the women workers with the administration of pension and sick funds, and other benefits. It was a complicated concept, as the factory sister had a lot of power. For Hållander and Norman the term has lost this historical connection. Instead the term has come to suggest a personal or political relationship between women – a feminist perspective on sisterhood whereby sisters support a struggle. At the same time, it urges the questions on a reorientation of feminist practice toward solidarity work and anticapitalist struggles.[7] A feminism without borders, fully engaged in with the realities of textile production.

6 Gerda Meyerson, *Arbeterskornas värld. Studier och erfarenhet* (Stockholm, 1917) p. 70–80.

7 Chandra Talpade Mohanty, Feminism without borders: *decolonizing theory, practicing solidarity* (Durham, 2003).

CHAPTER 21

Postscript: Launching an International Network of Home-based Workers During the COVID-19 Crisis

Chris Bonner, Jane Barrett, Janhavi Dave

In the chapter "Home-based Workers: Organizing from Local to Global" plans for the launch a global network of home-based workers' organizations – HomeNet International – were discussed. Whilst a representative working group was finalizing such plans, COVID-19 struck and disrupted them. And importantly, it decimated the livelihoods of home-based workers. However, home-based workers' organizations were determined to forge ahead. On February 24, 2021, HomeNet International became a reality. 80 home-based workers official delegates from 36 new affiliates in 20 countries came together in a virtual congress to launch their global network. They were joined by more than 400 observers including 200 home-based workers from affiliates and emerging affiliates, and more than 200 allies and supporters.

1 The Current Situation of Home-based Workers

HomeNet International's constituency consists of working poor home-based workers, a majority being women. These home-based workers' incomes are generally low and insecure, whether as own account workers or sub-contracted piece rate workers, and they have little access to legal and social protections. This means that when disaster strikes they have little to fall back on.

And so this was, and still is, with the COVID-19 disaster, as work and income dried up, leaving many with little or no means to support themselves and their families. In a twelve-city study by Women in Informal Employment (WIEGO) on the effects of the pandemic on workers in the informal economy, including home-based workers, one of the most shocking findings was the level of hunger reported.[1] HomeNet South Asia, in a similar study in seven countries

1 WIEGO. "The COVID-19 Crisis and the Informal Economy: Global Summary Report", June 2021. Accessible at www.wiego.org, last accessed 28 May 2021.

© CHRIS BONNER, JANE BARRETT, JANHAVI DAVE, 2022 | DOI:10.1163/9789004499614_024
This is an open access chapter distributed under the terms of the CC BY-NC-ND 4.0 license.

FIGURE 21.1 A group of Nubian home-based workers near Entebbe, Uganda receiving food relief in October 2020 organized by HomeNet International during the pandemic

of South Asia with 394 home-based worker respondents, found that seventy per cent had no income during the lockdown, used up all their savings and went into debt.[2] Both these studies were carried out in 2020, but in 2021 as new waves of the pandemic hit, the slow recovery from this stalled. On International Workers' Day 2021, in a global webinar organized by HomeNet International, home-based workers reported on their current situation. They spoke of "lost work", "no orders", "grief and depression", "lack of food", "family eats once a day", " products piling up", "no money to go to hospital", "on-line education difficult to afford for children", "government provides no support for HBWs", amongst others. For many, their main support is from their organizations, for both physical and mental wellbeing.

On the more positive side home-based workers in established and stronger organizations, were better able to sustain themselves, as their organizations were able to change supply chains from international to domestic, and focus

2 HomeNet South Asia, "Impact of Covid-19 on Women Home-based Workers in South Asia", December, 2020. Accessible at: www.hnsa.org.in, last accessed 26 May 2021.

on different products. Janhavi Dave, HomeNet International Coordinator, further noted,

> […] the membership of many grassroots organizations increased during the pandemic. The reason for that was that they were the only ones who were able to create access to government assistance programmes or food, and coming together and having a joint voice for demanding things like social protection.[3]

It is in this context that HomeNet International was launched, and has taken its first steps towards a strong global voice for home-based workers.

2 The Congress

During the early months of the pandemic home-based workers' organizations were busy with relief and recovery activities. Mobilizing for the formation of HomeNet International was not possible, and the nascent global network turned to supporting humanitarian relief efforts, holding virtual events to build unity and solidarity across the diverse regions, and promoting the demands of home-based workers for inclusion in government assistance programmes, compensation from brands, and social protection measures.

However, as noted above, the benefits of organizing were becoming clearer, including the need for, and benefits of, global solidarity, and a global voice. Once the decision was taken to launch HomeNet International virtually, the Interim International Working Group (IIWG), leading the process towards congress, began to mobilize and formally recruit affiliates.

Organizing the congress was practically and politically challenging. Although the IIWG, assisted by WIEGO, was gaining experience in organizing on–line meetings and workshops, organizing a congress was more complex. There were practical issues to overcome. A union congress would normally take place over two to three full days, but in this case affiliates were separated by time and space. The time differences stretched over fourteen hours. So whilst delegates in Nicaragua logged on at 6.30 in the morning for a two and a half hour session on two consecutive days, those from the Philippines joined the congress at 20.30 in the evening when they would normally be preparing for bed. This

3 WIEGO, "The Creation of HomeNet International", May 2021, available at www.wiego.org, last accessed 26 May 2021.

limited the time available for decision-making and direct participation. Apart from the obvious difficulties facing home-based worker participants- poor internet connections, data and device limitations, electricity outages and so forth- interpretation had to be provided in seventeen languages.

These practical limitations created political challenges. How could a sense of solidarity and camaraderie across diverse organizations infuse the congress without formal and informal face-to-face interactions? How could one adopt a founding constitution without time for a full debate, or the opportunity to hold caucus meetings and negotiations to settle differences? How could fair elections be organized where not all delegates had their own devices and where poll facilities on the internet platform were all in English?

Mobilization, planning and preparation were key to mitigating these challenges, and the IIWG, together with WIEGO, worked hard to ensure practical difficulties were minimized. Politically, it was important before the congress to include activities that would help build a common identity and solidarity. With such diversity amongst the affiliates in size (from small groups of 50 to over 300,000 members), political, economic and cultural context, and organizational history, this was just as important as taking organizational decisions. To this end, songs, poems, messages and reports from the different regions in many languages formed an important part of the proceedings- all prepared in advance by the affiliates and presented through video and powerpoint. Sharing the struggle history of the home-based workers' movement was another important element in solidarity building, with long-time supporters of the movement providing insights and lessons learnt. Ela Bhatt, now in her late eighties and recognised as the founder of the home-based workers' movement, recounted some of the early history, including the struggle for global recognition and how the ILO Convention on Home-Work (C177) was adopted. And, participants were surprised to learn that in 1994, prior to the ILO discussions, an earlier version of HomeNet International was formed, but that it failed to transform into a democratic global network of membership-based organizations.

Ensuring that key decisions were made to allow HomeNet International to move forward meant a tight agenda, firm chairing and good preparation. The constitution presented at congress was the product of a two-year participatory process. A spirit of cooperation across the regions meant that final changes proposed in regional preparatory meetings, also held virtually, were settled prior to congress. Similarly, affiliates agreed to appoint a transitional leadership committee, rather than to try and hold elections virtually. In addition, congress approved all new affiliates, appointed an International Coordinator, approved affiliation fees and laid out a broad agenda for HomeNet International over the next two years.

3 Future Prospects

An immediate internal priority for HomeNet International is to continue solidarity building across diverse affiliates and regions. This is the foundation on which future development rests. The new leadership committee, at the time of writing (May 2021), has met three times and begun a programme of activities focusing on sharing experiences on important common issues such as the COVID-19 situation, recovery demands, social protection, the solidarity economy, and livelihood strategies. It is also focused on developing governance and operational structures, policies and systems that meet the needs of affiliates, and, as a democratic worker organization, ensures membership is informed and involved.

With the on-going pandemic, the future of working poor home-based workers, and the resilience of their organizations remain uncertain, but the experience to date of HomeNet International and its affiliates provides for cautious optimism. Raising the visibility of home-based workers so that they gain recognition as workers and have a global voice is an important function of HomeNet International. The focus on the growing number of home-based workers – especially newer forms of non industrial home based workers such as teleworkers and digital platform workers- outlined in a recent ILO Report,[4] and fuelled further by the pandemic, could be the start of more widespread recognition of the value of all home-based work and the need for worker rights and protection. Concentrating on what unites all home-based workers, industrial and non-industrial, rather than on divisions of class and culture could provide the basis for issue-based solidarity and tactical alliances in the struggle of all home-based workers worldwide for decent work. Drawing on the lessons of history as recorded in this unique book, will be critical to this struggle for decent work.

4 ILO, "Working from Home. From Invisibility to Decent Work", Geneva, 2021.

Shared Dreams

With a word I express what I
want to achieve

Homeworkers in equal chains

We are so many, so we started
to put together

A vast puzzle for social change.

The first one said Visibility

A second said Recognition,
and so,

Many of us managed to
connect
in the struggle for solidarity.

Organization said another, and
the other replied

But we are so many scattered
around

Someone else thought, we are
tireless.

Unity can only be achieved
through our work.

Our rights cried another, we
are like all others

© PATRICIA COÑOMAN CARRILLO, 2022 | DOI:10.1163/9789004499614_025
This is an open access chapter distributed under the terms of the CC BY-NC-ND 4.0 license.

Rights with justice and equality
Not just because I work from
home

In a global world.

To globalize all hopes, with a

HomeNet International

We are many in a world that,

Without looking on creeds or
races

We all struggle to be
recognized.

With International Convention

We can't forget that after so
much work

What we will be able to attain

So that we can break the
chains

That have prevented us from
moving ahead.

PATYLU

Bibliography

Abreu, Alice, Rangel de Paiva. and Bila Sorj, "Good Housewives: Seamstresses in the Brazilian Garment Industry", in Eileen Boris and Elisabeth Prügl (eds), *Home workers in Global Perspective*, (New York and London, 1996), pp. 93–110.

Adams-Prassl, Abi and Janine Berg, *When home affects pay: An analysis of the gender pay gap among crowdworkers* (2017), available at: www.dx.doi.org, last accessed 1 June 2021.

Agarwala, Rina, "From Work to Welfare: A New Class Movement in India", *Critical Asian Studies*, 38 (2006), pp. 419–44.

Agarwala, Rina, "Resistance and Compliance in the Age of Globalization: Indian Women and Labour Organizations", *Annals of the American Academy of Political and Social Science*, 610 (2007), pp. 143–59.

Agrawal, Ajay, John Horton, Nicola Lacetera and Elizabeth Lyons, "Digitization and the Contract Labor Market: A research agenda", NBER Working Paper No. 19525 (2013).

Agriantoni, Christina, "Βιομηχανία", in Kostas Kostis and Socrates Petmezas (eds), *Η ανάπτυξη της ελληνικής οικονομίας κατά τον 19° αιώνα (1830–1914)* (Athens, 2006), pp. 219–51.

Agriantoni, Christina, "Οικονομία και εκβιομηχάνιση στην Ελλάδα του 19ου αιώνα", in Vassilis Kremmydas (ed.), *Εισαγωγή στη νεοελληνική οικονομική ιστορία (18ος–20ός αι.)* (Athens, 1999), pp. 145–76.

Agriantoni, Christina, *Οι απαρχές της εκβιομηχάνισης στην Ελλάδα τον 19° αιώνα* (Athens, 1986).

Ahmad, Zubeida M. and Martha F. Loutfi, *ILO Programme on Rural Women* (Geneva, December 1980).

Akhtar, Sajjad and Joann Vanek, "Home-Based Workers in Pakistan: Statistics and Trends", WIEGO Statistical Brief No. 9 (Cambridge, MA, 2013), available at www.wiego.org, last accessed 28 May 2021.

Aktiebolaget Erikson & Larson, Borås 1892–1942: En minnesskrift (Göteborg, 1942).

Aleksynska, Mariya, Anastasia Bastrakova and Natalia M. Kharchenko, *Work on Digital Labour Platforms in Ukraine: Issues and Policy Perspectives* (Geneva, 2018).

Marcel Allexandre, *L'industrie à domicile salariée* (Université Caen, 1906).

Ameeriar, Lalaie, "Pedagogies of Affect: Docility and Deference in the Making of Immigrant Women Subjects", *Signs: Journal of Women in Culture and Society*, 40 (2015), pp. 467–86.

Anderson, Margo, "The history of women and the history of statistics", *Journal of Women's History*, 4 (1992), pp. 14–36.

Andersson-Skog, Lena, "In the shadow of the Swedish welfare state: Women and the service sector", *Business History Review*, 81 (2007), pp. 451–70.

Appadurai, Arjun, *Modernity at Large: Cultural Dimensions of Globalization* (Minneapolis, 1996).

Appelbaum, Richard P. and Brad Christerson "Cheap labor strategies and export-oriented industrialization: Some lessons from the East Asia/Los Angeles apparel connection", *International Journal of Urban and Regional Research* 21 (1997), pp. 202–17.

Arnold, David, "Global goods and local usages: The small world of the Indian sewing machine, 1875–1952", *Journal of Global History*, 6:3 (2011), pp. 407–29.

Atasü-Topçuoğlu, Reyhan, "Home-Based Work and Informal Sector in the Period of Globalization: An Analysis through Capitalism and Patriarchy: The Case of Turkey", Master's thesis, The Graduate School of Social Sciences, Middle East Technical University (2005).

Atilgan, Saniye, "Evden Içeri Bir Ev: Ev Eksenli Üretimve Kadin Emeği", *Birikim* 217 (2007), pp. 134–40.

Audoux, Marguerite, *Marie-Claire's Workshop* (New York, 1920).

Avdela, Efi and Psarra Angelika, *Ο φεμινισμός στην Ελλάδα του Μεσοπολέμου: Μία ανθολογία* (Athens, 1985).

Avdela, Efi, "Contested Meanings: Protection and Resistance in Labour Inspectors' Reports in 20th c. Greece", *Gender & History*, 9:2 (1997), pp. 310–32.

Avdela, Efi, "L'histoire des femmes au sein de l'historiographie grecque contemporaine", in Gisela Bock and Anne Cova (eds), *Ecrire l'histoire des femmes en Europe du Sud, XIXe–XXe siècles* (Oeiras, 2003), pp. 81–96.

Avdela, Efi, *Le genre entre classe et nation : Essai d'historiographie grecque* (Paris, 2006).

Avrane, Colette, *Ourières à Domicile: Le combat pour un salaire minimum sous la Troisième Républicque* (Rennes, 2013).

Axelsson, Majgull, *Svenska textilarbetareförbundet 1949–1971* (Stockholm, 1991).

Bach, Robert L., Jennifer B. Bach and Timothy Triplett, "The Flotilla Entrants: Latest and most controversial", *Cuban Studies*, 11 (1981), pp. 29–48.

Backer, Larry, "Rights and Accountability in Development (Raid) v. Das Air and Global Witness v. Afrimex: Small Steps Towards an Autonomous Transnational Legal System for the Regulation of Multinational Corporations", *Melbourne Journal of International Law*, 10 (2009), pp. 258–307.

Bakalaki, Alexandra, and Elegmitou Eleni, *Η εκπαίδευση εις τα του οίκου και τα γυναικεία καθήκοντα: Από την ίδρυση του ελληνικού κράτους έως την εκπαιδευτική μεταρρύθμιση* (Athens, 1987).

Balaban, Utku and Esra Sarioğlu, "Home-Based Work in Istanbul: Varieties of Organization and Patriarchy", Working Paper, Social Policy Forum, Boğaziçi University (2008).

Balakrishnan Radhika, *The Hidden Assembly Line: Gender Dynamics of Subcontracted Work in a Global Economy* (Bloomfield, 2001).

Baldwin, Richard, "Global Supply Chains: Why They Emerged, Why They Matter, and Where They are Going", CTEI Working Paper (2011), available at www.ideas.repec.org, last accessed 2 June 2021.

Ballestrero, Maria Vittoria, *Dalla tutela alla parità: La legislazione italiana sul lavoro delle donne* (Bologna, 1979).

Barrientos, Stephanie and Sally Smith, "Do Workers Benefit from Ethical Trade? Assessing Codes of Labour Practice in Global Production Systems", *Third World Quarterly*, 28:4 (2007), pp. 713–29.

Barrientos, Stephanie and Sally Smith, "The ETI Code of Labour Practice: Do Workers Really Benefit?" Institute of Development Studies: University of Sussex (Sussex, 2006), pp. 1–32. Available at www.ethicaltrade.org, last accessed 28 May 2021.

Baylina, Mireia and Michaela Schier, "Home work in Germany and Spain: Industrial restructuring and the meaning of home work for women", *Geo Journal*, 56 (2002), pp. 295–304.

Beck, Joseph, *Die Schweizerische Hausindustrie: Ihre Soziale Und Wirtschaftliche Lage* (Zürich, 1909).

Benería, Lourdes and Marta I. Roldan, *The Crossroads of Class and Gender: Industrial Homework, Subcontracting, and Household Dynamics in Mexico City* (Chicago, 1987).

Benería, Lourdes, "Shifting the Risk: New Employment Patterns, Informalization, and Women's Work", *International Journal of Politics, Culture and Society*, 15 (2001), pp. 27–54.

Benería, Lourdes, *Gender, Development and Globalization: Economics as if All People Mattered* (New York and London, 2013).

Benería, Lourdes and Martha I. Roldan, "The Crossroads of Class and Gender: Industrial Outwork, Subcontracting, and the Household Dynamics in Mexico City", CTEI Working Papers series (Geneva, 2011).

Berg, Janine, "Income security in the on-demand economy: Findings and policy lessons from a survey of crowdworkers", *Comparative Labor Law and Policy Journal*, 37: 3 (2016), pp. 543–76.

Berg, Janine, Marianne Furrer, Ellie Harmon, Uma Rani and M. Six Silberman, *Digital labour platforms and the future of work: Towards decent work in the online world* (Geneva, 2018).

Berg, Maxine and Pat Hudson, *Manufacture in Town and Country Before the Factory* (Cambridge, 2002).

Bernhardt, Thomas and Milberg, William, Economic and Social Upgrading in Global Value Chains: Analysis of Horticulture, Apparel, Tourism and Mobile Telephones Capturing the Gains, Working Paper No. 2011/06, available at www.papers.ssrn.com, last accessed 28 May 2021.

Betti, Eloisa, "Gendering political violence in early Cold War Italy: The case of Bologna", in Pau Casanellas and Anna Sofia Ferreira (eds), *Violência política no século XX: Um balanço* (Lisbon, 2017).

Betti, Eloisa, "Lavoro a domicilio e relazioni di genere negli anni Cinquanta: Appunti sul caso Bolognese", in Ida Fazio, Anna Badino and Fiorella Imprenti (eds), *Genesis*, 2 (2015), pp. 107–33.

Betti, Eloisa, "Women's Working Conditions and Job Precariousness in Historical Perspective: The Case of Italian Industry during the Economic Boom (1958–1963)", in Isabella Agárdi, Berteke Waaldijk and Carla Salvaterra (eds), *Making Sense, Crafting History: Practices of Producing Historical Meaning* (Pisa, 2010), pp. 175–205.

Betti, Eloisa, *Le ombre del fordismo: Sviluppo industriale, occupazione femminile e precarietà del lavoro nel trentennio glorioso (Bologna, Emilia-Romagna, Italia)* (Bologna, 2020).

Ela Bhatt, "The invisibility of Home-Based work", in Andrea Menefee Singh and Anita Kelles (eds.) *Invisible Hands: Women in Home-based production* (New Delhi, 1987).

Ela, Bhatt, *We are poor but so many: The story of self employed women in India* (New Delhi, 2006).

Bhatty, Zarina, *The Economic Role and Status of Women in the Beedi Industry in Allahabad, India* (Fort Lauderdale, 1981).

Billikopf, Gregorio, *Labor Management in Agriculture: Cultivating Personnel Productivity*, 2nd edition (California, 2003).

Bonner, Chris, Pat Horn and Renana Jhabvala, "Informal Women Workers Open ILO Doors through Transnational Organizing, 1980s to 2010s", in Eileen Boris, Dorothea Hoehtker and Susan Zimmermann (eds), *Women's ILO: Transnational Networks, Global Labour Standards and Gender Equality* (Leiden, 2018), pp. 176–201.

Boris, Eileen and Cynthia R. Daniels (eds), *Homework: historical and contemporary perspectives on paid labor at home* (Urbana, 1989).

Boris, Eileen and Elisabeth Prügl (eds), *Homeworkers in Global Perspective: Invisible No More* (New York, 1996).

Boris, Eileen, *Home to Work: Motherhood and the politics of industrial homework in the United States* (New York, 1994).

Boris, Eileen, *Making the Woman Worker: Precarious Labour and the Fight for Global Standards, 1919–2019* (New York, 2019).

Bouvier, Jeanne, *La lingerie et les lingères* (Paris, 1928).

Bouvier, Jeanne, *Mes Mémoires: Une syndicaliste féministe, 1876–1935* (Paris, 1983 [1936]).

Bowles, Samuel and Herbert Gintis, *Schooling in Capitalist America* (London, 1976).

Boxer, Marilyn, "Women in Industrial Homework: The Flowermakers of Paris in the Belle Epoque", *French Historical Studies*, 12:3 (1982), pp. 401–23.

Boxer, Marilyn, "Protective legislation and home industry: The marginalization of women workers in late nineteenth–early twentieth-century France", *Journal of Social History*, 20 (1986), pp. 45–65.

Boyd, Monica, "Family and Personal Networks in International Migration: Recent Developments and New Agendas", *International Migration Review*, 23 (1989), pp. 638–70.

Blackburn, Sheila C., "'No Necessary Connection with Homework': Gender and Sweated Labour, 1840–1909", *Social History*, 22:3 (1997), pp. 269–85.

Breman, Jan, "Labour, Get Lost: A Late-Capitalist Manifesto', *Economic and Political Weekly*, 30 (1995).

Breman, Jan, "An Informalized Labour System: End of Labour Market Dualism", *Economic and Political Weekly*, 36 (December 2001–January 2002), pp. 4804–21.

Brusco, Sebastiano, "The Emilian model: productive decentralization and social integration", *Cambridge Journal of Economics*, 6 (1982), pp. 167–84.

Burchielli, Rosaria, Annie Delaney, and Maria Montesano, "Regulatory Challenges in the Australian Garment Industry: Human Rights in a Post-Ruggie Environment", *Labour & Industry: A Journal of the Social and Economic Relations of Work*, 23:1 (2013), pp. 69–88.

Burman, Barbara (ed.), *The Culture of Sewing: Gender, Consumption and Home Dressmaking* (Oxford, 1999).

Cafagna, Lucio, *Dualismo e sviluppo nella storia d'Italia* (Venice, 1989).

Carr, Marilyn, Martha Alter Chen and Jane Tate, "Globalization and Home-Based Workers", *Feminist Economics*, 6:3 (2000), pp. 123–42.

Carr, Marilyn and Martha Chen, 'Globalization, Social Exclusion and Work: With Special Reference to Informal Employment and Gender', Working Paper no. 20, World Commission on the Social Dimension of Globalization, International Labour Office (Geneva, 2004).

Carré, Françoise, "Defining and Categorizing Organizations of Informal Workers in Developed and Developing Countries", WIEGO Organizing Brief, No. 8, September 2013, available at www.wiego.org.

Carstensen, Fred V., *American enterprise in foreign markets: Studies of Singer and International Harvester in imperial Russia* (Chapel Hill, 1984).

Casson, Mark and Godley Andrew, "Revisiting the Emergence of Modern Business Enterprise: Entrepreneurship and the Singer Global Distribution System", *Journal of Management Studies*, 44:7 (2007), pp. 1064–77.

Centre for Indian Trade Unions (CITU), *Findings from Survey on Home-based Workers* (Delhi, 2013).

Chakrabarty, Dipesh, "Adda, Calcutta: Dwelling in Modernity", *Public Culture*, 11 (1999), pp. 109–45.

Chakravarty, Lalita "Emergence of an Industrial Labour Force in a Dual Economy: British India, 1880–1920", *Indian Economic and Social History Review* 15:3 (1978).

Chandrasekhar, C.P. *Financial Liberalization and the New Dynamics of Growth in India*, Third World Network, Global Economy Series, 13 (2008); available at www.twn.my last accessed 2 June 2021.

Chandrasekhar, C.P. and Jayati Ghosh, "Growth, Employment Patterns and Inequality in Asia: A Case Study of India", ILO Asia-Pacific Working Paper Series (Bangkok, 2014).

Chen, Martha, Jennifer Sebstad and Lesley O'Connell, "Counting the Invisible Workforce: The Case of Homebased Workers", *World Development*, 27:3 (1999).

Chen, Martha, "Informalization of labour markets Is formalization the answer?" in S. Shahra Razavi (ed.), *The Gendered Impacts of Liberalization: Towards "Embedded Liberalism"?* (New York, 2009), pp. 191–218.

Chen, Martha, *Informal Economy Monitoring Study Sector Report: Home Based Workers* (Cambridge, MA, 2014).

Chen, Martha and Shalini Sinha, "Home-Based Workers and Cities", *Environment and Urbanization*,28:2(2016), pp. 343–58.

Cherry, Miriam, "Beyond misclassification: The digital transformation of work", *Comparative Labor Law and Policy Journal*, 37: 3 (2016), pp. 544–77.

Choudary, Sangeet Paul, "The architecture of digital labour platforms: Policy recommendations on platform design for worker well-being", ILO Future of Work Working Paper Series (2018).

Çinar, Emine Mine, "Unskilled Urban Migrant Women and Disguised Employment: Homeworking Women in Istanbul, Turkey", *World Development*, 22 (1994), pp. 369–80.

Coffin, Judith C., "Consumption, Production and Gender: The Sewing Machine in Nineteenth Century France", in Laura Frader and Sonya O. Rose (eds), *Gender and Class in Modern Europe* (Ithaca, 1996), pp. 111–41.

Coffin, Judith C., "Credit, Consumption and Images of Women's Desires: Selling the Sewing Machine in Late Nineteenth Century France", *French Historical Studies*, 18:3 (1994), pp. 749–83.

Coffin, Judith C., *The Politics of Women's Work: The Paris Garment Trades, 1750–1915* (Princeton, N.J., 1996).

Colli, Andrea and Michelangelo Vasta (eds), *Forms of Enterprise in 20th Century Italy: Boundaries, Structures and Strategies* (Cheltenham, 2010).

Collins, Hugh, "The Productive Disintegration of Labour Law", *Industrial Law Journal*, 26:4 (1997), pp. 295–309.

Investigation Committee of the Women's Industrial Council, *Home Industries of Women in London: Report of an Inquiry* (1908).

Coşkun, Gülsüm, "Building women home-based workers' organizations in Turkey", Special Issue on Globalization(s) and Labour in China and India *Global Labour Journal*, 1 (2010), pp. 212–16.

Cranford, Cynthia. J., Leah. F Vosko., & Nancy, Zukewich, "The gender of precarious employment in Canada", *Relations Industrielles/Industrial Relations*, 58 (2003), pp. 454–82.

Crow, Graham and Graham Allan, "Constructing the Domestic Sphere: The Emergence of the Modern Home in Post-war Britain", in Helen Corr, Lynn Jamieson and Karin Gwinn Wilkins (eds), *Politics of Everyday Life: Continuity and Change in Work and the Family* (Basingstoke, 1990), pp. 11–36.

Crowston, Claire Haru, *Fabricating Women: The Seamstresses of Old Regime France, 1675–1791* (London and Durham, 2001).

Cunningham, Wendy and Carlos R. Gomez, *The Home as Factory Floor: Employment and Remuneration of Home-based Worker*, available at www.elibrary.worldbank.org, last accessed 23 August 2019.

Curli, Barbara, "Dalla Grande Guerra alla Grande crisi: I lavori delle donne", in Stefano Musso (ed.), *Storia del lavoro in Italia: Il lavoro nell'età industriale* (Rome, 2015), pp. 201–51.

Cutrufelli, Maria Rosa, *Operaie senza fabbrica* (Rome, 1977).

Dahmén, Erik, *Svensk industriell företagarverksamhet: Kausalanalys av den industriella utvecklingen 1919–1939*, I and II (Stockholm, 1950).

Dallalfar, Arlene, "Iranian Women as Immigrant Entrepreneurs", *Gender and Society*, 8 (1994), pp. 541–61.

Damodaran, Sumangala, "Global Production, Employment Conditions and Decent Work: Evidence from India's Informal Sector", ILO Working Paper (New Delhi, 2010).

Dart, Jon, "Home-based Work and Leisure Spaces: Settee or Work-Station?", *Leisure Studies*, 25 (2006), pp. 313–28.

Das Gupta, Tania *et al* (eds.), *Race and Racialization: Essential Readings*, second edn (Toronto, 2018).

Das Gupta, Tania, "Political Economy of Gender, Race, and Class: Looking at South Asian Immigrant Women in Canada", *Canadian Ethnic Studies*, 26 (1994), pp. 59–73.

De Cristofaro, Marcello, *Il lavoro a domicilio* (Padua, 1978).

de la Cruz-Fernández, Paula A., "Marketing the Hearth: Ornamental Embroidery and the Building of the Multinational Singer Sewing Machine Company", *Enterprise and Society*, 15:3 (2014), pp. 442–71.

de la Cruz-Fernández, Paula A., "Multinationals and Gender: Singer Sewing Machine and Marketing in Mexico, 1890–1930", *Business History Review*, 89 (Autumn 2015), pp. 531–49.

De Soto, Hernando, *The Other Path: The Invisible Revolution in the Third World* (New York, 1989).

de Souza, Flavia Fernandes, "Entre a convivência e a retribuição: Trabalho e subordinação nos significados sociais da prestação de serviços domésticos (cidade do rio de janeiro, 1870–1900", *Revista de História Comparada*, 4:1 (2010), p. 93–126.

de Villegas, Gisela Schneider, "Home work: A case for social protection", *International Labour Review*, 129:4 (1990).

Dedeoğlu, Saniye, *Women Workers in Turkey: Global Industrial Production in Istanbul* (New York, 2012).

Del Giudice, Sandro and Galvano Pizzol (eds), *Ristrutturazione produttiva e lavoro a domicilio : Indagine sul decentramento produttivo dell'industria tessile, dell'abbigliamento e delle calzature in provincia di Treviso* (Verona, 1975).

DeLanda, Manuel, *A New Philosophy of Society: Assemblage Theory and Social Complexity* (London, 2006).

Delaney, Annie et al., *Homeworking Women: A Gender Justice Perspective* (London, 2019).

Delaney, Annie, "Organizing homeworkers: Women's collective strategies to improve participation and social change", PhD dissertation, La Trobe University, 2009.

Deleuze, Gilles and Felix Guattari, *A Thousand Plateaus: Capitalism and Schizophrenia,* (London, 1988 [1980]).

Dev, S. Mahendra and N. Chandrasekhara Rao, "Food Processing and Contract Farming in Andhra Pradesh: A Small Farmer Perspective", *Economic and Political Weekly*, 40:26 (2005), pp. 2705–13.

Dialeti, Androniki, Eleni Fournaraki, and Glafki Gotsi, "Εισαγωγή", in Androniki Dialeti, Eleni Fournaraki, and Glafki Gotsi (eds), *Το φύλο στην ιστορία: Αποτιμήσεις και παραδείγματα* (Athens, 2015), pp. 7–52.

Dickerson, Kitty, *Textiles and apparel in the global economy*, third edn (Upper Saddle River, N.J., 1999).

Easterlin, Richard, *Growth Triumphant: The Twenty-First Century in Historical Perspective* (Ann Arbor, MI, 1998).

Edwards, Linda N. and Elizabeth Field-Hendrey, "Home-Based Work and Women's Labor Force Decisions", *Journal of Labor Economics*, 1:20 (2002).

Egels-Zandén, Niklas and Henrik Lindholm, "Do Codes of Conduct Improve Worker Rights in Supply Chains? A Study of Fair Wear Foundation", *Journal of Cleaner Production*, 107 (2015).

Elyachar, Julia, *Markets of Dispossession: NGOs' Economic Development, and the State in Cairo* (Durham, NC, 2005).

Eraydin, Ayda and Asuman, Erendil, "The Role of Female Labour in Industrial Restructuring: New Production Processes and Labour Market Relations in the Istanbul Clothing Industry", *Palace and Culture*, 6 (1999), pp. 259–72.

Ethical Trading Initiative (ETI), "Home Workers and Home Working: An Introduction" (2010), www.ethicaltrade.org, last accessed 28 May 2021.

Eyck, Kim V., "Flexibilizing Employment: An Overview", SEED Working Paper 41 (Geneva, 2003).

Farge, Arlette, *Le goût de l'archive* (Paris, 1986).

Federici, Silvia, *Revolution at Point Zero: Housework, Reproduction and Feminist Struggle* (Oakland, 2012).

Fenwick, Tara J. "Transgressive Desires: New Enterprising Selves in the New Capitalism", *Work, Employment and Society*, 16 (2002), pp. 703–23.

Fiedler, Franz, *Die Heimarbeit und deren Bekämpfung in der Kleider-und Wäsche-Industrie* (1908).

Foucault, Michel, "The Confession of the Flesh" (a conversation), in Colin Gordon (ed.), *Power/Knowledge: Selected Interviews and other writings 1972–1977* (London, 1980), pp. 194–228.

Foucault, Michel, "Nietzsche, Genealogy, History", in Paul Rabinow (ed.), *The Foucault Reader* (Harmondsworth, 1986), pp. 76–100.

Fougstedt, Gunnar, Holger Berndtson, and Sigvard Lindståhl, *Industrins storleksstruktur i Finland* (Helsingfors, 1961).

Fournaraki, Eleni and Yannis Yannitsiotis, "Three Decades of Women's and Gender History in Greece: An Account", *Aspasia, The International Yearbook of Central, Eastern, and Southeastern European Women's and Gender History*, 7 (2013), pp. 162–73.

Frey, Luigi (ed.), *Lavora a domicilio e decentramento dell'attività produttiva nei settori tessile e dell'abbigliamento in Italia* (Milan, 1975).

Frierson, Elisabeth, "Cheap and easy: The creation of the consumer culture in late Ottoman society", in Donald Quataert (ed.), *Consumption studies and the history of the Ottoman Empire: An introduction* (New York, 2000), pp. 243–60.

Fulcher, James, *Capitalism: A Very Short Introduction* (Oxford, 2004).

Fundamentals, *Insights into the Working Conditions in India's Garment Industry* (Geneva, 2015).

Gandhi, Nandita and Nandita Shah, "Women Workers and Industrial Restructuring in Two Industries in Mumbai", in Bharati Ray (ed.), *Women of India: Colonial and Post-Colonial Periods* (New Delhi, 2005), pp. 320–50.

Ganguly, Keya, *States of Exception: Everyday Life and Postcolonial identity* (Minneapolis, 2001).

Gereffi, G., J. Humphrey, and T. Sturgeon, "The Governance of Global Value Chains", *Review of International Political Economy*, 12:1 (2005), pp. 78–104.

Gereffi, Gary *et al.* (eds), *Commodity Chains and Global Capitalism* (Westport CT, 1994).

Gereffi, Gary, "The Organization of Buyer-Driven Global Commodity Chains: How U.S. Retailers Shape Overseas Production Networks", *Commodity Chains and Global Capitalism*, 95:122 (1994).

Ghosh, Jayati, *Never Done and Poorly Paid: Women's Work in Globalizing India,* (Delhi, 2009).

Ghosh, Jayati, "Globalization, Export-oriented Employment for Women and Social Policy: A Case Study of India", *Social Scientist,* 30 (2002), pp. 17–60.

Ghosh, Jayati, "Informalization and Women's Workforce Participation: A Consideration of Recent Trends in Asia", in Shahra Razavi (ed.), *The Gendered Impacts of Liberalization: Towards "Embedded Liberalism?"* (New York, 2009), pp. 1–36.

Gibbon, Peter and Stefano Ponte, *Trading Down: Africa, Global Value Chains and the Global Economy* (Philadelphia, 2005).

Giles, Wenona and Valery Preston, "The Domestication of Women's Work: A Comparison of Chinese and Portuguese Immigrant Women Homeworkers", *Studies in Political Economy*, 51 (1996), pp. 147–81.

Godley, Andrew, "Homeworking and the Sewing Machine in the British Clothing Industry 1850–1905", in Barbara Burman (ed.), *The Culture of Sewing: Gender, Consumption and Home Dressmaking* (Oxford, 1999), pp. 255–68.

Godley, Andrew, "Pioneering Foreign Direct Investment in British Manufacturing", *Business History Review*, 73 (1999), pp. 394–429.

Godley, Andrew, "The development of the clothing industry: Technology and fashion", *Textile History*, 28 (1997), pp. 3–10.

Godley, Andrew, "The Development of the U.K. Clothing Industry, 1850–1950: Output and Productivity Growth", *Business History*, 37 (1995), pp. 46–63.

Godley, Andrew, "The Global Diffusion of the Sewing Machine", *Research in Economic History*, 2 (2001), pp. 1–45.

Godley, Andrew, *Fabricating Consumers: The Sewing Machine in Modern Japan (Berkeley, 2011).*

Graziani, Augusto, "Dualismo e sottosviluppo nell'economia italiana", *Nord e Sud,* 2 (1963), pp. 24–32.

Green, Nancy, "Fashion, Flexible Specialization and the Sweatshop: A Historical Problem", *in* Daniel E. Bender, Richard A. Greenwald (eds), *Sweatshop USA: The American Sweatshop in Historical and Global Perspective* (New York, 2003), pp. 37–55.

Green, Nancy, *Du Sentier à la 7e Avenue: La Confection et les immigrés, Paris–New York 1880–1980* (Paris, 1998).

Green, Nancy, *Ready to Wear, Ready to Work: A Century of Industry Immigrants in Paris and New York* (Durham and London, 1997).

Grenander-Nyberg, Gertrud, "Sömnadsindustrien: En översikt av dess uppkomst och utveckling i Sverige", in Torsten Althin (ed.), *Daedalus: Tekniska museets årsbok* (Stockholm, 1946), pp. 75—120.

Gråbacke, Carina, and Jan Jörnmark, *Den textila modeindustrin i Göteborgsregionen: En Kartläggning* (Göteborg,2008).

Gråbacke, Carina, *Kläder, shopping och flärd: Modebranschen i Stockholm 1945–2010* (Stockholm, 2015).

Haavisto, Pirkko, *Suomen Vaatetusteollisuus: Kehitys vuosina 1965–1978 ja kehitysvaihtoehdot vuoteen 1990* (Helsinki, 1980).

Hadziiossif, Christos, "Το προσφυγικό σοκ, οι σταθερές και οι μεταβολές της ελληνικής οικονομίας", in Christos Hadziiosif (ed.), *Ιστορία της Ελλάδας τον 20ό αιώνα: Ο μεσοπόλεμος, 1922–1940*, vol. B1 (Athens, 2002), pp. 9–57.

Hadziiossif, Christos, *Η γηραιά σελήνη: Η βιομηχανία στην ελληνική οικονομία (1830–1940)* (Athens, 1993).

Hantzaroula, Pothiti, *Σμιλεύοντας την υποταγή: Οι έμμισθες οικιακές εργάτριες στην Ελλάδα το α΄ μισό του 20ού αιώνα* (Athens, 2012).

Hara, Kotaro, Abigail Adams, Kristy Milland, Saiph Savage, Chris Callison-Burch and Jeffrey P. Bigham, "A data-driven analysis of workers' earning on AMT", *CHI 2018: Proceedings of the Annual Conference on Human Factors in Computing Systems* (Montreal, 2018).

Hart, Vivien, *Bound by Our Constitution: Women, Workers, and the Minimum Wage* (Princeton, 1994).

Hartsock, Nancy, "Globalization and Primitive Accumulation: The Contribution of David Harvey's Dialectical Marxism", in Noel Castrée and Derek Gregory (eds), *David Harvey: A Critical Reader* (Oxford, 2006), pp. 167–90.

Hattatoğlu, Dilek, "Eveksenliçalişmastratejileri" Aynur Ilyasoğlu and Nebahat Akgökçe (eds), *Yerlibirfeminizmedoğru* (Istanbul, 2001), pp. 173–204.

Hausen, Karin, "Technical Progress and Women's Labour in the Nineteenth Century: The Social History of the Sewing Machine", in George G. Iggers (ed.), *The Social History of Politics. Critical Perspectives in West German Historical Writing since 1945* (Dover N.H., 1985), pp. 259–81.

Hemmings, Clare, *Why Stories Matter: The Political Grammar of Feminist Theory* (Durham, 2011).

Hiebert, Daniel, "Economic Associations of Immigrant Self-Employment in Canada", *International Journal of Entrepreneurial Behaviour and Research*, 8 (2002), pp. 93–112.

Hiralal Kalpana, "The 'Invisible' Workers of the Informal Economy: A Case Study of Home-based Workers in Kwazulu/Natal, South Africa", *Journal of Social Sciences*, 23:1 (2010), pp. 29–37.

Hsiung, Ping-Chun, *Living Rooms as Factories: Class, Gender, and the Satellite Factory System in Taiwan* (Philadelphia, 1996).

Hughes, Kendra, "Strengthening the Movement of Home-based Workers", Case Study, WIEGO, 2016, available at www.wiego.org, last accessed 30 September 2021.

Humphrey, John and Hubert Schmitz, "How does insertion in global value chains affect upgrading in Industrial clusters?" *Regional Studies*, 36:9 (2002), pp. 1017–27.

Huynh, Phu, "Employment, Wages and Productivity in Asia's Garment sector: Finding New Drivers of Competitiveness", Working Paper Series, ILO Regional Office for Asia and Pacific (Bangkok, 2015), pp. 11–3.

IKEA and ILO, "Employment Relationships and Working Conditions in an IKEA Rattan Supply Chain" (2015), available at www.ilo.org, last accessed 12 December 2020.

International Labour Organisation (ILO), "Purchasing practices and working conditions in global supply chains: Global Survey results", INWORK Issue Brief, No. 10 (2017), available at www.ilo.org, last accessed 12 December 2020.

International Labour Organisation (ILO), "Report of the Conference: Seventeenth International Conference of Labour Statisticians" (Geneva, 2003), available at www.ilo.org, last accessed 12 December 2020.

Ingalls Lewis, Susan, "Business or Labour? Blurred Boundaries in the Careers of Self-Employed Needlewomen in Mid-Nineteenth-Century Albany", in Beth Harris (ed.), *Famine and Fashion: Needlewomen in Nineteenth Century* (London, 2005), p. 217–41.

International Labour Organization (ILO), "The Future of Work in Textile, Clothing, Leather and Footwear", Working Paper 326 (Geneva, 2019).

International Labour Organization (ILO), *Employment, incomes and equity: A strategy for increasing productive employment in Kenya* (Geneva, 1972).

International Labour Organization (ILO), *Minimum Wages in the Global Garment Industry,* International Labour Organization Research Note (Geneva, 2015).

International Labour Organization (ILO), *Women and Men in the Informal Economy: A Statistical Picture, second edition* (Geneva, 2013).

Irani, Lilly, "Difference and Dependence among Digital Workers: The Case of Amazon Mechanical Turk", *South Atlantic Quarterly*, 114:1 (2015), pp. 225–34.

Isacson, Maths, and Lars Magnusson, *Proto-Industrialization in Scandinavia: Craft Skills in the Industrial Revolution* (Leamington Spa, 1987).

Işler, Sarioğlou Ayşen, "My faithful machine: The role of technology in daily life, The case of Singer sewing machine in Turkey", MA Thesis (School of Social Sciences, Middle East Technical University, 2011).

Jamal, Amina, "Situating South Asian Immigrant Women in the Canadian/Global Economy", *Canadian Woman Studies*, 18 (1998), pp. 26–33.

Janzén, Gustaf, *Svenska textilarbetareförbundet: Minnesskrift 1898–1923* (1923).

Janwadi Mahila Samiti, *Survey of Home-based Workers in Delhi* (Delhi, 2008).

Jha, Praveen and Paris Yeros, "Global Agricultural Value Systems in the South: Some Critical Issues at the Current Juncture", *Agrarian South: Journal of Political Economy*, 8 (2019), pp. 1–16.

Jha, Praveen, "Global Production Networks: What's Labour Got To Do With It?", in Hoffer, Frank et al (eds), *Monetary Markets, Labour and Development Festschrift for Hansjörg Herr* (Marburg, 2016).

Jhabvala, Renana, "Informal Workers and the Economy", *Indian Journal of Industrial Relations*, 48:3 (2013).

Jhabvala, Renana and Jane Tate, "Out of the Shadows: Home-based Workers Organize for International Recognition", *Seeds*, 18 (1996), pp. 1–28.

Kabeer, Naila, *Reversed Realities: Gender Hierarchies in Development Thought* (London and New York, 1994).

Kabeer, Naila, *The Power to Choose: Bangladeshi Women and Labour Market Decisions in London and Dhaka* (London, 2002).

Khan, Candy "The closed door: credentialized society and immigrant experiences", *Canadian Issues: Foreign Credential Recognition*, Spring (2007), pp. 63–6.

Klein, Naomi, *No Logo* (Toronto, 1999).

Koch, Heinrich, *Die Deutsche Hausindustrie* (Mönchen-Gladbach,1905).

Kolozova, Katerina, *Towards a Radical Metaphysics of Socialism: Marx and Laruelle* (Brooklyn, 2015).

Kongvichakarn Lae Pan, *Sarubponkarnsuksakarnjangngan Lae Sapapkantumngan* Kong purubnganpaitumteeban Nai pratedthai (Bangkok, 1986).

Kraatari, Eliza, "Finnish Cottage Industry and Cultural Policy: A Historical View", *Nordisk Kulturpolitisk Tidsskrift*, 1 (2013), pp. 137–52.

Kriedte, Peter, Hans Medick and Jürgen Schlumbohm, *Industrialization before Industrialization: Rural Industry in the Genesis of Capitalism* (Cambridge, 1981).

Kristensson, Folke, *Studier i Svenska Textila Industriers Struktur* (Stockholm, 1946).

Krom Sawasdeekarn Lae Kumkrong Rangngan, *Phrarachabunyat Kumkrongrangngan Rubnganpaitumteeban* (Bangkok, 2013).

Kupferberg, Feiwel, "The Established and the Newcomers: What Makes Immigrant and Women Entrepreneurs so Special?", *International Review of Sociology*, 13 (2003), pp. 89–104.

Kupferschmidt, Uri M., "The Social History of the Sewing Machine in the Middle East", *Die Welt des Islams*, 44:2 (2004), pp. 195–213.

Kyaga, Ulrika, *Swedish Fashion 1930–1960: Rethinking the Swedish Textile and Clothing Industry* (Stockholm, 2017).

Lappalainen, Piippa, and Mirja Almay, *Kansakunnan Vaatettajat* (Helsinki, 1996).

Lazo, Lucita (ed.), *Practical Actions for the Social Protection of Homeworkers in Thailand* (Bangkok, 1996), pp. 94–110.

Lee, MinKyung., Daniel Kusbit, Evan Metsky and Laura A. Dabbish, "Working with machines: The impact of algorithmic and data-driven management on human workers", *CHI 2015: Proceedings of the 33rd Annual ACM Conference on Human Factors in Computing Systems* (Seoul, 2015).

Lettieri, Alberto, "La república de la opinión: Poder político y sociedad civil de Buenos Aires entre 1852 y 1861", *Revista de Indias*, 57:210 (1997), p.475–510.

Liernur, Juan F., "La ciudad efímera", in Juan F. Liernur and Graciela Silvestri (comp.), *El umbral de la metrópolis: Transformaciones técnicas y cultura en la modernización de Buenos Aires (1870–1930)* (Buenos Aires, 1993), p. 177–222.

Lipartito, Kenneth and Lisa Jacobson (eds), *Hidden Capitalism: Beyond, Below, and Outside the Visible Market* (Philadelphia, 2019).

Liu, Jinghzou, "The Precarious Nature of Work in the Context of Canadian Immigration: An Intersectional Analysis", *Canadian Ethnic Studies*, 51 (2019), pp. 169–85.

Lobel, Orly, "Rethinking Traditional Alignments: Privatization and Participatory Citizenship", in Clare Dalton (ed.), *Progressive Lawyering, Globalization and Markets: Rethinking Ideology and Strategy* (New York, 2007).

Lund-Thomsen, Peter and Adam Lindgreen, "Corporate Social Responsibility in Global Value Chains: Where Are We Now and Where Are We Going?" *Journal of Business Ethics*, 123:1 (2013), pp. 11–22.

Lutz, Vera, "The growth process in a dual economic system", *Banca Nazionale del lavoro Quarterly Review*, 9 (1958), pp. 279–324.

Mahmud, Simeen, "Home-Based Workers in Bangladesh: Statistics and Trends", WIEGO Statistical Brief No. 12 (Cambridge, MA, 2013), available at www.wiego.org, last accessed 28 May 2021.

Maifreda, Germano, *La disciplina del lavoro: operai, macchine e fabbriche nella storia italiana* (Milan, 2007).

Maitra, Srabani, "Perspectives on Work and Family Lives: Exploring the Lived Experiences of South Asian Immigrant Mothers Working from Home in Toronto", in Sangha, Jasjit K. and Tahira Gonsalves (eds), *South Asian Mothering: Negotiating Culture, Family and Selfhood* (Toronto, 2013), pp. 149–64.

Maitra, Srabani, "Points of Entry: Examining the Conditions of South Asian Immigrant Women's Entry into Enclave Entrepreneurship in Toronto", *South Asian Diaspora*, 5 (2013), pp. 123–37.

Mares, Radu, "The Limits of Supply Chain Responsibility: A Critical Analysis of Corporate Responsibility Instruments", *Nordic Journal of International Law*, 79 (2010), pp. 193–244.

Mariucci, Luigi, *Il lavoro decentrato: Discipline legislative e contrattuali* (Milan, 1979).

Marmier, Xavier, *Buenos Aires y Montevideo en 1850* (Buenos Aires, 1948).

Marshall, Shelley, "A Comparison of Four Experiments in Extending Labour Regulation to Non-Standard and Informal Workers", *International Journal of Comparative Labour Law and Industrial Relations*, 3 (2018), pp. 281–311.

Martens, Margaret Hosmer and Swasti Mitter (eds), *Women in trade unions: Organizing the unorganized* (Geneva, 1994).

Marx, Karl, "Theses on Feuerbach", in Karl Marx and Friedrich Engels, *The German Ideology*, trans. Roy Pascal (London, 1938 [1845]).

Marx, Karl, *Capital Volume One: A Critical Analysis of Capitalist Production* (Delhi, 2018 [1887]).

Massé, Gladys, "Inmigrantes y nativos en la ciudad de Buenos Aires al promediar el siglo XIX", *Población de Buenos Aires: Revista semestral de datos y estudios demográficos*, 4 (2006), pp. 9–25.

Massé, Gladys, "Participación Económica Femenina en el Mercado de Trabajo Urbano al promediar el Siglo XIX", *La Aljaba, segunda época*, 1 (1996), pp. 81–103.

Massé, Gladys, Reinterpretación del fenómeno migratorio hacia la ciudad de Buenos Aires a mediados del siglo XIX., PhD dissertation (Universidad de Luján, 1993).

Mattera, Paolo, "Legislazione sociale e welfare", in Stefano Musso (ed.), *Storia del lavoro in Italia: Il Novecento, 1945–2000* (Rome, 2015), pp. 378–415.

Mazumdar, Indrani, *Women Workers and Globalization: Emergent Contradictions in India* (Kolkata, 2007).

Mazumdar, Indrani, *Approach paper: Vulnerabilities of women home based workers* (New Delhi, 2005).

Mazumdar, Indrani, *Home-based Work in 21st Century India* (Delhi, 2018).

Medick, Hans, "The Proto-Industrial Family Economy: The Structural Function of Household and Family during the Transition from Peasant Society to Industrial Capitalism", *Social History*, 1 (1976), pp. 291–315.

Meesithi, Chalit and Poonsap S. Tulaphan, *Purubnganpaitumteeban Nai Pratedtai: Sitthi Lae Karn Ronnarong Nayobai* (Bangkok, 2006).

Mehrotra, Santosh K and Mario Biggeri, 'A cross-country analysis of industrial outwork in Asia' in Mehrotra Santosh K. and Mario Biggeri, *Asian Informal Workers: Global risks, local protection* (Abingdon, 2007).

Meyerson, Gerda, *Arbeterskornas värld. Studier och erfarenhet* (Stockholm, 1917).

Mies, Maria, "Capitalist Development and Subsistence Reproduction: Rural Women in India", *Bulletin of Concerned Asian Scholars*, 12 (1980), pp. 2–14.

Mies, Maria, "Dynamics of Sexual Division of Labour and Capital Accumulation: Women Lace Workers of Narsapur", *Economic and Political Weekly*, 16 (1981), pp. 487–500.

Mies, Maria, *The Lace Makers of Narsapur: Indian Housewives Produce for the World Market* (London, 1982).

Milberg, William and Matthew Amengual, *Economic development and working conditions in export processing zones: A survey of trends* (Geneva, 2008).

Miller, Marla, "Gender, Artisanry, and Craft Tradition in Early New England: The View through the Eye of a Needle", *The William and Mary Quarterly*, 60:4 (2003), pp. 743–76.

Ministero del bilancio e della programmazione, *Conferenza sull'occupazione femminile* (Rome, 1968).

Ministry of Statistics and Programme Implementation (MoSPI), *Report of Independent Group on Home Based Work* (Delhi, 2008).

Mirchandani, Kiran et al., "The Paradox of Training and Learning in a Culture of Contingency", in Livingstone, David W, Kiran Mirchandani and Peter Harold Sawchuk (eds), *The Future of Lifelong Learning and Work: Critical Perspectives* (Rotterdam, 2008), pp. 171–84.

Moore, Niamh, Andrea Salter, Liz Stanley and Maria Tamboukou, *The Archive Project: Archival Research in the Social Sciences* (London, 2016).

Määttä, Paula, *The ILO Principle of Equal Pay and its Implementation* (Tampere, 2008).

Nari, Marcela, "El trabajo a domicilio y las obreras (1890–1918)", *Razón y Revolución*, no. 10 (2002). p.1–13.

National Council of Applied Economic Research (NCAER), *Report on Assessing the Prospects for India's Textile and Clothing Sector, for Ministry of Textiles, Government of India and Confederation of Indian Textile Industry* (2009); available at www.texmin.nic.in last accessed 2 June 2021.

National Economic and Social Development Board, *The Sixth National Economic and Social Development Plan (1987–1991)* (Bangkok, n.d.), available at www.nesdc.go.th, last accessed 23 August 2017.

National Statistical Office, *The 2007 Home Work Survey* (Bangkok, 2007).

Navdi, K., "Globalization and poverty: How can global value chain research inform the policy debate?" *Institute of Development Studies Bulletin*, 35:1 (2004), pp. 1–11.

van Nederveen Meerkerk, Elise, *Women, Work and Colonialism in the Netherlands and Java: Comparisons, Contrasts and Connections, 1830–1940* (Cham, 2019).

Nelson, Lichtenstein and Jill M. Jensen, *The ILO from Geneva to the Pacific Rim* (Geneva, 2016).

Newman, Janet, *Working the Spaces of Power: Activism, Neoliberalism and Gendered Labour* (London, 2012).

Nilsson, Malin, *Taking work home: Labour dynamics of women industrial homeworkers in Sweden during the second industrial revolution* (Gothenburg, 2015).

Nilsson, Malin, "Seasonal variation of hours worked in home-based industrial production: Evidence from Sweden 1912". *Economic and Industrial Democracy*, 40:4 (2019) pp. 838–66.

Nilsson, Malin, "Needles and Cribs: Becoming a First-time Mother and Starting Industrial Homework in Early Twentieth-century Sweden", *Journal of Family History*, 45:3 (2020), pp. 334–53.

Nirathron, Narumol *et al.*, *Karnsuksakarnkumnod Uttrakatobtan Kong Purubnganpai-tumteeban Naipratedtai* (Bangkok, 2015).

Nolan, Justine, "Business and Human Rights: The Challenge of Putting Principles into Practice and Regulating Global Supply Chains", *Alternative Law Journal*, 42:1 (2017), pp. 42–46.

OECD, *OECD Due Diligence Guidance for Responsible Supply Chains in the Garment and Footwear Sector* (Paris 2018).

OECD, *OECD Guidelines for Multinational Enterprises* (Paris, 2013).

Offen, Karen, "'Powered by a Woman's Foot': A Documentary Introduction to the Sexual Politics of the Sewing Machine in Nineteenth Century France", *Women's Studies International Forum*, 11:2 (March 1988), pp. 93–101.

Oldenziel, Ruth and Mikael Hård, *Consumers, tinkerers, rebels: The people who shaped Europe* (New York, 2013).

Olsson, Kent, *En västsvensk industrihistoria: tiden fram till 1950* (Göteborg, 2012).

Papadiamantis, Alexandros, "Πατέρα στο σπίτι!" (1895); *Άπαντα*,v. Γ′ (Athens, 1984).

Papadogiannis, Nikolaos, "Gender in modern Greek historiography", *Historein*, 16:1–2 (2017), pp. 74–101.

Papastefanaki, Leda, "Labour in economic and social history: The viewpoint of gender in Greek historiography", *Genesis: Rivista della Societá Italiana delle Storiche*, 15:2 (2016), pp. 59–83.

Papastefanaki, Leda, "Μισθωτή εργασία", in Kostas Kostis and Socrates Petmezas (eds), *Η ανάπτυξη της ελληνικής οικονομίας κατά τον 19° αιώνα (1830–1914)* (Athens, 2006), pp. 253–91.

Papastefanaki, Leda, *Εργασία, τεχνολογία και φύλο στην ελληνική βιομηχανία: Η κλωστοϋφαντουργία του Πειραιά, 1870–1940* (Herakleion, 2009).

Parasassi, Maurizio and Giorgio Ruffolo, *La disoccupazione in Italia: relazione sintetica delle indagini e degli studi promossi dalla Commissione parlamentare d'inchiesta sulla disoccupazione* (Bologna, 1954).

Pedersen, Esben Rahbek and Mette Andersen, "Safeguarding Corporate Social Responsibility (CSR) in Global Supply Chains: How Codes of Conduct Are Managed in Buyer–Supplier Relationships", *Journal of Public Affairs*, 6:3–4 (2006), pp. 228–40.

Petmezas, Socrates, "Patterns of Protoindustrialization in the Ottoman Empire: The Case of Eastern Thessaly", *Journal of European Economic History*, 19:3 (1990), pp. 575–603.

Pieper, Anton and Prashasti Putri, "No excuses for home work: Working conditions in the Indonesian leather and footwear sector" (2017), available at www.labourbehindthelabel.net, last accessed 12 December 2020.

Pingali, Prabhu, "Westernization of Asian Diets and the Transformation of Food Systems: Implications for Research and Policy", *Food Policy*, 32:3 (2007), pp. 281–98.

Pio, Edwina, "Ethnic Minority Migrant Women Entrepreneurs and the Imperial Imprimatur", *Women in Management Review*, 22 (2007), pp. 631–49.

Piore, Michael and Charles Sabel, *The second industrial divide: possibilities for prosperity* (New York, 1984).

Pita, Valeria, "Nos termos de suas benfeitoras: encontros entre trabalhadoras e as senhoras da sociedade de beneficência, Buenos Aires, 1852–1870", *Revista Mundos do Trabalho*, 1:2 (2009), pp. 41–75.

Pita, Valeria, *La casa de laslocas: Una historia social del Hospital de Mujeres Dementes, Buenos Aires, 1852–1890* (Rosario, 2012).

Portes, Alejandro "Modes of Structural Incorporation and Present Theories of Immigration", in Mary M. Kritz, Charles B. Keely, and Silvano M. Tomasi (eds), *Global Trends in Migration* (New York, 1981), pp. 279–97.

Portes, Alejandro and Robert L. Bach, "Immigrant Earnings: Cuban and Mexican Immigrants in the United States", *International Migration Review*, 14 (1980), pp. 315–41.

Portes, Alejandro and Robert L. Bach, The Latin Journey: Cuban and Mexican Immigrants in the United States (Berkeley, CA, 1985).

Prügl, Elisabeth, "Home-based Workers: A Comparative Exploration of Mies's Theory of Housewifization", *Frontiers: A Journal of Women Studies*, 17 (1996), pp. 114–35.

Prügl, Elisabeth, "Biases in Labor Law", in Eileen Boris and Elisabeth Prügl (eds), *Homeworkers in Global Perspective: Invisible No More* (Abingdon, 1996), pp. 203–19.

Prügl, Elisabeth, *The Global Construction of Gender: Home-based Work in the Political Economy of the 20th Century* (New York, 1999).

Prügl, Elisabeth and Eileen Boris, "Introduction", in Boris, Eileen and E. Prügl (eds), *Home workers in global perspective: Invisible no more* (New York and London, 1996), pp. 3–18.

Prügl, Elisabeth and Irene Tinker, "Microentrepreneurs and Homeworkers: Convergent Categories", *World Development*, 25 (1997), pp. 1471–82.

Pun, Ngai, *Women Factory Workers in a Global Workspace* (Durham and London, 2005).

Puthai (Special Issue), *Rangngannokrabob Nai Krungthepmahanakorn* (Bangkok, 1994).

Quataert, Donald, *Manufacturing and Technology Transfer in the Ottoman Empire 1800–1914* (Istanbul, 1992).

Quensel, C.-E., "Antalet förvärvsarbetande gifta kvinnor i Sverige några kommentarer till data från folkräkningen 1945", *Ekonomisk Tidskrift*, 53 (1951), pp. 244–57.

Rao, K S Chalapati and Biswajit Dhar, "FDI into India's Manufacturing Sector via M&As: Trends and Composition", Working Paper 161, Institute for Studies in Industrial Development (New Delhi, 2014).

Rao, N.C. and Sukti Dasgupta, "Nature of Employment in Food Processing Sector", *Economic and Political Weekly*, 44:17 (2009), pp. 109–15.

Raveendran, Govindan, Ratna M. Sudarshan and Joann Vanek, "Home-Based Workers in India: Statistics and Trends", *WIEGO Statistical Brief*, 10 (Cambridge, MA 2013).

Raveendran, Govindan and Joann Vanek, "Home-Based Workers in Nepal: Statistics and Trends", *WIEGO Statistical Brief*, 11 (Cambridge, MA, 2013).

Rawling, Michael, "Cross-jurisdictional and other Implications of Mandatory Clothing Retailer Obligations", *Australian Journal of Labour Law*, 27:3 (2014), pp. 191–215.

Reitz, Jeffrey G., "Tapping immigrants' skills: New directions for Canadian immigration policy in the knowledge economy", *Choices*, 11 (2005), pp. 1–18.

Rodgers, Gerry *et al.*, *The ILO and The Quest for Social Justice, 1919–2009* (Ithaca, 2009).

Romero, Luis A. and Hilda Sábato, "Artesanos, oficiales, operarios: trabajocalificadoen Buenos Aires. 1854–1887", in Diego Armus (ed.), *Mundourbano y cultura popular* (Buenos Aires, 1990), pp. 219–50.

Romero, Luis A. and Hilda Sábato, *Los trabajadores de Buenos Aires: La experiencia del mercado: 1850 –1880* (Buenos Aires, 1992).

Rosal, Miguel, "La esclavituden Buenos Aires y susfuentes", paper presented to the round table: Fontes para o estudo da escravidão, em 5º EncontroEscravidão e Liberdade no Brasil Meridional, Universidade Federal do Rio Grande do Sul (UFRGS) (2011).

Rosenblat, Alex and Luke Stark, "Algorithmic Labor and Information Asymmetries: A Case Study of Uber's Drivers", *International Journal of Communication*, 10 (2016), pp. 3758–84.

Rowbotham, Sheila and Swasti Miller, *Dignity and Daily Bread: New forms of economic organizing among poor women in the Third World and the First* (London, 1994).

Roy, Satyaki, *Garments Industry in India: A study of two clusters* (New Delhi, 2009).

Roy, Tirthankar, "Sardars, Jobbers, Kanganies: The Labour Contractor and Indian Economic History", Modern Asian Studies 42:5 (2008).

Ruiz, Luz Vega, "Home work: Towards a new regulatory framework?" *International Labour Review*, 131:2 (1992).

Sadiq, Kareem, "Race, Ethnicity and Immigration in the Workplace: Visible Minority Experiences and Workplace Diversity Initiatives", *Canadian Issues: Immigration and the Intersections of Diversity*, Spring (2005), pp. 61–6.

Salmi, Minna, "Finland is Another World", in Eileen Boris and Elisabeth Prügl (eds), *Homeworkers in Global Perspective: Invisible No More* (Abingdon: 1996), pp. 143–67.

Samiou, Dimitra, "Svolou, Maria", in Francisca de Haan, Krasimira Daskalova, and Anna Loutfi (eds), *Biographical Dictionary of Women's Movements and Feminisms in Central, Eastern, and South Eastern Europe: 19th and 20th Centuries* (New York, 2005), pp. 552–57.

Sarioğlu, Esra, "Gendering the organization of home-based work in Turkey: Classical versus familial patriarchy", *Gender, Work & Organization*, 20 (2013), pp. 479–97.

Sarpong, Sam, "Sweatshops and the Duty of Care: To What Extent? The Case of Bangladesh", *Stakeholders, Governance and Responsibility* (*Developments in Corporate Governance and Responsibility*, 14 (2018), pp. 229–47.

Sarti, Rafaella, Anna Bellavitis and Manuela Martini (eds), *What is Work? Gender at the Crossroads of Home, Family and Business from the Early Modern Era to the Present* (New York and London, 2018).

Schwartz, Cowan Ruth, "The 'Industrial Revolution' in the Home: Household Technology and Social Change in the 20th Century", *Technology and Culture*, 17:1 (1976), pp. 1–23.

Schwartzman, Robert (ed.), *Aktiebolaget Schwartzman & Nordström* (Göteborg, 1943).

Schön, Lennart, *An Economic History of Modern Sweden*, Routledge Explorations in Economic History 54 (2012).

Scott, Joan W., *Gender and the Politics of History* (New York, 1988).

Shaw, Malcolm, *International Law* (Cambridge, 2008).

Sidhom, Hamadi "Le travail feminin à domicile, taux de chômage et productivité : Le cas de la Tunisie", in Jacques Charmes and Mohamed Saïb Musette (eds), *Reflets de l'économie sociale* (Alger, 2006), pp. 199–223.

Silberman, M. Six and Lilly Irani, "Operating an employer reputation system: Lessons from Turkopticon, 2008–2015", in *Comparative Labor Law and Policy Journal*, 37:3 (2016), pp. 505–41.

Simons, Penelope and Audrey Macklin, *The Governance Gap: Extractive Industries, Human Rights and the Home State Advantage* (London, 2014).

Simonton, Deborah, *A history of European women's work: 1700 to the present* (London, 1998).

Singh, Andréa Menefee and Anita Kelles-Viitanen, *Invisible Hands: Women in Home-based Production* (New Delhi, 1987).

Sinha, Shalini and Firoza Mehrotra, "Working in the Shadows: Women Home Workers in the Global Supply Chain", HNSA (2016), available at www.hnsa.org.in, last accessed 2 June 2021.

SOMO and ICN, *Maid in India: Young Dalit Girls Continue to Suffer Exploitation in India's Garment Industry* (Amsterdam, 2012).

Spooner, Dave, "Challenges and Experiences in Organizing Home-Based Workers in Bulgaria", *WIEGO Organizing Brief*, 7 (2013), available at www.wiego.org, last accessed 12 December 2020.

Srivastava, Ravi, "Changing Employment Conditions of the Indian Workforce and Implications for Decent Work", *Global Labour Journal*, 3 (2012), pp. 63–90.

Standing, Guy, *Global Labour Flexibility: Seeking Distributive Justice* (London, 1999).

Standing, Guy, "Global Feminization through Flexible Labor: A Theme Revisited", *World Development*, 27:3 (1999), pp. 583–602.

Statistics Canada, *Women in Canada: A Gender-based Statistical Report* (Ottawa, 2015).

Statistics Canada, *Working from Home: An Update* (Ottawa, 2016).

Sturgeon, Timothy, "From Commodity Chains to Value Chains: Inter-disciplinary Theory-Building", *Frontiers of Commodity Chain Research* (2009), pp. 1–30.

Sumnakngan Sathiti Haengchart, *Karn Sumruaj Karnrubnganmatumteeban* (Bangkok, 2007).

Surya, Deva, "Guiding Principles on Business and Human Rights: Implications for Companies", *European Company Law*, 9:2 (2012), pp. 101–9.

Svanberg, Johan, "Migration at the multi-level intersection of industrial relations: The Schleswig-Holstein Campaign and the Swedish garment industry in the early 1950s", *Scandinavian Economic History Review*, 66 (2018), pp. 54–72.

Svensk Hemindustri [*Le Travail à Domicile En Suède*] (Stockholm, 1917).

Swaminathan, Padmini, "Introduction", in Padmini Swaminathan (ed.), *Women and Work: Essays from Economic and Political Weekly* (Hyderabad, 2012), pp. 1–17.

Tamboukou, Maria, *Gendering the memory of work: women workers' narratives* (London, 2016).

Tamboukou, Maria, *Sewing, Fighting and Writing: Radical Practices in Work, Politics and Culture* (London, 2015).

Tamil Nadu Manual Workers Welfare Board and 13 Other Boards, "Information Handbook Under 'Right to Information Act 2005' "; available at www.tn.gov.in, last accessed 27 November 2020.

Tartanoğlu, Şafak, "The Voluntary Precariat in the Value Chain: The Hidden Patterns of Home-Based Garment Production in Turkey", *Competition & Change*, 22 (2017), pp. 1–18.

Taylor, Michael *et al.*, (eds), *The Geography of Multinationals: Studies in the Spatial Development and Economic Consequences of Multinational Corporations* (London, 1982).

Technopak, *Study on "Garment Sector to Understand Their Requirement for Capacity Building"* (Delhi, 2018).

Tejani, Sheba and William Milberg, "Global Defeminization? Industrial Upgrading and Manufacturing Employment in Developing Countries", *Feminist Economics*, 22:2 (2016), pp. 24–54.

Thanachaisethawut, Bundit (ed.), *Leowlunglaena Kodmaikumkrong Sitthi Purubngan-paitumteeban* (Bangkok, 2007).

Tilly, Chris, Rina Agarwala, Sarah Mosoetsa, Pun Ngai, Carlos Salas and Hina Sheikh, *Informal Worker Organizing as a Strategy for Improving Subcontracted Work in the Textile and Apparel Industries of Brazil, South Africa, India and China* (Los Angeles, 2013).

Tilly, Louise, A. and Joan W Scott, *Women, Work and Family* (New York, 1978).

Toffanin, Tania, *Fabbriche invisibili: storie di donne, lavoranti a domicilio* (Verona, 2016).

Toffler, Alvin, *The third wave* (New York, 1980).

Tommasetta, Leonardo, *Il lavoro a domicilio nell'Emilia-Romagna* (Bologna, 1977).

Tragellis, Christos, *Η Καλλονή της Λέσβου μέσα από παλιές φωτογραφίες* (Athens, 2009).

Trubeck, David, "New Governance and Legal Regulation: Complementarity, Rivalry or Transformation", SSRN *Electronic Journal*, 13:3 (2006), pp. 1–27.

Tulaphan, Poonsap S. *et al.*, "Rangngannokrabob Lae Karnkumkrongthangsungkom: Koraneesuksa Purubnganpaitumteeban", in N. Ativanichpong (ed.), *Rangngan Kub Kwammaipentham: Punha Lae Tang-ok* (Bangkok, 2012), pp. 3–1 to 3–64.

Turcotte, Martin. *Working at home: An update* (Ottawa, 2010).

UNESCAP, *Sustainable Social Development in a Period of Rapid Globalization: Challenges, Opportunities and Policy Options* (Bangkok, 2002).

Unni, Jeemol and Suma Scaria, "Government Structure and Labour Market Outcomes in Garment Embellishment Chains", Working Papers id: 3061, eSocialSciences (2010).

Valette, Aline, "Le travail des femmes: Ouvrières et syndicats", *La Fronde*, 10 July 1898.

Von Broembsen, Marlese, "Constitutionalizing labour rights: Informal home workers in global value chains", *The International Journal of Comparative Labour Law and Industrial Relations*, 34:3 (2018), pp. 257–80.

Vosko, Leah F., *Managing the Margins: Gender, Citizenship, and the International Regulation of Precarious Employment* (New York, 2010).

Walton-Roberts, Margaret and Daniel Hiebert, "Immigration, Entrepreneurship, and the Family: Indo-Canadian Enterprise in the Construction Industry of Greater Vancouver", Canadian Journal of Regional Science, 20 (1997), pp. 119–40.

Walton-Roberts, Margaret and Geraldine Pratt, "Mobile Modernities: A South Asian Family Negotiates Immigration, Gender and Class in Canada", *Gender Place and Culture*, 12 (2005), pp. 173–95.

Wasserman, Fabio, "Prensa, política y orden social en Buenos Aires durante la década de 1850", *Revista Historia y Comunicación Social*, 20:1 (2015). p.173–187.

Wazir Advisors, *Existing FTAs and Their Impact on Indian Textile Exports* (Delhi, 2016).

Weeks, Kathy, *The Problem with Work: Feminism, Marxism, Antiwork Politics, and Postwork Imaginaries* (Durham, 2011).

Weil, David, *The Fissured Workplace: Why Work Became so Bad for so Many and What Can Be Done to Improve It* (Cambridge, 2014).

White, Jenny, *Money Makes Us Relatives: Women's Labour in Urban Turkey* (Austin, 1994).

Wick, Ingeborg, *Women Working in the Shadows: The Informal Economy and Export Processing Zones* (Munich, 2010).

WIEGO, "Commemorating Twenty Years of the ILO Home Work Convention 177 (1996–2016)", available at www.wiego.org, last accessed 28 May 2021.

WIEGO, "Decent Work for Home workers in Global Supply Chains: Platform of Demands" (2016), available at www.wiego.org, last access 12 December 2020.

WIEGO, "Strengthening the Movement of Home-based Workers", Workers on the Move (2016), available at www.wiego.org, last accessed 28 May 2021.

WIEGO, "Winning Legal Rights for Thailand's Home-based Workers", Impact Brief (2015), available at www.wiego.org, last accessed 28 May 2021.

William Milberg & Deborah Winkler, "Economic and Social Upgrading in Global Production Networks: Problems of Theory and Measurement" *International Labour Review*, 150: 3–4 (2011), pp. 341–65.

Wilson, Perry, *Women in 20th century Italy* (Basingstoke, 2009).

Workers Rights Consortium, *Global Wage Trends for Apparel Workers, 2001–2011* (Washington, D.C., 2013).

World Bank, *Stitches to Riches: Apparel Employment, Trade and Economic Development in South Asia* (Washington 2016).

Zangheri, Renato, "Caratteri dell'economia Emiliano-Romagnola", in *Atti dell'Accademia delle scienze dell'istituto di Bologna, Rendiconti,* LXVI (1978).

Zhou, M., "Pakistan's Hidden Workers: Wages and Conditions of Home-based Workers and the Informal Economy" (Geneva, 2017), available at www.ilo.org, last accessed 28 May 2021.

Ziogou-Karastergiou, Sidiroula, *Η μέση εκπαίδευση των κοριτσιών στην Ελλάδα (1830–1893)* (Athens, 1986).

Özgüler, Verda Canbey, "Home-Based Woman Workers: The Case of Turkey/Eskisehir", *International Journal of Business and Social Science* (Anadolu University), 3:19 (2012), pp. 1–10.

Index

www.ingramcontent.com/pod-product-compliance
Lightning Source LLC
LaVergne TN
LVHW021724021026
849161LV00004BA/669